Presidential Power
DOCUMENTS DECODED

The ABC-CLIO series *Documents Decoded* guides readers on a hunt for new secrets through an expertly curated selection of primary sources. Each book pairs key documents with in-depth analysis, all in an original and visually engaging side-by-side format. But *Documents Decoded* authors do more than just explain each source's context and significance—they give readers a front-row seat to their own investigation and interpretation of each essential document line by line.

Presidential Power
DOCUMENTS DECODED

Brian M. Harward

Documents Decoded

ABC-CLIO™

An Imprint of ABC-CLIO, LLC
Santa Barbara, California • Denver, Colorado

Library of Congress Cataloging-in-Publication Data

Names: Harward, Brian M.
Title: Presidential power : documents decoded / Brian M. Harward.
Description: Santa Barbara, California : ABC-CLIO, 2016. | Series: Documents decoded |
   Includes bibliographical references and index.
Identifiers: LCCN 2015030765 | ISBN 9781610698290 (hardback : acid-free paper) |
   ISBN 9781610698306 (ebook)
Subjects: LCSH: Executive power—United States—History—Sources. | Presidents—United States—History—
   Sources. | BISAC: POLITICAL SCIENCE / Government / Executive Branch. | POLITICAL SCIENCE /
   Political Process / Leadership.
Classification: LCC JK516 .P728 2016 | DDC 352.23/50973—dc23
LC record available at http://lccn.loc.gov/2015030765

ISBN: 978–1–61069–829–0
EISBN: 978–1–61069–830–6

20 19 18 17 16   1 2 3 4 5

This book is also available on the World Wide Web as an eBook.
Visit www.abc-clio.com for details.

ABC-CLIO
An Imprint of ABC-CLIO, LLC

ABC-CLIO, LLC
130 Cremona Drive, P.O. Box 1911
Santa Barbara, California 93116-1911

This book is printed on acid-free paper ∞

Manufactured in the United States of America

Contents

Introduction

In 2003, after U.S. forces invaded Iraq, news outlets reported shocking evidence of the torture, abuse, and brutal treatment of prisoners held at a U.S. detention facility in Iraq called Abu Ghraib. In condemning the actions, President George W. Bush stated that the detainees' treatment at Abu Ghraib was not consistent with U.S. policy. However, the human rights abuses appeared to many international organizations, such as Amnesty International and the Red Cross, to be reflective of a systematic pattern of abuse of detainees held by U.S. forces rather than isolated incidents. In response, Congress passed the Detainee Treatment Act of 2005, a measure that—among other things—prohibited the "cruel, inhuman, or degrading treatment or punishment" of detainees held by U.S. forces.

While Congress debated the legislation, President Bush threatened to veto the measure, indicating that the legislation would tie the hands of interrogators and thereby impede the president's ability to keep the nation safe from terrorists' plots. When the bill passed with a veto-proof majority, Bush signed it into law. However, as he did so, he also issued something called a "signing statement." In that signing statement, Bush declared, "[t]he executive branch shall construe [the provision] relating to detainees in a manner consistent with the constitutional authority of the President to supervise the unitary executive branch and as Commander in Chief and consistent with the constitutional limitations on the judicial power, which will assist in achieving the shared objective of the Congress and the President . . . of protecting the American people from further terrorist attacks."

It was clear that though the measure was now law, the president would not execute the law as directed by Congress. His view was that his role as commander in chief permitted no congressional intrusion on his authority over the executive branch, especially during a time of war. The reference to the "unitary executive" reflected a view of executive power that insulates the president from congressional or judicial encroachments on the office's exclusive authority to execute the law. Insofar as Congress sought to limit that authority by setting policy for intelligence agencies under the president's control, Bush believed, Congress violated the separation of powers. The view the president had of his unfettered authority to prosecute the war on terror gave rise to a series of national security policies that arguably violated statutory, constitutional, and international law.

On March 2, 2009, just a few weeks after taking office, President Obama released a series of memoranda written by Justice Department attorneys under President George W. Bush. The memos were drafted by Office of Legal Counsel attorneys for the purpose of providing legal justifications for what may have been extraconstitutional actions by President Bush after the September 11, 2001, terrorist attacks in the United States. Among the documents were justifications for the use of torture against suspected terrorists in (apparent) violation of U.S. statutory and international law; justifications for the rendition of detained terror suspects to secret prisons in foreign countries; justifications for warrantless wiretaps and electronic surveillance in violation of the Foreign Intelligence Surveillance Act and U.S. constitutional guarantees; justifications for the indefinite detention of suspected enemy combatants, including U.S. citizens; and legal justifications for disregarding congressional attempts to curb executive prerogative in the fight against terrorism. A common theme in each of the memos was that the president, as commander in chief during a time of national crisis, had broad discretionary powers to pursue such actions—even if they contravened domestic or international law.

Of particular interest to lawmakers were the memos justifying the use of the so-called enhanced interrogation techniques such as waterboarding, sleep deprivation, and forced stress positions. Historically, these techniques would have met the definition of torture and therefore deemed illegal actions, subject to criminal prosecution. But under the Bush administration, the harsh methods were employed by interrogators under the legal authority provided by the Justice Department officials. As the world learned of the legal reasoning contained in the memos, many called for the investigation and indictment of intelligence personnel who tortured terror suspects.

The memos were released in response to a Freedom of Information Act lawsuit brought by the American Civil Liberties Union. In confronting the decision of whether to release the secret memos, the Obama administration faced a dilemma: they wanted to publicly repudiate what they perceived to be the illegal policies of the Bush administration (and thereby confirm the stance Obama had taken as a candidate), but they also did not want to reveal intelligence secrets or upset morale in the agencies responsible for counterterrorism. In his remarks at the State Department two days after taking office, President Obama promised to "send an unmistakable signal that our actions in defense of liberty will be as just as our cause, and that we . . . will uphold our fundamental values as vigilantly as we protect our security. Once again, America's moral example must be the bedrock and the beacon of our global leadership." But, as he decided to release the memos, President Obama declined to pursue legal action against the Bush administration officials who authorized the illegal activities. He indicated that it was time for the country to "look forward, not backward" and that those who "acted reasonably and relied upon legal advice from the Department of Justice" would not be prosecuted.

Many Democrats in Congress were not satisfied. In response, on March 5, 2009, a Senate inquiry into the use of torture by American intelligence agencies was initiated. Five years later, in December 2014, the Senate Select Committee on Intelligence released its 6,000-page report. Among the report's key findings was the conclusion that the enhanced interrogation techniques used by intelligence officials in the Bush administration neither assisted in acquiring useful intelligence nor generated cooperation from detainees. In addition, the report concluded that the program was conducted without oversight and without proper legal authority, and ultimately did grave damage to the nation's standing in the world. To date, no legal action has been taken against those who followed the legal advice of the Justice Department officials, and no formal sanctions have been brought against the authors of the memos, though subsequent memoranda repudiated the legal reasoning.

Many were concerned that once broad, emergency powers were claimed by the executive, they would become regularized—as opposed to remaining extraordinary—to "lay about like a loaded weapon" as precedent for future extra-constitutional action by other presidents. Indeed, as several cases in this volume document, many of the policies enacted by the Bush administration were continued, and in some cases even extended, under the Obama administration. In many respects, it is clear that crises—like imminent threats to national security—often require extraordinary executive powers not deemed appropriate, or even legal, during ordinary times. Seventeenth-century political philosopher John Locke recognized the necessity of these "prerogative powers" of an executive officer. He wrote that sometimes an executive must "act according to discretion, for the public good, without the prescription of the law, and sometimes even against it." The challenge, however, is whether a system of constitutionalism, marked by limited governmental power and the rule of law, is able to survive those moments of great insecurity and concentrated power. In fact, this is a core concern of this volume and the reason we must come to understand the political and legal contexts in which the events included in this book took place: from Lincoln's actions during the Civil War, to FDR during World War II, Truman in the Korean War, and Nixon during Vietnam and the Watergate era. It becomes all the more pressing a question when one considers the present context, where the threat posed by international terrorism seems likely to exist indefinitely. Under what conditions is extraordinary executive action—Lockean prerogative—appropriate, even necessary? What limits are to be placed on a president while the nation is in a state of perpetual crisis? Are lawmakers even inclined to restrain presidents during such times when the public demands swift, decisive action? Even if lawmakers were so inclined, are our laws sufficient to address the threats while restraining executive power within a constitutional system? What obligations do citizens have in such contexts? Keep these questions—and others you might have—in mind as you review the cases included in this volume.

* * *

Constitutionalism—the rule of law—binds political authority to a set of formal constraints. In the United States, our constitution constrains the exercise of political power to prevent grave risks to constitutional government. When we explore specific examples of challenges to the rule of law in the United States, such as when presidents take actions that lie beyond the formal constraints laid down in the Constitution, we might perceive those actions as threats to our system of separated powers and self-governance.

But how, exactly, does the Constitution constrain political behavior? What is the mechanism by which presidents, for example, are restrained by constitutionalism? By most popular accounts, the Supreme Court of the United States and its power of judicial review would provide the means of "policing" our constitutional government. But that view may make too much of the role of the courts in resolving challenges to the constitutional order; in fact, many of the most important challenges to constitutional government in the United States were resolved with only limited involvement by the courts. And when the courts do take action, they are rarely the final arbiter of constitutional meaning. As the example described above suggests, courts were rather peripheral to the resolution of the president's use of enhanced interrogation techniques; rather, Congress, media outlets, interest groups, the public, and so on played key roles in constraining extralegal action by the executive branch. What we can learn from that example, then, is that the constraints that constitutionalism places on public officials are, in many important respects, conditioned by the willingness of the political order to apply the constraints.

As political scientist Keith Whittington (2009) argues, there is no perspective external to politics from which to define those constraints, and there is no nonpolitical mechanism available to enforce those constraints. Both our interpretation of constitutional obligations and the maintenance of the constitutional "form" occur within our political practices. Constitutionalism, then, can only be understood in a political context; constitutional meaning is made and remade through political struggle. That means that challenges to constitutionalism posed by emergency powers of executives, for example, and the means by which we attempt to constrain those actions must both be found within the political order itself.

In this book, we will consider the constitutional order through the lens of challenges to that order, typically in the form of critical, discrete events that reveal competition among separated institutions sharing powers. But while the events are themselves singular, focusing events, they are very often reflections of broader political forces rather than concrete law or court doctrine. Unlike other areas of law, consideration of the separation of powers and extraconstitutional action by executives very often does not involve the application of clear rules that are laid down in the constitutional text itself. Thus, in cases dealing with separated powers, judicial resolutions are only part of the on-going "dialogue" among the branches of government. Typically, resolutions to these "hard cases" are provided by other political actors. As Justice Robert H. Jackson noted in an important separation of powers case, *Youngstown Sheet and Tube v. Sawyer* (1952):

A judge . . . may be surprised at the poverty of really useful and unambiguous authority applicable to concrete problems of executive power as they actually present themselves.

In the same concurring opinion, Justice Jackson reveals the importance of understanding the political—as opposed to the strictly legal—nature of executive power:

No appraisal of [the president's] necessities is realistic which overlooks that he heads a political system, as well as a legal system. Party loyalties and interests, sometimes more binding than law, extend his effective control into branches of government other than his own, and he often may win, as a political leader, what he cannot command under the Constitution.

—*Youngstown Sheet and Tube v. Sawyer* (1952) (J. Jackson concurring)

Once we come to understand that constitutionalism and the rule of law as political concepts as much as legal ideals, we can begin to see how at different times over our nation's history executive power has been broadened, constrained, or justified, even as the constitutional text itself has not changed. So, our exploration of presidential power begins with this simple, but important, principle: law and politics are deeply connected. The meaning, context, and consequence of executive actions, for example, are understood in light of what the political system permits, even if those actions appear to have no textual basis in the Constitution itself. Again, in *Youngstown Sheet and Tube*, Justice Jackson reminded us of "the gap [that] exists between the President's paper powers and his real powers." So, when we speak of the constitutionality of an action, we are really referring to the action's propriety as a part of a constitutional *system* or *order* rather than its consistency with the *actual text* of the Constitution.

* * *

When we explore the multiple dimensions of executive power in our constitutional system, it is customary to identify its sources, including expressed and implied powers. Expressed powers are those powers presidents have that have a textual basis in the Constitution, typically in Article II. Implied powers, like the implied powers of Congress, are derivative of those expressed powers. It is indeed the case, however, that even with respect to expressed powers, competing views of executive power arise. Consequently, many presidential powers derived from expressed authority are similarly contested. But none is more controversial than a claim of inherent presidential power. Claims of inherent presidential power to act are those that most challenge the constitutional order because the claims are based on illimitable authority and therefore fundamentally challenge the idea of the rule of law. Truman, Nixon, and George W. Bush all invoked inherent powers, and in each case, their claims were rebuked by Congress or the courts. Understandably, the invocation of inherent presidential authority to act is less common than justifying aggrandized presidential power under conditions of a national emergency. While the powers of the executive branch must—out of necessity—be enlarged during national crises, several of the cases discussed in this volume reveal the difficulty that emerges when an on-going crisis possibly gives rise to a permanent expansion of executive power.

As the discussion of the more recent documents regarding state secrets, targeted killings, electronic surveillance, war powers, and so on reveal, President Obama appeared as willing as his predecessor to maximize executive power. Though he did not invoke the language of the unitary executive, many of President Obama's antiterror policies were fundamentally consistent with that perspective. In some respect, that is not remarkable at all. The status quo Obama received upon taking office was a vast aggregation of executive power. And he inherited residual effects of that dramatic aggregation—such as the detainees being held in legal limbo at

Guantanamo Bay, Cuba. But, in other areas, like the use of drones, he expanded presidential authority. As those powers become regularized and institutionalized in an on-going state of emergency, the powers take hold and become the "new normal." That has dramatic consequences for constitutionalism.

The historical development of emergency powers during times of crisis has been episodic, punctuations along a trajectory of expanding presidential power. Nonetheless, there have been periods in the nation's history when the proper scope of executive power was understood to be strictly limited by the text of Article II of the Constitution. This literalist view of presidential power was largely undone by the vast demands placed upon the presidency, at least since the Great Depression. At no point in the modern era has a president embraced a limited view of presidential power. But even during eras in which the traditionalist, literal interpretation of executive power dominated, presidents took actions that pushed the boundaries (and sometimes exceeded the boundaries) of their formal, textual authority. Many of those occasions are discussed in the early chapters of this text. My expectation is that by exploring the historical examples of presidential power—even during an era dominated by a literalist view of the presidency—the reader will discover that the constitutional order is made and remade by multiple parties in a contested, evolutive process. And, as we will see, the U.S. Supreme Court certainly weighs in on that process and can shape it in important ways, but is by no means determinative. Constitutional meaning is understood as a repeated interaction with broad-based social movements, the courts, Congress, the public, parties and interest groups, and of course, the executive branch. But in that dynamic, evolutive, and repeated contestation, that which came prior shapes that which is contemporarily possible. Precedents matter for presidents, Congress, Courts, and citizens as they engage in constitutional contestation. The residuum of the resolution from the last exchange sets expectations and frames the parameters of what's possible in the current exchange. In that respect, one might see Nixon's actions—or the actions of Bush or Obama—as expressions of the accrual of powers rather than aberrant exercises of power. This dynamic is usefully captured by a passage in Justice Jackson's famous dissent in the *Korematsu* case (1944):

> Much is said of the danger to liberty from the Army program for deporting and detaining these citizens of Japanese extraction. But a judicial construction of the due process clause that will sustain this order is a far more subtle blow to liberty than the promulgation of the order itself. A military order, however unconstitutional, is not apt to last longer than the military emergency. But once a judicial opinion rationalizes such an order to show that it conforms to the Constitution, or rather rationalizes the Constitution to show that the Constitution sanctions such an order, the Court for all time has validated the principle. The principle then lies about like a loaded weapon, ready for the hand of any authority that can bring forward a plausible claim of an urgent need. Every repetition imbeds that principle more deeply in our law and thinking and expands it to new purposes. A military commander may overstep the bounds of constitutionality, and it is an incident. But if we review and approve, that passing incident becomes the doctrine of the Constitution. There it has a generative power of its own, and all that it creates will be in its own image.

Certainly, if claims of inherent power are successful and validated by the constitutional order, there is no limit to executive prerogative. In that respect, moments of constitutional resilience in the face of claims of inherent power are reassuring for those suspicious of illimitable power of an executive. The actions of Truman during the Korean War, Nixon's impoundment of funds and domestic spying, and Bush's detainee policies were each challenged and limited in important respects. In the case of emergency powers specifically, however, we have seen Jackson's concerns prove prescient: the extreme crisis situations of the past gave rise to broad accretions of executive power, and the subsequent validation and repetition imbedded those principles to justify more recent policies of extraordinary rendition, targeted extrajudicial killings, and torture, for example. As many of the vignettes collected here will demonstrate, presidential power is constructed less by the office's Article II "paper powers" as Jackson put it, and more by what the constitutional *order* permits. Put another way, the president's ability to take particular actions is conditioned by the willingness and ability of Congress and the courts to take actions to constrain the president. Insofar as Congress lacks the incentive or capacity to restrain executive prerogative, or courts have "neither sword nor purse, merely judgment" and must rely on the executive branch to enforce their rulings, vast presidential power can pose dramatic challenges to a system of limited government under the rule of law.

So, we might be inclined to consider how Congress might assert more control over the unilateral actions of a president. Recall the premise with which I began: our constitutional order is made within politics. If constitutionalism is understood as constrained and maintained within politics, then the character of our politics and our political participation has implications for our constitutional order and, by extension, Congress's willingness to constrain executive overreach. But there are many difficulties that must be overcome to do so. Scholarly studies of representatives' voting behavior reveal that we are now experiencing the most ideologically polarized Congress since Reconstruction. Heightened polarization means that major legislative action will require supermajorities rather than simple majorities to overcome filibusters. As a consequence, the likelihood of congressional *inaction* on any particular policy issue is *high* and the likelihood of congressional *reaction* to presidential unilateralism is *low*. Ideological polarization in Congress, then, invites presidents to extend executive power through unilateralism rather than bargaining with members of Congress. That is something that should concern both parties, because it reveals the difficulties that inhere in constraining executive prerogative even when majorities in Congress are inclined to do so. And the absence of congressional constraint becomes the tacit approval of executive authority. Thus, the polarized character of our contemporary politics limits our constitutional order, or more precisely, expands the set of possible unilateral actions of presidents that are impervious to constraints. One of the key challenges we face, then, is to find ways to invigorate congressional resilience in the face of presidential unilateralism—and that implicates each of us as citizens.

* * *

In this volume, we explore the contingent nature of the constitutional order through the in-depth consideration of the documents that shaped historical challenges to that order. Students will be led through the history of each "focusing event," complete with attention to the personalities involved, the social, political, and economic forces at play, the specific events that gave shape to the conflict, and ultimately, its consequences for the constitutional order. The Nazi saboteurs case, for example, begins in the dead of night on a Long Island beach as a rubber raft floats ashore after being deployed by a German U-Boat. That story serves to set the jurisprudential context for *Ex Parte Quirin*, which in turn provides background for the role of tribunals in Guantanamo detainee cases. Or the story of Fred Korematsu gives a face and a personal history for readers to associate with the internment camps and the expression of executive power during wartime. Truman's decision during the Korean War to seize the nation's steel mills is considered as well. The plumbers, of course, figure in the Watergate affair, as the downing of a secret CIA flight over Honduras begins the unraveling of the arms for hostages deal. The George W. Bush era policies on Guantanamo detainees and the infamous "torture memo" are represented as a means to consider more recent examples of extraconstitutionalism. Finally, the targeted killing of American citizen and terror suspect Anwar al-Awlaki and the continuation of the program of warrantless wiretaps are explored as examples of the Obama administration's exercise of executive power.

There are certainly many examples of the expression of executive power throughout U.S. history; not each warrants its own separate treatment. Consequently, there may be some actions, events, or cases that the reader might expect to find that perhaps may not appear here. My hope is that those are few. I have tried to include as many expressions of the scope and limit of presidential power as I could within reason. Just as I had to discern which cases stand for larger principles in the exercise or constraint of presidential power, it was clear that there are certain cases that are simply too important to not include—even if they do not stand as proxy for a larger principle. Again, in that category, choices had to be made as to which were in and which were out and I experienced the regrettable consequence of excluding some that I would have preferred to have included. Nonetheless, those that are compiled here are, in my judgment, critical cases and themes that reflect key moments, ideas, and perspectives on the history of presidential power in the United States.

These 64 critical cases not only present moments of constitutional contestation and the high ideals of constitutional law, but they also reveal key actions by the media, citizens, and public officials that confronted assertions of presidential prerogative. In that sense, these vignettes reveal the dynamism and fluidity of the political environment as it anticipates, acquiesces, and sometimes prevails over executive actions that can pose grave challenges to our constitutional system.

Presidential Power
DOCUMENTS DECODED

Declaration of Neutrality

George Washington's Proclamation

April 22, 1793

INTRODUCTION

Among the first tests of executive power confronting the United States under its new constitutional order was the challenge posed by war between Great Britain and France. The difficulty for President Washington was that the new nation could ill afford becoming entangled in yet another war. In particular, Washington was not inclined to go to war against Great Britain, the nation's greatest security threat, but also its largest trading partner. Under the terms of a 1778 treaty, however, the United States seemed to be obliged to come to the aid of France. According to Secretary of the Treasury Alexander Hamilton, however, the terms of that treaty were no longer obligatory since the French Revolution ushered in a new government in France—one that was not a party to the treaty. Furthermore, Washington and others were concerned that private citizens, ship owners, and seamen would be inclined to become war profiteers, siding with Great Britain or France. A policy of strict neutrality that criminalized such private conduct, Washington reasoned, would prevent the private action of profiteers from drawing the United States into the war. Neutrality, or impartiality, was the general consensus among Washington's cabinet and the president issued the proclamation after just a few days of debate among his cabinet.

The issuance of the proclamation, however, was done in the absence of congressional input. The president had unilaterally changed the terms of a treaty in what he perceived to be a national emergency. By what authority the president could do so, however, was the subject of considerable debate. Specifically, James Madison (and Thomas Jefferson) argued that the president could not lawfully determine for himself that the treaty did not oblige the United States to go to war. The power to declare war, he wrote, was vested in Congress by the Constitution and was not a power that the president had. It was Madison's view that the proclamation infringed on congressional prerogative over decisions regarding war and peace. The president could, however, maintain legal order and the existing treaties until such a time when Congress could convene to take up the issue of war. By this view, Madison seemed to suggest that what the president did was legally defensible, if understood as not infringing on congressional prerogative.

Whereas it appears that a state of war exists between Austria, Prussia, Sardinia, Great Britain, and the United Netherlands of the one part and France on the other, and the duty and interest of the United States require that they should with sincerity and good faith adopt and pursue a conduct friendly and impartial toward the belligerent powers:

I have therefore thought fit by these presents to declare the disposition of the United States to observe the conduct aforesaid toward those powers respectively, and to exhort and warn the citizens of the United States carefully to avoid all acts and proceedings whatsoever which may in any manner tend to contravene such disposition.

And I do hereby also make known that whosoever of the citizens of the United States shall render himself liable to punishment or forfeiture under the law of nations by committing, aiding, or abetting hostilities against any of the said powers, or by carrying to any of them those articles which are deemed contraband by the modern usage of nations, will not receive the protection of the United States against such punishment or forfeiture; and further, that I have given instructions to those officers to whom it belongs to cause prosecutions to be instituted against all persons who shall, within the cognizance of the courts of the United States, violate the law of nations with respect to the powers at war, or any of them.

In testimony whereof I have caused the seal of the United States of America to be affixed to these presents, and signed the same with my hand. Done at the city of Philadelphia, the 22d day of April, 1793, and of the Independence of the United States of America the seventeenth.

Source: *A Compilation of the Messages and Papers of the Presidents*, Prepared under the direction of the Joint Committee on printing, of the House and Senate Pursuant to an Act of the Fifty-Second Congress of the United States (New York: Bureau of National Literature, Inc., 1897).

Hamilton's perspective on the constitutionality of the proclamation differed from Madison's a great deal. By Hamilton's reading of Article II, the president was vested with not only all executive authority but prerogative powers as well. Hamilton argued that while there are certain exceptions to the president's executive authority, such as the Constitution's grant of authority to Congress to declare war and to the Senate to ratify treaties, they are only exceptions. Generally, Hamilton wrote, it is the executive's prerogative to interpret and execute the nation's treaty obligations, even when doing so might infringe on congressional authority over war and peace.

President Washington never officially endorsed either approach, as either one permitted the action he took. The Hamiltonian and Madisonian approaches simply justified the action differently. Madison's justification was that this was necessary in order to maintain the lawful arrangements until Congress could determine what to do. In that respect, Washington acted deferentially to the legislature. In Hamilton's view, the proclamation was lawful because it was within the executive's prerogative powers to issue the proclamation. Its issuance, according to Hamilton, was, therefore, within the constitutional duty of the president to execute the law.

These two perspectives on executive power largely set the terms for much of the debates we observe today over executive power. Hamiltonian justifications for broad executive authority beyond the reach of congressional control are common defenses for presidential unilateralism in the contemporary era. The Jeffersonian and Madisonian perspectives of an executive circumscribed by congressional authority unless events hold that would justify prerogative powers are generally among those articulated in opposition to the Hamiltonian views.

The Alien and Sedition Acts

An Act Respecting Alien Enemies

July 6, 1798

INTRODUCTION

The war between France and Great Britain continued to have dramatic consequences for the new nation. During the American Revolution, France had been a key ally of the American colonies. However, after the Revolution, America developed significant trade agreements and treaties with its former colonial power, Great Britain. The new country could not afford to be drawn into war between the two powers. Two views—one sympathetic to Britain and one sympathetic to France—emerged. The Democratic-Republicans, led by Thomas Jefferson, were pro-French. They saw the Revolutionary government in France as a powerful force for democratic governance in its war against the British monarchy. There were many in the United States, however, who feared that if the country aligned itself with the French, the Reign of Terror would be replicated on U.S. soil. The Reign of Terror was a period of systematic eradication of the enemies of the French Revolution. For roughly 10 years, the revolutionary tribunal of the French government executed, usually by guillotine, tens of thousands of its political enemies. The Federalists, led by President John Adams, were staunchly anti-France and used this fear of a reignition of the Reign of Terror as a means to generate support for Federalist policies or, more accurately, weaken opposition to Federalist policies. To that end, the Federalist Congress passed (and the Federalist president Adams signed) a series of bills designed to weaken the political opposition. These acts became known as the Alien and Sedition Acts of 1798.

Among the set of bills comprising the Alien and Sedition Acts of 1798 was the Alien Act that allowed the president complete discretion to (1) determine which noncitizens posed a potential threat to the United States and (2) deport those persons without review, even during peacetime. Another law (the Sedition Act) made it a crime to publish or declaim any criticism of the U.S. government that would stir rebellion (sedition). While those laws were allowed to expire after their enactment, the act excerpted here, known as the Alien Enemies Act, is the only one of the original Alien and Seditions Acts that remains on the books. It permits the detention and deportation of the so-called enemy aliens, people who are subjects of hostile nations or governments.

SECTION 1. Be it enacted by the Senate and House of Representatives of the United States of America in Congress assembled, **That whenever there shall be a declared war between the United States and any foreign nation or government, or any invasion or predatory incursion shall be perpetrated, attempted, or threatened against the territory of the United States, by any foreign nation or government, and the President of the United States shall make public proclamation of the event, all natives, citizens, denizens, or subjects of the hostile nation or government, being males of the age of fourteen years and upwards, who shall be within the United States, and not actually naturalized, shall be liable to be apprehended, restrained, secured and removed, as alien enemies.**

And the **President of the United States shall be, and he is hereby authorized, in any event, as aforesaid, by his proclamation thereof, or other public act, to direct the conduct to be observed, on the part of the United States, towards the aliens who shall become liable, as aforesaid; the manner and degree of the restraint to which they shall be subject, and in what cases, and upon what security their residence shall be permitted, and to provide for the removal of those, who, not being permitted to reside within the United States, shall refuse or neglect to depart therefrom; and to establish any other regulations which shall be found necessary in the premises and for the public safety:** Provided, that aliens resident within the United States, who shall become liable as enemies, in the manner aforesaid, and who shall not be chargeable with actual hostility, or other crime against the public safety, shall be allowed, for the recovery, disposal, and removal of their goods and effects, and for their departure, the full time which is, or shall be stipulated by any treaty, where any shall have been between the United States, and the hostile nation or government, of which they shall be natives, citizens, denizens or subjects: and where no such treaty shall have existed, the President of the United States may ascertain and declare such reasonable time as may be consistent with the public safety, and according to the dictates of humanity and national hospitality.

SEC. 2. And be it further enacted, That after any proclamation shall be made as aforesaid, it shall be the duty of the several courts of the United States, and of each state, having criminal jurisdiction, and of the several judges and justices of the courts of the United States, and they shall be, and are hereby respectively, authorized upon complaint, against any alien or alien enemies, as aforesaid, who shall be resident and at large within such jurisdiction or district, to the danger of the public peace or safety, and contrary to the tenor or intent of such proclamation, or other regulations which **the President of the United States shall and may establish in the premises, to cause such alien or aliens to be duly apprehended and convened before such court, judge or justice; and after a full examination and hearing on such**

These measures were adopted when war with France appeared imminent. The detention and deportation of noncitizens when invasion is threatened, or when war is declared, is a powerful tool at the disposal of the president in a time of heightened insecurity. This Alien Enemies Act grants the executive branch the sole discretionary authority to determine the "threat status" of any noncitizen simply because of that person's alienage and without consideration of whether or not that person has committed any particular enemy action. Subsequent court decisions have determined that courts may not review the president's determination of whether a noncitizen poses a threat.

The Enemy Aliens Act has been used many times since its adoption as an exercise of broad executive power, including during the War of 1812 and World Wars I and II. Since its adoption, courts have generally expanded its reach by limiting court review of executive actions pursuant to the act. It is important to note that during World War II, the policies of exclusion and internment of Japanese Americans after the bombing of Pearl Harbor were grounded in part on President Roosevelt's authority pursuant to the Enemy Aliens Act of 1798.

When the Alien and Sedition Acts of 1798 were adopted, the Alien Act was never enforced, though the Sedition Act was only enforced against Democratic-Republican critics of the Federalist government. Thomas Jefferson drafted the Kentucky Resolutions, which made the argument that the acts were unconstitutional grants of power to the federal government in violation of the 10th Amendment, which reserves those powers not delegated by the national government to states. Though the Alien Act and the Sedition Act were not challenged in court, public sentiment against them doomed their enforcement and set the stage for a huge electoral loss for the Federalists in the election of 1800. Only the Enemy Aliens Act remains good law.

complaint, and sufficient cause therefor appearing, shall and may order such alien or aliens to be removed out of the territory of the United States, or to give sureties of their good behaviour, or to be otherwise restrained, conformably to the proclamation or regulations which shall and may be established as aforesaid, and may imprison, or otherwise secure such alien or aliens, until the order which shall and may be made, as aforesaid, shall be performed.

SEC. 3. And be it further enacted, That it shall be the duty of the marshal of the district in which any alien enemy shall be apprehended, who by the President of the United States, or by order of any court, judge or justice, as aforesaid, shall be required to depart, and to be removed, as aforesaid, to provide therefor, and to execute such order, by himself or his deputy, or other discreet person or persons to be employed by him, by causing a removal of such alien out of the territory of the United States; and for such removal the marshal shall have the warrant of the President of the United States, or of the court, judge or justice ordering the same, as the case may be.

APPROVED, July 6, 1798.

Source: An Act Respecting Alien Enemies. *U.S. Statutes at Large*, 1 (1798): 577.

The Louisiana Purchase

Thomas Jefferson's Letter to John C. Breckinridge

August 12, 1803

INTRODUCTION

The Louisiana Purchase was a land deal between the United States and France that doubled the size of the United States. The total price of the sale of the 827,000 acres of land west of the Mississippi was $15 million. France claimed the area west of the Mississippi in the late 17th century, and named it Louisiana after King Louis XIV. At the end of the French and Indian War, France ceded control over the region to Spain. Though the area was under Spanish control, American settlers began to populate the region. By 1801, Spain recognized that authority over the area was untenable and ceded control back to the French. But French control over New Orleans, in particular, unsettled many in the United States, particularly the Federalists, among whom anti-French sentiment ran deep. But even Jefferson was disinclined to permit Napoleon to have a foothold in the region and deny the United States use of its ports. Jefferson then charged James Monroe and ambassador to France Robert Livingston with negotiating with Napoleon for the purchase of New Orleans. The two were sent to the negotiations with instructions to pay up to $10 million. But by 1803, the situation for France had changed dramatically. The Treaty of Amiens was signed in 1802, but the peace was short-lived. War broke out between Britain and France again on May 18, 1803, as the Napoleonic Wars were beginning. Napoleon was convinced by his advisers that it was better to forego his plans for an American empire in exchange for the European campaign. The money from the sale of France's land holdings would be brought to bear for the war effort. So, Monroe and Livingston were presented with an offer they couldn't refuse—827,000 acres (including New Orleans) for $15 million. Though this deal was not within the terms of their instructions, they acted quickly to accept the land deal. The deal was announced officially on July 4, 1803.

DEAR SIR, The enclosed letter, tho' directed to you, was intended to me also, and was left open with a request, that when perused, I would forward it to you. **It gives me occasion to write a word to you on the subject of Louisiana, which being a new one, an interchange of sentiments may produce correct ideas before we are to act on them.**

Our information as to the country is very incompleat; we have taken measures to obtain it in full as to the settled part, which I hope to receive in time for Congress. The boundaries, which I deem not admitting question, are the high lands on the western side of the Missisipi enclosing all its waters,

From the time of the announcement of the purchase to the ratification of the treaty of purchase in October 1803, there was a great deal of debate regarding the constitutionality of the purchase by Jefferson. It was not a foregone conclusion that the president could do this, as there was no provision in the Constitution that permitted the acquisition of a territory by a treaty. Moreover, there was little known about the region (including its boundaries that would have to be negotiated with England and Spain over several years), as the Lewis and Clark expedition would not explore the area until 1804.

the Missouri of course, and terminating in the line drawn from the northwestern point of the Lake of the Woods to the nearest source of the Missipi, as lately settled between Gr Britain and the US. We have some claims, to extend on the sea coast Westwardly to the Rio Norte or Bravo, and better, to go Eastwardly to the Rio Perdido, between Mobile & Pensacola, the antient boundary of Louisiana. These claims will be a subject of negociation with Spain, and if, as soon as she is at war, we push them strongly with one hand, holding out a price in the other, we shall certainly obtain the Floridas, and all in good time. In the meanwhile, without waiting for permission, we shall enter into the exercise of the natural right we have always insisted on with Spain, to wit, that of a nation holding the upper part of streams, having a right of innocent passage thro' them to the ocean. We shall prepare her to see us practise on this, & she will not oppose it by force.

Objections are raising to the Eastward against the vast extent of our boundaries, and propositions are made to exchange Louisiana, or a part of it, for the Floridas. But, as I have said, we shall get the Floridas without, and I would not give one inch of the waters of the Mississippi to any nation, because I see in a light very important to our peace the exclusive right to its navigation, & the admission of no nation into it, but as into the Potomak or Delaware, with our consent & under our police. These federalists see in this acquisition the formation of a new confederacy, embracing all the waters of the Missipi, on both sides of it, and a separation of its Eastern waters from us. These combinations depend on so many circumstances which we cannot foresee, that I place little reliance on them. We have seldom seen neighborhood produce affection among nations. The reverse is almost the universal truth. Besides, if it should become the great interest of those nations to separate from this, if their happiness should depend on it so strongly as to induce them to go through that convulsion, why should the Atlantic States dread it? But especially why should we, their present inhabitants, take side in such a question? When I view the Atlantic States, procuring for those on the Eastern waters of the Missipi friendly instead of hostile neighbors on its Western waters, I do not view it as an Englishman would the procuring future blessings for the French nation, with whom he has no relations of blood or affection. **The future inhabitants of the Atlantic & Missipi States will be our sons. We leave them in distinct but bordering establishments. We think we see their happiness in their union, & we wish it. Events may prove it otherwise; and if they see their interest in separation, why should we take side with our Atlantic rather than our Missipi descendants? It is the elder and the younger son differing. God bless them both, & keep them in union, if it be for their good, but separate them, if it be better.**

The inhabited part of Louisiana, from Point Coupee to the sea, will of course be immediately a territorial government, and soon a State. But above that, the best use we can make of the country for some time, will be to give establishments in it to the Indians on the East side of the Missipi, in exchange for their present country, and open land offices in the last, & thus make this acquisition the means of filling up the Eastern side, instead of drawing off its population. When we shall be full on this side, we may lay off a range of States on the Western bank from the head to the mouth, & so, range after range, advancing compactly as we multiply.

This treaty must of course be laid before both Houses, because both have important functions to exercise respecting it. They, I presume, will see their duty to their country in ratifying & paying for it, so as to secure a good which would otherwise probably be never again in their power. But I suppose they must then appeal to *the nation* for an additional article to the Constitution, approving & confirming an act which the nation had not previously authorized. The constitution has made no provision for our holding foreign territory, still less for incorporating foreign nations into our Union. The Executive in seizing the fugitive occurrence which so much advances the good of their country, have done an act beyond the Constitution. The Legislature in casting behind them metaphysical subtleties, and risking themselves like faithful servants, must ratify & pay for it, and throw

Many Federalists, especially those in New England, were particularly critical of the land deal. In their view, they stood to lose much of their political authority with the huge increase in land, and by extension, people who would then be given representation in Congress. They were so distraught that some Federalists even floated the idea of New England secession from the Union.

The Louisiana Purchase was, by all accounts, the most consequential act of Jefferson's presidency, even as it was considered by many Federalists (and, as is evident here, even by Jefferson himself) to be unconstitutional. Though in this passage we see that Jefferson plainly saw it as an "as act beyond the Constitution," he thought it was justified as a necessary action for future generations. Jefferson is typically considered to have been a so-called strict constructionist of constitutional meaning. Not one to read into the constitutional text meaning that is neither explicit nor clearly implicit, Jefferson seems to have made an exception to his general rule of constitutional interpretation. In fact, he was reported to have once remarked to his cabinet, "the less we say about constitutional difficulties [of the Purchase] the better, and that what is necessary for surmounting them must be done sub silentio." While the Constitution does not abide the action, Jefferson seems to say, pragmatism demands it. The Senate went on to ratify the treaty on October 20 by a vote of 24-7.

themselves on their country for doing for them unauthorized what we know they would have done for themselves had they been in a situation to do it. It is the case of a guardian, investing the money of his ward in purchasing an important adjacent territory; & saying to him when of age, I did this for your good; I pretend to no right to bind you: you may disavow me, and I must get out of the scrape as I can: I thought it my duty to risk myself for you. But we shall not be disavowed by the nation, and their act of indemnity will confirm & not weaken the Constitution, by more strongly marking out its lines.

We have nothing later from Europe than the public papers give. I hope yourself and all the Western members will make a sacred point of being at the first day of the meeting of Congress; for *vestra res agitur.*

Accept my affectionate salutations & assurances of esteem & respect.

Source: *Old South Leaflets*, Vol. VI, Issues 126–150 (New York: Burt Franklin), 60–62.

Andrew Jackson and the Cherokee Indian Cases

Worcester v. Georgia

March 3, 1832

INTRODUCTION

In Federalist No. 78, Alexander Hamilton wrote that the U.S. Supreme Court is the "least dangerous to the political rights of the Constitution because it will be least in a capacity to annoy or injure them." It possesses, he argued, "no influence over either the sword or the purse, and can take no active resolution whatever. It may truly be said to have neither force nor will, but merely judgment; and must ultimately depend upon the aid of the executive arm even for the efficacy of its judgments." This view of contingent and dependent judicial power is reflective of the thesis that constitutional meaning is an ongoing *dialogue* among citizens, officials, institutions, and interests. That is, the U.S. Supreme Court may make decisions, but in no real sense will those decisions be final. One way in which the decision might not be the ultimate say on constitutional meaning is through congressional reaction, either by writing a new statute or by initiating a constitutional amendment procedure. Another way court decisions may be limited could be through noncompliance by states. Some states in the South, for instance, reacted to the 1954 *Brown v. Board of Education* decision with laws and actions that discouraged compliance with the court's decision. Each of the 11 Southern states adopted laws after Brown meant to preserve segregation, rather than comply with the court's desegregation decision. Yet another way the court's decision could be limited in its impact is through executive inaction. Courts may decide, but executive action is required to ensure the decision is implemented. Again, as an example, only after congressional and executive action were Southern states forced to comply with Brown.

The Cherokee Indian cases also reveal the requisite coordinated action of institutions to ensure compliance with court decisions. Two cases comprise the Cherokee Indian cases: *Cherokee Nation v. Georgia* (1831) and *Worcester v. Georgia* (1832). Both cases dealt with laws passed in many Southern states that invalidated federal treaties with Native American tribes, including the Cherokee. While anti–Native American sentiment spurred much of the legislation aimed at nullifying the federal treaties, the discovery of gold on Cherokee land in northern mountains of Georgia in 1829 gave further incentive for states to pass laws that limited Native American rights, including their land claims. The state laws also authorized the forced removal of the Cherokee from their lands. President Andrew Jackson, a former Indian fighter, was wholeheartedly supportive of these state laws as well as the interests of the states in claiming the land from the Cherokee, independent of the federal treaties and statutes that guaranteed that land to the Native American tribes.

Worcester v. Georgia (1832)

MARSHALL, C. J. This cause, in every point of view in
which it can be placed, is of the deepest interest.

The defendant is a State, a member of the Union, which has exercised the powers of government over a people who deny its jurisdiction, and are under the protection of the United States.

The plaintiff is a citizen of the State of Vermont, condemned to hard labor for four years in the penitentiary of Georgia under color of an act which he alleges to be repugnant to the Constitution, laws, and treaties of the United States.

The legislative power of a State, the controlling power of the Constitution and laws of the United States, the rights, if they have any, the political existence of a once numerous and powerful people, the personal liberty of a citizen, all are involved in the subject now to be considered. . . .

In this case, Vermont missionary Samuel Worcester and his family refused to abide by a Georgia statute that required them to receive a permit from state of Georgia to reside on Cherokee land. Worcester's argument was that the state laws violated federal law governing Native American rights and land claims. The state of Georgia disagreed and sentenced the missionary to four years of hard labor in prison for violating the state law. The issue before the court, then, was whether the state of Georgia could make policies dealing with Native Americans that contravene federal treaties with those groups.

We must inquire and decide whether the act of the Legislature of Georgia under which the plaintiff in error has been persecuted and condemned, be consisted with, or repugnant to the Constitution, laws and treaties of the United States.

It has been said at the bar that the acts of the Legislature of Georgia seize on the whole Cherokee country, parcel it out among the neighboring counties of the State, extend her code over the whole country, abolish its institutions and its laws, and annihilate its political existence.

If this be the general effect of the system, let us inquire into the effect of the particular statute and section on which the indictment is founded.

It enacts that "all white persons, residing within the limits of the Cherokee Nation on the 1st day of March next, or at any time thereafter, without a license or permit from his excellency the governor . . . and who shall not have taken the oath hereinafter required, shall be guilty of a high misdemeanor, and upon conviction thereof, shall be punished by confinement to the penitentiary at hard labor for a term not less than four years." . . .

The extraterritorial power of every Legislature being limited in its action to its own citizens or subjects, the very passage of this act is an assertion of jurisdiction over the Cherokee Nation, and of the rights and powers consequent on jurisdiction.

The first step, then, in the inquiry which the Constitution and the laws impose on this court, is an examination of the rightfulness of this claim. . . .

From the commencement of our government Congress has passed acts to regulate trade and intercourse with the Indians; which treat them as nations, respect their rights, and manifest a firm purpose to afford that protection which treaties stipulate. **All these acts, and especially that of 1802, which is still in force, manifestly consider the several Indian nations as distinct political communities, having territorial boundaries, within which their authority is exclusive, and having a right to all the lands within those boundaries, which is not only acknowledged, but guaranteed by the United States . . . .**

The Cherokee Nation, then, is a distinct community, occupying its own territory, with boundaries accurately described, in which the laws of Georgia can have no force, and which the citizens of Georgia have no right to enter but with the assent of the Cherokees themselves or in conformity with treaties and with the acts of Congress. The whole intercourse between the United States and this nation is, by our Constitution and laws, vested in the government of the United States.

The act of the State of Georgia under which the plaintiff in error was prosecuted is consequently void, and the judgment a nullity. . . . The Acts of Georgia are repugnant to the Constitution, laws, and treaties of the United States.

They interfere forcibly with the relations established between the United States and the Cherokee Nation, the regulation of which according to the settled principles of our Constitution, are committed exclusively to the government of the Union.

Here, Chief Justice Marshall calls attention to the Native American tribes and lands as political entities distinct from states in the same way foreign countries are distinct from states. In that respect, all treaties, policies, and negotiations with those Native communities must be carried out exclusively by the federal government. According to Chief Justice Marshall, the Constitution, like the Articles of Confederation before it, grants the federal government the authority to negotiate policy with Native Americans, not states. Insofar as the state of Georgia wrote laws that affected policy dealing with Native communities, such as the licensing law, Georgia exceeded its authority under the Constitution. As a result, the laws of the state of Georgia that limit Cherokee rights are unconstitutional.

The court's decision in *Worcester v. Georgia* fell upon deaf ears, however. It was never enforced in Georgia and was ignored by President Andrew Jackson. In fact, President Jackson was reported to have said about the ruling, "John Marshall has made his decision, now let him enforce it." Even if the quote is apocryphal, the president exercised institutional power by not acting to comply with the decision. In that sense, Jackson forced the court to recognize the limits of its own institutional authority and its dependency on other political branches to make policy.

The forced removal of Native Americans from the Southeastern United States had begun under the authority of the Indian Removal Act, which was passed by Congress and signed by the president in 1830. Only the Cherokee Nation was successful in resisting the forced removal in federal court. Though they were successful in pressing their claims in the *Worcester v. Georgia* case, the political tide of congress and the president counteracted their gains in court. Without Jackson's support to uphold the court's decision, Cherokee rights were not protected. Ultimately, the forced removal of the Cherokee began in 1838, resulting in the death of 4,000 Cherokee on the Trail of Tears.

They are in direct hostility with treaties, repeated in a succession of years, which mark out the boundary that separates the Cherokee country from Georgia; guarantee to them all the land within their boundary; solemnly pledge the faith of the United States to restrain their citizens from trespassing on it; and recognize the pre-existing power of the nation to govern itself.

They are in equal hostility with the acts of Congress for regulating this intercourse, and giving effect to the treaties.

The forcible seizure and abduction of the plaintiff, who was residing in the nation with its permission, and by authority of the President of the United States, is also a violation of the acts which authorize the chief magistrate to exercise this authority. . . .

Judgment reversed.

Source: *Worcester v. Georgia*, 31 U.S. (6 Pet.) 515 (1832).

Polk Sends Troops to the U.S.-Mexico Border

James Polk's Request for a Declaration of War

May 11, 1846

INTRODUCTION

In the waning days of his administration, President Tyler sent to Congress a resolution for the annexation of Texas. That measure passed the Congress in March 1845 and Texas became a state in December 1845. The annexation of Texas was vehemently opposed by Mexico, which threatened to go to war with the United States if the latter moved ahead with statehood for Texas. Though annexation occurred, the Mexicans did not make good on their threat of war. Dispute over the border between the two countries intensified, however. The Mexican government severed diplomatic relations with the United States when American forces moved into a territory along the Rio Grande near Matamoros, Mexico, that was disputed between Texas and Mexico. In response, Mexican military personnel crossed the Rio Grande, into the area the United States claimed was its own territory and killed or injured 16 U.S. soldiers. That action led Polk to seek a declaration of war from Congress, and on May 13, war was declared.

To the Senate and House of Representatives:

The existing state of the relations between the United States and Mexico renders it proper that I should bring the subject to the consideration of Congress. In my message at the commencement of your present session the state of these relations, the causes which led to the suspension of diplomatic intercourse between the two countries in March, 1845, and the long-continued and unredressed wrongs and injuries committed by the Mexican Government on citizens of the United States in their persons and property were briefly set forth.

The strong desire to establish peace with Mexico on liberal and honorable terms, and the readiness of this Government to regulate and adjust our boundary and other causes of difference with that power on such fair and equitable principles as would lead to permanent relations of the most friendly nature, induced me in September last to seek the reopening of diplomatic relations between the two countries.

Upon an invasion of the United States, it .... stands to reason that the president would have the constitutional authority to act swiftly (and unilaterally) to repel the invasion including, perhaps, invading the territory of the enemy. But what if it is not clear that the territory that was invaded was U.S. territory? If it was not, then no invasion of the United States occurred and no unilateral military retaliation by the president could be supported by the Constitution. As then representative Abraham Lincoln pointed out in a letter to his former law partner, "That soil was not ours; and Congress did not annex it or attempt to annex it. But to return to your position: Allow the President to invade a neighboring nation, whenever *he* shall deem it necessary to repel an invasion, and you allow him to do so, *whenever he may choose to say* he deems it necessary for such purpose—and you allow him to make war at pleasure. Study to see if you can fix *any limit* to his power in this respect.... Your view ... places our President where Kings have always stood" (emphasis in the original). Very clearly, Lincoln saw this action as unconstitutional unless Polk could provide evidence that the exact location of the hostilities fell within U.S. territory. In fact, Lincoln introduced a resolution, later referred to as the *spot resolution*, that challenged Polk to clarify with precision where the attacks occurred. Though Lincoln's bill did not pass the House, later, in early 1848, the House did pass an amendment censuring Polk for "unnecessarily and unconstitutionally" beginning the Mexican War. Polk responded to Lincoln and other Whig criticism by claiming that those who do not support the troops in battle with Mexico are treasonous.

Every measure adopted on our part had for its object the furtherance of these desired results. In communicating to Congress a succinct statement of the injuries which we had suffered from Mexico, and which have been accumulating during a period of more than twenty years, every expression that could tend to inflame the people of Mexico or defeat or delay a pacific result was carefully avoided. An envoy of the United States repaired to Mexico with full powers to adjust every existing difference. But though present on the Mexican soil by agreement between the two Governments, invested with full powers, and bearing evidence of the most friendly dispositions, his mission has been unavailing. **The Mexican Government not only refused to receive him or listen to his propositions, but after a long-continued series of menaces have at last invaded our territory and shed the blood of our fellow-citizens on our own soil.**

On the 10th of November, 1845, Mr. John Slidell, of Louisiana, was commissioned by me as envoy extraordinary and minister plenipotentiary of the United States to Mexico, and was entrusted with full powers to adjust both the questions of the Texas boundary and of indemnification to our citizens. The redress of the wrongs of our citizens naturally and inseparably blended itself with the question of boundary. The settlement of the one question in any correct view of the subject involves that of the other. I could not for a moment entertain the idea that the claims of our much-injured and long-suffering citizens, many of which had existed for more than twenty years, should be postponed or separated from the settlement of the boundary question.

Mr. Slidell arrived at Vera Cruz on the 30th of November, and was courteously received by the authorities of that city. But the Government of General Herrera was then tottering to its fall.... The Government of General Herrera, there is good reason to believe, was sincerely desirous to receive our minister; but it yielded to the storm raised by its enemies, and on the 21st of December refused to accredit Mr. Slidell upon the most frivolous pretexts.

...General Herrera yielded the Government to General Paredes without a struggle, and on the 30th of December resigned the Presidency. This revolution was accomplished solely by the army, the people having taken little part in the contest; and thus the supreme power in Mexico passed into the hands of a military leader.

Determined to leave no effort untried to effect an amicable adjustment with Mexico, I directed Mr. Slidell to present his credentials to the Government of General Paredes and ask to be officially received by him. . . . Mr. Slidell, in obedience to my direction, addressed a note to the Mexican minister of foreign relations, under date of the 1st of March last, asking to be received by that Government in the diplomatic character to which he had been appointed. This minister in his reply, under date of the 12th of March, reiterated the arguments of his predecessor, and in terms that may be considered as giving just grounds of offense to the Government and people of the United States denied the application of Mr. Slidell. Nothing therefore remained for our envoy but to demand his passports and return to his own country.

Thus the Government of Mexico, though solemnly pledged by official acts in October last to receive and accredit an American envoy, violated their plighted faith and refused the offer of a peaceful adjustment of our difficulties. Not only was the offer rejected, but the indignity of its rejection was enhanced by the manifest breach of faith in refusing to admit the envoy who came because they had bound themselves to receive him. . . . The Mexican Government refused all negotiation, and have made no proposition of any kind.

In my message at the commencement of the present session I informed you that upon the earnest appeal both of the Congress and convention of Texas I had ordered an efficient military force to take a position "between the Nueces and the Del Norte." This had become necessary to meet a threatened invasion of Texas by the Mexican forces, for which extensive military preparations had been made. The invasion was threatened solely because Texas had determined, in accordance with a solemn resolution of the Congress of the

United States, to annex herself to our Union, and under these circumstances it was plainly our duty to extend our protection over her citizens and soil.

. . .The movement of the troops to the Del Norte was made by the commanding general under positive instructions to abstain from all aggressive acts toward Mexico or Mexican citizens and to regard the relations between that Republic and the United States as peaceful unless she should declare war or commit acts of hostility indicative of a state of war. He was specially directed to protect private property and respect personal rights.

The Army moved from Corpus Christi on the 11th of March, and on the 28th of that month arrived on the left bank of the Del Norte opposite to Matamoras, where it encamped on a commanding position, which has since been strengthened by the erection of fieldworks. . . .

The Mexican forces at Matamoras assumed a belligerent attitude, and on the 12th of April General Ampudia, then in command, notified General Taylor to break up his camp within twenty-four hours and to retire beyond the Nueces River, and in the event of his failure to comply with these demands announced that arms, and arms alone, must decide the question. But no open act of hostility was committed until the 24th of April. On that day General Arista, who had succeeded to the command of the Mexican forces, communicated to General Taylor that "he considered hostilities commenced and should prosecute them." A party of dragoons of 63 men and officers were on the same day dispatched from the American camp up the Rio del Norte, on its left bank, to ascertain whether the Mexican troops had crossed or were preparing to cross the river, "became engaged with a large body of these troops, and after a short affair, in which some 16 were killed and wounded, appear to have been surrounded and compelled to surrender."

The grievous wrongs perpetrated by Mexico upon our citizens throughout a long period of years remain unredressed, and solemn treaties pledging her public faith for this redress have been disregarded. A government either unable or unwilling to enforce the execution of such treaties fails to perform one of its plainest duties.

. . .

But now, after reiterated menaces, Mexico has passed the boundary of the United States, has invaded our territory and shed American blood upon the American soil. She has proclaimed that hostilities have commenced, and that the two nations are now at war.

As war exists, and, notwithstanding all our efforts to avoid it, exists by the act of Mexico herself, we are called upon by every consideration of duty and patriotism to vindicate with decision the honor, the rights, and the interests of our country.

In later communications with Congress, the embattled Polk continued his defense of his call for a declaration of war. He again reiterates that it was brought on by Mexico through aggression and invasion of U.S. sovereign territory. Those who challenge that state of affairs give aid and comfort to the enemy by sewing discord in the United States over the legal authority of the commander in chief to prosecute the Mexican War.

Anticipating the possibility of a crisis like that which has arrived, instructions were given in August last, "as a precautionary measure" against invasion or threatened invasion, authorizing General Taylor, if the emergency required, to accept volunteers, not from Texas only, but from the States of Louisiana, Alabama, Mississippi, Tennessee, and Kentucky, and corresponding letters were addressed to the respective governors of those States. These instructions were repeated, and in January last, soon after the incorporation of "Texas into our Union of States," General Taylor was further "authorized by the President to make a requisition upon the executive of that State for such of its militia force as may be needed to repel invasion or to secure the country against apprehended invasion." On the 2d day of March he was again reminded, "in the event of the approach of any considerable Mexican force, promptly and efficiently to use the authority with which he was clothed to call to him such auxiliary force as he might need." War actually existing and our territory having been invaded, General Taylor, pursuant to authority vested in him by my direction, has called on the governor of Texas for four regiments of State troops, two to be mounted and two to serve on foot, and on the governor of

Louisiana for four regiments of infantry to be sent to him as soon as practicable.

Though Lincoln and other Whigs argued aggressively and even voted to censure the president for his actions leading to the war, they generally voted in favor of the declaration of war and voted to appropriate funds for weapons and provisions for the military.

In further vindication of our rights and defense of our territory, I invoke the prompt action of Congress to recognize the existence of the war, and to place at the disposition of the Executive the means of prosecuting the war with vigor, and thus hastening the restoration of peace. To this end I recommend that authority should be given to call into the public service a large body of volunteers to serve for not less than six or twelve months unless sooner discharged. A volunteer force is beyond question more efficient than any other description of citizen soldiers, and it is not to be doubted that a number far beyond that required would readily rush to the field upon the call of their country. I further recommend that a liberal provision be made for sustaining our entire military force and furnishing it with supplies and munitions of war.

The most energetic and prompt measures and the immediate appearance in arms of a large and overpowering force are recommended to Congress as the most certain and efficient means of bringing the existing collision with Mexico to a speedy and successful termination.

After Mexico City fell into American hands in late 1847, the United States and Mexico signed the Treaty of Guadalupe Hidalgo the next spring, which ended the hostilities. The terms of the treaty allowed the United States to purchase the areas that would become the states of California and New Mexico and established the Rio Grande as the border between Texas and Mexico. Curiously, in reporting on the terms of the treaty to Congress, Polk did not continue to claim that the initial hostilities occurred on U.S. soil. Rather, he said, it was the agreement reached with Mexico (and subsequent Senate ratification) that determined the Rio Grande to be the boundary. In addition, Mexico ceded previously held territory to the United States, including what would become Arizona, Utah, Nevada, and portions of Wyoming and Colorado.

In making these recommendations I deem it proper to declare that it is my anxious desire not only to terminate hostilities speedily, but to bring all matters in dispute between this Government and Mexico to an early and amicable adjustment; and in this view I shall be prepared to renew negotiations whenever Mexico shall be ready to receive propositions or to make propositions of her own.

. . .

JAMES K. POLK.

Source: James D. Richardson, *A Compilation of the Messages and Papers of the Presidents*, Volume 4: James Knox Polk (Washington, DC: Government Printing Office).

The Blockade of Southern Ports

Abraham Lincoln's Proclamation

April 19, 1861

INTRODUCTION

Historians continue to debate the precise causes of the Civil War. There is general agreement, however, that a principal cause was the deep division between Northern States and Southern States over whether slavery would be prohibited in those territories that had yet to be admitted to the Union. Abraham Lincoln campaigned for the presidency at least in part on the platform of refusing to permit slavery in the new states. Lincoln garnered a plurality of the electoral vote and was elected president on November 6, 1860. In reaction, South Carolina seceded from the Union even before Lincoln's inauguration. South Carolina's example was followed quickly by several other Southern states. Ultimately, those states of the Deep South were joined by others of the upper South to comprise the Confederate States of America (CSA). By the time Lincoln gave his first inaugural address on March 4, 1861, a new CSA Constitution was drafted and ratified by the Southern states and Jefferson Davis was elected to a six-year term as president of the Confederacy. For Lincoln, and most of the population in the North, the secession was not considered legal; rather, the Southern states were understood to be in rebellion against the Union—an entity of which they remained member states.

Whereas an insurrection against the Government of the United States has broken out in the States of South Carolina, Georgia, Alabama, Florida, Mississippi, Louisiana, and Texas, and the laws of the United States for the collection of the revenue cannot be effectually executed therein conformably to that provision of the Constitution which requires duties to be uniform throughout the United States; and

Whereas a combination of persons engaged in such insurrection have threatened to grant pretended letters of marque to authorize the bearers thereof to commit assaults on the lives, vessels, and property of good citizens of the country lawfully engaged in commerce on the high seas and in waters of the United States; and

Whereas an Executive proclamation has been already issued requiring the persons engaged in these disorderly proceedings to desist therefrom, calling out a militia force for the purpose

The Civil War began when Confederate canon fired upon Fort Sumter, the federal garrison in the Charleston Harbor, South Carolina. The assault began in reaction to Lincoln's efforts to resupply the troops stationed at the fort. Lincoln felt that he had an obligation to provide protection for federal property in secessionist areas, which included Fort Sumter. The Fort fell on April 12, 1861, and within days, President Lincoln issued two proclamations. One called for a special session of Congress and 75,000 troops to put down the insurrection that had begun. Another proclamation initiated a naval blockade of Southern ports to deny the largely agrarian Confederacy supplies it would require to successfully prosecute a war.

of repressing the same, and convening Congress in extraordinary session to deliberate and determine thereon:

Now, therefore, I, Abraham Lincoln, President of the United States, with a view to the same purposes before mentioned and to the protection of the public peace and the lives and property of quiet and orderly citizens pursuing their lawful occupations until Congress shall have assembled and deliberated on the said unlawful proceedings or until the same shall have ceased, **have further deemed it advisable to set on foot a blockade of the ports within the States aforesaid, in pursuance of the laws of the United States and of the law of nations in such case provided. For this purpose a competent force will be posted so as to prevent entrance and exit of vessels from the ports aforesaid. If, therefore, with a view to violate such blockade, a vessel shall approach or shall attempt to leave either of the said ports, she will be duly warned by the commander of one of the blockading vessels, who will indorse on her register the fact and date of such warning, and if the same vessel shall again attempt to enter or leave the blockaded port she will be captured and sent to the nearest convenient port for such proceedings against her and her cargo as prize as may be deemed advisable.**

And I hereby proclaim and declare that if any person, under the pretended authority of the said States or under any other pretense, shall molest a vessel of the United States or the persons or cargo on board of her, such person will be held amenable to the laws of the United States for the prevention and punishment of piracy.

In witness whereof I have hereunto set my hand and caused the seal of the United States to be affixed.

It was under the authority of this proclamation that a number of vessels, along with their cargoes, were seized by Union gunships. When the interdictment of the vessels was challenged in court, the cases became known as the Prize Cases. At issue in those cases was whether the federal government —in this case, the executive branch—had the authority to enforce a blockade of ports and seize enemy property when not at war with a foreign power. The constitutional authority of the declaration of war rests with the Congress. But Congress was out of session and had not declared war.

Done at the city of Washington, this 19th day of April, A.D. 1861, and of the Independence of the United States the eighty-fifth.

ABRAHAM LINCOLN.

Source: Abraham Lincoln, Proclamation 81 – Declaring a Blockade of Ports in Rebellious States, April 19, 1861. Online by Gerhard Peters and John T. Woolley, *The American Presidency Project*. http://www.presidency.ucsb.edu/ws/?pid=70101.

President Lincoln had blockaded the ports and seized the property of both American and foreign vessels that attempted to run the blockades in the absence of that formal declaration of war. But under international law, only port closures—not blockades—were authorized. Lincoln's cabinet was split over the issue of whether to block or close the Southern ports. The distinction was important, as a closure meant absolutely no import or export. A blockade, however, would allow certain neutral nonbelligerents access to trade. This latter alternative was Britain's clear preference, as British traders stood to lose all commercial enterprise with the entire region. Lincoln saw the wisdom in not giving the British any more reason to put their full support behind the insurrection and opted for the blockade rather than (the more clearly legal) closure.

When the legality of the action was considered by the U.S. Supreme Court in the Prize Cases, the majority ruled in favor of Lincoln's approach. As to the question of whether the president may take military action in defense of the nation without congressional approval, Justice Grier ruled that "the President was bound to meet [war] in the shape it presented itself; without waiting for Congress to baptize it with a name." This war, he reasoned, was characterized by belligerents who, while not foreign, were at war with the Union. Consequently, he wrote, they were "liable to be treated as enemies, though not foreigners. They have cast off their allegiance and made war on their Government, and are nonetheless enemies because they are traitors." As a result, "the President, in fulfilling his duties as Commander-in-chief in suppressing an insurrection . . . must determine what degree of force the crisis demands. The proclamation of blockade is itself official and conclusive evidence to the Court that a state of war existed which demanded and authorized a recourse to such a measure under the circumstances peculiar to the case."

The Prize Cases reflect the principle that the president can use exceptional means to defend against an attack by a foreign nation in the absence of congressional action. In this case, however, the Union was not under attack from a foreign enemy—the enemy emerged as an insurrection from within the Union. The majority's decision in the Prize Cases determined that the distinction does not matter. The president's power over national security is extensive—independent of the source of the insecurity.

The Arrest of John Merryman

Ex Parte Merryman

May 25, 1861

INTRODUCTION

The short period of time between the fall of Fort Sumter on April 12, 1861, and the emergency session of Congress held on July 4, 1861, was a remarkable period in the history of American presidential power. During that 10-week period, President Lincoln exercised substantial executive prerogative power by calling up thousands of state militias, imposing a blockade on Southern ports, authorizing the appropriation of funds for the military, expanding the size of the army and navy, and even unilaterally suspending the writ of habeas corpus. Each of the actions was taken without authorization from Congress and without the formal declaration of war from Congress. Though Congress eventually authorized the president's actions, Lincoln had acted with wide-ranging power and autonomy to face the challenge to the Union posed by the domestic rebellion. Historically, Lincoln's actions during this period reflect the prerogative power of presidents as envisioned by John Locke. You will recall Locke's formulation of prerogative as "doing public good without a rule." In fact, Locke reasons, sometimes presidents must, of necessity, act not only in the absence of a rule, but they must take actions that contravene a rule. Lincoln's suspension of the *great writ* of *habeas corpus* is an important example of a president acting in contravention of a constitutional rule. The privilege of *habeas corpus* permits someone who has been detained by government to challenge the lawfulness of their detention in court. It is a protection afforded individuals against arbitrary detention by governmental authorities that dates back centuries and is one of the most important constraints placed upon government in the interest of individual liberty.

During this short period of time after the beginning of hostilities, it was critical for the fate of the Union to keep Washington, DC, from falling into the hands of the Confederacy. That challenge looked more and more difficult as Virginia, which is separated from the Capital by the Potomac River, voted to secede less than a week after the fall of Sumter. The only way the Union could defend the Capital, then, was a supply line that went through Maryland. Lincoln recognized that in order to preserve the Union, Maryland would have to remain under Union control. However, after Federal troops en route to DC were attacked by a Baltimore mob, and the prosecessionist Maryland governor called for a secession vote in the state legislature, Lincoln took action. He authorized the Federal military authorities to secure the transportation lines through Maryland by all necessary means, including by suspending habeas corpus. John Merryman was arrested on the suspicion that he was a member of armed secessionist organization and transported to Fort McHenry in the Baltimore Harbor. Merryman immediately sought counsel and petitioned for a writ of habeas corpus challenging his detention as a violation of his 5th Amendment guarantee of due process. Chief Justice of the Supreme Court Roger B. Taney (a native Marylander, and the author of the infamous Dred Scott decision that, in large part, led to the Civil War) granted Merryman his writ of habeas corpus. The military official, General Cadwalader, to whom the writ was given, however, refused to appear to defend the actions of the government, citing presidential authority to suspend habeas relief in times of insurrection or rebellion.

Before the Chief Justice of the Supreme Court of the United States, at Chambers.

The application in this case for a writ of *habeas corpus* is made to me under the 14th section of the Judiciary Act of 1789, which renders effectual for the citizen the constitutional privilege of the *habeas corpus*. That act gives to the Courts of the United States, as well as to each Justice of the Supreme Court, and to every District Judge, power to grant writs of *habeas corpus* for the purpose of an inquiry into the cause of commitment. **The petition was presented to me at Washington, under the impression that I would order the prisoner to be brought before me there, but as he was confined in Fort McHenry, at the city of Baltimore, which is in my circuit, I resolved to hear it in the latter city, as obedience to the writ, under such circumstances, would not withdraw Gen. Cadwalader, who had him in charge, from the limits of his military command.**

It is important to remember that Chief Justice Roger Taney is hearing this case under the statutory authority (Judiciary Act of 1789) given federal judges and justices of the U.S. Supreme Court to hear *habeas* petitions under their original jurisdiction. You may recall the 1803 case, *Marbury v. Madison,* in which the Marshall Court ruled that Section 13 of the Judiciary Act of 1789 unconstitutionally expanded the original jurisdiction of the Court by granting it the authority to issue (as an original action) *writs of mandamus.* Presumably, the power to issue (again, as an original action) writs of habeas corpus would also be unconstitutional. One might be perplexed, then, to learn that Chief Justice Taney heard and decided this case under the legal authority of a provision, the twin of one which was determined to have unconstitutionally expanded the court's original jurisdiction 60 years prior.

The petition presents the following case: The petitioner resides in Maryland, in Baltimore county. While peaceably in his own house, with his family, it was at two o'clock, on the morning of the 25th of May, 1861, entered by an armed force, professing to act under military orders. He was then compelled to rise from his bed, taken into custody, and conveyed to Fort McHenry, where he is imprisoned by the commanding officer, without warrant from any lawful authority.

The commander of the fort, Gen. George Cadwalader, by whom he is detained in confinement, in his return to the writ, does not deny any of the facts alleged in the petition.

The case, then, is simply this: A military officer residing in Pennsylvania issues an order to arrest a citizen of Maryland, upon vague and indefinite charges, without any proof, so far as appears. Under this order his house is entered in the night; he is seized as a prisoner, and conveyed to Fort McHenry, and there kept in close confinement. And when a *habeas corpus* is served on the commanding officer, requiring him to produce the prisoner before a Justice of the Supreme Court, in order that he may examine into the legality of the imprisonment, the answer of the officer is that he is authorized by the President to suspend the writ of *habeas corpus* at his discretion, and, in the exercise of that discretion, suspends it in this case, and on that ground refuses obedience to the writ.

As the case comes before me, therefore, I understand that the President not only claims the right to suspend the writ of *habeas corpus* himself, at his discretion, but to delegate that discretionary power to a military officer, and to leave it to him to determine whether he will or will not obey judicial process that may be served upon him.

No official notice has been given to the courts of justice, or to the public, by proclamation or otherwise, that the President claimed this power, and had exercised it in the manner stated in the return. And I certainly listened to it with some surprise, for I had supposed it to be one of those points of constitutional law upon which there is no difference of opinion, and that it was admitted on all hands that the privilege of the writ could not be suspended except by act of Congress.

Being thus officially notified that the privilege of the writ has been suspended under the orders and by the authority of the President, and believing as I do that the President has exercised a power which he does not possess under the Constitution, a proper respect for the high office he fills requires me to state plainly and fully the grounds of my opinion, in order to show that I have not ventured to question the legality of this act without a careful and deliberate examination of the whole subject.

Article I of the Constitution, the legislative article, includes the following provision: "The privilege of the writ of habeas corpus shall not be suspended, unless when in cases of rebellion or invasion the public safety may require it." Since the constitutional protection against suspending habeas relief is included in the legislative article, it would seem to be a limitation on Congress. But could a president suspend *habeas* protections? That was the issue before the court in this case.

The clause in the Constitution which authorizes the suspension of the privilege of the writ of *habeas corpus* is in the ninth section of the first article. This article is devoted to the Legislative Department of the United States, and has not the slightest reference to the Executive Department.

The great importance which the framers of the Constitution attached to the privilege of the writ of *habeas corpus*, to protect the liberty of the citizen, is proved by the fact that its suspension, except in cases of invasion and rebellion, is first in the list of prohibited powers; and even in these cases the power is denied and its exercise prohibited unless the public safety shall require it. It is true that in the cases mentioned Congress is of necessity the judge of whether the public safety does or does not require it; and its judgment is conclusive. But the introduction of these words is a standing admonition to the legislative body of the danger of suspending it and of the extreme caution they should exercise before they give the Government of the United States such power over the liberty of a citizen.

It is the second article of the Constitution that provides for the organization of the Executive Department, and enumerates the powers conferred on it, and prescribes its duties. And if the high power over the liberty of the citizens now claimed was intended to be conferred on the President, it would undoubtedly be found in plain words in this article. But there is not a word in it that can furnish the slightest ground to justify the exercise of the power.

He is not empowered to arrest anyone charged with an offence against the United States, and whom he may, from the evidence before him, believe to be guilty; nor can he authorize any officer, civil or military, to exercise this power, for the fifth article of the amendments to the Constitution expressly provides that no person "shall be deprived of life, liberty, or property without due process of law;" that is, judicial process.

With such provisions in the Constitution, expressed in language too clear to be misunderstood by any one, I can see no ground whatever for supposing that the President, in any emergency or in any state of things, can authorize the suspension of the privilege of the writ of *habeas corpus*, or arrest a citizen, except in aid of the judicial power. He certainly does not faithfully execute the laws if he takes upon himself legislative power by suspending the writ of *habeas corpus*— and the judicial power, also, by arresting and imprisoning a person without due process of law. Nor can any argument be drawn from the nature of sovereignty, or the necessities of government for self-defense, in times of tumult and danger. The Government of the United States is one of delegated and limited powers. It derives its existence and authority altogether from the Constitution, and neither of its branches—executive, legislative or judicial—can exercise any of the powers of government beyond those specified and granted.

The right of the subject to the benefit of the writ of *habeas corpus,* it must be recollected, was one of the great points in controversy during the long struggle in England between arbitrary government and free institutions, and must therefore have strongly attracted the attention of statesmen engaged in framing a new and, as they supposed, a freer government than the one which they had thrown off by the Revolution.

But the documents before me show that the military authority in this case has gone far beyond the mere suspension of the privilege of the writ of *habeas corpus.* It has, by force of arms, thrust aside the judicial authorities and officers to whom the Constitution has confided the power and duty of interpreting and administering the laws, and substituted a military government in its place, to be administered and executed by military officers.

I can only say that if the authority which the Constitution has confided to the judiciary department and judicial officers may thus upon any pretext or under any circumstances be usurped by the military power at its discretion, the people of the United States are no longer living under a Government of laws, but every citizen holds life, liberty, and property at the will and pleasure of the army officer in whose military district he may happen to be found.

In Taney's view, Merryman was due immediate relief from his imprisonment because only Congress could suspend habeas corpus and only under very limited circumstances when invasion, rebellion, or the public safety demands it. Nonetheless, Taney faced severe limitations in ensuring the Lincoln administration acted on his decision granting Merryman relief. Indeed, the military authority simply ignored the decision of the court. Here, Taney seems resigned to the fact that he could not enforce the decision.

In such a case my duty was too plain to be mistaken. I have exercised all the power which the Constitution and laws confer on me, but that power has been resisted by a force too strong for me to overcome. It is possible that the officer who has incurred this grave responsibility may have misunderstood his instructions, and exceeded the authority intended to be given him. I shall, therefore, order all the proceedings in this case, with my opinion, to be filed and recorded in the Circuit Court of the United States for the District of Maryland, and direct the clerk to transmit a copy, under seal, to the President of the United States. It will then remain for that high officer, in fulfilment of his constitutional obligation to "take care that the laws be faithfully executed," to determine what measures he will take to cause the civil process of the United States to be respected and enforced.

R. B. Taney,

Chief Justice of the Supreme Court of the United States

Source: *Ex Parte Merryman*, 17 F. Cas. 144 (C.C.D. Md. 1861) (No. 9487).

President Lincoln was well aware of the constitutional difficulties that attended his decision to suspend the writ of habeas corpus. Indeed, he recognized that his constitutional obligation to "take care that the laws be faithfully executed" was in many respects in tension with what he perceived as his larger obligation to preserve the Union. In stark terms, Lincoln asked, "are all the laws, *but one*, to go unexecuted, and the government itself to go to pieces, lest that one be violated?" That is, he understood the guarantee of habeas protection as secondary to the more important requirement that he "preserve, protect, and defend the Constitution of the United States." Circumstances demanded that he bracket specific requirements and protections in order to preserve the whole. The dilemma, though, was striking. Both Taney and Lincoln presented defensible and principled positions on the weighty issue. Years later, a justice of the Supreme Court, Robert H. Jackson, would remark "[h]ad Mr. Lincoln scrupulously observed the Taney policy, I do not know whether we would have had any liberty, and had the Chief Justice adopted Mr. Lincoln's philosophy as the philosophy of law, I again do not know whether we would have had any liberty." For its part, though, Congress later authorized many of Lincoln's unilateral actions taken during that 10-week period.

Lincoln Uses War Powers to Free the Slaves

Abraham Lincoln's Emancipation Proclamation

January 1, 1863

INTRODUCTION

In a letter to the influential newspaper editor and abolitionist, Horace Greeley, President Lincoln wrote the following: "I would save the Union. I would save it the shortest way under the Constitution.... If I could save the Union without freeing any slave I would do it, and if I could save it by freeing all the slaves I would do it; and if I could save it by freeing some and leaving others alone I would also do that. What I do about slavery, ... I do because I believe it helps to save the Union; and what I forbear, I forbear because I do not believe it would help to save the Union. I have here stated my purpose according to my view of official duty; and I intend no modification of my oft-expressed personal wish that all men everywhere could be free."

There are at least two important issues to note about this passage. First, many historians and abolitionist contemporaries of Lincoln's took his ambivalence to mean that Lincoln was not interested in freeing the slaves, or that he would do so only slowly and deliberately. Others argue that Lincoln drew a distinction between his official duty as a president and his preferences as a private citizen. That is, he saw his obligation to his constitutional office as separable from the set of strongly held beliefs and preferences he may have for a particular policy (even the issue of slavery). The Union was at stake; extraconstitutional action and prerogative power by the president could only be justified when the constitutional order itself was imperiled—not when the moral and political preferences of the president demanded the action. Second, this letter was written in August 1862. By that time, Lincoln was already reviewing drafts of what would become the Emancipation Proclamation of January 1, 1863.

A difficulty arose, however, as the proclamation itself could run afoul of other constitutionally protected liberties retained by the people, even in the states that had voted to secede. Recall that the federal government did not recognize those states as having left the Union. As a result, the individuals in those states retained protections from action by the federal government, and in particular, due process protections against the taking of private property (which would have included slaves). Lincoln's position was that the Constitutional dilemma could be avoided by the invocation of the war powers of the president as commander in chief.

By the President of the United States of America:

A Proclamation.

Whereas, on the twenty-second day of September, in the year of our Lord one thousand eight hundred and sixty-two, a proclamation was issued by the President of the United States, containing, among other things, the following, to wit:

"That on the first day of January, in the year of our Lord one thousand eight hundred and sixty-three, **all persons held as slaves within any State or designated part of a State, the people whereof shall then be in rebellion against the United States, shall be then, thenceforward, and forever free**; and the Executive Government of the United States, including the military and naval authority thereof, will recognize and maintain the freedom of such persons, and will do no act or acts to repress such persons, or any of them, in any efforts they may make for their actual freedom.

"That the Executive will, on the first day of January aforesaid, by proclamation, designate the States and parts of States, if any, in which the people thereof, respectively, shall then be in rebellion against the United States; and the fact that any State, or the people thereof, shall on that day be, in good faith, represented in the Congress of the United States by members chosen thereto at elections wherein a majority of the qualified voters of such State shall have participated, shall, in the absence of strong countervailing testimony, be deemed conclusive evidence that such State, and the people thereof, are not then in rebellion against the United States."

Now, therefore I, Abraham Lincoln, President of the United States, by virtue of the power in me vested as Commander-in-Chief, of the Army and Navy of the United States in time of actual armed rebellion against the authority and government of the United States, and as a fit and necessary war measure for suppressing said rebellion, do, on this first day of January, in the year of our Lord one thousand eight hundred and sixty-three, and in accordance with my purpose so to do publicly proclaimed for the full period of one hundred days, from the day first above mentioned, order and designate as the States and parts of States wherein the people thereof respectively, are this day in rebellion against the United States, the following, to wit:

Because Lincoln justified the issuance of the Emancipation Proclamation as an extension of his war powers, it could only apply to slaves held in areas controlled by the enemy. That is, slaves in areas under Union control were not freed by the proclamation. This is because under international laws of war, the precedent of the Prize Cases, and the authority granted Congress in Art. 1, Section 8 of the Constitution, the national government could seize enemy property when its seizure is necessary to prosecute the war. Without the authority granted by that war power, the seizure of the property of Southern slaveholders would violate the 5th Amendment. Ironically, then, the proclamation only freed those slaves in regions where the federal government could not actually free them and left in bondage slaves in regions where federal authority remained.

Arkansas, Texas, Louisiana, (except the Parishes of St. Bernard, Plaquemines, Jefferson, St. John, St. Charles, St. James Ascension, Assumption, Terrebonne, Lafourche, St. Mary, St. Martin, and Orleans, including the City of New Orleans) Mississippi, Alabama, Florida, Georgia, South Carolina, North Carolina, and Virginia, (except the forty-eight counties designated as West Virginia, and also the counties of Berkley, Accomac, Northampton, Elizabeth City, York, Princess Ann, and Norfolk, including the cities of Norfolk and Portsmouth[)], and which excepted parts, are for the present, left precisely as if this proclamation were not issued.

And by virtue of the power, and for the purpose aforesaid, I do order and declare that all persons held as slaves within said designated States, and parts of States, are, and henceforward shall be free; and that the Executive government of the United States, including the military and naval authorities thereof, will recognize and maintain the freedom of said persons.

And I hereby enjoin upon the people so declared to be free to abstain from all violence, unless in necessary self-defence; and I recommend to them that, in all cases when allowed, they labor faithfully for reasonable wages.

This passage proved to be the most consequential element of the Emancipation Proclamation. Aside from its obvious symbolic value—the federal government has declared to be free all slaves in regions of the country that were in rebellion—the proclamation encouraged African Americans to take up the Union cause by enlisting in the military. As a result, Black regiments proliferated, and ultimately comprised roughly 10% of all Union Navy and Army personnel. You will note, however, that the passage refers to their role as support personnel, and not as combat troops. Due to discriminatory practices in the military, Black soldiers were not deployed into battle to the extent they might have been. The 54th Massachusetts Infantry Regiment, however, would become one of the most celebrated units in the Union Army after leading the assault on Ft. Wagner in South Carolina. The Black unit lost half its number in the assault, but through its sacrifice dispelled a great deal of cynicism about the abilities of Black troops in combat.

And I further declare and make known, that such persons of suitable condition, will be received into the armed service of the United States to garrison forts, positions, stations, and other places, and to man vessels of all sorts in said service.

And upon this act, sincerely believed to be an act of justice, warranted by the Constitution, upon military necessity, I invoke the considerate judgment of mankind, and the gracious favor of Almighty God.

In witness whereof, I have hereunto set my hand and caused the seal of the United States to be affixed.

Done at the City of Washington, this first day of January, in the year of our Lord one thousand eight hundred and sixty three, and of the Independence of the United States of America the eighty-seventh.

By the President: ABRAHAM LINCOLN

Source: Abraham Lincoln, Emancipation Proclamation, January 1, 1863, Presidential Proclamations, 1791–1991, Record Group 11, General Records of the United States Government, National Archives.

The Emancipation Proclamation did not free all of the slaves in the United States. Rather, it emancipated only those slaves held in states of the Confederacy. Lincoln felt that the South could only be defeated with the abolition of slavery. Therefore, it was justified as a war measure to save the Union. As the quote from the letter to Horace Greeley indicates, the goal was the preservation of the constitutional order, not the abolition of slavery. Insofar as the taking of rebels' *property* was required for the successful prosecution of the war, the actions were justified. But the proclamation's constitutionality, though not really in question due to precedent and the laws of war, was never decided in court. Slavery was abolished by the 13th Amendment, which removed all need to inquire into the legality of the Emancipation Proclamation.

Lincoln's Defense of the Suspension of Habeas Corpus

Abraham Lincoln's Letter to Erastus Corning

June 12, 1863

INTRODUCTION

Lincoln's reaction to Taney's decision in *Ex Parte Merryman* was to simply ignore it. In fact, when the special session of Congress convened in July 1861, Lincoln only gave a general defense of his actions, including the suspension of habeas corpus. As a result, when historians review Lincoln's own writings for a window into his perspective, many turn to this letter from Lincoln to Erastus Corning. The so-called Corning letter was a reply to a group of Democrats in New York, led by Corning, who had protested the Lincoln administration's detention and trial by the military commission of Clement Vallandigham. The New York Democrats met and passed a series of resolutions calling for Lincoln to discontinue what they perceived to be unconstitutional actions, including the arrest and trial of their colleague from Ohio. Vallandigham was a leader of the Ohio Democratic Party and a vocal opponent of Lincoln and the war. He had been detained and tried by military authorities for "publicly expressing sympathy for those in arms against the Government of the United States, and declaring disloyal sentiments and opinions, with the object and purpose of weakening the power of the Government in its efforts to suppress an unlawful rebellion" (*Ex Parte Vallandigham*, 68 U.S. 1 Wall. 243 243 (1863)). In this letter, we see Lincoln offering a vigorous defense of the extraordinary actions taken by his administration in order to quell the rebellion. It is thought that the force of this letter, which will become immediately apparent, was in large part due to Lincoln's concerns that Northerners—particularly Northern Democrats who refused to support the war— would prove as responsible for the fall of the Union as the Confederacy itself.

Abraham Lincoln

Executive Mansion, Washington

Hon. Erastus Corning and Others.

Gentlemen:

Your letter of May 19, inclosing the resolutions of a public meeting held at Albany, New York, on the 16th of the same month, was received several days ago.

The resolutions, as I understand them, are resolvable into two propositions—first, the expression of a purpose to sustain the cause of the Union, to secure peace through victory, and to support the administration in every constitutional and lawful measure to suppress the rebellion; and, secondly, a declaration of censure upon the administration for supposed unconstitutional action, such as the making of military arrests. And from the two propositions a third is deduced, which is that the gentlemen composing the meeting are resolved on doing their part to maintain our common government and country, despite the folly or wickedness, as they may conceive, of any administration. This position is eminently patriotic, and as such I thank the meeting, and congratulate the nation for it. My own purpose is the same; so that the meeting and myself have a common object, and can have no difference, except in the choice of means or measures for effecting that object.

The meetings, by their resolutions, assert and argue that certain military arrests, and proceedings following them, for which I am ultimately responsible, are unconstitutional. I think they are not.

Prior to my installation here it had been inculcated that any State had a lawful right to secede from the national Union, and that it would be expedient to exercise the right whenever the devotees of the doctrine should fail to elect a president to their own liking. I was elected contrary to their liking; and, accordingly, so far as it was legally possible, they had taken seven States out of the Union, had seized many of the United States forts, and had fired upon the United States Flag, all before I was inaugurated, and, of course, before I had done any official act whatever. The rebellion thus began soon ran into the present civil war; and, in certain respects, it began on very unequal terms between the parties.

The insurgents had been preparing for it more than thirty years, while the government had taken no steps to resist them. The former had carefully considered all the means which could be turned to their account. It undoubtedly was a well-pondered reliance with them that in their own unrestricted effort to destroy Union, Constitution and law, all together, the government would, in great degree, be restrained by the same

In very clear terms, Lincoln is arguing that constitutional protections, such as free speech, free press, and habeas relief, provide cover for insurgents bent on dissolution of the Union. To enforce those protections and thereby limit the president in the face of such rebellion was to play into the hands of the Confederacy. In short, those who criticized his efforts he saw as aiding and abetting the Confederacy.

Constitution and law from arresting their progress. Their sympathizers pervaded all departments of the government and nearly all communities of the people. **From this material, under cover of "liberty of speech," "liberty of the press," and "habeas corpus," they hoped to keep on foot amongst us a most efficient corps of spies, informers, suppliers, and aiders and abettors of their cause in a thousand ways.** They knew that in times such as they were inaugurating, by the Constitution itself the "*habeas corpus*" might be suspended; but they also knew they had friends who would make a question as to who was to suspend it; meanwhile their spies and others might remain at large to help on their cause. Or if, as has happened, the Executive should suspend the writ without ruinous waste of time, instances of arresting innocent persons might occur, as are always likely to occur in such cases; and then a clamor could be raised in regard to this, which might be at least of some service to the insurgent cause. It needed no very keen perception to discover this part of the enemy's program, so soon as by open hostilities their machinery was fairly put in motion.

Lincoln portrays himself as "forced" into this position by threats to the public safety and the Union. In addition, reliance upon civilian courts for the trial of, for instance, sedition, would be inadequate. Keep this argument in mind when we consider the case of *Ex Parte Milligan* (1866).

Yet, thoroughly imbued with a reverence for the guaranteed rights of individuals, I was slow to adopt the strong measures which by degrees I have been forced to regard as being within the exceptions of the Constitution, and as indispensable to the public safety. Nothing is better known to history than that courts of justice are utterly incompetent to such cases. Civil courts are organized chiefly for trials of individuals, or, at most, a few individuals acting in concert—and this in quiet times, and on charges of crimes well defined in the law. Even in times of peace bands of horse-thieves and robbers frequently grow too numerous and powerful for the ordinary courts of justice. But what comparison, in numbers, have such bands ever borne to the insurgent sympathizers even in many of the loyal States? Again, a jury too frequently has at least one member more ready to hang the panel than to hang the traitor.

And yet again, he who dissuades one man from volunteering, or induces one soldier to desert, weakens the Union cause as much as he who kills a Union soldier in battle. Yet this dissuasion or inducement may be so conducted as to be no defined crime of which any civil court would take cognizance. Ours is a case of rebellion—so called by the resolutions before me—in fact, a clear, flagrant, and gigantic case of rebellion; and the provision of the Constitution that "the privilege of the writ of *habeas corpus* shall not be suspended unless when, in cases of rebellion or invasion, the public safety may require it," is the provision which specially applies to our present case. This provision plainly attests the understanding of those who made the Constitution that ordinary courts of justice are inadequate to "cases of rebellion"—attests their purpose that, in such cases, men may be held in custody whom the courts, acting on ordinary rules, would discharge. *Habeas corpus* does not discharge men who are proved to be guilty of defined crime; and its suspension is allowed by the Constitution on purpose that men may be arrested and held who cannot be proved to be guilty of defined crime, "when, in cases of rebellion or invasion, the public safety may require it."

This is precisely our present case—a case of rebellion wherein the public Safety does require the suspension. Indeed, arrests by process of courts and arrests in cases of rebellion do not proceed altogether upon the same basis. The former is directed at the small percentage of ordinary and continuous perpetration of crime, while the latter is directed at sudden and extensive uprisings against the government, which, at most, will succeed or fail in no great length of time. In the latter case arrests are made not so much for what has been done, as for what probably would be done. The latter is more for the preventive and less for the vindictive than the former. In such cases the purposes of men are much more easily understood than in cases of ordinary crime. **The man who stands by and says nothing when the peril of his government is discussed, cannot be misunderstood. If not hindered, he is sure to help the enemy; much more if he talks ambiguously—talks for his country with "buts," and "ifs" and "ands."**

Lincoln suggests that not only are critics of the government a threat to the prosecution of the war, but so too are those who remain silent or who equivocate in their support. Both those who remain silent and those who speak with " 'buts,' and 'ifs' and 'ands' " give comfort to the enemy. Patriotic fervor is the only protection against the sneaking sedition that Lincoln observes in the Northern Democrats, like Vallandigham and Corning. Moreover, he continues, had he acted preemptively in certain cases, the Union would have been more secure.

Of how little value the constitutional provision I have quoted will be rendered if arrests shall never be made until defined crimes shall have been committed, may be illustrated by a few notable examples: General John C. Breckenridge, General Robert E. Lee, General Joseph E. Johnston, General John B. Magruder, General William B. Preston, General Simon B. Buckner, and Commodore Franklin Buchanan, now occupying the very highest places in the rebel war service, were all within the power of the government since the rebellion began, and were nearly as well known to be traitors then as now. Unquestionably if we had seized and held them, the insurgent cause would be much weaker. But no one of them had then committed any crime defined in the law. Every one of them, if arrested, would have been discharged on *habeas corpus* were the writ allowed to operate. **In view of these and similar cases, I think the time not unlikely to come when I shall be blamed for having made too few arrests rather than too many.**

Lincoln seems to suggest that he came late to these justifiable measures and perhaps did not employ them to their full extent. One can imagine the reaction from the Peace Democrats, like Corning, who received this letter. This letter is not about encouraging healthy democratic debate on the weighty issues of presidential power during wartime; this was about silencing those who would dissent.

By the third resolution the meeting indicates their opinion that military arrests may be constitutional in localities where rebellion actually exists, but that such arrests are unconstitutional in localities where rebellion or insurrection does not actually exist. They insist that such arrests shall not be made "outside of the lines of necessary military occupation and the scenes of insurrection." Inasmuch, however, as the Constitution itself makes no such distinction, I am unable to believe that there is any such constitutional distinction.

Mr. Vallandigham avows his hostility to the war on the part of the Union; and his arrest was made because he was laboring, with some effect, to prevent the raising of troops, to encourage desertions from the army, and to leave the rebellion without an adequate military force to suppress it. He was not arrested because he was damaging the political prospects of the administration or the personal interests of the commanding general, but because he was damaging the army, upon the existence and vigor of which the life of the nation depends. He was warring upon the military, and this gave the military constitutional jurisdiction to lay hands upon him. If Mr. Vallandigham was not damaging the military power of the country, then his arrest was made on mistake of fact, which I would be glad to correct on reasonably satisfactory evidence.

Long experience has shown that armies cannot be maintained unless desertion shall be punished by the severe penalty of death. The case requires, and the law and the
Constitution sanction, this punishment. Must I shoot a
simple-minded soldier boy who deserts, while I must not
touch a hair of a wily agitator who induces him to desert?
I think that, in such a case, to silence the agitator and save the
boy is not only constitutional, but withal a great mercy.
If I be wrong on this question of constitutional power, my error
lies in believing that certain proceedings are constitutional
when, in cases of rebellion or invasion, the public safety
requires them, which would not be constitutional when, in
absence of rebellion or invasion, the public safety does not
require them: in other words, that the Constitution is not in its
application in all respects the same in cases of rebellion or
invasion involving the public safety, as it is in times of profound peace and public security. The Constitution itself makes
the distinction, and **I can no more be persuaded that the
government can constitutionally take no strong measures
in time of rebellion, because it can be shown that the same
could not be lawfully taken in time of peace, than I can be
persuaded that a particular drug is not good medicine for
a sick man because it can be shown to not be good food
for a well one. Nor am I able to appreciate the danger
apprehended by the meeting, that the American people will
by means of military arrests during the rebellion lose the
right of public discussion, the liberty of speech and the
press, the law of evidence, trial by jury, and *habeas
corpus* throughout the indefinite peaceful future which
I trust lies before them, any more than I am able to believe
that a man could contract so strong an appetite for emetics
during temporary illness as to persist in feeding upon them
during the remainder of his healthful life.**

This is an interesting passage in that Lincoln's argument may not be as persuasive as he would like to think. Surely, one can imagine the addictive qualities of medicines that continue to pull at the patient long after the illness has been cured. In this metaphor, he seems remarkably unaware of the effect that a strong medicine, like exceptional executive powers, may be desired by a political community long after the crisis is over.

One of the resolutions expresses the opinion of the meeting
that arbitrary arrests will have the effect to divide and distract those who should be united in suppressing the rebellion,
and I am specifically called on to discharge Mr. Vallandigham. I regard this as, at least, a fair appeal to me on the
expediency of exercising a constitutional power which
I think exists. In response to such appeal I have to say, it gave

me pain when I learned that Mr. Vallandigham had been arrested (that is, I was pained that there should have seemed to be a necessity for arresting him), and that it will afford me great pleasure to discharge him so soon as I can by any means believe the public safety will not suffer by it.

The scrappiness of the Corning letter reveals a Lincoln committed to ensuring that the Democratic Party recognizes that opposing the war itself is equivalent to giving aid and comfort to the Confederacy. To that end, the letter marshals the full force of patriotic fervor to crush the seditious elements of the Peace Democrats. In the months that followed, the message appeared to have been received and the political landscape shifted. Northern Democrats lost many seats and in 1864 would nominate a prowar candidate to run against Lincoln for the presidency. This shift in emphasis would coincide with a softening of rhetoric from Lincoln as well, as we will see in later chapters.

I further say that, as the war progress, it appears to me, opinion and action, which were in great confusion at first, take shape and fall into more regular channels, so that the necessity for arbitrary dealing with them gradually decreases. I have every reason to desire that it should cease altogether, and far from the least is my regard for the opinions and wishes of those who, like the meeting at Albany, declare their purpose to sustain the government in every constitutional and lawful measure to suppress the rebellion. Still, I must continue to do so much as may seem to be required by the public safety.

A. Lincoln.

Source: Edward McPherson, *The Political History of the United States of America during the Great Rebellion*, 2nd edition (Washington, DC: Phip & Solomons, 1865), 163–167.

Limits on Trials by Military Commissions

Ex Parte Milligan

April 3, 1866

INTRODUCTION

More than a year after Lincoln suspended the writ of *habeas corpus* along the resupply lines into the nation's capital, he issued a second proclamation suspending the privilege under the authority granted him by Congress through the passage of the Habeas Corpus Act of 1863. However, neither Lincoln's proclamation nor the Habeas Corpus Act itself authorized the trial of civilians by military commissions. Nonetheless, under the authority of Lincoln's proclamation, Lambdin Milligan was arrested in Indiana on October 5, 1864, for "[conspiring] against the government, [affording] aid and comfort to rebels, and [inciting] the people to insurrection" (*Ex parte Milligan*, 71 U.S. 4 Wall. 2 (1866)). Along with four other *sons of liberty*, Milligan had been a conspirator in a plot to break into a federal weapons arsenal for the purpose of using the weapons to free Confederate soldiers held in Union prisoner-of-war camps. After his arrest, he was brought before a military commission, tried, found guilty of all charges against him, and sentenced to death by hanging.

Mr. Justice DAVIS delivered the opinion of the court.

The controlling question in the case is this: upon the facts stated in Milligan's petition and the exhibits filed, had the military commission mentioned in it jurisdiction legally to try and sentence him? Milligan, not a resident of one of the rebellious states or a prisoner of war, but a citizen of Indiana for twenty years past and never in the military or naval service, is, while at his home, arrested by the military power of the United States, imprisoned, and, on certain criminal charges preferred against him, tried, convicted, and sentenced to be hanged by a military commission, organized under the direction of the military commander of the military district of Indiana. **Had this tribunal the legal power and authority to try and punish this man?**

No graver question was ever considered by this court, nor one which more nearly concerns the rights of the whole people, for it is the birthright of every American citizen when charged with crime to be tried and punished according to law. By the

This, of course, is the key constitutional question in the Milligan case. Milligan was arrested on October 5, 1864, and sentenced to be hanged on May 9, 1865. In the interim, President Lincoln died and was succeeded by President Johnson, who upheld Milligan's sentence. At the last possible moment, Milligan petitioned for habeas relief, was granted a stay (his sentence was commuted, by Johnson, to life in prison), and the Court agreed to hear the case in March 1866.

protection of the law, human rights are secured; withdraw that protection and they are at the mercy of wicked rulers or the clamor of an excited people. If there was law to justify this military trial, it is not our province to interfere; if there was not, it is our duty to declare the nullity of the whole proceedings. The decision of this question does not depend on argument or judicial precedents, numerous and highly illustrative as they are. These precedents inform us of the extent of the struggle to preserve liberty and to relieve those in civil life from military trials. The founders of our government were familiar with the history of that struggle, and secured in a written constitution every right which the people had wrested from power during a contest of ages. By that Constitution and the laws authorized by it, this question must be determined. The provisions of that instrument on the administration of criminal justice are too plain and direct to leave room for misconstruction or doubt of their true meaning. Those applicable to this case are found in that clause of the original Constitution which says "That the trial of all crimes, except in case of impeachment, shall be by jury," and in the fourth, fifth, and sixth articles of the amendments.

Remember that this case was decided a full year after the Civil War ended. Justice Davis is writing here with an eye on the military conflict of the Civil War, for sure, but the effect of the decision would not live up to the rhetoric of this passage. Because the hostilities had ended, the real effect of this decision was to release a few pro-Confederate conspirators from prison. It did not present a powerful constitutional bulwark against executive overreach, irrespective of its language here. One might argue, however, that the power of this passage lies not in its practical effect but in its admonition to future presidents and in granting future Congresses, courts, and citizens the authority to constrain executive power. Perhaps, but as we will discover, we've yet to see such constraints employed in meaningful ways during times of crisis.

The Constitution of the United States is a law for rulers and people, equally in war and in peace, and covers with the shield of its protection all classes of men, at all times and under all circumstances. No doctrine involving more pernicious consequences was ever invented by the wit of man than that any of its provisions can be suspended during any of the great exigencies of government. Such a doctrine leads directly to anarchy or despotism, but the theory of necessity on which it is based is false, for the government, within the Constitution, has all the powers granted to it which are necessary to preserve its existence, as has been happily proved by the result of the great effort to throw off its just authority.

Have any of the rights guaranteed by the Constitution been violated in the case of Milligan?, and, if so, what are they?

Every trial involves the exercise of judicial power, and from what source did the military commission that tried him derive their authority? Certainly no part of judicial power of the country was conferred on them, because the Constitution expressly vests it "in one supreme court and such inferior courts as the Congress may from time to time ordain and establish," and it is not pretended that the commission was a court ordained and established by Congress. They cannot justify on the mandate of the President, because he is controlled by law, and has his appropriate sphere of duty, which is to execute, not to make, the laws, and there is "no unwritten criminal code to which resort can be had as a source of jurisdiction."

But it is said that the jurisdiction is complete under the "laws and usages of war."

It can serve no useful purpose to inquire what those laws and usages are, whence they originated, where found, and on whom they operate; they can never be applied to citizens in states which have upheld the authority of the government, and where the courts are open and their process unobstructed. This court has judicial knowledge that, in Indiana, the Federal authority was always unopposed, and its courts always open to hear criminal accusations and redress grievances, and no usage of war could sanction a military trial there for any offence whatever of a citizen in civil life in nowise connected with the military service. Congress could grant no such power, and, to the honor of our national legislature be it said, it has never been provoked by the state of the country even to attempt its exercise. One of the plainest constitutional provisions was therefore infringed when Milligan was tried by a court not ordained and established by Congress and not composed of judges appointed during good behavior.

Why was he not delivered to the Circuit Court of Indiana to be proceeded against according to law? No reason of necessity could be urged against it, because Congress had declared penalties against the offences charged, provided for their punishment, and directed that court to hear and determine them. And soon after this military tribunal was ended, the Circuit Court met, peacefully transacted its business, and adjourned. It needed no bayonets to protect it, and required no military aid to execute its judgments. It was held in a state, eminently distinguished for patriotism, by judges commissioned during the Rebellion, who were provided with juries, upright, intelligent, and selected by a marshal appointed by the President. The government had no right to conclude that Milligan, if guilty, would not receive in that court merited punishment, for its records disclose that it was constantly engaged in the trial of similar offences, and was never interrupted in its administration of criminal justice. If it was dangerous, in the distracted condition of affairs, to leave Milligan unrestrained of his liberty because he "conspired against the government, afforded aid and comfort to rebels, and incited the people to insurrection," the law said arrest him, confine him closely, render him powerless to do further mischief, and then present his case to the grand jury of the district, with proofs of his guilt, and, if indicted, try him according to the course of the common law. If this had been done, the Constitution would have been vindicated, the law of 1863 enforced, and the securities for personal liberty preserved and defended.

It is claimed that martial law covers with its broad mantle the proceedings of this military commission. The proposition is this: that, in a time of war, the commander of an armed force (if, in his opinion, the exigencies of the country demand it, and of which he is to judge) has the power, within the lines of his military district, to suspend all civil rights and their remedies and subject citizens, as well as soldiers to the rule of *his will,* and, in the exercise of his lawful authority, cannot be restrained except by his superior officer or the President of the United States.

Martial law established on such a basis destroys every guarantee of the Constitution, and effectually renders the "military independent of and superior to the civil power"—the attempt to do which by the King of Great Britain was deemed by our fathers such an offence that they assigned it to the world as one of the causes which impelled them to declare their independence. Civil liberty and this kind of martial law cannot endure together; the antagonism is irreconcilable, and, in the conflict, one or the other must perish.

This nation, as experience has proved, cannot always remain at peace, and has no right to expect that it will always have wise and humane rulers sincerely attached to the principles of the Constitution. Wicked men, ambitious of power, with hatred of liberty and contempt of law, may fill the place once occupied by Washington and Lincoln, and if this right is conceded, and the calamities of war again befall us, the dangers to human liberty are frightful to contemplate. If our fathers had failed to provide for just such a contingency, they would have been false to the trust reposed in them. They knew—the history of the world told them—the nation they were founding, be its existence short or long, would be involved in war; how often or how long continued human foresight could not tell, and that unlimited power, wherever lodged at such a time, was especially hazardous to freemen. For this and other equally weighty reasons, they secured the inheritance they had fought to maintain by incorporating in a written constitution the safeguards which time had proved were essential to its preservation. Not one of these safeguards can the President or Congress or the Judiciary disturb, except the one concerning the writ of habeas corpus.

It is essential to the safety of every government that, in a great crisis like the one we have just passed through, there should be a power somewhere of suspending the writ of habeas corpus. Unquestionably, there is then an exigency which demands that the government, if it should see fit in the exercise of a proper discretion to make arrests, should not be required to produce the persons arrested in answer to a writ of habeas corpus. The Constitution goes no further. It does not say, after a writ of habeas corpus is denied a citizen, that he shall be tried otherwise than by the course of the common law; if it had intended this result, it was easy, by the use of direct words, to have accomplished it.

But it is insisted that the safety of the country in time of war demands that this broad claim for martial law shall be sustained. If this were true, it could be well said that a country, preserved at the sacrifice of all the cardinal principles of liberty, is not worth the cost of preservation. Happily, it is not so.

It will be borne in mind that this is not a question of the power to proclaim martial law when war exists in a community and the courts and civil authorities are overthrown. Nor is it a question what rule a military commander, at the head of his army, can impose on states in rebellion to cripple their resources and quell the insurrection.

> On [Indiana's] soil there was no hostile foot; if once invaded, that invasion was at an end, and, with it, all pretext for martial law. Martial law cannot arise from a *threatened* invasion. The necessity must be actual and present, the invasion real, such as effectually closes the courts and deposes the civil administration.

It is difficult to see how the *safety* for the country required martial law in Indiana. If any of her citizens were plotting treason, the power of arrest could secure them until the government was prepared for their trial, when the courts were open and ready to try them.

It follows from what has been said on this subject that there are occasions when martial rule can be properly applied. If, in foreign invasion or civil war, the courts are actually closed, and it is impossible to administer criminal justice according to law, *then*, on the theatre of active military operations, where war really prevails, there is a necessity to furnish a substitute for the civil authority, thus overthrown, to preserve the safety of the army and society, and as no power is left but the military, it is allowed to govern by martial rule until the laws can have their free course. As necessity creates the rule, so it limits its duration, for, if this government is continued *after* the courts are reinstated, it is a gross usurpation of power. Martial rule can never exist where the courts are open and in the proper and unobstructed exercise of their jurisdiction. It is also confined to the locality of actual war. Because, during the late Rebellion, it could have been enforced in Virginia, where the national authority was overturned and the courts driven out, it does not follow that it should obtain in Indiana, where that authority was never disputed and justice was always administered. And so, in the case of a foreign invasion, martial rule may become a

Here is the court's decision, then. The writ of habeas corpus had not been suspended by Congress; therefore, Milligan must be released, or tried in civilian court. The executive has no constitutional authority to detain and try by means of a military commission a civilian in areas where the civil courts of the United States are open and functioning. The military commission cannot try civilians when those civilians could, like Milligan and his coconspirators, be tried through civil courts in Indianapolis, for example. At the time of Milligan's detention, the civil courts in Indiana were open for business and could have heard his case under the procedures required by the 1863 Habeas Corpus Act.

necessity in one state when, in another, it would be "mere lawless violence."

If the military trial of Milligan was contrary to law, then he was entitled, on the facts stated in his petition, to be discharged from custody by the terms of the act of Congress of March 3d, 1863. But it is insisted that Milligan was a prisoner of war, and therefore excluded from the privileges of the statute. **It is not easy to see how he can be treated as a prisoner of war when he lived in Indiana for the past twenty years, was arrested there, and had not been, during the late troubles, a resident of any of the states in rebellion. If in Indiana he conspired with bad men to assist the enemy, he is punishable for it in the courts of Indiana.**

Source: *Ex Parte Milligan*, 71 U.S. (4 Wall.) 2 (1866).

In all, the *Ex Parte Milligan* decision limits the ability of presidents to institute military commissions to try civilians in areas where the domestic courts are open. Four members of the court concurred in the judgment, but separated themselves from Davis in at least one important respect. Davis suggested, in dicta, that even Congress could not sanction military commissions where the civilian courts are open. The concurrence, written by Justice Chase, however, was more permissive of congressional action: "We think that the power of Congress, in such times and in such localities, to authorize trials for crimes against the safety and security of the national forces, may be derived from its constitutional authority to raise and support armies and to declare war...." As we will see, the issue of congressionally authorized military commissions has arisen a few times since the Civil War—most notably during World War II and after 9/11.

The Impeachment of Andrew Johnson

Benjamin Butler's Opening Argument

February 24, 1868

INTRODUCTION

A group of former abolitionists in Congress, known as the Radical Republicans, sought to transform the postwar South from a system of apartheid to a more democratic political, economic, and social community. To this end, they passed a Civil Rights Act which was intended to eradicate the so-called Black Codes that had been passed by White Southerners resistant to African American suffrage. The Civil Rights Act granted basic civil liberties and rights to African Americans, including the right to hold property, serve on a jury, and vote. Andrew Johnson, who had assumed the office of the president upon the death of Abraham Lincoln on April 15, 1865, vetoed the measure because, he said, it would sow "discord among the races." When the Congress narrowly overrode his veto, there began a series of very public bitter disputes between President Johnson and the Radical Republicans in control of the House and Senate, which ultimately led to Johnson's impeachment.

Though he supported the Union during the Civil War, Johnson was from the South and was not inclined to support the Reconstruction Acts as passed by the Radical Republicans, like Thaddeus Stevens, Charles Sumner, and Benjamin Butler. Johnson thought that the acts, which, among other things, ensured access to the ballot box for the newly freed slaves, were not within the power of the federal government, and therefore unconstitutional. As a result, he first vetoed them, and then when those vetoes were overridden, he refused to enforce their provisions. At every turn, Johnson sought to limit the entire reconstruction project of the Radical Republicans. One of the acts that was vetoed and then overridden by Congress was the Tenure in Office Act. This act required Senate approval for the removal of any official who required Senate approval for appointment. That meant that if the president wanted to remove a cabinet official, he would have to receive Senate approval to do so.

Secretary of War Edwin Stanton was a key Republican supporter of the reconstruction measures. In fact, Stanton had taken action to require the military commanders from the reconstruction districts to report to Congress, and not the president. Incensed by this, Johnson unilaterally removed Stanton from office and replaced him with a new secretary of war. Eventually, Stanton refused to be removed and barricaded himself into his office to await Senate approval of his removal. Within days, 11 articles of impeachment were passed in the House. The trial began in the Senate in March, with the chief justice of the U.S. Supreme Court Salmon P. Chase presiding. The House managers of the impeachment proceedings Rep. Stevens and Butler made the case for impeachment.

The CHIEF JUSTICE. Gentlemen, Managers of the House of Representatives, you will now proceed in support of the articles of impeachment. Senators will please give their attention.

Opening Argument of Mr. Butler, of Massachusetts, one of the Managers on the impeachment of the President.

Mr. President and Gentlemen of the Senate:

The onerous duty has fallen to my fortune to present to you, imperfectly as I must, the several propositions of fact and law upon which the House of Representatives will endeavor sustain the cause of the people against the President of the United States, now pending at your bar.

The high station of the accused, the novelty of the proceeding, the gravity of the business, the importance of the questions to be presented to your adjudication, the possible momentous result of the issues, each and all must plead for me to claim your attention for as long a time as your patience may endure.

Now, for the first time in the history of the world, has a nation brought before its highest tribunal its chief magistrate for trial and possible deposition from office upon charges of maladministration of the powers and duties of that office. In other times and in other lands it has been found that despotism could only be tempered by assassination, and nations living under constitutional governments even have found no mode by which to rid themselves of a tyrannical, imbecile, or faithless ruler, save by overturning the very foundation and framework of the Government itself. And but recently, in one of the most civilized and powerful governments of the world, from which our own institutions have been largely modeled, we have seen a nation submit for years to the rule of an insane king, because its constitution contained no method for his removal.

This, them, is the plain and inevitable issue before the Senate and the American people:

Has the President, under the Constitution, the more kingly prerogative at will to remove from office and suspend from office indefinitely, all executive officers of the United States, either civil, military, or naval, at any and all times, and fill the vacancies with creatures of his own appointment, for his own purposes, without any restraint whatever, or possibility of restraint by the Senate or by Congress through laws duly enacted.

The House of Representatives, in behalf of the people, join this issue by affirming that the exercise of such powers is a high misdemeanor in office.

If the affirmative is maintained by the respondent, then, so far as the first eight articles are concerned—unless such corrupt purposes are shown as will of themselves make the exercise of a legal power a crime—the respondent must go, and ought to go quit and free.

Therefore, by these articles and answers thereto, the momentous question, here and now, is raised whether the *presidential office itself (if it has the prerogatives and power claimed for it) ought, in fact, to exist as a part of the constitutional government of a free people,* while by the last three articles the simpler and less important inquiry is to be determined, whether Andrew Johnson has so conducted himself that he ought longer to hold any constitutional office whatever. The latter sinks to merited insignificance compared with the grandeur of the former.

In the 2d of March, 1867, the tenure-of-office act provided, in substance, that all civil officers duly qualified to act by appointment, with the advice and consent of the Senate, shall be entitled to hold such office until a successor shall have been in like manner appointed and duly qualified, except has herein otherwise provided, to wit: "provided that the Secretaries shall hold their office during the term of the President by whom they may have been appointed, and for one month thereafter, subject to removal by and with the advice and consent of the senate.

So the President of the United States, with a determination to assert at all hazards the tremendous power of removal of every officer, without the consent of the Senate, did not deem it "material or necessary" that the Senate should know that he had suspend Mr. Stanton indefinitely against the provisions of the tenure of office act, with full intent, at all hazards to remove him, and that the solemn deliberations of the Senate, which the President of the United States was then calling upon them to make in a matter of the highest governmental concern, were only to be of use in case they suited his purposes; that it was not "material or necessary" for the Senate to know that its high decisions was futile and useless that the President was playing fast and loose with this branch of the Government—which was never before done save by himself.

If Andrew Johnson never committed any other offense—if we know nothing of him save from this avowal—we should have a full picture of his mind and heart, painted in colors of living light, so that no man will ever mistake his mental and moral lineaments hereafter.

Instead of open and frank dealing as becomes the head of a great Government in every relation of life, and especially needful from the highest executive officer of the Government to the highest legislative branch thereof; instead of a manly, straightforward bearing, claiming openly and distinctly the rights which he believed pertained to his high office, and yielding to the other branches, fairly and justly, those which belong to them, we find him, upon this position he must stand before the Senate and the country if they believe his answer, which I do not, that he had at that time these intents and purposes in his mind and they are not the subterfuge and evasion and after-thought which a criminal brought to bay makes to escape the consequences of his acts.

Article ten alleges that, intending to set aside the rightful authority and powers of Congress, and to bring into disgrace and contempt the Congress of the United States, and to destroy confidence in and to excite odium against Congress and its laws, he, Andrew Johnson, President of the United States, made divers speeches set out therein, whereby he brought the office of President into contempt, ridicule and disgrace.

In recent months, Johnson had publically declared his contempt for the Congress as the bitterness continued to grow between the two branches. He declared Congress to be a "body hanging on the verge of the Government" and that it was "pretending to be a Congress when, in fact, it was not a Congress." Moreover, he suggested that it was "a Congress which had done everything to be for the Union when its every step and act tended to perpetuate disunion ... and make a disruption of the States inevitable." The House managers of the impeachment proceedings thought that saying these things was prelude to tyranny—and an *overthrow of Congress* by the executive.

The issue, them, finally, is this: that those utterances of his, in the manner and form in which they are alleged to have been made, and under the circumstances and at the time they were made, are decent and becoming the President of the United States, and do not tend to bring the office into ridicule and disgrace.

You will find these denunciations had a deeper meaning than mere expressions of opinion. It may be taken as an axiom in the affairs of nations that no usurper has ever seized upon the Legislature of his country until he has familiarized the people with the possibility of so doing by vituperating and decrying it. Denunciatory attacks upon the Legislature have always preceded, slanderous abuse of the individuals composing it have always accompanied, a seizure by a despot of the legislative power of a country. That the attempt of Andrew Johnson to overthrow Congress has failed is because of the want of ability and power not of malignity and will.

By murder most foul he succeeded to the Presidency, and is the elect of an assassin to that high office, and not of the people.

To the bar of this high tribunal, invested with all its great power and duties, the House of Representatives has brought the President of the United States by the most solemn form of accusation, charging him with high crimes and misdemeanors in office, as set forth in the several articles which I have thus feebly presented to your attention.

The acts set out in the first eight articles are but the culmination of a series of wrongs, malfeasances, and usurpations committed by the respondent, and therefore need to be examined in the light of his precedent and concomitant acts to grasp their scope and design. The last three articles presented show the perversity and malignity with which he acted, so that the man, as he is known to us may be clearly spread upon the record to be seen and known of all men hereafter.

Who does not know that when Congress met and undertook to legislate upon the very subject of reconstruction of which he had advised them in his message, which they alone had the constitutional power to do, Andrew Johnson last afore-said again changed his course, and declared that Congress had no power to legislate upon that subject? **Who does not know that when Congress, assuming its rightful power to propose amendments to the Constitution, had passed such an amendment, and had submitted it to the States as a measure of pacification, Andrew Johnson advised and counseled the Legislatures of the States lately in rebellion, as well as others, to reject the amendment, so that it might not operate as a law, and thus establish equality of right in the members of the Electoral College and in the number of the Representatives to the Congress of the United States?**

Of particular note here is the reference to the recent passage by the Congress of the 14th Amendment to the Constitution. The amendment guaranteed the equal protection of the laws to all individuals and prevented states from depriving the life, liberty, or property of citizens without due process of law. After it was sent to the states for ratification, Johnson discouraged Southern states from supporting the amendment. Of the Southern states, only Tennessee voted to ratify. That refusal ultimately led to the Reconstruction Acts and the passage of a statute that required the former Confederate states to ratify the 14th Amendment in order to receive representation in the federal government.

Lest any one should doubt the correctness of this piece of history or the truth of this common fame we shall show you that while the Legislature of Alabama was deliberating upon the reconsideration of the vote whereby it had rejected the constitutional amendment, the fact being brought to the knowledge of Andrew Johnson and his advice asked, he, by a telegraphic message under his own hand, *here to be produced*, to show his intent and purposes, advised the Legislature against passing the amendment, and to remain firm in their opposition to Congress. We shall show like advice of Andrew Johnson, upon the same subject, to the Legislature of South Carolina, and this, too, in the winter of 1867, after the action of Congress in proposing the constitutional amendment had been sustained in the previous election by an overwhelming majority. Thus we charge that Andrew Johnson, President of the United States, not only endeavors to thwart the constitutional action of Congress and bring it to naught, but also to hinder and oppose the execution of the will of the loyal people of the United States expressed, in the only mode by which it can be done, through the ballot-box, in the election of their Representatives. Who does not know that from the hour he began these his usurpations of power he everywhere denounced Congress, the legality and constitutionality of its action, and defied its legitimate powers, and for that purpose, announced his intentions and carried out his purpose, as far as he was able, of removing every true man from office who sustained the Congress of the United States? And it is to carry out this plan of action that he claims the unlimited power of removal, for the illegal exercise of which he stands before you this day.

These and his concurrent acts show conclusively that his attempt to get the control of the military force of the Government, by the seizing of the Department of War, was done in pursuance his general design if it were possible, to overthrow the Congress of the United States; and he now claims by his answer the right to control at his own will, for the execution of this very design, every officer of the Army, Navy, civil, and diplomatic service of the United States. He asks you here, Senators, by your solemn adjudication, to confirm him in that right, to invest him with that power, to be used with the intents and for the purposes which he has already shown.

The responsibility is with you; the safeguards of the Constitution against usurpation are in your hands; and the hopes of free institutions wait upon your verdict. The House of Representatives has done its duty. We have presented the facts in the constitutional manner; we have brought the criminal to your bar, and demand judgment at your hands for his so great crimes.

The impeachment trial lasted 11 days and ended when the two-thirds of the Senate required for impeachment was missed by one vote. Johnson remained in office and would go on to complete his term. Though he seemed to have been chastened a bit in his public feud with Congress, the president continued to veto reconstruction laws only to have them overridden by Congress. Ironically, after completing his term in the White House, Johnson ran for the House, lost, and then ran for the Senate and won. Johnson returned to the scene of his own impeachment trial for a short period and thereby became the only sitting Senator to have been president.

Never again, if Andrew Johnson goes quit and free this day, can the people of this or any other country by constitutional checks or guards stay the usurpations of executive power.

I speak, therefore, not the language of exaggeration, but the words of truth and soberness, that the future political welfare and liberties of all men hang trembling on the decision of the hour.

Source: Trial of Andrew Johnson, President of the United States, Vol. 1 (Washington, DC: Government Printing Office), 87–94.

The Spanish-American War

William McKinley's Address to Congress

April 11, 1898

INTRODUCTION

As the nation approached a new century, many began to look beyond the borders of the United States for acquisition of new lands, dominance in international trade, development of a massive naval force, and, in short, empire building. That desire, though not shared by all in the United States, would run up against other powerful imperial forces, like that of Spain. When McKinley took office, he inherited from Grover Cleveland a difficult situation in international affairs. Cuba was controlled by Spain through extraordinarily repressive means. That repression led to a massive revolt by Cuban nationalists in 1895. Spain responded to the insurrection by herding hundreds of thousands of Cubans into concentration camps where approximately 100,000 Cubans perished. The events presaged a response from many American citizens that put immense pressure on the McKinley administration to come to the aid of the Cubans.

For his part, McKinley wanted an end to the Spanish-Cuban conflict and applied pressure on Spain to come to an agreement that would both satisfy Cuba and protect American investments on the island. In late 1897, such a resolution seemed possible when Spain agreed to close the concentration camps and granted some autonomy to Cuba. However, those concessions by Spain angered pro-Spanish factions on Cuba who responded by rioting in the capital city of Havana in January 1898. In order to protect U.S. interests in the region, McKinley sent a new warship, the USS *Maine,* to the Havana Harbor. On February 15, 1898, the USS *Maine* exploded and sank to the bottom of the harbor, killing 260 of its crew. While investigations into the explosion commenced, many in the United States blamed Spain. Those charges appeared to be confirmed when preliminary inquiries revealed that the source of the explosion appeared to be a Spanish mine in the Cuban harbor. Subsequent investigations revealed that the explosion was a result of ammunitions aboard the ship. Nonetheless, Spain was blamed and the war cry went up: "Remember the Maine! To Hell with Spain!" On April 11, President McKinley gave the following address to a joint session of Congress.

To the Congress of the United States:

Obedient to that precept of the Constitution which commands the President to give from time to time to the Congress information of the state of the Union and to recommend to their consideration such measures as he shall judge necessary and expedient, it becomes my duty to now address your body with regard to the grave crisis that has arisen in the relations of the United States to Spain by reason of the warfare that for more than three years has raged in the neighboring island of Cuba.

The present revolution is but the successor of other similar insurrections which have occurred in Cuba against the dominion of Spain, extending over a period of nearly half a century, each of which during its progress has subjected the United States to great effort and expense in enforcing its neutrality laws, caused enormous losses to American trade and commerce, caused irritation, annoyance, and disturbance among our citizens, and, by the exercise of cruel, barbarous, and uncivilized practices of warfare, shocked the sensibilities and offended the humane sympathies of our people.

Since the present revolution began, in February, 1895, this country has seen the fertile domain at our threshold ravaged by fire and sword in the course of a struggle unequaled in the history of the island and rarely paralleled as to the numbers of the combatants and the bitterness of the contest by any revolution of modern times where a dependent people striving to be free have been opposed by the power of the sovereign state.

Our people have beheld a once prosperous community reduced to comparative want, its lucrative commerce virtually paralyzed, its exceptional productiveness diminished, its fields laid waste, its mills in ruins, and its people perishing by tens of thousands from hunger and destitution. We have found ourselves constrained, in the observance of that strict neutrality which our laws enjoin and which the law of nations commands, to police our own waters and watch our own seaports in prevention of any unlawful act in aid of the Cubans.

Our trade has suffered, the capital invested by our citizens in Cuba has been largely lost, and the temper and forbearance of our people have been so sorely tried as to beget a perilous unrest among our own citizens, which has inevitably found its expression from time to time in the National Legislature, so that issues wholly external to our own body politic engross attention and stand in the way of that close devotion to domestic advancement

that becomes a self-contained commonwealth whose primal maxim has been the avoidance of all foreign entanglements. All this must needs awaken, and has, indeed, aroused, the utmost concern on the part of this Government, as well during my predecessor's term as in my own.

In these passages, McKinley is arguing that the United States is bound by international law and treaty obligations to remain neutral. But those obligations may be cast aside in the face of wholesale human suffering of the scale Cuba has experienced through the Cuban War of Independence.

In April, 1896, the evils from which our country suffered through the Cuban war became so onerous that my predecessor made an effort to bring about a peace through the mediation of this Government in any way that might tend to an honorable adjustment of the contest between Spain and her revolted colony, on the basis of some effective scheme of self-government for Cuba under the flag and sovereignty of Spain. It failed through the refusal of the Spanish government then in power to consider any form of mediation or, indeed, any plan of settlement which did not begin with the actual submission of the insurgents to the mother country, and then only on such terms as Spain herself might see fit to grant. The war continued unabated. The resistance of the insurgents was in no wise diminished.

The efforts of Spain were increased. The peasantry, including all dwelling in the open agricultural interior, were driven into the garrison towns or isolated places held by the troops.

The raising and movement of provisions of all kinds were interdicted. The fields were laid waste, dwellings unroofed and fired, mills destroyed, and, in short, everything that could desolate the land and render it unfit for human habitation or support was commanded by one or the other of the contending parties and executed by all the powers at their disposal.

By the time the present Administration took office, a year ago, reconcentration (so called) had been made effective over the better part of the four central and western provinces—Santa Clara, Matanzas, Havana, and Pinar del Rio.

The agricultural population to the estimated number of 300,000 or more was herded within the towns and their immediate vicinage, deprived of the means of support, rendered destitute of shelter, left poorly clad, and exposed to the most unsanitary conditions. As the scarcity of food increased with the devastation of the depopulated areas of production, destitution and want became misery and starvation. Month by month the death rate increased in an alarming ratio. By March, 1897, according to conservative estimates from official Spanish sources, the mortality among the reconcentrados from starvation and the diseases thereto incident exceeded 50 per cent of their total number.

The case he is making is one of military engagement for humanitarian purposes. Indeed, that was very much the sense among contemporary observers—that the U.S. government went to war in 1898 for Cuban human rights. Later, especially after the yellow journalism and incorrect investigation into the explosion on board the Maine, historians turned to other explanations for the Spanish-American War, including the empire-building interest the United States had in constructing a canal through Central America.

The war in Cuba is of such a nature that, short of subjugation or extermination, a final military victory for either side seems impracticable. The alternative lies in the physical exhaustion of the one or the other party, or perhaps both. The prospect of such a protraction and conclusion of the present strife is a contingency hardly to be contemplated with equanimity by the civilized world, and least of all by the United States, affected and injured as we are, deeply and intimately, by its very existence.

The forcible intervention of the United States as a neutral to stop the war, according to the large dictates of humanity and following many historical precedents where neighboring states have interfered to check the hopeless sacrifices of life by internecine conflicts beyond their borders, is justifiable on rational grounds. It involves, however, hostile constraint upon both the parties to the contest, as well to enforce a truce as to guide the eventual settlement.

The grounds for such intervention may be briefly summarized as follows:

First. In the cause of humanity and to put an end to the barbarities, bloodshed, starvation, and horrible miseries now existing there, and which the parties to the conflict are either unable or unwilling to stop or mitigate. It is no answer to say this is all in another country, belonging to another nation, and is therefore none of our business. It is specially our duty, for it is right at our door.

Second. We owe it to our citizens in Cuba to afford them that protection and indemnity for life and property which no government there can or will afford, and to that end to terminate the conditions that deprive them of legal protection.

Third. The right to intervene may be justified by the very serious injury to the commerce, trade, and business of our people and by the wanton destruction of property and devastation of the island.

Fourth, and which is of the utmost importance. The present condition of affairs in Cuba is a constant menace to our peace and entails upon this Government an enormous expense. With such a conflict waged for years in an island so near us and with which our people have such trade and business relations; when the lives and liberty of our citizens are in constant danger and their property destroyed and themselves ruined; where our trading vessels are liable to seizure and are seized at our very door by war ships of a foreign nation; the expeditions of filibustering that we are powerless to prevent altogether, and the irritating questions and entanglements thus arising—all these and others that I need not mention, with the resulting strained relations, are a constant menace to our peace and compel us to keep on a semi war footing with a nation with which we are at peace.

These elements of danger and disorder already pointed out have been strikingly illustrated by a tragic event which has deeply and justly moved the American people. I have already transmitted to Congress the report of the naval court of inquiry on the destruction of the battle ship *Maine* in the harbor of Havana during the night of the 15th of February. The destruction of that noble vessel has filled the national heart with inexpressible horror. Two hundred and fifty-eight brave sailors and marines and two officers of our Navy, reposing in the fancied security of a friendly harbor, have been hurled to death, grief and want brought to their homes and sorrow to the nation.

The naval court of inquiry, which, it is needless to say, commands the unqualified confidence of the Government, was unanimous in its conclusion that the destruction of the *Maine* was caused by an exterior explosion—that of a submarine mine. It did not assume to place the responsibility. That remains to be fixed.

Several investigations occurred; among them was a Spanish investigation. Initially, it was thought that a submarine mine in the harbor caused the explosion. Later, evidence of an internal explosion in the forward ammunition magazines was found. If the later finding was correct, it certainly did not follow that the explosion, while tragic, was "proof of a state of things in Cuba."

In any event, the destruction of the *Maine*, by whatever exterior cause, is a patent and impressive proof of a state of things in Cuba that is intolerable. That condition is thus shown to be such that the Spanish Government cannot assure safety and security to a vessel of the American Navy in the harbor of Havana on a mission of peace, and rightfully there.

Sure of the right, keeping free from all offense ourselves, actuated only by upright and patriotic considerations, moved neither by passion nor selfishness, the Government will continue its watchful care over the rights and property of American citizens and will abate none of its efforts to bring about by peaceful agencies a peace which shall be honorable and enduring. If it shall hereafter appear to be a duty imposed by our obligations to ourselves, to civilization, and humanity to intervene with force, it shall be without fault on our part and only because the necessity for such action will be so clear as to command the support and approval of the civilized world.

The long trial has proved that the object for which Spain has waged the war cannot be attained. The fire of insurrection may flame or may smolder with varying seasons, but it has not been and it is plain that it cannot be extinguished by present methods. The only hope of relief and repose from a condition which can no longer be endured is the enforced pacification of Cuba. In the name of humanity, in the name of civilization, in behalf of endangered American interests which give us the right and the duty to speak and to act, the war in Cuba must stop.

In view of these facts and of these considerations I ask the Congress to authorize and empower the President to take measures to secure a full and final termination of hostilities between the Government of Spain and the people of Cuba, and to secure in the island the establishment of a stable government, capable of maintaining order and

observing its international obligations, insuring peace and tranquility and the security of its citizens as well as our own, and to use the military and naval forces of the United States as may be necessary for these purposes.

And in the interest of humanity and to aid in preserving the lives of the starving people of the island I recommend that the distribution of food and supplies be continued and that an appropriation be made out of the public Treasury to supplement the charity of our citizens.

The issue is now with the Congress. It is a solemn responsibility. I have exhausted every effort to relieve the intolerable condition of affairs which is at our doors. Prepared to execute every obligation imposed upon me by the Constitution and the law, I await your action.

WILLIAM McKINLEY.

Source: U.S. Department of State, Papers Relating to Foreign Affairs (Washington, DC, 1898), 750–760.

It is important to keep in mind that this is not technically a call for a declaration of war; rather, McKinley is asking for support in intervening in the conflict in Cuba. Within days, Congress granted the request and authorized the president to issue an ultimatum to the Spanish to leave Cuba. When he did, the Spanish interpreted that as a declaration of war. By late April, Congress declared war and the Spanish-American War had begun. The war would last just over three months. After a cease fire in August, the war ended on December 10, 1898, with the signing of the Treaty of Paris. Under the terms of the treaty, the United States acquired Puerto Rico, Guam, and the Philippines. In addition, Cuba became a protectorate of the United States. Due to his successful prosecution of the war and leadership in securing the votes necessary to ratify the treaty in the Senate and the expansionist effect of the terms of the treaty, President McKinley was credited with a dramatic expansion of the foreign policy making role of the president. The United States was now on the cusp of being a dominant power.

The Square Deal

Teddy Roosevelt's Address in New York
September 7, 1903

INTRODUCTION

By the turn of the 20th century, the United States had developed a massive transportation infrastructure that generated a transformation of the American economic, political, and social life. No longer was the economic system predominantly rural and agricultural; rather, the country was becoming rapidly urbanized as the industrial era took hold and manufacturing developed on an unprecedented scale. This shift contributed to a robust economy as the United States became the world's leading exporter of critically important materials, including steel, petroleum, and grains. It was a time of dramatic demographic shifts as well, as immigrants from all over the world began to come to the United States in search of jobs. At the same time that immigrants poured in, U.S. citizens also began to move into the cities, eventually crowding and overpopulating the nascent urban infrastructure. By the time Teddy Roosevelt took office in 1901, the population of the United States had more than doubled in just three decades. The rapid large-scale industrialization and overcrowding of cities that attended the shift in the economic structures led to many problems, including poor working conditions in manufacturing, the spread of cholera and dysentery in the cities, and dramatic inequities in the distribution of wealth driven by huge corporate profits and the political dominance of a few major industries. Many political reformers in the United States began to look for ways to ameliorate the grave economic and social ills facing the nation.

Teddy Roosevelt came into office with the goal of using the power of government to address these issues. Regulation of big business, in particular, would prove to be a powerful tool in the president's tool kit. But governmental regulation of the private marketplace was rather limited at the time; in fact, the U.S. Supreme Court, dominated by former railroad attorneys, who were largely probusiness, decided several cases that limited the reach of federal and state regulations. As a result, Roosevelt would be striking new ground in his efforts. But he was no radical reformer. Roosevelt was sensitive to the need for corporate profit and investment. He also recognized that workers' rights, while important, could not be permitted to destroy enterprise. Governmental regulation could be the benevolent intermediary, he thought, fending off socialist tendencies and saving industry from its more destructive practices. The reforms Roosevelt enacted included reinvigorating the Sherman Antitrust Act, which the court had gutted through its earlier decisions; food and drug safety legislation; and the creation of environmental conservation measures. These three elements comprised a perspective that he labeled a *square seal*—fair treatment for all from corporate monopolies, securing consumer health, and protecting the environment.

In speaking on Labor Day at the annual fair of the New York State Agricultural Association, it is natural to keep especially in mind the two bodies who compose the majority of our people and upon whose welfare depends the welfare of the entire State. If circumstances are such that thrift, energy, industry, and forethought enable the farmer, the tiller of the soil, on the one hand, and the wage-worker on the other, to keep themselves, their wives, and their children in reasonable comfort, then the State is well off, and we can be assured that the other classes in the community will likewise prosper. On the other hand, if there is in the long run a lack of prosperity among the two classes named, then all other prosperity is sure to be more seeming than real.

It has been our profound good fortune as a nation that hitherto, disregarding exceptional periods of depression and the normal and inevitable fluctuations, there has been on the whole from the beginning of our government to the present day a progressive betterment alike in the condition of the tiller of the soil and in the condition of the man who, by his manual skill and labor, supports himself and his family, and endeavors to bring up his children so that they may be at least as well off as, and, if possible, better off than, he himself has been. There are, of course, exceptions, but as a whole the standard of living among the farmers of our country has risen from generation to generation, and the wealth represented on the farms has steadily increased, while the wages of labor have likewise risen, both as regards the actual money paid and as regards the purchasing power which that money represents.

Side by side with this increase in the prosperity of the wage-worker and the tiller of the soil has gone on a great increase in prosperity among the business men and among certain classes of professional men; and the prosperity of these men has been partly the cause and partly the consequence of the prosperity of farmer and wage-worker. It cannot be too often repeated that in this country, in the long run, we all of us tend to go up or go down together. If the average of well-being is high, it means that the average wage-worker, the average farmer, and the average business man are all alike well-off. If the average shrinks, there is not one of these classes which will not feel the shrinkage. Of course, there are always some men who are not affected by good times, just as there are some men who are not affected by bad times. But speaking broadly, it is true that if prosperity comes, all of us tend to share more or less therein, and that if adversity comes each of us, to a greater or less extent, feels the tension.

Unfortunately, in this world the innocent frequently find themselves obliged to pay some of the penalty for the misdeeds of the guilty; and so if hard times come, whether they be due to our own fault or to our misfortune, whether they be due to some burst of speculative frenzy that has caused a portion of the business world to lose its head—a loss which no legislation can possibly supply—or whether they be due to any lack of wisdom in a portion of the world of labor—in each case, the trouble once started is felt more or less in every walk of life. It is all-essential to the continuance of our healthy national life that we should recognize this community of interest among our people. **The welfare of each of us is dependent fundamentally upon the welfare of all of us, and therefore in public life that man is the best representative of each of us who seeks to do good to each by doing good to all; in other words, whose endeavor it is not to represent any special class and promote merely that class's selfish interests, but to represent all true and honest men of all sections and all classes and to work for their interests by working for our common country.**

We can keep our government on a sane and healthy basis, we can make and keep our social system what it should be, only on condition of judging each man, not as a member of a class, but on his worth as a man. It is an infamous thing in our American life, and fundamentally treacherous to our institutions, to apply to any man any test save that of his personal worth, or to draw between two sets of men any distinction save the distinction of conduct, the distinction that marks off those who do well and wisely from those who do ill and foolishly. There are good citizens and bad citizens in every class as in every locality, and the attitude of decent people toward great public and social questions should be determined, not by the accidental questions of employment or locality, but by those deep-set principles which represent the innermost souls of men.

This communitarian appeal was typical of much of the progressive era reforms, and served as a justification—on egalitarian principles—for governmental action to rectify grievous social and economic ills. In other speeches calling for a square deal, Roosevelt picked up similar themes. For example, later in his famous 1910 New Nationalism speech, he says the following: "I stand for the square deal. But when I say that I am for the square deal, I mean not merely that I stand for fair play under the present rules of the game, but that I stand for having those rules changed so as to work for a more substantial equality of opportunity and of reward for equally good service."

The failure in public and in private life thus to treat each man on his own merits, the recognition of this government as being either for the poor as such or for the rich as such, would prove fatal to our Republic, as such failure and such recognition have always proved fatal in the past to other republics. A healthy republican government must rest upon individuals, not upon classes or sections. As soon as it becomes government by a class or by a section, it departs from the old American ideal.

Many qualities are needed by a people which would preserve the power of self-government in fact as well as in name. Among these qualities are forethought, shrewdness, self-restraint, the courage which refuses to abandon one's own rights, and the disinterested and kindly good sense which enables one to do justice to the rights of others. Lack of strength and lack of courage and unfit men for self-government on the one hand; and on the other, brutal arrogance, envy—in short, any manifestation of the spirit of selfish disregard, whether of one's own duties or of the rights of others, are equally fatal.

In the history of mankind many republics have risen, have flourished for a less or greater time, and then have fallen because their citizens lost the power of governing themselves and thereby of governing their state; and in no way has this loss of power been so often and so clearly shown as in the tendency to turn the government into a government primarily for the benefit of one class instead of a government for the benefit of the people as a whole. Again and again in the republics of ancient Greece, in those of medieval Italy and medieval Flanders, this tendency was shown, and wherever the tendency became a habit it invariably and inevitably proved fatal to the state. In the final result, it mattered not one whit whether the movement was in favor of one class or of another.

Roosevelt's pragmatism is evident here, as he makes the case for avoiding the excesses of labor reform and the excesses of corporate profit. The regulatory measures he promoted as part of his legislative agenda, including the Food and Drug Act, the Meat Inspection Act, the Elkins Act, and the Hepburn Act, sought to secure the square deal for workers as much as industrialists, and for consumers as much as producers.

The outcome was equally fatal, whether the country fell into the hands of a wealthy oligarchy which exploited the poor or whether it fell under the domination of a turbulent mob which plundered the rich. In both cases there resulted violent alternations between tyranny and disorder, and a final complete loss of liberty to all citizens—destruction in the end overtaking the class which had for the moment been victorious as well as that which had momentarily been defeated. The death-knell of the Republic had rung as soon as the active power became lodged in the hands of those who sought, not to do justice to all citizens, rich and poor alike, but to stand for one special class and for its interests as opposed to the interests of others. The reason why our future is assured lies in the fact that our people are genuinely skilled in and fitted for self-government and therefore will spurn the leadership of those who seek to excite this ferocious and foolish class antagonism. The average American knows not only that he himself intends to do what is right, but that his average fellow countryman has the same intention and the same power to make his intention effective. He knows, whether he be business man, professional man, farmer, mechanic, employer, or wage-worker, that the welfare of each of these men is bound up with the welfare of all the others; that each is neighbor to the other, is actuated by the same hopes and fears, has fundamentally the same ideals, and that all alike have much the same virtues and the same faults. Our average fellow citizen is a sane and healthy man who believes in decency and has a wholesome mind. He therefore feels an equal scorn alike for the man of wealth guilty of the mean and base spirit of arrogance toward those who are less well off, and for the man of small means who in his turn either feels, or seeks to excite in others the feeling of mean and base envy for those who are better off. The two feelings, envy and arrogance, are but opposite sides of the same shield, but different developments of the same spirit. . . .

The line of cleavage between good citizenship and bad citizenship separates the rich man who does well from the rich man who does ill, the poor man of good conduct from the poor man of bad conduct. This line of cleavage lies at right angles to any such arbitrary line of division as that separating one class from another, one locality from another, or men with a certain degree of property from those of a less degree of property. The good citizen is the man who, whatever his wealth or his poverty, strives manfully to do his duty to himself, to his family, to his neighbor, to the States; who is incapable of the baseness which manifests itself either in arrogance or in envy, but who while demanding justice for himself is no less scrupulous to do justice to others. It is because the average American citizen, rich or poor, is of just this type that we have cause for our profound faith in the future of the Republic.

There is no worse enemy of the wage-worker than the man who condones mob violence in any shape or who preaches class hatred; and surely the slightest acquaintance with our industrial history should teach even the most short-sighted that the times of most suffering for our people as a whole, the times when business is stagnant, and capital suffers from shrinkage and gets no return from its investments, are exactly the times of hardship, and want, and grim disaster among the poor. If all the existing instrumentalities of wealth could be abolished, the first and severest suffering would come among those of us who are least well-off at present. The wage-worker is well off only when the rest of the country is well-off; and he can best contribute to this general well-being by showing sanity and a firm purpose to do justice to others.

In his turn, the capitalist who is really a conservative, the man who has forethought as well as patriotism, should heartily welcome every effort, legislative or otherwise, which has for its object to secure fair dealing by capital, corporate or individual, toward the public and toward the employee. Such laws as the franchise-tax law in this State, which the Court of Appeals recently unanimously decided constitutional—such a law as that passed in Congress last year for the purpose of establishing a Department of Commerce and Labor, under which there should be a bureau to oversee and secure publicity from the great corporations which do an interstate business—such a law as that passed at the same time for the regulation of the great highways of commerce so as to keep these roads clear on fair terms to all producers in getting their goods to market—these laws are in the interest not merely of the people as a whole, but of the propertied classes. For in no way is the

The agency to which Roosevelt refers is the Interstate Commerce Commission (ICC), a regulatory apparatus that set rates for the shipment of goods (largely by rail) that affect interstate commerce and secured transparency in the financial records of the interstate carriers.

stability of property better assured than by making it patent to our people that property bears its proper share of the burdens of the State; that property is handled not only in the interest of the owner, but in the interest of the whole community.

Among ourselves we differ in many qualities of body, head, and heart; we are unequally developed, mentally as well as physically. But each of us has the right to ask that he shall be protected from wrongdoing as he does his work and carries his burden through life. No man needs sympathy because he has to work, because he has a burden to carry. Far and away the best prize that life offers is the chance to work hard at work worth doing; and this is a prize open to every man, for there can be no better worth doing than that done to keep in health and comfort and with reasonable advantages those immediately dependent upon the husband, the father, or the son. There is no room in our healthy American life for the mere idler, for the man or the woman whose object it is throughout life to shirk the duties which life ought to bring. Life can mean nothing worth meaning, unless its prime aim is the doing of duty, the achievement of results worth achieving. A recent writer has finely said: "After all, the saddest thing that can happen to a man is to carry no burdens. To be bent under too great a load is bad; to be crushed by it is lamentable; but even in that there are possibilities that are glorious. But to carry no load at all—there is nothing in that. No one seems to arrive at any goal really worth reaching in this world who does not come to it heavy laden."

Surely from our own experience each one of us knows that this is true. From the greatest to the smallest, happiness and usefulness are largely found in the same soul, and the joy of life is won in its deepest and truest sense only by those who have not shirked life's burdens. The men whom we most delight to honor in all this land are those who, in the iron years from '61 to '65, bore on their shoulders the burden of saving the Union. They did not choose the easy task. They did not shirk the difficult duty. Deliberately and of their own free will they strove for an ideal, upward and onward across the stony slopes of greatness. They did the hardest work that was then to be done; they bore the heaviest burden that any generation of Americans ever had to bear; and because they did this they have won such proud joy as it has fallen to the lot of no other men to win, and have written their names forevermore on the golden honor-roll of the nation. As it is with the soldier, so it is with the civilian. To win success in the business world, to become a first-class mechanic, a successful farmer, an able lawyer or doctor, means that the man has devoted his best energy and power through long years to the achievement of his ends. So it is in the life of the family, upon which in the last analysis the whole welfare of the nation rests. The man or woman who, as bread-winner and home-maker, or as wife and mother, has done all that he or she can do, patiently and uncomplainingly, is to be honored; and is to be envied by all those who have never had the good fortune to feel the need and duty of doing such work. The woman who has borne, and who has reared as they should be reared, a family of children, has in the most emphatic manner deserved well of the Republic. Her burden has been heavy, and she has been able to bear it worthily only by the possession of resolution, of good sense, of conscience, and of unselfishness. But if she has borne it well, then to her shall come the supreme blessing, for in the words of the oldest and greatest of books, "Her children shall rise up and call her blessed;" and among the benefactors of the land, her place must be with those who have done the best and the hardest work, whether as law-givers or as soldiers, whether in public or private life.

This is not a soft and easy creed to preach. It is a creed willingly learned only by men and women who, together with the softer virtues, possess also the stronger; who can do, and dare, and die at need, but who while life lasts will never flinch from their allotted task. You farmers, and wage-workers, and business men of this great State, of this mighty and wonderful nation, are gathered together today, proud of your State and still prouder of your nation, because your forefathers and predecessors have lived up to just this creed. You have received from their hands a great inheritance, and you will leave an even greater inheritance to your children, and your children's children, provided only that you practice alike in your private and your public lives the strong virtues that have given us as a people greatness in the past. It is not enough to be well-meaning and kindly, but weak; neither is it enough to be strong, unless morality and decency go hand in hand with strength. We must possess the qualities which make us do our duty in our homes and among our neighbors, and in addition we must possess the qualities which are indispensable to the make-up of every great and masterful nation—the qualities of courage and hardihood, of individual initiative and yet of power to combine for a common end, and above all, the resolute determination to permit no man and no set of men to sunder us one from the other by lines of caste or creed or section.

We must act upon the motto of all for each and each for all. There must be ever present in our minds the fundamental truth that in a republic such as ours the only safety is to stand neither for nor against any man because he is rich or because he is poor, because he is engaged in one occupation or another, because he works with his brains or because he works with his hands. We must treat each man on his worth and merits as a man. **We must see that each is given a square deal, because he is entitled to no more and should receive no less. Finally, we must keep ever in mind that a republic such as ours can exist only by virtue of the orderly liberty which comes through the equal domination of the law over all men alike, and through its administration in such resolute and fearless fashion as shall teach all that no man is above it and no man below it.**

Among the most successful reforms was the Roosevelt administration's efforts to break up monopolistic business entities. To do so, they didn't have to go through Congress because a statute was already in place—the Sherman Antitrust Act of 1890. Previous pro-business court decisions had limited its usefulness, however. Consequently, one can imagine that Roosevelt's line "no man above [the law]" may refer to the corporate monopolies that proliferated in the absence of prosecution under existing statute. Roosevelt's attorney general began successfully prosecuting these cases, and by the end of his presidency, Roosevelt had filed 43 antitrust lawsuits, effectively turning the Sherman Antitrust Act into a powerful weapon against anticompetitive practice by corporations.

Source: *The Works of Theodore Roosevelt.* Presidential Addresses and State Papers, Part Two (New York: P.F. Collier & Son, 1901), 466–481.

Teddy Roosevelt's Views Coalesce

The "New Nationalism" Speech
August 31, 1910

INTRODUCTION

It is evident from Teddy Roosevelt's *square deal* that he thought that governmental involvement in the market could be a force for justice and fairness in society. That perspective becomes even more evident in this New Nationalism speech he delivered several years later to a group of Civil War veterans at a commemorative event in Osawatomie, Kansas, in 1910. Here and elsewhere, Roosevelt makes a powerful case for an activist alternative to a theory of limited, or negative, government. President Taft, who was the sitting president when TR delivered this speech, saw executive power as simply that which was specifically granted the office by the Constitution—no more and no less. Taft wrote "[t]he true view of the Executive function is, as I conceive it, that the President can exercise no power which cannot be fairly and reasonably traced to some specific grant of power or justly implied ... [and] ... [s]uch specific grant must be either in the Federal Constitution or in an act of Congress passed in pursuance thereof" (*Our Chief Magistrate and His Powers*, 1916). Later, when Taft became the chief justice of the U.S. Supreme Court, he continued to hold to this literalist perspective on executive power, writing that the proper role of the president is to simply execute the laws passed by Congress.

Roosevelt, however, saw the presidency as a *bully pulpit* that granted the occupant significant political authority and opportunity for moral leadership on consequential issues facing the country. Scholars refer to this perspective as the stewardship theory of executive power. Stewardship theory is premised upon a philosophy of positive government and heightened presidential power in the absence of specific limits and prescriptions. It is an approach that counsels presidents to be aggressive in asserting the powers of the office. While Taft's view of executive power would relegate the president to a functionary of Congress or an executor of congressional preferences, the stewardship view invites presidents to take action with the authority of inherent and implied powers. As you read the text of this famous speech, you will notice how aggressively Roosevelt is making this call to governmental action to combat growing economic inequalities and the political influence of corporate interests.

There have been two great crises in our country's history: first, when it was formed, and then, again, when it was perpetuated; and, in the second of these great crises—in the time of stress and strain which culminated in the Civil War, on the outcome of which depended the justification of what had been done earlier, you men of the Grand Army, you men who fought through the Civil War, not only did you justify your generation, but you justified the wisdom of Washington and Washington's colleagues. If this Republic had been founded by them only to be split asunder into fragments when the strain came, then the judgment of the world would have been that Washington's work was not worth doing. It was you who crowned Washington's work, as you carried to achievement the high purpose of Abraham Lincoln.

Of that generation of men to whom we owe so much, the man to whom we owe most is, of course, Lincoln. Part of our debt to him is because he forecast our present struggle and saw the way out. He said:

"I hold that while man exists it is his duty to improve not only his own condition, but to assist in ameliorating mankind."

And again:

"Labor is prior to, and independent of, capital. Capital is only the fruit of labor, and could never have existed if labor had not first existed. Labor is the superior of capital, and deserves much the higher consideration."

If that remark was original with me, I should be even more strongly denounced as a Communist agitator than I shall be anyhow. It is Lincoln's. I am only quoting it; and that is one side; that is the side the capitalist should hear. Now, let the working man hear his side.

"Capital has its rights, which are as worthy of protection as any other rights. . . . Nor should this lead to a war upon the owners of property. Property is the fruit of labor; . . . property is desirable; is a positive good in the world."

And then comes a thoroughly Lincolnlike sentence:

"Let not him who is houseless pull down the house of another, but let him work diligently and build one for himself, thus by example assuring that his own shall be safe from violence when built."

It seems to me that, in these words, Lincoln took substantially the attitude that we ought to take; he showed the proper sense of proportion in his relative estimates of capital and labor, of human rights and property rights. Above all, in this speech, as in many others, he taught a lesson in wise kindliness and charity; an indispensable lesson to us of to-day. But this wise kindliness and charity never weakened his arm or numbed his heart. We cannot afford weakly to blind ourselves to the actual conflict which faces us today. The issue is joined, and we must fight or fail.

In every wise struggle for human betterment one of the main objects, and often the only object, has been to achieve in large measure equality of opportunity. In the struggle for this great end, nations rise from barbarism to civilization, and through it people press forward from one stage of enlightenment to the next. One of the chief factors in progress is the destruction of special privilege. The essence of any struggle for healthy liberty has always been, and must always be, to take from some one man or class of men the right to enjoy power, or wealth, or position, or immunity, which has not been earned by service to his or their fellows. That is what you fought for in the Civil War, and that is what we strive for now.

At many stages in the advance of humanity, this conflict between the men who possess more than they have earned and the men who have earned more than they possess is the central condition of progress. In our day it appears as the struggle of freemen to gain and hold the right of self-government as against the special interests, who twist the methods of free government into machinery for defeating the popular will. At every stage, and under all circumstances, the essence of the struggle is to equalize opportunity, destroy privilege, and give to the life and citizenship of every individual the highest possible value both to himself and to the commonwealth.

Many observes of this speech were struck by its stridency. Some labeled it communistic; others thought it was a powerful critique of his fellow Republican, Taft. Clearly, it was a call to bring the power of government to bear on addressing critical economic and social ills.

Practical equality of opportunity for all citizens, when we achieve it, will have two great results. First, every man will have a fair chance to make of himself all that in him lies; to reach the highest point to which his capacities, unassisted by special privilege of his own and unhampered by the special privilege of others, can carry him, and to get for himself and his family substantially what he has earned. Second, equality of opportunity means that the commonwealth will get from every citizen the highest service of which he is capable. No man who carries the burden of the special privileges of another can give to the commonwealth that service to which it is fairly entitled.

Here, Roosevelt reminds the audience of his square deal from several years prior—the core of which included antitrust regulation, consumer safety, and environmental conservation.

I stand for the square deal. But when I say that I am for the square deal, I mean not merely that I stand for fair play under the present rules of the game, but that I stand for having those rules changed so as to work for a more substantial equality of opportunity and of reward for equally good service.

Exactly as the special interests of cotton and slavery threatened our political integrity before the Civil War, so now the great special business interests too often control and corrupt the men and methods of government for their own profit. We must drive the special interests out of politics. That is one of our tasks to-day. For every special interest is entitled to justice, but not one is entitled to a vote in Congress, to a voice on the bench, or to representation in any public office. The Constitution guarantees protection to property, and we must make that promise good. But it does not give the right of suffrage to any corporation.

It is necessary that laws should be passed to prohibit the use of corporate funds directly or indirectly for political purposes; it is still more necessary that such laws should be thoroughly enforced. **Corporate expenditures for political purposes, and especially such expenditures by public service corporations, have supplied one of the principal sources of corruption in our political affairs.**

In 1819, the U.S. Supreme Court held that corporations enjoy certain protections under the Constitution. In a case from the late 1880s, the court was reported to hold that corporations were guaranteed the equal protection of the laws under the 14th Amendment in the same way an individual might be afforded those protections. In recent years, the idea of corporate personhood has become a very controversial subject in the context of restrictions government may place on campaign contributions, for example.

It has become entirely clear that we must have government supervision of the capitalization, not only of public service corporations, including, particularly, railways, but of all corporations doing an interstate business.

I believe that the officers, and, especially, the directors, of corporations should be held personally responsible when any corporation breaks the law.

Combinations in industry are the result of an imperative economic law which cannot be repealed by political legislation. The effort at prohibiting all combination has substantially failed. The way out lies, not in attempting to prevent such combinations, but in completely controlling them in the interest of the public welfare. For that purpose the Federal Bureau of Corporations is an agency of first importance. Its powers, and, therefore, its efficiency, as well as that of the Interstate Commerce Commission, should be largely increased. **The Hepburn Act, and the amendment to the act in the shape in which it finally passed Congress at the last session, represent a long step in advance, and we must go yet further.**

The Hepburn Act of 1906 invigorated the Interstate Commerce Commission, allowing it to set the rates for goods shipped by railroads (rather than permitting the lines themselves, or the states in which they held powerful sway, to set their own rates).

It is hardly necessary to me to repeat that I believe in an efficient army and a navy large enough to secure for us abroad that respect which is the surest guarantee of peace. A word of special warning to my fellow citizens who are as progressive as I hope I am. I want them to keep up their interest in our international affairs; and I want them also continually to remember Uncle Sam's interests abroad. Justice and fair dealings among nations rest upon principles identical with those which control justice and fair dealing among the individuals of which nations are composed, with the vital exception that each nation must do its own part in international police work. I believe in national friendships and heartiest good will to all nations; but national friendships, like those between men, must be founded on respect as well as on liking, on forbearance as well as upon trust. I should be heartily ashamed of any American who did not try to make the American government act as justly toward the other nations in international relations as he himself would act toward any individual in private relations. I should be heartily ashamed to see us wrong a weaker power, and I should hang my head forever if we tamely suffered wrong from a stronger power.

Conservation means development as much as it does protection. I recognize the right and duty of this generation to develop and use the natural resources of our land; but I do not recognize the right to waste them, or to rob, by wasteful use, the generations that come after us.

I believe that the natural resources must be used for the benefit of all our people, and not monopolized for the benefit of the few, and here again is another case in which I am accused of taking a revolutionary attitude. Conservation is a great moral issue, for it involves the patriotic duty of insuring the safety and continuance of the nation. Let me add that the health and vitality of our people are at least as well worth conserving as their forests, waters, lands, and minerals, and in this great work the national government must bear a most important part.

I have spoken elsewhere also of the great task which lies before the farmers of the country to get for themselves and their wives and children not only the benefits of better farming, but also those of better business methods and better conditions of life on the farm. The burden of this great task will fall, as it should, mainly upon the great organizations of the farmers themselves. I am glad it will, for I believe they are all well able to handle it. In particular, there are strong reasons why the Departments of Agriculture of the various states, the United States Department of Agriculture, and the agricultural colleges and experiment stations should extend their work to cover all phases of farm life, instead of limiting themselves, as they have far too often limited themselves in the past, solely to the question of the production of crops.

The right to regulate the use of wealth in the public interest is universally admitted. Let us admit also the right to regulate the terms and conditions of labor, which is the chief element of wealth, directly in the interest of the common good. The fundamental thing to do for every man is to give him a chance to reach a place in which he will make the greatest possible contribution to the public welfare. Understand what I say there. Give him a chance, not push him up if he will not be pushed. Help any man who stumbles; if he lies down, it is a poor job to try to carry him; but if he is a worthy man, try your best to see that he gets a chance to show the worth that is in him. No man can be a good citizen unless he has a wage more than sufficient to cover the bare cost of living, and hours of labor short enough so after his day's work is done he will have time and energy to bear his share in the management of the community, to help in carrying the general load. We keep countless men from being good citizens by the conditions of life by which we surround them. We need comprehensive workman's compensation acts, both State and national laws to regulate child labor and work for women, and, especially, we need in our common schools not merely education in book-learning, but also practical training for daily life and work. We need to enforce better sanitary conditions for our workers and to extend the use of safety appliances for workers in industry and commerce, both within and between the States. Also, friends, in the interest of the working man himself, we need to set our faces like flint against mob-violence just as against corporate greed; against violence and injustice and lawlessness by wage-workers just as much as against lawless cunning and greed and selfish arrogance of employers.

Remember what I said about excess in reformer and reactionary alike. If the reactionary man, who thinks of nothing but the rights of property, could have his way, he would bring about a revolution; and one of my chief fears in connection with progress comes because I do not want to see our people, for lack of proper leadership, compelled to follow men whose intentions are excellent, but whose eyes are a little too wild to make it really safe to trust them.

I do not ask for the over centralization; but I do ask that we work in a spirit of broad and far-reaching nationalism where we work for what concerns our people as a whole. We are all Americans. Our common interests are as broad as the continent. I speak to you here in Kansas exactly as I would speak in New York or Georgia, for the most vital problems are those which affect us all alike. The National Government belongs to the whole American people, and where the whole American people are interested, that interest can be guarded effectively only by the National Government. The betterment which we seek must be accomplished, I believe, mainly through the National Government.

Note that Roosevelt is arguing that the president is responsible for dealing with the pressing problems in society—as *the* steward of the public welfare—but so too are other institutions of the federal government. Each, he argues, must be solicitous of the public good and not of any particular sector. Hence, the stewardship theory of the presidency is reflective of this idea that the powers of the executive branch should be exercised for the good of the nation to ameliorate social, environmental, economic, and political problems.

The American people are right in demanding that New Nationalism, without which we cannot hope to deal with new problems. The New Nationalism puts the national need before sectional or personal advantage. This New Nationalism regards the executive power as the steward of the public welfare. It demands of the judiciary that it shall be interested primarily in human welfare rather than in property, just as it demands that the representative body shall represent all the people rather than any one class or section of the people.

I believe in shaping the ends of government to protect property as well as human welfare. I am far from underestimating the importance of dividends; but I rank dividends below human character. Again, I do not have any sympathy with the reformer who says he does not care for dividends. Of course, economic welfare is necessary, for a man must pull his own weight and be able to support his family. I know well that the reformers must not bring upon the people economic ruin, or the reforms themselves will go down in the ruin. Those who oppose reform will do well to remember that ruin in its worst form is inevitable if our national life brings us nothing better than swollen fortunes for the few and the triumph in both politics and business of a sordid and selfish materialism.

The progressive era was well under way as proposals like the direct primary began to gain support. The 17th Amendment, which provided for the direct election of senators, for example, was one example of the power of the progressives. The collective effect of such proposals was to weaken the hold that parties had over voters and policy. Soon after this address, Roosevelt became the face of the progressive movement within the Republican Party. During the election of 1912, Roosevelt opted to challenge the incumbent Taft for the Republican nomination. Taft, however, held control of most of the party leaders. Soon after the convention, Roosevelt founded the Progressive Party—later named the Bull Moose Party—and was nominated by that party for the presidency. Though he would go on to lose the election to Woodrow Wilson, the swift successes of the Progressive Party heralded the rise of a new kind of politics, a new commitment to democratic practices, and a new role for the federal government in the economic marketplace.

If our political institutions were perfect, they would absolutely prevent the political domination of money in any part of our affairs. **We need to make our political representatives more quickly and sensitively responsive to the people whose servants they are. More direct action by the people in their own affairs under proper safeguards is vitally necessary. The direct primary is a step in this direction, if it is associated with a corrupt-services act effective to prevent the advantage of the man willing recklessly and unscrupulously to spend money over his more honest competitor.** It is particularly important that all moneys received or expended for campaign purposes should be publicly accounted for, not only after election, but before election as well. Political action must be made simpler, easier, and freer from confusion for every citizen.

The object of government is the welfare of the people. The material progress and prosperity of a nation are desirable chiefly so long as they lead to the moral and material welfare of all good citizens. We must have—I believe we have already—a genuine and permanent moral awakening, without which no wisdom of legislation or administration really means anything; and, on the other hand, we must try to secure the social and economic legislation without which any improvement due to purely moral agitation is necessarily evanescent. No matter how honest and decent we are in our private lives, if we do not have the right kind of law and the right kind of administration of the law, we cannot go forward as a nation. That is imperative; but it must be an addition to, and not a substitute for, the qualities that make us good citizens. In the last analysis, the most important elements in any man's career must be the sum of those qualities which, in the aggregate, we speak of as character. If he has not got it, then no law that the wit of man can devise, no administration of the law by the boldest and strongest executive, will avail to help him. The prime problem of our nation is to get the right type of good citizenship, and, to get it, we must have progress, and our public men must be genuinely progressive.

Source: *The Works of Theodore Roosevelt*, Vol. 19 (New York: P.F. Collier & Son, 1926), 10–30.

The "New Freedom" Approach

Woodrow Wilson's First Inaugural Address

March 4, 1913

INTRODUCTION

Teddy Roosevelt and Woodrow Wilson ran against each other in the election of 1912. Both were considered progressives, but approached their progressive politics with different perspectives on the proper role of the federal government in the marketplace and the proper distribution of power between states and the federal government. Roosevelt's New Nationalism called for extensive federal regulation of the economy on behalf of the public good while Wilson's New Freedom platform was premised on the idea that those who regulate government were very likely to be in the pockets of those they were charged with regulating. Wilson's New Freedom called for the lowering of protective tariffs, an improved banking system, and stronger antitrust legislation. Unlike the New Nationalism of Roosevelt, Wilson's program was not driven by an abiding interest in reducing inequalities for social and economic justice; rather, he wanted to ensure fair competition to allow maximum opportunity for citizens' success.

Wilson's view of executive power was a dramatic departure from the literalist perspective of his predecessor, Taft, and for that matter rather distinct from the general shift toward congressional dominance that characterized the separation of powers since Lincoln. Curiously, in the late 1880s, Wilson had written that Congress had become the dominant branch of government. But by the time he ran for the presidency, his view on executive power shifted and became much more akin to that of TR. He held to the view that presidents were endowed with broad inherent powers to act—powers conditioned only by specific, clearly expressed limits on that power imposed by the Constitution or by statute passed in pursuance of the Constitution. A professor of politics and then president of Princeton University until he assumed the governorship of New Jersey, Wilson wrote extensively on executive power. In his 1908 book titled *Constitutional Government,* he reasoned that since the president is the only public official to have been voted on by all of the electorate, the president is endowed with a greater capacity and obligation to act on behalf of the whole. The president, Wilson argued, "is the representative of no constituency, but of the whole people . . . he speaks for no special interest . . . [and] . . . his is the only voice in national affairs." As a result of this perspective, Wilson's view of executive power stands in sharp contrast to almost every other executive that preceded him, and his effect on the powers that subsequent occupants of the office could claim would become significant.

THERE has been a change of government. It began two years ago, when the House of Representatives became Democratic by a decisive majority. It has now been completed. The Senate about to assemble will also be Democratic.

The offices of President and Vice-President have been put into the hands of Democrats. What does the change mean? That is the question that is uppermost in our minds to-day. That is the question I am going to try to answer, in order, if I may, to interpret the occasion.

It means much more than the mere success of a party. The success of a party means little except when the Nation is using that party for a large and definite purpose. No one can mistake the purpose for which the Nation now seeks to use the Democratic Party. It seeks to use it to interpret a change in its own plans and point of view. Some old things with which we had grown familiar, and which had begun to creep into the very habit of our thought and of our lives, have altered their aspect as we have latterly looked critically upon them, with fresh, awakened eyes; have dropped their disguises and shown themselves alien and sinister. Some new things, as we look frankly upon them, willing to comprehend their real character, have come to assume the aspect of things long believed in and familiar, stuff of our own convictions. We have been refreshed by a new insight into our own life.

We see that in many things that life is very great. It is incomparably great in its material aspects, in its body of wealth, in the diversity and sweep of its energy, in the industries which have been conceived and built up by the genius of individual men and the limitless enterprise of groups of men. It is great, also, very great, in its moral force. Nowhere else in the world have noble men and women exhibited in more striking forms the beauty and the energy of sympathy and helpfulness and counsel in their efforts to rectify wrong, alleviate suffering, and set the weak in the way of strength and hope. We have built up, moreover, a great system of government, which has stood through a long age as in many respects a model for those who seek to set liberty upon foundations that will endure against fortuitous change, against storm and accident. Our life contains every great thing, and contains it in rich abundance.

But the evil has come with the good, and much fine gold has been corroded. With riches has come inexcusable waste.

Wilson, a Democrat, was elected to office in the wake of a split Republican Party. Recall that Roosevelt had left the party to run as the nominee of the Progressive *Bull Moose* Party, while Taft ran for reelection as the incumbent Republican. Wilson won an Electoral College landslide—carrying 40 states—but he did so with just over 40% of the vote. Roosevelt and Taft earned 27% and 23% of the popular vote, respectively. The Socialist candidate, Eugene Debs, garnered 6%.

We have squandered a great part of what we might have used, and have not stopped to conserve the exceeding bounty of nature, without which our genius for enterprise would have been worthless and impotent, scorning to be careful, shamefully prodigal as well as admirably efficient. We have been proud of our industrial achievements, but we have not hitherto stopped thoughtfully enough to count the human cost, the cost of lives snuffed out, of energies overtaxed and broken, the fearful physical and spiritual cost to the men and women and children upon whom the dead weight and burden of it all has fallen pitilessly the years through. The groans and agony of it all had not yet reached our ears, the solemn, moving undertone of our life, coming up out of the mines and factories, and out of every home where the struggle had its intimate and familiar seat. With the great Government went many deep secret things which we too long delayed to look into and scrutinize with candid, fearless eyes. The great Government we loved has too often been made use of for private and selfish purposes, and those who used it had forgotten the people.

At last a vision has been vouchsafed us of our life as a whole. We see the bad with the good, the debased and decadent with the sound and vital. With this vision we approach new affairs. Our duty is to cleanse, to reconsider, to restore, to correct the evil without impairing the good, to purify and humanize every process of our common life without weakening or sentimentalizing it. There has been something crude and heartless and unfeeling in our haste to succeed and be great. Our thought has been "Let every man look out for himself, let every generation look out for itself," while we reared giant machinery which made it impossible that any but those who stood at the levers of control should have a chance to look out for themselves. We had not forgotten our morals. We remembered well enough that we had set up a policy which was meant to serve the humblest as well as the most powerful, with an eye single to the standards of justice and fair play, and remembered it with pride. But we were very heedless and in a hurry to be great.

We have come now to the sober second thought. The scales of heedlessness have fallen from our eyes. We have made up our minds to square every process of our national life again with the standards we so proudly set up at the beginning and have always carried at our hearts. Our work is a work of restoration.

We have itemized with some degree of particularity the things that ought to be altered and here are some of the chief items: A tariff which cuts us off from our proper part in the commerce of the world, violates the just principles of taxation, and makes the Government a facile instrument in the hand of private interests; a banking and currency system based upon the necessity of the Government to sell its bonds fifty years ago and perfectly adapted to concentrating cash and restricting credits; an industrial system which, take it on all its sides, financial as well as administrative, holds capital in leading strings, restricts the liberties and limits the opportunities of labor, and exploits without renewing or conserving the natural resources of the country; a body of agricultural activities never yet given the efficiency of great business undertakings or served as it should be through the instrumentality of science taken directly to the farm, or afforded the facilities of credit best suited to its practical needs; watercourses undeveloped, waste places unreclaimed, forests untended, fast disappearing without plan or prospect of renewal, unregarded waste heaps at every mine. We have studied as perhaps no other nation has the most effective means of production, but we have not studied cost or economy as we should either as organizers of industry, as statesmen, or as individuals.

Nor have we studied and perfected the means by which government may be put at the service of humanity, in safeguarding the health of the Nation, the health of its men and its women and its children, as well as their rights in the struggle for existence. This is no sentimental duty. The firm basis of government is justice, not pity. These are matters of justice. **There can be no equality or opportunity, the first essential of justice in the body politic, if men and women and children be not shielded in their lives, their very vitality, from the consequences of great industrial and social processes which they cannot alter, control, or singly cope with.**

Tariff reform was one of the first actions he took upon assuming office. His view was that high tariffs encouraged monopolies and increased costs to consumers. The result of his efforts was the Underwood-Simmons Act, the most significant tariff reduction measure in 50 years. Another Progressive Movement policy victory—the progressive income tax—was made possible by the ratification of the 16th Amendment just weeks prior to his inaugural.

Wilson would oversee massive policy changes, many of which were the result of Roosevelt's New Nationalism and square deal initiatives years prior. Labor laws governing working conditions, banking reform and the Federal Reserve Act, the Clayton Antitrust Act, the establishment of the Federal Trade Commission to investigate anticompetitive business practice, and several other policies grew out of the progressive movement's attention to the economic and social ills that attended vast concentrations of power and wealth in the hands of a few.

Society must see to it that it does not itself crush or weaken or damage its own constituent parts. The first duty of law is to keep sound the society it serves. Sanitary laws, pure food laws, and laws determining conditions of labor which individuals are powerless to determine for themselves are intimate parts of the very business of justice and legal efficiency.

These are some of the things we ought to do, and not leave the others undone, the old-fashioned, never-to-be-neglected, fundamental safeguarding of property and of individual right. This is the high enterprise of the new day: To lift everything that concerns our life as a Nation to the light that shines from the hearthfire of every man's conscience and vision of the right. It is inconceivable that we should do this as partisans; it is inconceivable we should do it in ignorance of the facts as they are or in blind haste. We shall restore, not destroy. We shall deal with our economic system as it is and as it may be modified, not as it might be if we had a clean sheet of paper to write upon; and step by step we shall make it what it should be, in the spirit of those who question their own wisdom and seek counsel and knowledge, not shallow self-satisfaction or the excitement of excursions whither they cannot tell. Justice, and only justice, shall always be our motto.

And yet it will be no cool process of mere science. The Nation has been deeply stirred, stirred by a solemn passion, stirred by the knowledge of wrong, of ideals lost, of government too often debauched and made an instrument of evil. The feelings with which we face this new age of right and opportunity sweep across our heartstrings like some air out of God's own presence, where justice and mercy are reconciled and the judge and the brother are one. We know our task to be no mere task of politics but a task which shall search us through and through, whether we be able to understand our time and the need of our people, whether we be indeed their spokesmen and interpreters, whether we have the pure heart to comprehend and the rectified will to choose our high course of action.

This is not a day of triumph; it is a day of dedication. Here muster, not the forces of party, but the forces of humanity.

Men's hearts wait upon us; men's lives hang in the balance; men's hopes call upon us to say what we will do. Who shall live up to the great trust? Who dares fail to try? I summon all honest men, all patriotic, all forward-looking men, to my side. God helping me, I will not fail them, if they will but counsel and sustain me!

Source: Library of Congress. Manuscript Division. *The Papers of Woodrow Wilson.*

The Espionage Act of 1917

Woodrow Wilson's State of the Union Address

December 7, 1915

INTRODUCTION

When the Great War broke out in Europe in August 1914, President Wilson counseled a policy of neutrality for the United States. The struggling U.S. economy, however, required the exportation of goods—including munitions—to European countries, specifically the British and French, in violation of a general policy of neutrality. This sparked a confrontation with Germany that erected a naval blockade to prevent the shipment of goods. In May 1915, a German U-Boat torpedoed and sank the *Lusitania*, a British passenger vessel, killing over 1,000 civilians. Among the dead were 128 American citizens. By 1917, Congress declared war on Germany and the United States joined the Allied forces in World War I.

In this State of the Union address, U.S. involvement in the Great War was still two years away, and the *Lusitania* had not yet been attacked. Nonetheless, President Wilson proposes a massive troop increase and preparedness effort in case of war. Though he is careful to distinguish why the United States would be drawn into a fight (recall that the official policy was neutrality at this time), he argues that under certain circumstances, war would be necessary to protect free nations. In this speech, he notes: "[g]reat democracies are not belligerent. They do not seek or desire war. Their thought is of individual liberty and of the free labor that supports life and the uncensored thought that quickens it. Conquest and dominion are not in our reckoning, or agreeable to our principles. But just because we demand unmolested development and the undisturbed government of our own lives upon our own principles of right and liberty, we resent, from whatever quarter it may come, the aggression we ourselves will not practice. We insist upon security in prosecuting our self-chosen lines of national development. We do more than that. We demand it also for others. We do not confine our enthusiasm for individual liberty and free national development to the incidents and movements of affairs which affect only ourselves. We feel it wherever there is a people that tries to walk in these difficult paths of independence and right." This obligation of free nations to repel aggressors and ensure collective development and undisturbed governance would come to frame the basis for the League of Nations. The League of Nations was an international organization of states dedicated to world peace founded at the end of World War I, in large measure due to the vision and support of President Wilson.

As he is proposing large-scale military preparedness, he is mindful that munitions and troops are not the only requisite elements of a nation at war. This excerpt from his address is a call for legal measures by which dissent could be silenced at home. In two years' time, Congress responded to his plea and passed the Espionage Act of 1917. Recall that the Alien and Sedition Acts of 100 years prior were similar examples of government prohibiting the expression of "false, scandalous, and malicious" criticisms of government. Those acts, however, were not challenged in court, as you will recall. When he took office, President Jefferson simply pardoned those who had been convicted of violating the laws. In this case, Wilson was calling for the imposition of similar statutes during war. The constitutionality of the measure, once the nation was at war and the Espionage Act was implemented, then turned on whether the speech (or conduct that was paired with the speech) could be abridged in a time of national emergency.

GENTLEMEN OF THE CONGRESS:

I have spoken to you to-day, Gentlemen, upon a single theme, the thorough preparation of the nation to care for its own security and to make sure of entire freedom to play the impartial role in this hemisphere and in the world which we all believe to have been providentially assigned to it. I have had in my mind no thought of any immediate or particular danger arising out of our relations with other nations. We are at peace with all the nations of the world, and there is reason to hope that no question in controversy between this and other Governments will lead to any serious breach of amicable relations, grave as some differences of attitude and policy have been land may yet turn out to be. I am sorry to say that the gravest threats against our national peace and safety have been uttered within our own borders. **There are citizens of the United States, I blush to admit, born under other flags but welcomed under our generous naturalization laws to the full freedom and opportunity of America, who have poured the poison of disloyalty into the very arteries of our national life; who have sought to bring the authority and good name of our Government into contempt, to destroy our industries wherever they thought it effective for their vindictive purposes to strike at them, and to debase our politics to the uses of foreign intrigue.**

Internal enemies present both a national security threat and a compelling target for political leaders. The difficulty, of course, lies in determining an actual security threat from that of political dissent. Neutralizing enemy belligerents may be necessary for securing the homeland; arresting political enemies for their critique of government and military authority may not be as justifiable.

Their number is not great as compared with the whole number of those sturdy hosts by which our nation has been enriched in recent generations out of virile foreign stock; but it is great enough to have brought deep disgrace upon us and to have made it necessary that we should promptly make use of processes of law by which we may be purged of their corrupt distempers. America never witnessed anything like this before. It never dreamed it possible that men sworn into its own citizenship, men drawn out of great free stocks such as supplied some of the best and strongest elements of that little, but how heroic, nation that in a high day of old staked its very life to free itself from every entanglement that had darkened the fortunes of the older nations and set up a new standard here, that men of such origins and such free choices of allegiance would ever turn in malign reaction against the Government and people who bad welcomed and nurtured them and seek to make this proud country once more a hotbed of European passion. A little while ago such a thing would have seemed incredible. Because it was incredible we made no preparation for it. We would have been almost ashamed to prepare for it, as if we were suspicious of ourselves, our own comrades and neighbors! But the ugly and incredible thing has actually come about and we are without adequate federal laws to deal with it. **I urge you to enact such laws at the earliest possible moment and feel that in doing so I am urging you to do nothing less than save the honor and self-respect of the nation. Such creatures of passion, disloyalty, and anarchy must be crushed out.**

They are not many, but they are infinitely malignant, and the hand of our power should close over them at once. They have formed plots to destroy property, they have entered into conspiracies against the neutrality of the Government, they have sought to pry into every confidential transaction of the Government in order to serve interests alien to our own. **It is possible to deal with these things very effectually. I need not suggest the terms in which they may be dealt with.**

I wish that it could be said that only a few men, misled by mistaken sentiments of allegiance to the governments under which they were born, had been guilty of disturbing the self-possession and misrepresenting the temper and principles of the country during these days of terrible war, when it would seem that every man who was truly an American would instinctively make it his duty and his pride to keep the scales of judgment even and prove himself a partisan of no nation but his own. But it cannot. There are some men among us, and many resident abroad who, though born and bred in the United States and calling themselves Americans, have so forgotten themselves and their honor as citizens as to put their passionate sympathy with one or the other side in the great European conflict above their regard for the peace and dignity of the United States. They also preach and practice disloyalty. No laws, I suppose, can reach corruptions of

The Espionage Act of 1917 was amended in 1918 by the Sedition Act, which extended the prohibitions to include the obstruction of enlistment of military personnel, promoting insubordination in the military, and dissemination of false statements with the purpose of interfering with military operations. Across a range of cases arising under the Espionage Act and Sedition Act, the U.S. Supreme Court routinely ruled in favor of government and against those who were charged with interfering with the war effort.

The implication was clear. Among the provisions in the Espionage Act that Congress eventually adopted was a measure that made the dissemination of information with the intent to interfere with military operations punishable by death.

the mind and heart; but I should not speak of others without also speaking of these and expressing the even deeper humiliation and scorn which every self-possessed and thoughtfully patriotic American must feel when lie thinks of them and of the discredit they are daily bringing upon us.

While we speak of the preparation of the nation to make sure of her security and her effective power we must not fall into the patent error of supposing that her real strength comes from armaments and mere safeguards of written law. It comes, of course, from her people, their energy, their success in their undertakings, their free opportunity to use the natural resources of our great home land and of the lands outside our continental borders which look to us for protection, for encouragement, and for assistance in their development; from the organization and freedom and vitality of our economic life. The domestic questions which engaged the attention of the last Congress are more vital to the nation in this its time of test than at any other time. We cannot adequately make ready for any trial of our strength unless we wisely and promptly direct the force of our laws into these all-important fields of domestic action. A matter which it seems to me we should have very much at heart is the creation of the right instrumentalities by which to mobilize our economic resources in any time of national necessity.

For what we are seeking now, what in my mind is the single thought of this message, is national efficiency and security. We serve a great nation. We should serve it in the spirit of its peculiar genius. It is the genius of common men for self-government, industry, justice, liberty and peace. We should see to it that it lacks no instrument, no facility or vigor of law, to make it sufficient to play its part with energy, safety, and assured success. In this we are no partisans but heralds and prophets of a new age.

Source: Arthur S. Link, ed., *The Papers of Woodrow Wilson*, Vol. 35, 1915–1916 (Princeton, NJ: Princeton University Press, 1980), 293–310.

The expediency and definitiveness of swift, efficient justice is often appealing to government and the public alike in times of national emergency. Since its enactment, the Espionage Act of 1917 has been used by government to root out spies (such as Aldrich Ames and Robert Hanssen), prosecute those who release information (such as the recent cases of Bradley Manning and Edward Snowden), and silence opposition. A public insufficiently attentive to the chilling effect of such prohibitions grants presidents wide discretion for its use. In fact, as in the examples of the Red Scare that followed World War I and the Pentagon Papers case from the Vietnam era, the employment of such prohibitive measures by government is often desired by a public that feels threatened.

The Delegation of Congressional Power

J. W. Hampton & Co. v. United States

April 9, 1928

INTRODUCTION

In Federalist No. 47, James Madison wrote: "The accumulation of powers, legislative, executive, or judiciary, in the same hands, whether of one, a few or many, and whether self-appointed, or elective, may justly be pronounced the very definition of tyranny...." He continues, "[W]here the whole power of one department is exercised by the same hands which possess the whole power of another department, the fundamental principles of a free constitution are subverted."

Thus, by Madison's reasoning, each branch of government must avoid exercising power granted other branches. As an example, for the president to have the power to both legislate and execute, or implement, the legislation would amount to a violation of constitutional principle because concentrations of power reduce the opportunities for the checks and balances that typically attend a system of separated institutions sharing power.

But there is a further difficulty for democratic government when the legislative branch grants broad powers to the executive to implement legislation. Governmental power is held in trust; as citizens, we grant our consent to that governmental authority. When Congress cedes its lawmaking authority to another branch, the consent of the governed may be violated. This concern reflects an ancient legal principle that would presumably prohibit Congress from delegating its powers over legislation to another branch of government. This principle of nondelegation roughly means that *a power once delegated cannot be redelegated.* That is, the citizens have delegated legislative authority to the Congress. By this maxim, Congress must not then redelegate that legislative authority to another body. However, nowhere in the Constitution do we find Congress prohibited from delegating its power to the executive or judicial branches. As a result, the question of what delegations of lawmaking power are consistent with democracy has been left for the courts to determine.

Mr. Chief Justice TAFT delivered the opinion of the Court.

In this case, the Tariff Act of 1922 included a provision (Sect. 315 of Title III) that authorized the president to equalize the differences in the costs of production of certain U.S. and foreign products by setting duties imposed under the act. J. W. Hampton and Co. was required to pay an extra duty on barium dioxide under the terms of the president's proclamation (under the authority delegated to the president by the statute). The company sued, challenging the constitutionality of the delegation of legislative power from Congress to the executive.

J. W. Hampton, Jr., & Co. made an importation into New York of barium dioxide which the collector of customs assessed at the dutiable rate of six cents per pound. This was two cents per pound more than that fixed by statute. The rate was raised by the collector by virtue of the proclamation of the President issued under, and by authority of, section 315 of title 3 of the Tariff Act of September 21, 1922, which is the so-called flexible tariff provision.

The issue here is as to the constitutionality of section 315, upon which depends the authority for the proclamation of the President and for two of the six cents per pound duty collected from the petitioner. The contention of the taxpayers is that the section is invalid in that it is a delegation to the President of the legislative power, which by article 1, § 1 of the Constitution, is vested in Congress, the power being that declared in section 8 of article 1, that the Congress shall have power to lay and collect taxes, duties, imposts and excises.

First. It seems clear what Congress intended by section 315. Its plan was to secure by law the imposition of customs duties on articles of imported merchandise which should equal the difference between the cost of producing in a foreign country the articles in question and laying them down for sale in the United States, and the cost of producing and selling like or similar articles in the United States, so that the duties not only secure revenue, but at the same time enable domestic producers to compete on terms of equality with foreign producers in the markets of the United States. It may be that it is difficult to fix with exactness this difference, but the difference which is sought in the statute is perfectly clear and perfectly intelligible. Because of the difficulty in practically determining what that difference is, **Congress seems to have doubted that the information in its possession was such as to enable it to make the adjustment accurately, and also to have apprehended that with changing conditions the difference might vary in such a way that some readjustments would be necessary to give effect to the principle on which the statute proceeds. To avoid such difficulties, Congress adopted in section 315 the method of describing with clearness what its policy and plan was and then authorizing a member of the executive branch to carry out its policy and plan and to find the changing difference from time to time and to make the adjustments necessary to conform the duties to the standard underlying that policy and plan.** As it was a matter of great importance, it concluded to give by statute to the President, the chief of the executive branch, the function of determining the difference as it might vary. He was provided with a body of investigators who were to assist him in

If Congress were to keep for itself the power to fix rates, or impose duties as events, conditions, or markets warrant, one can imagine Congress could do little else. Delegation can be understood in this sense as a division of labor under fluid conditions or conditions of uncertainty.

obtaining needed data and ascertaining the facts justifying readjustments. There was no specific provision by which action by the President might be invoked under this act, but it was presumed that the President would through this body of advisers keep himself advised of the necessity for investigation or change, and then would proceed to pursue his duties under the act and reach such conclusion as he might find justified by the investigation and proclaim the same, if necessary.

The well-known maxim 'Delegata potestas non potest delegari,' applicable to the law of agency in the general and common law, is well understood and has had wider application in the construction of our federal and state Constitutions than it has in private law. Our Federal Constitution and state Constitutions of this country divide the governmental power into three branches. The first is the legislative, the second is the executive, and the third is the judicial, and the rule is that in the actual administration of the government Congress or the Legislature should exercise the legislative power, the President or the state executive, the Governor, the executive power, and the courts or the judiciary the judicial power, and in carrying out that constitutional division into three branches it is a breach of the national fundamental law if Congress gives up its legislative power and transfers it to the President, or to the judicial branch, or if by law it attempts to invest itself or its members with either executive power or judicial power. This is not to say that the three branches are not co-ordinate parts of one government and that each in the field of its duties may not invoke the action of the two other branches in so far as the action invoked shall not be an assumption of the constitutional field of action of another branch. **In determining what it may do in seeking assistance from another branch, the extent and character of that assistance must be fixed according to common sense and the inherent necessities of the governmental co-ordination.**

The field of Congress involves all and many varieties of legislative action, and Congress has found it frequently necessary to use officers of the executive branch within defined limits, to secure the exact effect intended by its acts of

While there have been a few occasions of the courts using the nondelegation doctrine to bar Congress from ceding plenary legislative authority to other branches, by and large, courts have approved the congressional grants. This passage explains part of the reason why. Congress, the court seems to say, is permitted to delegate powers to the other branches if those delegations are exercises of Congress's legislative authority, rather than wholesale abdications of legislative power.

legislation, by vesting discretion in such officers to make public regulations interpreting a statute and directing the details of its execution, even to the extent of providing for penalizing a breach of such regulations.

Congress may feel itself unable conveniently to determine exactly when its exercise of the legislative power should become effective, because dependent on future conditions, and it may leave the determination of such time to the decision of an executive.

Again, one of the great functions conferred on Congress by the Federal Constitution is the regulation of interstate commerce and rates to be exacted by interstate carriers for the passenger and merchandise traffic. The rates to be fixed are myriad. If Congress were to be required to fix every rate, it would be impossible to exercise the power at all. Therefore, common sense requires that in the fixing of such rates Congress may provide a Commission, as it does, called the Interstate Commerce Commission, to fix those rates, after hearing evidence and argument concerning them from interested parties, all in accord with a general rule that Congress first lays down that rates shall be just and reasonable considering the service given and not discriminatory. As said by this Court in Interstate Commerce Commission v. Goodrich Transit Co., 224 U.S. 194, 214, 32 S. Ct. 436, 441 (56 L. Ed. 729):

> The Congress may not delegate its purely legislative power to a commission, but, having laid down the general rules of action under which a commission shall proceed, it may require of that commission the application of such rules to particular situations and the investigation of facts, with a view to making orders in a particular matter within the rules laid down by the Congress.

The same principle that permits Congress to exercise its rate-making power in interstate commerce by declaring the rule which shall prevail in the legislative fixing of rates, and enables it to remit to a rate-making body created in accordance with its provisions the fixing of such rates, justifies a similar provision for the fixing of customs duties on imported merchandise.

Here is the standard the court came to apply ·······
in delegation cases—the intelligible principle standard. It is rather vague and certainly accommodating of broad grants of discretionary authority by Congress to the president. As a result of this broad standard, the president's discretion in regulatory affairs and in implementing congressional statutes has expanded considerably. There are many reasons for this, not the least of which has been technological changes that require the specialization of experts rather than congressional (nonexpert) policy making. As that discretion has expanded, courts have routinely upheld those delegations despite the ancient maxim. Keep this dynamic in mind as you review the history and consequence of the *Chevron* doctrine, discussed in a later chapter.

If Congress shall lay down by legislative act an intelligible principle to which the person or body authorized to fix such rates is directed to conform, such legislative action is not a forbidden delegation of legislative power.

If it is thought wise to vary the customs duties according to changing conditions of production at home and abroad, it may authorize the Chief Executive to carry out this purpose, with the advisory assistance of a Tariff Commission appointed under congressional authority.

While Congress could not delegate legislative power to the President, this act did not in any real sense invest the President with the power of legislation, because nothing involving the expediency or just operation of such legislation was left to the determination of the President. What the President was required to do was merely in execution of the act of Congress. It was not the making of law. He was the mere agent of the lawmaking department to ascertain and declare the event upon which its expressed will was to take effect.

The judgment of the Court of Customs Appeals is affirmed.

Source: *J.W. Hampton, Jr. & Co. v. United States*, 276 U.S. 394 (1928).

FDR's First 100 Days

Franklin D. Roosevelt's First Inaugural Address
March 4, 1933

INTRODUCTION

When the U.S. stock market crashed in 1929 setting in motion a cascade of economic crises that came to be known as the Great Depression, President Herbert Hoover's prescription for dealing with the worldwide economic downturn was for government to stay out of the way and let it run its course. Meanwhile, unemployment hit 25%, bread lines and soup kitchens proliferated, foreclosures filled the ranks of the homeless, and banks and other industries were shuttered. By 1933, the United States was at its lowest point during the Great Depression. The era of laissez faire economics and governmental restraint in the private marketplace fell away in the face of the dramatic and tragic realities of the Great Depression. The long period of Republican control of the federal government that began with Lincoln ended with Franklin Delano Roosevelt's election in 1932. The three most recent presidents, Harding, Coolidge, and Hoover, each enjoyed solid Republican majorities, but by Hoover's second term, the shift to Democratic control was underway. With Roosevelt's election, the New Deal realignment—a sharp, dramatic, and enduring change in the voting patterns of major blocs of voters—had taken hold. Armed with overwhelming Democratic majorities in both chambers of Congress, FDR set the federal government on a course of aggressive engagement with the economy in order to pull the country out of the economic crisis.

I am certain that my fellow Americans expect that on my induction into the Presidency I will address them with a candor and a decision which the present situation of our Nation impels. This is preeminently the time to speak the truth, the whole truth, frankly and boldly. Nor need we shrink from honestly facing conditions in our country today. This great Nation will endure as it has endured, will revive and will prosper. **So, first of all, let me assert my firm belief that the only thing we have to fear is fear itself—nameless, unreasoning, unjustified terror which paralyzes needed efforts to convert retreat into advance. In every dark hour of our national life a leadership of frankness and vigor has met with that understanding and support of the people themselves which is essential to victory. I am convinced that you will again give that support to leadership in these critical days.**

The country was on the verge of complete social and economic collapse as it struggled with the worst economic depression in history. In some cities, such as Detroit, unemployment had reached 50%. The banking system was virtually nonexistent; even the U.S. Treasury did not have sufficient funds to pay government workers. In order to restore consumer confidence and end the panic that had gripped the country, Roosevelt and his advisors initiated a plan for a New Deal, several measures of which were introduced and enacted within the president's first 100 days in office. This passage, among the most famous of FDR's quotes, reflects the role that consumer confidence has to play in dragging the economy out of depression.

In such a spirit on my part and on yours we face our common difficulties. They concern, thank God, only material things. Values have shrunken to fantastic levels; taxes have risen; our ability to pay has fallen; government of all kinds is faced by serious curtailment of income; the means of exchange are frozen in the currents of trade; the withered leaves of industrial enterprise lie on every side; farmers find no markets for their produce; the savings of many years in thousands of families are gone.

More important, a host of unemployed citizens face the grim problem of existence, and an equally great number toil with little return. Only a foolish optimist can deny the dark realities of the moment.

Yet our distress comes from no failure of substance. We are stricken by no plague of locusts. Compared with the perils which our forefathers conquered because they believed and were not afraid, we have still much to be thankful for. Nature still offers her bounty and human efforts have multiplied it. Plenty is at our doorstep, but a generous use of it languishes in the very sight of the supply. Primarily this is because rulers of the exchange of mankind's goods have failed through their own stubbornness and their own incompetence, have admitted their failure, and have abdicated. Practices of the unscrupulous money changers stand indicted in the court of public opinion, rejected by the hearts and minds of men.

True they have tried, but their efforts have been cast in the pattern of an outworn tradition. Faced by failure of credit they have proposed only the lending of more money. Stripped of the lure of profit by which to induce our people to follow their false leadership, they have resorted to exhortations, pleading tearfully for restored confidence. They know only the rules of a generation of self-seekers. They have no vision, and when there is no vision the people perish.

The money changers have fled from their high seats in the temple of our civilization. We may now restore that temple to the ancient truths. The measure of the restoration lies in the extent to which we apply social values more noble than mere monetary profit.

Happiness lies not in the mere possession of money; it lies in the joy of achievement, in the thrill of creative effort. The joy and moral stimulation of work no longer must be forgotten in the mad chase of evanescent profits. These dark days will be worth all they cost us if they teach us that our true destiny is not to be ministered unto but to minister to ourselves and to our fellow men.

Recognition of the falsity of material wealth as the standard of success goes hand in hand with the abandonment of the false belief that public office and high political position are to be valued only by the standards of pride of place and personal profit; and there must be an end to a conduct in banking and in business which too often has given to a sacred trust the likeness of callous and selfish wrongdoing. Small wonder that confidence languishes, for it thrives only on honesty, on honor, on the sacredness of obligations, on faithful protection, on unselfish performance; without them it cannot live. Restoration calls, however, not for changes in ethics alone. This Nation asks for action, and action now.

Our greatest primary task is to put people to work. This is no unsolvable problem if we face it wisely and courageously. It can be accomplished in part by direct recruiting by the Government itself, treating the task as we would treat the emergency of a war, but at the same time, through this employment, accomplishing greatly needed projects to stimulate and reorganize the use of our natural resources.

Hand in hand with this we must frankly recognize the overbalance of population in our industrial centers and, by engaging on a national scale in a redistribution, endeavor to provide a better use of the land for those best fitted for the land. The task can be helped by definite efforts to raise the values of agricultural products and with this the power to purchase the output of our cities. It can be helped by preventing realistically the tragedy of the growing loss through foreclosure of our small homes and our farms. It can be helped

The immediacy and desirability of extensive corrective measures was clear to most observers. As a result of the flurry of New Deal legislation passed during the first 100 days of his presidency, Roosevelt would set a new standard by which all subsequent presidents' first few months in office are measured. Thanks to FDR, the first 100 days is perceived to be a yardstick for measuring the success of a new president. Their political power, presumably, is at its apogee during the so-called honeymoon period following inauguration. There is nothing magical about the 100 days, but FDR's aggressive actions during this period established the benchmark for declaring early presidential success or failure.

The Banking Act of 1933 was among the most significant of the new laws passed during the first 100 days. The act established the Federal Deposit Insurance Corporation (FDIC), which insured the deposits of individuals in their local banks. Another law established the Securities and Exchange Commission (SEC) to regulate investment banks and prevent the abuse that prevailed prior to 1929. These measures went a long way toward overcoming the panic that had crippled the country's banking system.

by insistence that the Federal, State, and local governments act forthwith on the demand that their cost be drastically reduced. It can be helped by the unifying of relief activities which today are often scattered, uneconomical, and unequal. It can be helped by national planning for and supervision of all forms of transportation and of communications and other utilities which have a definitely public character. There are many ways in which it can be helped, but it can never be helped merely by talking about it. **We must act and act quickly.**

Finally, in our progress toward a resumption of work we require two safeguards against a return of the evils of the old order: **there must be a strict supervision of all banking and credits and investments, so that there will be an end to speculation with other people's money; and there must be provision for an adequate but sound currency.**

These are the lines of attack. I shall presently urge upon a new Congress, in special session, detailed measures for their fulfillment, and I shall seek the immediate assistance of the several States.

Through this program of action we address ourselves to putting our own national house in order and making income balance outgo. Our international trade relations, though vastly important, are in point of time and necessity secondary to the establishment of a sound national economy. I favor as a practical policy the putting of first things first. I shall spare no effort to restore world trade by international economic readjustment, but the emergency at home cannot wait on that accomplishment.

The basic thought that guides these specific means of national recovery is not narrowly nationalistic. It is the insistence, as a first consideration, upon the interdependence of the various elements in and parts of the United States—a recognition of the old and permanently important manifestation of the American spirit of the pioneer. It is the way to recovery. It is the immediate way. It is the strongest assurance that the recovery will endure.

In the field of world policy I would dedicate this Nation to the policy of the good neighbor—the neighbor who resolutely respects himself and, because he does so, respects the rights of others—the neighbor who respects his obligations and respects the sanctity of his agreements in and with a world of neighbors.

If I read the temper of our people correctly, we now realize as we have never realized before our interdependence on each other; that we cannot merely take but we must give as well; that if we are to go forward, we must move as a trained and loyal army willing to sacrifice for the good of a common discipline, because without such discipline no progress is made, no leadership becomes effective. We are, I know, ready and willing to submit our lives and property to such discipline, because it makes possible a leadership which aims at a larger good. This I propose to offer, pledging that the larger purposes will bind upon us all as a sacred obligation with a unity of duty hitherto evoked only in time of armed strife.

With this pledge taken, I assume unhesitatingly the leadership of this great army of our people dedicated to a disciplined attack upon our common problems.

Action in this image and to this end is feasible under the form of government which we have inherited from our ancestors. **Our Constitution is so simple and practical that it is possible always to meet extraordinary needs by changes in emphasis and arrangement without loss of essential form. That is why our constitutional system has proved itself the most superbly enduring political mechanism the modern world has produced. It has met every stress of vast expansion of territory, of foreign wars, of bitter internal strife, of world relations.**

This appeal to constitutionalism is a prelude to the passage to follow. Here, he is suggesting that the genius of our constitutional system is its dynamism and flexibility for adapting to the critical events of the time. He might be speaking to the U.S. Supreme Court here, suggesting that their reluctance to permit the federal government the authority to regulate the economy would have devastating consequences.

It is to be hoped that the normal balance of Executive and legislative authority may be wholly adequate to meet the unprecedented task before us. But it may be that an unprecedented demand and need for undelayed action may call for temporary departure from that normal balance of public procedure.

I am prepared under my constitutional duty to recommend the measures that a stricken Nation in the midst of a stricken world may require. These measures, or such other measures as the Congress may build out of its experience and wisdom, I shall seek, within my constitutional authority, to bring to speedy adoption.

But in the event that the Congress shall fail to take one of these two courses, and in the event that the national emergency is still critical, I shall not evade the clear course of duty that will then confront me. **I shall ask the Congress for the one remaining instrument to meet the crisis—broad Executive power to wage a war against the emergency, as great as the power that would be given to me if we were in fact invaded by a foreign foe.**

The exigencies of this crisis, he suggests, make it comparable to placing the country on war footing. The executive branch is given emergency powers under such conditions. New Dealers believed that wide discretion would be needed to meet the needs presented by this crisis. It would not be long before the U.S. Supreme Court rejected that view in a series of cases involving the power of government to regulate commerce and the power of Congress to delegate to the executive branch certain legislative powers.

For the trust reposed in me I will return the courage and the devotion that befit the time. I can do no less.

We face the arduous days that lie before us in the warm courage of national unity; with the clear consciousness of seeking old and precious moral values; with the clean satisfaction that comes from the stern performance of duty by old and young alike. We aim at the assurance of a rounded and permanent national life.

We do not distrust the future of essential democracy. The people of the United States have not failed. In their need they have registered a mandate that they want direct, vigorous action. They have asked for discipline and direction under leadership. They have made me the present instrument of their wishes. In the spirit of the gift I take it.

In this dedication of a Nation we humbly ask the blessing of God. May He protect each and every one of us. May He guide me in the days to come.

Source: Franklin D. Roosevelt, Inaugural Address, March 4, 1933. Online by Gerhard Peters and John T. Woolley, *The American Presidency Project*. http://www.presidency.ucsb.edu/ws/?pid=14473.

The Four Horsemen

Carter v. Carter Coal Co.

May 18, 1936

INTRODUCTION

The Republican Party controlled the presidency and both chambers of Congress when the Great Depression hit in 1929. As the nation and the world slumped further into the depression, President Hoover continued to apply the same principles of economics and approaches to regulation that had been applied in the years leading up to the depression with unambiguously poor results. The American public had had enough, and voted the Republican incumbent out of office and elected Franklin Delano Roosevelt by a wide margin, almost 60%. The New Deal programs that FDR initiated—many in the first 100 days—became extremely popular. The newly established Tennessee Valley Authority, for example, brought electrification to the rural South, and the Works Progress Administration and the Civilian Conservation Corps employed thousands of previously impoverished citizens. The country began to get back on its feet by the election of 1936. Voters rewarded FDR with an even greater margin of electoral victory and a larger Democratic majority in Congress. As noted earlier, the New Deal realignment was occurring. However, the federal judiciary was quite removed from those electoral shifts. U.S. Supreme Court judges and other federal judges have life tenure and are therefore somewhat insulated from the electoral influences that shape the political branches of government. Therefore, while the country had moved on and embraced the New Deal, the Supreme Court and its Republican-appointed majority reflected the preferences and policies of the previous coalition. In fact, the recent Hoover appointments meant that FDR would not get to make a single appointment to the court until his second term as president. He would not get a pro–New Deal majority on the court until 1940—seven years after he first took office.

Within days of taking office, FDR initiated a series of measures that comprised the core of the New Deal. The national government was asserting broad new powers to regulate the economy. In passing these measures, Congress and the president relied on a number of expressed and implied constitutional powers, including the power to regulate interstate commerce and the taxing and spending power of Congress. Those powers, however, were thought by many in the GOP to run afoul of the 10th Amendment, which reserves to the states those powers not delegated to the national government. To the U.S. Supreme Court, which was dominated by Republican appointees, the federal government sought to exercise power denied to it by the Constitution. To FDR and the New Dealers in Congress, these were thoroughly constitutional powers that the government must have in order to drag the country out of the Great Depression. As soon as the new measures were implemented, the business interests opposed to the New Deal brought legal challenges, and the appeals were heard by a sympathetic core of four (sometimes five) conservative justices known to their critics as the *four horsemen*: Justices Van Devanter, McReynolds, Sutherland, and Butler. This collection was sometimes joined by a fifth vote, Justice Owen Roberts, to comprise the conservative bulwark against the New Deal legislation. The stage was set for the New Deal realignment to confront the conservative judiciary with life tenure.

MR. JUSTICE SUTHERLAND delivered the opinion of the Court.

In this U.S. Supreme Court case, *Carter v. Carter Coal Co.* (1936), the court considered the constitutionality of the Guffey Coal Act, formally known as the Bituminous Con-servation Act of 1935. Congress passed the act in order to stabilize the coal mining industry through a series of regulations cov-ering, among other things, the pricing of coal, wage and labor conditions, and collec-tive bargaining. It also established a Commis-sion to oversee the implementation of the guidelines. A stockholder in the Carter Coal Company, James Carter, sued to enjoin the company's compliance with the Guffey Coal Act's provisions. His suit, along with several others that challenged the act, was consoli-dated on appeal to the court.

Section 1 . . . declares that the mining and distribution of bituminous coal throughout the United States by the pro-ducer are affected with a national public interest, and that the service of such coal in relation to industrial activ-ities, transportation facilities, health and comfort of the people, conservation by controlled production and eco-nomical mining and marketing, maintenance of just and rational relations between the public, owners, producers and employees, the right of the public to constant and adequate supplies of coal at reasonable prices, and the general welfare of the nation, require that the bituminous coal industry should be regulated as the act provides.

These, it may be conceded, are objects of great worth; but are they ends the attainment of which has been committed by the Constitution to the federal government? This is a vital ques-tion, for nothing is more certain than that beneficent aims, however great or well directed, can never serve in lieu of constitutional power.

The ruling and firmly established principle is that the powers which the general government may exercise are only those specifically enumerated in the Constitution and such implied powers as are necessary and proper to carry into effect the enumerated powers. Whether the end sought to be attained by an act of Congress is legitimate is wholly a matter of con-stitutional power, and not at all of legislative discretion. Legislative congressional discretion begins with the choice of means, and ends with the adoption of methods and details to carry the delegated powers into effect. The distinction between these two things—power and discretion—is not only very plain, but very important. For while the powers are rigidly limited to the enumerations of the Constitution, the means which may be employed to carry the powers into effect are not restricted, save that they must be appropriate, plainly adapted to the end, and not prohibited by, but consis-tent with, the letter and spirit of the Constitution. *McCulloch v. Maryland,* 4 Wheat. 316, 421. Thus, it may be said that, to a constitutional end, many ways are open, but to an end not within the terms of the Constitution, all ways are closed.

The proposition, often advanced and as often discredited, that the power of the federal government inherently extends to purposes affecting the nation as a whole with which the states severally cannot deal or cannot adequately deal, and the related notion that Congress, entirely apart from those powers delegated by the Constitution, may enact laws to promote the general welfare, have never been accepted, but always definitely rejected, by this court.

But the proposition that there are legislative powers affecting the Nation as a whole which belong to, although not expressed in the grant of powers, is in direct conflict with the doctrine that this is a government of enumerated powers. That this is such a government clearly appears from the Constitution, independently of the Amendments, for otherwise there would be an instrument granting certain specified things made operative to grant other and distinct things. This natural construction of the original body of the Constitution is made absolutely certain by the Tenth Amendment. This amendment, which was seemingly adopted with prescience of just such contention as the present, disclosed the widespread fear that the National Government might, under the pressure of a supposed general welfare, attempt to exercise powers which had not been granted.

[T]he general purposes which the act recites . . . are beyond the power of Congress except so far, and only so far, as they may be realized by an exercise of some specific power granted by the Constitution. Proceeding by a process of elimination which it is not necessary to follow in detail, we shall find no grant of power which authorizes Congress to legislate in respect of these general purposes unless it be found in the commerce clause—and this we now consider.

Since the validity of the act depends upon whether it is a regulation of interstate commerce, the nature and extent of the power conferred upon Congress by the commerce clause becomes the determinative question in this branch of the case.

The commerce clause vests in Congress the power—"To regulate Commerce with foreign Nations, and among the several States, and with the Indian Tribes." The function to be exercised is that of regulation. The thing to be regulated is the commerce described. In exercising the authority conferred by this clause of the Constitution, Congress is powerless to regulate anything which is not commerce, as it is powerless to do anything about commerce which is not regulation.

No distinction is more popular to the common mind, or more clearly expressed in economic and political literature, than that between manufacture and commerce. Manufacture is transformation—the fashioning of raw materials into a change of form for use. The functions of commerce are different.... If it be held that the term includes the regulation of all such manufactures as are intended to be the subject of commercial transactions in the future, it is impossible to deny that it would also include all productive industries that contemplate the same thing. The result would be that Congress would be invested, to the exclusion of the States, with the power to regulate not only manufactures, but also agriculture, horticulture, stock raising, domestic fisheries, mining—in short, every branch of human industry.

The fact that an article is manufactured for export to another State does not, of itself, make it an article of interstate commerce, and the intent of the manufacturer does not determine the time when the article or product passes from the control of the State and belongs to commerce....

That commodities produced or manufactured within a state are intended to be sold or transported outside the state does not render their production or manufacture subject to federal regulation under the commerce clause. To hold otherwise would nationalize all industries, it would nationalize and withdraw from state jurisdiction and deliver to federal commercial control the fruits of California and the South, the wheat of the West and its meats, the cotton of the South, the shoes of Massachusetts and the woolen industries of other States, at the very inception of their production or growth, that is, the fruits unpicked, the cotton and wheat ungathered, hides and flesh of cattle yet "on the hoof," wool yet unshorn, and coal yet unmined, because they are in varying percentages destined for and surely to be exported to States other than those of their production.

Mining is not interstate commerce, but, like manufacturing, is a local business subject to local regulation and taxation.... Its character in this regard is intrinsic, is not affected by the intended use or disposal of the product, is not controlled by contractual engagements, and persists even though the business be conducted in close connection with interstate commerce.

But § 1 (the preamble) of the act now under review declares that all production and distribution of bituminous coal "bear upon and directly affect its interstate commerce", and that regulation thereof is imperative for the protection of such commerce. The contention of the government is that the labor provisions of the act may be sustained in that view.

That the production of every commodity intended for interstate sale and transportation has some effect upon interstate commerce may be, if it has not already been, freely granted, and we are brought to the final and decisive inquiry, whether here that effect is direct, as the "preamble" recites, or indirect. The distinction is not formal, but substantial in the highest degree...

Whether the effect of a given activity or condition is direct or indirect is not always easy to determine. The word "direct" implies that the activity or condition invoked or blamed shall operate proximately—not mediately, remotely, or collaterally—to produce the effect. It connotes the absence of an efficient intervening agency or condition. And the extent of the effect bears no logical relation to its character. **The distinction between a direct and an indirect effect turns not upon the magnitude of either the cause or the effect, but entirely upon the manner in which the effect has been brought about.** If the production by one man of a single ton of coal intended for interstate sale and shipment, and actually so sold and shipped, affects interstate commerce

Among the first New Deal cases to reach the court was *Panama Refining v. Ryan* (1935). In that case, the court struck portions of the National Industrial Recovery Act as a violation of the nondelegation doctrine. Then, just a few days later, a series of other New Deal measures fell at the hands of the court. The court found that Congress could not use the power to regulate interstate commerce to regulate business activities—such as manufacturing, refining, or mining—that were strictly local and had only an indirect effect on interstate commerce. This was known as the direct-indirect effects test that the court developed to limit the power of the national government to regulate business. In this case, the court extended its application of the direct-indirect effects test to mean that Congress could not regulate anything that had to do with the manufacturing of goods, only the distribution of those products. That is, it is in fact the *kind* of activity that is at issue, not simply its effect on interstate commerce that matters. Mining and production, for example, is always only indirectly related to interstate commerce and therefore beyond the reach of the federal government. But, if in the course of regulating distribution the regulations affected production, Congress could not regulate—only states can by virtue of the 10th Amendment. This case reflects the application of this doctrine and demonstrates the severe limits the court placed on the New Deal legislation that FDR and congressional Democrats supported.

indirectly, the effect does not become direct by multiplying the tonnage, or increasing the number of men employed, or adding to the expense or complexities of the business, or by all combined. It is quite true that rules of law are sometimes qualified by considerations of degree, as the government argues. But the matter of degree has no bearing upon the question here, since that question is not what is the extent of the local activity or condition, or the extent of the effect produced upon interstate commerce?, but what is the relation between the activity or condition and the effect?

Much stress is put upon the evils which come from the struggle between employers and employees over the matter of wages, working conditions, the right of collective bargaining, etc., and the resulting strikes, curtailment and irregularity of production and effect on prices, and it is insisted that interstate commerce is greatly affected thereby. But, in addition to what has just been said, the conclusive answer is that the evils are all local evils over which the federal government has no legislative control. The relation of employer and employee is a local relation. At common law, it is one of the domestic relations. The wages are paid for the doing of local work. Working conditions are obviously local conditions. The employees are not engaged in or about commerce, but exclusively in producing a commodity. And the controversies and evils which it is the object of the act to regulate and minimize are local controversies and evils affecting local work undertaken to accomplish that local result. Such effect as they may have upon commerce, however extensive it may be, is secondary and indirect. An increase in the greatness of the effect adds to its importance. It does not alter its character.

The government's contentions in defense of the labor provisions are really disposed of adversely by our decision in the *Schechter* case, *supra*. **The only perceptible difference between that case and this is that, in the *Schechter* case, the federal power was asserted with respect to commodities which had come to rest after their interstate transportation, while here the case deals with commodities at rest before interstate commerce has begun.** That difference is without significance. The federal regulatory power

In *Schecter Poultry Corp. v. U.S.* (1935), the court ruled that the slaughtering and selling of chicken by Schechter brothers in a Brooklyn slaughterhouse was a strictly local activity that was beyond the reach of congressional authority over interstate commerce. Specifically, the court found that the poultry slaughter business had only an indirect effect on interstate commerce. The chickens, though once in a stream of interstate commerce, had come to "rest" in the slaughterhouse, thus ending federal authority over them. If Schecter is understood to establish the terminus of federal power over interstate commerce, *Carter v. Carter Coal Co.*, then, can be understood as establishing where federal authority begins.

ceases when interstate commercial intercourse ends; and, correlatively, the power does not attach until interstate commercial intercourse begins. There is no basis in law or reason for applying different rules to the two situations. [I]f the commerce clause could be construed to reach transactions having an indirect effect upon interstate commerce, the federal authority would embrace practically all the activities of the people, and the authority of the state over its domestic concerns would exist only by sufferance of the federal government.

A reading of the entire opinion makes clear what we now declare, that the want of power on the part of the federal government is the same whether the wages hours of service, and working conditions, and the bargaining about them, are related to production before interstate commerce has begun or to sale and distribution after it has ended.

It is so ordered.

Source: *Carter v. Carter Coal Co.*, 298 U.S. 238 (1936).

Presidents and Foreign Affairs

U.S. v. Curtiss-Wright Export Co.

December 21, 1936

INTRODUCTION

In the mid-1960s, political scientists generally agreed that it was useful to think about presidential power as reflective of not one but two presidencies: one presidency directed toward domestic affairs and the other toward foreign affairs and national defense. The premise was that presidents enjoy far greater latitude in foreign affairs than in domestic policy. One important study demonstrated that presidents had much better success getting their foreign affairs polices through Congress than their domestic agenda. In recent years, the Two Presidencies thesis has received some criticism for being time-bound (reflective of congressional deference to the executive branch during the Cold War), but its central proposition that there is a difference in presidential power with respect to domestic and foreign affairs remains. One of the reasons it's been such a powerful explanation of presidential power is because in a 1936 case, the U.S. Supreme Court upheld the principle that Congress may delegate broader discretionary authority to the president in foreign affairs than it may in domestic affairs. If you recall the discussion of the nondelegation doctrine earlier, you will no doubt recognize that this 1936 decision expands presidential power by granting Congress the ability to cede its own authority. This decision authorizes the explicit congressional delegation of power to the president in foreign affairs. But those explicit delegations of power are *in addition to* congressional inaction in the face of the exercise of presidential unilateral power in foreign affairs. The effect of both sources of presidential discretion is to widen the scope of executive power a great deal.

MR. JUSTICE SUTHERLAND delivered the opinion of the Court.

It is contended that, by the Joint Resolution, the going into effect and continued operation of the resolution was conditioned (a) upon the President's judgment as to its beneficial effect upon the reestablishment of peace between the countries engaged in armed conflict in the Chaco; (b) upon the making of a proclamation, which was left to his unfettered discretion, thus constituting an attempted substitution of the President's will for that of Congress; (c) upon the making of a proclamation putting an end to the operation of the resolution, which again was left to the President's unfettered discretion, and (d) further, that the extent of its operation in particular cases was subject to limitation and exception by the President, controlled by no standard. **In each of these particulars, appellees urge that Congress abdicated its essential functions and delegated them to the Executive.**

Whether, if the Joint Resolution had related solely to internal affairs, it would be open to the challenge that it constituted an unlawful delegation of legislative power to the Executive we find it unnecessary to determine. The whole aim of the resolution is to affect a situation entirely external to the United States and falling within the category of foreign affairs. The determination which we are called to make, therefore, is whether the Joint Resolution, as applied to that situation, is vulnerable to attack under the rule that forbids a delegation of the lawmaking power. In other words, assuming (but not deciding) that the challenged delegation, if it were confined to internal affairs, would be invalid, may it nevertheless be sustained on the ground that its exclusive aim is to afford a remedy for a hurtful condition within foreign territory?

It will contribute to the elucidation of the question if we first consider the differences between the powers of the federal government in respect of foreign or external affairs and those in respect of domestic or internal affairs. That there are differences between them, and that these differences are fundamental, may not be doubted.

The two classes of powers are different both in respect of their origin and their nature. The broad statement that the federal government can exercise no powers except those specifically enumerated in the Constitution, and such implied powers as are necessary and proper to carry into effect the enumerated powers, is categorically true only in respect of our internal affairs. In that field, the primary purpose of the Constitution was to carve from the general mass of legislative powers then possessed by the states such portions as it was thought desirable to vest in the federal government, leaving those not included in the enumeration still in the states. *Carter v. Carter Coal Co.,* 298 U.S. 238, 294. **That this doctrine applies only to powers which the states had is self-evident. And since the states severally never**

Between 1932 and 1935, Paraguay and Bolivia were involved in a military conflict over the oil-rich region of the Chaco. In an effort to minimize the level of fighting, Congress passed, in 1934, a resolution that authorized the president to proscribe the sale of U.S. manufactured weapons and munitions to those nations with any limitations and exceptions he deemed appropriate. Through a proclamation pursuant to that resolution, FDR then authorized the secretary of state to enforce an embargo on the sale of arms to the region. Though FDR later rescinded that order, the Curtiss-Wright Export Co. was charged with conspiring to sell weapons to Bolivia while the embargo was in effect.

Here, we can see the court suggesting that there is a distinction between the delegation of power by Congress in domestic affairs and a delegation of power in foreign affairs —reflective of what would come to be known as the two presidencies thesis.

This passage and the reference to *Carter v. Carter Coal Co.* demonstrate the court's position on the 10th Amendment at this time. The 10th Amendment reserves those powers not delegated to the federal government by the Constitution to the states. While construing the amendment as a powerful brake on federal regulatory authority in Commerce Clause cases, such as *Carter v. Carter Coal Co.*, in this case, the court does not consider the 10th Amendment as a bulwark against federal power in foreign affairs. The assumption is that if the states did not have power over foreign affairs prior to the ratification of the Constitution, then that could not have been a power they retained. Therefore, federal power dominates the field.

possessed international powers, such powers could not have been carved from the mass of state powers, but obviously were transmitted to the United States from some other source. During the colonial period, those powers were possessed exclusively by, and were entirely under the control of, the Crown.

As a result of the separation from Great Britain by the colonies, acting as a unit, the powers of external sovereignty passed from the Crown not to the colonies severally, but to the colonies in their collective and corporate capacity as the United States of America. The Framers' Convention was called, and exerted its powers upon the irrefutable postulate that, though the states were several, their people, in respect of foreign affairs, were one.

It results that the investment of the federal government with the powers of external sovereignty did not depend upon the affirmative grants of the Constitution. The powers to declare and wage war, to conclude peace, to make treaties, to maintain diplomatic relations with other sovereignties, if they had never been mentioned in the Constitution, would have vested in the federal government as necessary concomitants of nationality.

Not only, as we have shown, is the federal power over external affairs in origin and essential character different from that over internal affairs, but participation in the exercise of the power is significantly limited. In this vast external realm, with its important, complicated, delicate and manifold problems, the President alone has the power to speak or listen as a representative of the nation. He makes treaties with the advice and consent of the Senate; but he alone negotiates. Into the field of negotiation the Senate cannot intrude, and Congress itself is powerless to invade it.

It is important to bear in mind that we are here dealing not alone with an authority vested in the President by an exertion of legislative power, but with such an authority plus the very delicate, plenary and exclusive power of the President as the sole organ of the federal government

in the field of international relations—a power which does not require as a basis for its exercise an act of Congress but which, of course, like every other governmental power, must be exercised in subordination to the applicable provisions of the Constitution. It is quite apparent that if, in the maintenance of our international relations, embarrassment—perhaps serious embarrassment—is to be avoided and success for our aims achieved, congressional legislation which is to be made effective through negotiation and inquiry within the international field must often accord to the President a degree of discretion and freedom from statutory restriction which would not be admissible were domestic affairs alone involved. Moreover, he, not Congress, has the better opportunity of knowing the conditions which prevail in foreign countries, and especially is this true in time of war. He has his confidential sources of information. He has his agents in the form of diplomatic, consular and other officials. Secrecy in respect of information gathered by them may be highly necessary, and the premature disclosure of it productive of harmful results.

The marked difference between foreign affairs and domestic affairs in this respect is recognized by both houses of Congress in the very form of their requisitions for information from the executive departments. In the case of every department except the Department of State, the resolution directs the official to furnish the information. In the case of the State Department, dealing with foreign affairs, the President is requested to furnish the information "if not incompatible with the public interest." A statement that to furnish the information is not compatible with the public interest rarely, if ever, is questioned.

When the President is to be authorized by legislation to act in respect of a matter intended to affect a situation in foreign territory, the legislator properly bears in mind the important consideration that the form of the President's action or, indeed, whether he shall act at all—may well depend, among other things, upon the nature of the confidential information which he has or may thereafter receive, or upon the effect

Here then, we come to a key passage in the court's decision. Note first that Sutherland makes reference to the cooperative powers enjoyed by the president—the power to exercise authority granted the office by Congress as well as plenary authority in certain foreign affairs by virtues of being the sole voice of the nation in foreign relations. Some have taken this to be a grant of exclusive power of the president over foreign affairs, but the holding of the court does not go that far. Rather, the court simply holds that relative to domestic policy, Congress has wider authority to delegate power to the president in foreign affairs.

Again, the court makes the distinction between its ruling in foreign relations and its earlier precedents regarding the delegation of discretion in domestic affairs. Just a few years prior, in a 1928 case, the court ruled that delegations would be allowed so long as Congress laid down an intelligible principle by which the executive could implement the legislative act.

which his action may have upon our foreign relations. **This consideration, in connection with what we have already said on the subject, discloses the unwisdom of requiring Congress in this field of governmental power to lay down narrowly definite standards by which the President is to be governed.**

In the light of the foregoing observations, it is evident that this court should not be in haste to apply a general rule which will have the effect of condemning legislation like that under review as constituting an unlawful delegation of legislative power. The principles which justify such legislation find overwhelming support in the unbroken legislative practice which has prevailed almost from the inception of the national government to the present day.

It is enough to summarize by saying that, both upon principle and in accordance with precedent, we conclude there is sufficient warrant for the broad discretion vested in the President to determine whether the enforcement of the statute will have a beneficial effect upon the reestablishment of peace in the affected countries; whether he shall make proclamation to bring the resolution into operation; whether and when the resolution shall cease to operate and to make proclamation accordingly, and to prescribe limitations and exceptions to which the enforcement of the resolution shall be subject.

The judgment of the court below must be reversed, and the cause remanded for further proceedings in accordance with the foregoing opinion.

Reversed.

Source: *United States v. Curtiss-Wright Export Corp.*, 299 U.S. 304 (1936).

The Court Packing Plan

Franklin D. Roosevelt's Fireside Chat

March 9, 1937

INTRODUCTION

In just two years' time, the conservative majority on the U.S. Supreme Court had struck down major provisions of 10 New Deal statutes. Never before or since has the court struck a similar number of laws in such quick succession. The court's decision in *Carter v. Carter Coal Co.*, however, would be FDR's last defeat at the hands of the four horsemen on the U.S. Supreme Court. Roosevelt had the clear backing of the electorate, winning his 1936 reelection with 98% of the electoral votes while Democrats swept 80% of the seats in both the House and the Senate. An emboldened Roosevelt thought it was time to take on the *nine old men* of the court, as he called them. Up to this time, he had not yet had the opportunity to appoint a single justice to the court. There was ample evidence that they might undo the entire New Deal unless FDR could get supporters of the measures on the bench. On March 9, 1937, FDR made the announcement excerpted here. He was poised to submit to Congress a plan to reorganize the federal court system. Among the changes he proposed was a plan to expand the number of lower court seats, provide expedited appellate review of constitutional cases, and allow lower court judges to preside in other, more burdened districts to help with the huge caseloads those districts were facing. But far more controversially, he proposed that Congress pass legislation creating one new seat on the U.S. Supreme Court for every current justice over the age of 70. The proposed measure would bring the total number of justices on the court to 15 and effectively dilute the vote strength of the conservative core of the court.

Last Thursday I described in detail certain economic problems which everyone admits now face the Nation. For the many messages which have come to me after that speech, and which it is physically impossible to answer individually, I take this means of saying "thank you."

Tonight, sitting at my desk in the White House, I make my first radio report to the people in my second term of office.

I am reminded of that evening in March, four years ago, when I made my first radio report to you. We were then in the midst of the great banking crisis.

Between 1933 and 1944, Roosevelt gave approximately 30 of these informal, conversational radio addresses to the nation. Almost 90% of all homes in America had a radio in these years before television, so he was able to speak directly to huge numbers of listeners. Though he did not give the talks next to a fireplace, the talks were given the name *fireside chats* by the White House—evoking an image of American families huddled by the fireside listening to FDR speak with them about important issues of the day.

Soon after, with the authority of the Congress, we asked the Nation to turn over all of its privately held gold, dollar for dollar, to the Government of the United States.

Today's recovery proves how right that policy was.

But when, almost two years later, it came before the Supreme Court its constitutionality was upheld only by a five-to-four vote. The change of one vote would have thrown all the affairs of this great Nation back into hopeless chaos. In effect, four Justices ruled that the right under a private contract to exact a pound of flesh was more sacred than the main objectives of the Constitution to establish an enduring Nation.

In 1933 you and I knew that we must never let our economic system get completely out of joint again—that we could not afford to take the risk of another great depression.

We also became convinced that the only way to avoid a repetition of those dark days was to have a government with power to prevent and to cure the abuses and the inequalities which had thrown that system out of joint.

We then began a program of remedying those abuses and inequalities—to give balance and stability to our economic system to make it bomb-proof against the causes of 1929.

Today we are only part-way through that program—and recovery is speeding up to a point where the dangers of 1929 are again becoming possible, not this week or month perhaps, but within a year or two.

Here, Roosevelt is criticizing the legal reasoning of several of the recent decisions by the Supreme Court. In those rulings, the court often decided that states, not the federal government, had the authority to regulate working conditions, set wages, and otherwise make policy to regulate the manufacturing of goods. To FDR, leaving states to do so was to invite the difficulties that beset the country under the Articles of Confederation—every state looking out for its own interests without attending to the welfare of the whole.

National laws are needed to complete that program. Individual or local or state effort alone cannot protect us in 1937 any better than ten years ago.

It will take time—and plenty of time—to work out our remedies administratively even after legislation is passed. To complete our program of protection in time, therefore, we cannot delay one moment in making certain that our National Government has power to carry through.

Four years ago action did not come until the eleventh hour. It was almost too late.

If we learned anything from the depression we will not allow ourselves to run around in new circles of futile discussion and debate, always postponing the day of decision.

The American people have learned from the depression. For in the last three national elections an overwhelming majority of them voted a mandate that the Congress and the President begin the task of providing that protection —not after long years of debate, but now.

After the 1936 election, for example, Democrats held 333 seats in the House against 89 GOP seats and 75 Senate seats to the GOP's 17. FDR received 60.8% of the popular vote, even more than he garnered in 1932. Surely, he saw these numbers as vindication for the New Deal that the conservative justices on the court were intent on dismantling.

The Courts, however, have cast doubts on the ability of the elected Congress to protect us against catastrophe by meeting squarely our modern social and economic conditions.

We are at a crisis in our ability to proceed with that protection. It is a quiet crisis. There are no lines of depositors outside closed banks. But to the far-sighted it is far-reaching in its possibilities of injury to America.

I want to talk with you very simply about the need for present action in this crisis—the need to meet the unanswered challenge of one-third of a Nation ill-nourished, ill-clad, ill-housed.

Last Thursday I described the American form of Government as a three horse team provided by the Constitution to the American people so that their field might be plowed. The three horses are, of course, the three branches of government— the Congress, the Executive and the Courts. Two of the horses are pulling in unison today; the third is not. Those who have intimated that the President of the United States is trying to drive that team, overlook the simple fact that the President, as Chief Executive, is himself one of the three horses.

It is the American people themselves who are in the driver's seat. It is the American people themselves who want the furrow plowed.

It is the American people themselves who expect the third horse to pull in unison with the other two.

In the last four years . . . [t]he Court has been acting not as a judicial body, but as a policy-making body.

When the Congress has sought to stabilize national agriculture, to improve the conditions of labor, to safeguard business against unfair competition, to protect our national resources, and in many other ways, to serve our clearly national needs, the majority of the Court has been assuming the power to pass on the wisdom of these Acts of the Congress—and to approve or disapprove the public policy written into these laws.

The Court in addition to the proper use of its judicial functions has improperly set itself up as a third House of the Congress—a super-legislature, as one of the justices has called it—reading into the Constitution words and implications which are not there, and which were never intended to be there.

We have, therefore, reached the point as a Nation where we must take action to save the Constitution from the Court and the Court from itself. We must find a way to take an appeal from the Supreme Court to the Constitution itself. We want a Supreme Court which will do justice under the Constitution—not over it. In our Courts we want a government of laws and not of men.

I want—as all Americans want—an independent judiciary as proposed by the framers of the Constitution. That means a Supreme Court that will enforce the Constitution as written —that will refuse to amend the Constitution by the arbitrary exercise of judicial power—amendment by judicial say-so. It does not mean a judiciary so independent that it can deny the existence of facts universally recognized.

What is my proposal? It is simply this: whenever a Judge or Justice of any Federal Court has reached the age of seventy and does not avail himself of the opportunity to retire on a pension, a new member shall be appointed by the President then in office, with the approval, as required by the Constitution, of the Senate of the United States.

That plan has two chief purposes. By bringing into the judicial system a steady and continuing stream of new and younger blood, I hope, first, to make the administration of all Federal justice speedier and, therefore, less costly; secondly, to bring to the decision of social and economic problems younger men who have had personal experience and contact with modern facts and circumstances under which average men have to live and work. **This plan will save our national Constitution from hardening of the judicial arteries.**

This emphasis on the age and frailty of the members of the Supreme Court did not sit well with many in the public. While voters were largely supportive of the New Deal, characterizing the court as feeble, slow, and aged did not serve the president well with public sentiment. In fact, when Chief Justice Hughes sent a letter to the Senate indicating that there was no backlog of cases, it undercut much of this line of argument.

The number of Judges to be appointed would depend wholly on the decision of present Judges now over seventy, or those who would subsequently reach the age of seventy.

If, for instance, any one of the six Justices of the Supreme Court now over the age of seventy should retire as provided under the plan, no additional place would be created. Consequently, although there never can be more than fifteen, there may be only fourteen, or thirteen, or twelve. And there may be only nine.

There is nothing novel or radical about this idea. It seeks to maintain the Federal bench in full vigor. It has been discussed and approved by many persons of high authority ever since a similar proposal passed the House of Representatives in 1869.

Why was the age fixed at seventy? Because the laws of many States, the practice of the Civil Service, the regulations of the Army and Navy, and the rules of many of our Universities and of almost every great private business enterprise, commonly fix the retirement age at seventy years or less.

The statute would apply to all the courts in the Federal system. There is general approval so far as the lower Federal courts are concerned. The plan has met opposition only so far as the Supreme Court of the United States itself is concerned. If such a plan is good for the lower courts it certainly ought to be equally good for the highest Court from which there is no appeal.

Those opposing this plan have sought to arouse prejudice and fear by crying that I am seeking to "pack" the Supreme Court and that a baneful precedent will be established.

What do they mean by the words "packing the Court"?

Let me answer this question with a bluntness that will end all honest misunderstanding of my purposes.

If by that phrase "packing the Court" it is charged that I wish to place on the bench spineless puppets who would disregard the law and would decide specific cases as I wished them to be decided, I make this answer: that no President fit for his office would appoint, and no Senate of honorable men fit for their office would confirm, that kind of appointees to the Supreme Court.

But if by that phrase the charge is made that I would appoint and the Senate would confirm Justices worthy to sit beside present members of the Court who understand those modern conditions, that I will appoint Justices who will not undertake to override the judgment of the Congress on legislative policy, that I will appoint Justices who will act as Justices and not as legislators—if the appointment of such Justices can be called "packing the Courts," then I say that I and with me the vast majority of the American people favor doing just that thing—now.

Is it a dangerous precedent for the Congress to change the number of the Justices? The Congress has always had, and will have, that power. The number of Justices has been changed several times before, in the Administrations of John Adams and Thomas Jefferson—both signers of the

Declaration of Independence—Andrew Jackson, Abraham Lincoln and Ulysses S. Grant.

Like all lawyers, like all Americans, I regret the necessity of this controversy. But the welfare of the United States, and indeed of the Constitution itself, is what we all must think about first. Our difficulty with the Court today rises not from the Court as an institution but from human beings within it. But we cannot yield our constitutional destiny to the personal judgment of a few men who, being fearful of the future, would deny us the necessary means of dealing with the present.

> **This plan of mine is no attack on the Court; it seeks to restore the Court to its rightful and historic place in our system of Constitutional Government and to have it resume its high task of building anew on the Constitution "a system of living law." The Court itself can best undo what the Court has done.**

Drawing attention to the age of the members of the Supreme Court was not the only track FDR took, of course. Here, and elsewhere, he makes a case based on constitutional interpretation. The formalism of the traditional legal theory that had dominated the court for decades had to be replaced with an approach to constitutional meaning that took account of the needs of contemporary society. Recall FDR's earlier argument that the president needed to be granted emergency, prerogative powers to meet the crisis posed by the Great Depression. The traditional legal theory would not permit such powers to be exercised. For the president to have such power, he would need a court that had a different view of constitutional meaning.

I have thus explained to you the reasons that lie behind our efforts to secure results by legislation within the Constitution. I hope that thereby the difficult process of constitutional amendment may be rendered unnecessary.

I am in favor of action through legislation:

First, because I believe that it can be passed at this session of the Congress.

Second, because it will provide a reinvigorated, liberal-minded Judiciary necessary to furnish quicker and cheaper justice from bottom to top.

Third, because it will provide a series of Federal Courts willing to enforce the Constitution as written, and unwilling to assert legislative powers by writing into it their own political and economic policies.

> **During the past half century the balance of power between the three great branches of the Federal Government, has been tipped out of balance by the**

FDR's proposal met with very little support in Congress. Part of the difficulty was that he did not consult with congressional leaders before making the plan public a month earlier, in February. While they were supportive of a change on the court, blindsiding Congress with a major proposal such as this was not well received. Both Republicans and Democrats rejected the president's proposal after hearings were held by the Senate Judiciary Committee. In the end, however, FDR got the results he wanted—a doctrinal shift on the court. That shift, however, came from the court itself and is typically referred to as "the switch in time that saved nine." Within a month, the court changed course on a number of key New Deal provisions. And in two months, retirements gave FDR his first opportunities to appoint new justices to the bench. The showdown between the president and the court was at an end, and a new approach to constitutional interpretation emerged on the court—one that was generally more deferential to legislative and executive power.

Courts in direct contradiction of the high purposes of the framers of the Constitution. It is my purpose to restore that balance. You who know me will accept my solemn assurance that in a world in which democracy is under attack, I seek to make American democracy succeed. You and I will do our part.

Source: Fireside Chats of Franklin D. Roosevelt, #9 On the Reorganization of the Judiciary. Franklin D. Roosevelt Presidential Library and Museum. Online at http://docs.fdrlibrary.marist.edu/030937.html.

The Four Freedoms

Franklin D. Roosevelt's Eighth State of the Union Address
January 6, 1941

INTRODUCTION

In FDR's first inaugural address, he issued an appeal for optimism in the depths of the world's greatest economic crisis. His "firm belief that the only thing we have to fear is fear itself" remains among his most famous lines. That theme of freedom from fear was picked up again in 1941, just months before the United States declared war against Japan. This time, "freedom from fear" refers specifically to freedom from fear of external attack. In this State of the Union address, FDR links that freedom from fear of external threat to freedom from want—securing for "every nation a healthy peacetime life for its inhabitants." The address, while primarily a speech about international affairs, yoked the two themes of political democracy and economic democracy together. This link, and the extension of the principles to "everywhere in the world," was quite deliberate. Just weeks after giving his Four Freedoms address, Roosevelt met with Winston Churchill regarding the war in Europe. The two leaders wanted to establish a set of core principles, or values, that would guide the Allies both in war and in its aftermath. The Atlantic Charter, issued in August 1941, was the result. The Four Freedoms address and the Atlantic Charter can be understood as in some important respects complimentary, reflecting the primacy of individual liberty, self-determination, economic justice, and state sovereignty based on the consent of the governed. New Deal interventionism in the marketplace and the Allies' fight against fascism in Europe were now joined.

Mr. President, Mr. Speaker, Members of the Seventy-seventh Congress:

I address you, the Members of the Seventy-seventh Congress, at a moment unprecedented in the history of the Union. I use the word "unprecedented," because at no previous time has American security been as seriously threatened from without as it is today.

Since the permanent formation of our Government under the Constitution, in 1789, most of the periods of crisis in our history have related to our domestic affairs. Fortunately, only one of these—the four-year War Between the States—ever threatened our national unity. Today, thank God, one hundred and thirty million Americans, in forty-eight States, have forgotten points of the compass in our national unity.

It is true that prior to 1914 the United States often had been disturbed by events in other Continents. We had even engaged in two wars with European nations and in a number of undeclared wars in the West Indies, in the Mediterranean and in the Pacific for the maintenance of American rights and for the principles of peaceful commerce. But in no case had a serious threat been raised against our national safety or our continued independence.

What I seek to convey is the historic truth that the United States as a nation has at all times maintained clear, definite opposition, to any attempt to lock us in behind an ancient Chinese wall while the procession of civilization went past. Today, thinking of our children and of their children, we oppose enforced isolation for ourselves or for any other part of the Americas.

Even when the World War broke out in 1914, it seemed to contain only small threat of danger to our own American future. But, as time went on, the American people began to visualize what the downfall of democratic nations might mean to our own democracy.

Every realist knows that the democratic way of life is at this moment being directly assailed in every part of the world—assailed either by arms, or by secret spreading of poisonous propaganda by those who seek to destroy unity and promote discord in nations that are still at peace.

During sixteen long months this assault has blotted out the whole pattern of democratic life in an appalling number of independent nations, great and small. The assailants are still on the march, threatening other nations, great and small.

Therefore, as your President, performing my constitutional duty to "give to the Congress information of the state of the Union," I find it, unhappily, necessary to report that the future and the safety of our country and of our democracy are overwhelmingly involved in events far beyond our borders.

Armed defense of democratic existence is now being gallantly waged in four continents. If that defense fails, all the population and all the resources of Europe, Asia, Africa and Australasia will be dominated by the conquerors.

No realistic American can expect from a dictator's peace international generosity, or return of true independence, or world disarmament, or freedom of expression, or freedom of religion—or even good business.

Roosevelt is assailing the isolationism that critics of his foreign policies sought. Many, for instance, thought that it was mainly a European conflict, and the United States ought to stay out of it. In criticizing the view that United States should stay out of the fight against fascism, he also calls for increased defense spending and the authority to provide assistance to those countries in the fight against Italy, Germany, and Japan.

Such a peace would bring no security for us or for our neighbors.

As a nation, we may take pride in the fact that we are soft-hearted; but we cannot afford to be soft-headed.

I have recently pointed out how quickly the tempo of modern warfare could bring into our very midst the physical attack which we must eventually expect if the dictator nations win this war.

There is much loose talk of our immunity from immediate and direct invasion from across the seas. Obviously, as long as the British Navy retains its power, no such danger exists. Even if there were no British Navy, it is not probable that any enemy would be stupid enough to attack us by landing troops in the United States from across thousands of miles of ocean, until it had acquired strategic bases from which to operate.

The first phase of the invasion of this Hemisphere would not be the landing of regular troops. **The necessary strategic points would be occupied by secret agents and their dupes—and great numbers of them are already here, and in Latin America.**

Within a year and a half, Nazi saboteurs would deploy out of German submarines and secretly come ashore in the United States with the intent to disrupt the Allied war effort by destroying key infrastructure. The trial of some of those saboteurs, as reviewed in *Ex Parte Quirin*, will be explored in an upcoming chapter.

As long as the aggressor nations maintain the offensive, they—not we—will choose the time and the place and the method of their attack.

That is why the future of all the American Republics is today in serious danger.

That is why this Annual Message to the Congress is unique in our history.

That is why every member of the Executive Branch of the Government and every member of the Congress faces great responsibility and great accountability.

The need of the moment is that our actions and our policy should be devoted primarily—almost exclusively—to meeting this foreign peril. For all our domestic problems are now a part of the great emergency.

The president now turns to a consideration of the principles that are derived from the domestic policies of the New Deal. His argument is that some of those same principles can be brought to bear in the international context, as they are universal values that secure human dignity and well-being.

Just as our national policy in internal affairs has been based upon a decent respect for the rights and the dignity of all our fellow men within our gates, so our national policy in foreign affairs has been based on a decent respect for the rights and dignity of all nations, large and small. And the justice of morality must and will win in the end.Our national policy is this:

First, by an impressive expression of the public will and without regard to partisanship, we are committed to all-inclusive national defense.

Second, by an impressive expression of the public will and without regard to partisanship, we are committed to full support of all those resolute peoples, everywhere, who are resisting aggression and are thereby keeping war away from our Hemisphere. By this support, we express our determination that the democratic cause shall prevail; and we strengthen the defense and the security of our own nation.

Third, by an impressive expression of the public will and without regard to partisanship, we are committed to the proposition that principles of morality and considerations for our own security will never permit us to acquiesce in a peace dictated by aggressors and sponsored by appeasers. We know that enduring peace cannot be bought at the cost of other people's freedom.

In the recent national election there was no substantial difference between the two great parties in respect to that national policy. No issue was fought out on this line before the American electorate. Today it is abundantly evident that American citizens everywhere are demanding and supporting speedy and complete action in recognition of obvious danger.

To change a whole nation from a basis of peacetime production of implements of peace to a basis of wartime production of implements of war is no small task. And the greatest difficulty comes at the beginning of the program, when new tools, new plant facilities, new assembly lines, and new ship ways must first be constructed before the actual materiel begins to flow steadily and speedily from them.

The Congress, of course, must rightly keep itself informed at all times of the progress of the program. **However, there is certain information, as the Congress itself will readily recognize, which, in the interests of our own security and those of the nations that we are supporting, must of needs be kept in confidence.**

This passage recalls John Jay's view, in Federalist No. 64, that "perfect secrecy and immediate dispatch are sometimes requisite . . . [the president should] be able to manage the business of intelligence in such a manner as prudence may suggest." Again, this is consistent with the view that presidents are privileged in many respects when it comes to foreign affairs—both in terms of their discretionary authority and how much information is obliged to be shared with Congress.

New circumstances are constantly begetting new needs for our safety. I shall ask this Congress for greatly increased new appropriations and authorizations to carry on what we have begun.

I also ask this Congress for authority and for funds sufficient to manufacture additional munitions and war supplies of many kinds, to be turned over to those nations which are now in actual war with aggressor nations.

Our most useful and immediate role is to act as an arsenal for them as well as for ourselves. They do not need man power, but they do need billions of dollars worth of the weapons of defense.

The time is near when they will not be able to pay for them all in ready cash. We cannot, and we will not, tell them that they must surrender, merely because of present inability to pay for the weapons which we know they must have.

A month prior to this address, FDR called for the United States to become the Arsenal of Democracy. The idea was to harness the power of U.S. industry to arm countries in their fights against Germany, Italy, and Japan. However, under 1930's statutes, the United States could not sell arms to belligerent nations. If FDR wanted to lend support to the Allied forces in Europe, he needed some other way to do it that would not run afoul of those Neutrality Acts. His lend-lease program became the mechanism. Lend-lease would equip Britain and other Allies with massive amounts of, among other items, arms, ships, vehicles, and food needed in their fight to hold off the Axis powers.

I recommend that we make it possible for those nations to continue to obtain war materials in the United States, fitting their orders into our own program. Nearly all their materiel would, if the time ever came, be useful for our own defense.

Let us say to the democracies: "We Americans are vitally concerned in your defense of freedom. We are putting forth our energies, our resources and our organizing powers to give you the strength to regain and maintain a free world. We shall send you, in ever-increasing numbers, ships, planes, tanks, guns. This is our purpose and our pledge."

The happiness of future generations of Americans may well depend upon how effective and how immediate we can make our aid felt. No one can tell the exact character of the emergency situations that we may be called upon to meet. The Nation's hands must not be tied when the Nation's life is in danger.

We must all prepare to make the sacrifices that the emergency—almost as serious as war itself—demands. Whatever stands in the way of speed and efficiency in defense preparations must give way to the national need.

A free nation has the right to expect full cooperation from all groups. A free nation has the right to look to the leaders of business, of labor, and of agriculture to take the lead in stimulating effort, not among other groups but within their own groups.

The best way of dealing with the few slackers or trouble makers in our midst is, first, to shame them by patriotic example, and, if that fails, to use the sovereignty of Government to save Government.

As men do not live by bread alone, they do not fight by armaments alone. Those who man our defenses, and those behind them who build our defenses, must have the stamina and the courage which come from unshakable belief in the manner of life which they are defending. The mighty action that we are calling for cannot be based on a disregard of all things worth fighting for.

The Nation takes great satisfaction and much strength from the things which have been done to make its people conscious of their individual stake in the preservation of democratic life in America. Those things have toughened the fibre of our people, have renewed their faith and strengthened their devotion to the institutions we make ready to protect.

Certainly this is no time for any of us to stop thinking about the social and economic problems which are the root cause of the social revolution which is today a supreme factor in the world.

For there is nothing mysterious about the foundations of a healthy and strong democracy. The basic things expected by our people of their political and economic systems are simple. They are:

Equality of opportunity for youth and for others.

Jobs for those who can work.

Security for those who need it.

The ending of special privilege for the few.

The preservation of civil liberties for all.

The enjoyment of the fruits of scientific progress in a wider and constantly rising standard of living.

These are the simple, basic things that must never be lost sight of in the turmoil and unbelievable complexity of our modern world. The inner and abiding strength of our economic and political systems is dependent upon the degree to which they fulfill these expectations.

Many subjects connected with our social economy call for immediate improvement. As examples:

We should bring more citizens under the coverage of old-age pensions and unemployment insurance.

We should widen the opportunities for adequate medical care.

We should plan a better system by which persons deserving or needing gainful employment may obtain it.

I have called for personal sacrifice. I am assured of the willingness of almost all Americans to respond to that call.

A part of the sacrifice means the payment of more money in taxes. In my Budget Message I shall recommend that a greater portion of this great defense program be paid for from taxation than we are paying today. No person should try, or be allowed, to get rich out of this program; and the principle of tax payments in accordance with ability to pay should be constantly before our eyes to guide our legislation.

If the Congress maintains these principles, the voters, putting patriotism ahead of pocketbooks, will give you their applause.

In the future days, which we seek to make secure, we look forward to a world founded upon **four essential human freedoms.**

The first is freedom of speech and expression—everywhere in the world.

The Four Freedoms, from which the speech takes its name, were written not by FDR's speechwriters, as is typical for the State of the Union addresses, but by Roosevelt himself. While the first three appear to be almost tacked on to a speech about international affairs, their inclusion here (and being followed by the fourth) demonstrates the degree to which he perceived issues of domestic economic and social justice to be connected to issues of international security. He felt that connection so strongly, in fact, that he included the phrase "everywhere in the world" over the objections of his closest advisors. Scholars believe his insistence on this universalization of freedoms to be attributable to the First Lady's considerable influence. Eleanor Roosevelt was a tireless supporter of human rights and economic and social justice around the world.

The second is freedom of every person to worship God in his own way—everywhere in the world.

The third is freedom from want—which, translated into world terms, means economic understandings which will secure to every nation a healthy peacetime life for its inhabitants—everywhere in the world.

The fourth is freedom from fear—which, translated into world terms, means a world-wide reduction of armaments to such a point and in such a thorough fashion that no nation will be in a position to commit an act of physical aggression against any neighbor—anywhere in the world.

That is no vision of a distant millennium. It is a definite basis for a kind of world attainable in our own time and generation. That kind of world is the very antithesis of the so-called new order of tyranny which the dictators seek to create with the crash of a bomb.

To that new order we oppose the greater conception—the moral order. A good society is able to face schemes of world domination and foreign revolutions alike without fear.

Since the beginning of our American history, we have been engaged in change—in a perpetual peaceful revolution—a revolution which goes on steadily, quietly adjusting itself to changing conditions—without the concentration camp or the quick-lime in the ditch. The world order which we seek is the cooperation of free countries, working together in a friendly, civilized society.

This nation has placed its destiny in the hands and heads and hearts of its millions of free men and women; and its faith in freedom under the guidance of God. Freedom means the supremacy of human rights everywhere. Our support goes to those who struggle to gain those rights or keep them. Our strength is our unity of purpose. To that high concept there can be no end save victory.

Source: Franklin D. Roosevelt Presidential Library. http://www.fdrlibrary.marist.edu/pdfs/fftext.pdf.

Pearl Harbor

Franklin D. Roosevelt's Request for a Declaration of War
December 7, 1941

INTRODUCTION

Article I, Section 8 grants Congress the authority to declare war. Upon that declaration, Article II, Section 2 vests the president with the power to wage war as commander in chief of the armed forces. On the face of it, these two constitutional provisions make collaboration assured in times of war. Congress declares war and appropriates funds to support it, while the president directs the armed forces as war is waged. But there is a tension here as well, in that presidents have initiated and sustained military engagements without congressional declarations of war. Though rare, there have also been occasions when Congress wanted to declare war but the president refused to go along. In this situation, at the onset of World War II, the two branches were fully committed to the same course.

The attack on Pearl Harbor by Japanese forces was surely the event that triggered Roosevelt's request for a declaration of war from Congress, but events prior to the attack had many in the United States preparing for war. In the mid-1930s, the Japanese Empire began a campaign to conquer China. By 1940, Japan had allied itself with Nazi Germany and Italy. The United States had remained neutral as the conflicts in Europe and Asia intensified. When Japan made the formal alliance with the Axis powers and invaded Indochina, threatening U.S. interests in the region, the United States responded by cutting off the shipment of important resources, such as oil, to Japan. Japan was so dependent on its imported oil that the embargo was considered a belligerent act. As Japan sought to secure its own sources of oil in Southeast Asia, it would threaten in a direct way U.S. interests and very likely draw the United States into war. Anticipating that reaction, Japanese military planners drew up plans for a surprise attack to hobble the ability of the United States to respond. As the Roosevelt administration engaged diplomatically with Japanese emissaries, the Emperor's military was planning an attack on the U.S. Pacific fleet in Hawaii. Just before 8:00 am local time, hundreds of Japanese fighter planes attacked the American Naval Base at Pearl Harbor. The attack lasted just two hours, but the devastation was massive. The nation was in shock.

Mr. Vice President, and Mr. Speaker, and Members of the Senate and House of Representatives:

Yesterday, December 7, 1941—a date which will live in infamy—the United States of America was suddenly and deliberately attacked by naval and air forces of the Empire of Japan.

The United States was at peace with that Nation and, at the solicitation of Japan, was still in conversation with its Government and its Emperor looking toward the maintenance of peace in the Pacific. Indeed, one hour after Japanese air squadrons had commenced bombing in the American Island of Oahu, the Japanese Ambassador to the United States and his colleague delivered to our Secretary of State a formal reply to a recent American message. **And while this reply stated that it seemed useless to continue the existing diplomatic negotiations, it contained no threat or hint of war or of armed attack.**

It will be recorded that the distance of Hawaii from Japan makes it obvious that the attack was deliberately planned many days or even weeks ago. During the intervening time the Japanese Government has deliberately sought to deceive the United States by false statements and expressions of hope for continued peace.

The attack yesterday on the Hawaiian Islands has caused severe damage to American naval and military forces. I regret to tell you that very many American lives have been lost. In addition American ships have been reported torpedoed on the high seas between San Francisco and Honolulu.

Yesterday the Japanese Government also launched an attack against Malaya.

Last night Japanese forces attacked Hong Kong.

Last night Japanese forces attacked Guam.

Last night Japanese forces attacked the Philippine Islands.

Last night the Japanese attacked Wake Island. And this morning the Japanese attacked Midway Island.

Japan has, therefore, undertaken a surprise offensive extending throughout the Pacific area. The facts of yesterday and today speak for themselves. The people of the United States

U.S. public opinion in the fall of 1941 was anticipating war with Japan over the issues that arose prior to the attack. U.S. embargoes of key resources and Japan's expansionist moves into Southeast Asia seemed to make war inevitable, but the attack of Pearl Harbor was a strike that the United States had not anticipated.

have already formed their opinions and well understand the implications to the very life and safety of our Nation.

As Commander in Chief of the Army and Navy I have directed that all measures be taken for our defense.

By the end of the attack, 18 U.S. warships and 300 airplanes were destroyed. The bombing raids left over 2,500 dead and 1,000 injured.

But always will our whole Nation remember the character of the onslaught against us.

No matter how long it may take us to overcome this premeditated invasion, the American people in their righteous might will win through to absolute victory. I believe that I interpret the will of the Congress and of the people when I assert that we will not only defend ourselves to the uttermost but will make it very certain that this form of treachery shall never again endanger us.

Hostilities exist. There is no blinking at the fact that our people, our territory, and our interests are in grave danger.

With confidence in our armed forces—with the unbounding determination of our people—we will gain the inevitable triumph—so help us God.

The next day, December 8, Congress voted to declare war on Japan. Within three days, the Axis powers of Germany and Italy would join Japan and declare war on the United States. The United States was now at war. Roosevelt, as commander in chief of the Army and Navy, would now assume greater powers than he had already been granted. But what happens to constitutional limits on executive power during times of war? The World War II era provided several challenges to those limits; usually, the Supreme Court was at the center of the discussion even as it would rarely constrain the president's prerogative.

I ask that the Congress declare that since the unprovoked and dastardly attack by Japan on Sunday, December 7, 1941, a state of war has existed between the United States and the Japanese Empire.

Source: U.S. Department of State, *Peace and War: United States Foreign Policy, 1931–1941* (Washington, DC: U.S. Government Printing Office, 1943), 838–839.

Operation Pastorius: The Nazi Saboteurs

Report of Operation

June 12, 1942

INTRODUCTION

For many years prior to World War II, Germany had operated training programs for spies and saboteurs. In the espionage schools, spies were taught the craft of stealing secrets and transmitting the information back to Germany. The sabotage training included instruction in the use of explosives and detonators for sabotage against enemy targets such as railroads, dams, canals, bridges, and factories. In September 1941, with the assistance of a double agent posing as a German spy, U.S. authorities uncovered a large Nazi spy ring operating in the United States. The sweep netted 30 German spies and set back the German espionage effort so much that Hitler insisted that something had to been done immediately. The Germans turned to their sabotage trainees. The sabotage program recruited Germans who had experience living in the United States to participate, some of whom had U.S. citizenship. Eight of its trainees left France for the United States to begin what was known as Operation Pastorius, named for the founder of the first German settlement in America. Four of the saboteurs had a destination of Ponte Vedra Beach, just south of Jacksonville, Florida. The other four were headed to Long Island. Their objectives included destroying key infrastructure and industrial sites while also committing (while minimizing civilian casualties) acts of terror through the destruction of bridges, locks, railroad depots, and in particular, Jewish-owned businesses in the United States. The leader of the Long Island group was George Dasch, a German-born U.S. citizen who had once served in the U.S. Army.

With one set of saboteurs en route to the Florida coast, Dasch and the other group set off for Long Island on May 28. Around midnight on June 12, 1942, their German U-boat, U-202, was within sight of Amagansett beach in the Hamptons, on Long Island, New York. The submarine had run aground as the Germans tried to get as close to shore as possible to lessen the distance the groups would have to row in their rubber raft, heavily loaded with four boxes of explosives. Though few of them were actually German soldiers, they all wore German military uniforms, because if they were apprehended upon arrival, they would be treated as prisoners of war rather than as spies. But, the saboteurs were instructed that they should attempt to overpower anyone they come across and place the prisoners (along with the team members' German uniforms) in the raft to be rowed back to the U-boat by the German sailors accompanying the group.

When the group reached the shore, they began to unload their raft and remove their German military uniforms. As they were doing so, however, John C. Cullen, a worker at the nearby Coast Guard station, approached the group. Instead of grabbing the Coast Guardsman, as instructed, Dasch engaged the man in small talk, made some vague threats, and eventually offered him money to "forget what you saw here." Meanwhile, the U-boat crewmembers left without the uniforms, which Dasch's team was busy burying in the sand, along with the boxes of explosives, and, oddly, a few easily identifiable German items that were brought along. When Cullen reached his station, he reported what had transpired on the beach. Without much effort, the Coast Guard officials were able to uncover the entire cache of explosives, detonators, and other instruments of sabotage, along with German cigarettes, a hat with a swastika, and a bottle of German schnapps. The saboteurs had left on foot, toward the train station to make their way to Manhattan (Fisher, Louis. 2005. *Nazi Saboteurs on Trial: A Military Tribunal and American Law*, 2nd ed. Lawrence, KS: Kansas University Press).

Summarized Introduction

The Sabotage Expedition, which was known to the German Secret Service as the Franz Daniel Pastorious Undertaking, consisted of eight men who were landed from U-boats on the East Coast of the USA in June 1942. The saboteurs were in two groups, the first being put ashore at Amagansett, Long Island on 13.6.4, while the second group was landed on the coast of Florida near Ponte Vedra, fifteen miles south of Jacksonville, on 17.6.42.

This report deals in detail with all the aspects of the case that might be of interest to the Security Service. The following points however are of sufficient interest to be summarized.

Within a day of the group's arrival in New York City, Dasch called the FBI to turn himself in. By this time, the FBI was certainly aware of the boxes of explosives and German paraphernalia found on the beach in the Hamptons. However, without giving them much information to go on, the FBI surprisingly listed his initial entreaties as low priority. After a few more days, Dasch left New York, booked a room at the Mayflower Hotel in Washington, DC, and made a call to the Justice Department to set up a face-to-face meeting with the FBI. With exceptionally little effort and virtually no investigation, the FBI was able to apprehend four Nazi saboteurs within a week. An independent investigation by the FBI led to the capture of the Ponte Vedra team on June 27.

It is abundantly evident that the leader of the first group of saboteurs, George John Dasch, had every intention of giving himself up to the American authorities and compromising the whole expedition, probably from the moment that it was first suggested to him in Germany that he should go to the USA on a sabotage assignment. Dasch's character is difficult to fathom. He was a strong left-wing supporter in the USA and both the FBI and the writer independently had the idea that he might be more than just a supporter of the left.

The submarine which landed one of the groups got into difficulties during the landing operation and went aground. It was only owing to the laziness or stupidity of the American coastguards that this submarine was not attacked by USA forces. The submarine went aground because it came in close to the shore to prevent the rubber boat containing the bulky sabotage supplies having to be rowed too far. The difficulty of safety of the rubber boat together with its contents, was the subject of acrimonious discussion between the German Secret Service and the U-boat High Command, when the submarine in the decision has been reached not to send submarines on pure sabotage expeditions in the future, but to include one or possibly two saboteurs among the normal crew of a submarine going on an operational trip. For this and other reasons it is most unlikely that in the future saboteurs will be landed with large stores of sabotage equipment. The equipment within the country concerned and will only bring with them such things as detonators, which occupy little space and cannot be manufactured by amateurs.

This sabotage expedition was better equipped with sabotage apparatus and better trained than any other expeditions of which the Security Service has heard. The German Secret Service attached the greatest importance to the success of the undertaking and were fortunate in having techniques among its members. Two members were machine tool fitters and were therefore in a far better position to commit sabotage to machinery than the usual type of saboteur employed by the German Secret Service.

One of the difficulties associated with the commission of acts of sabotage is to provide the saboteur with a mechanism by which he can get far away from the target before the sabotage occurs. The standard German method involves the use of a time clock. The type used in the Eastern Hemisphere has certain technical defects and does not always go off. A new type was given to the American saboteurs, but apart from this they were instructed in the manufacture of home-made delay mechanisms to be constructed from easily obtainable commodities such as tins of dried peas, lumps of sugar, and razor blades. This new technique is disturbing in that it removes one method of detecting saboteurs arriving in the country.

Another disturbing feature of this case is that the saboteurs were provided with abrasives for interfering with the lubrication systems of various types of machinery. (The provision of abrasives is somewhat childish as they could have easily obtained within the USA.) Until the equipment of the USA saboteurs was examined there was no evidence that the German Sabotage Service went in for any types of sabotage other than those done with incendiary or high explosive bombs. The interference with machinery by means of abrasives opens up a far wider field of possible German activities and will necessitate a close examination of cases which appear to be the work of disgruntled workmen or sailors.

The sabotage targets had been carefully thought out by the German Secret Service and were directed against real bottle necks in the American war industry.

Objectives of the Undertaking

This expedition was the first that Abw. II had sent to the USA. Its members had three objectives:

To commit sabotage

To lay the foundation of a German sabotage organization in the USA to be augmented by the further arrivals

To disseminate anti-war propaganda in the USA

These are all pure Abw. II functions and the members of the undertaking were specifically told that it was not part of their function to obtain military or political information.

Sabotage.

The task of the saboteurs was to slow down production at certain factories concerned with the American war effort, for which they were given specific targets; and to interfere with transportation systems, including railways and canals. They received special training for this latter purpose. Apart from interfering directly with the war effort, Abw. II hoped that the sabotage was not to be done in such a way that it appeared accidental, but was to be plainly recognizable as sabotage. In amplification of this scheme, the saboteurs were also instructed to carry out small acts of terrorism, such as the placing of incendiary bombs in suitcases left in luggage depots and in Jewish-owned shops. The saboteurs were however told that they must avoid killing or injuring people as this would not benefit Germany but would merely arouse indignation.

As regards to sabotage to the American war industry, the saboteurs were instructed to confine themselves to the light metal industry, interference with which would affect aircraft production.

The Foundation of a German Sabotage Organization in the USA.

This function was entrusted to the first group of the undertaking which landed at Long Island. Chicago was chosen as the headquarters of this organization, as German journalists returning to the Fatherland from the USA stated that this city seemed to be particularly against the war with Germany.

Dissemination of anti-war propaganda. **At least one of the saboteurs was instructed to establish contact with persons who appeared to be against the war and if possible to create an organization of such people to carry out anti-war propaganda. Another was told that if he heard persons indulging in anti-war talk, he was to agree with them and point out that the USA had no reason to be at war with Germany and that Germany wanted nothing from the USA.**

The day after the saboteurs were detained by authorities, headlines credited the FBI with nabbing the eight accomplices in the Nazi plot to sabotage American infrastructure. But a question remained—what to do with them? They were not prisoners of war, as they were not wearing the uniforms of an enemy combatant when they were apprehended. What, then, was their legal status and, consequently, what would the limits be to the military's authority over them? These are questions raised in the chapter on the *Ex Parte Quirin* case.

Source: German Saboteurs Landed in the USA from U-boats in 1942. Report of operation. SF54-7-234 LINK A; KV 3-413. UK National Archives. http://discovery.nationalarchives.gov.uk/details/r/C11602761. Contains public sector information licensed under the Open Government Licence v3.0.

Ex Parte Quirin

Franklin D. Roosevelt's Proclamation 2561

July 2, 1942

INTRODUCTION

Upon the capture of the Nazi saboteurs, many in Congress urged the Roosevelt administration to pursue the swift justice of a military tribunal as opposed to a civilian prosecution. Most had assumed that the prosecution of the saboteurs would occur in civilian court. Military tribunals had not been used since the Civil War and were unlikely to be reactivated in the absence of a declaration of martial law. Moreover, recall that the court's *Ex Parte Milligan* decision applied to this instance. In that case, the court determined that "martial rule can never exist where the courts are open and in the proper and unobstructed exercise of their jurisdiction. It is also confined to the locality of actual war." Roosevelt, however, was inclined to pursue the military tribunal option for at least two reasons. First, if the proceedings were open (as they might be in civilian court), national morale would be jeopardized because the public would discover how close the U-boats had been to shore and how poorly the FBI investigated the sabotage plan. Second, the maximum sentence prosecutors could get for the crime of sabotage was 30 years. The difficulty, however, was that the saboteurs never got the chance to engage in sabotage, so it was unlikely that prosecutors would even succeed on that count in civilian court. If they were found to have engaged in a conspiracy to commit the crime of sabotage (the far more likely outcome in civilian court), they would at most receive three years. Prosecution by military tribunal afforded the administration the secrecy they desired, the absence of appeal for the defendants, and the ability to sentence the conspirators to death. Within a week of their capture, President Roosevelt issued this proclamation establishing a military tribunal with the authority to depart from court-martial practices when necessary.

The reference to "the law of war" is important because it refers to a set of procedures that are not clearly defined by statute or international agreement. The alternative language, "articles of war," would have obliged the tribunal to a set of congressionally established procedural protections for the defendants. Consequently, the tribunal was authorized under this proclamation with a great deal of discretion to use the procedures it deemed appropriate as it prosecuted the defendants. For instance, under the rules established for the tribunal, only two-thirds of the commission had to vote to impose the death penalty. Under regular court-martial proceedings, the vote had to be unanimous.

By the President of the United States of America

A Proclamation

Whereas, the safety of the United States demands that all enemies who have entered upon the territory of the United States as part of an invasion or predatory incursion, or who have entered in order to commit sabotage, espionage, or other hostile or warlike acts, should be promptly tried in accordance **with the Law of War;**

Now, Therefore, I, Franklin D. Roosevelt, President of the United States of America and Commander in Chief of the

Army and Navy of the United States, by virtue of the authority vested in me by the Constitution and the statutes of the United States do hereby proclaim that all persons who are subjects, citizens, or residents of any Nation at war with the United States or who give obedience to or act under the direction of any such Nation and who during time of war enter or attempt to enter the United States or any territory or possession thereof, through coastal or boundary defenses, and are charged with committing or attempting or preparing to commit sabotage, espionage, hostile or warlike acts, or violations of the law or war, shall be subject to the law of war and to the jurisdiction of military tribunals; and that such persons **shall not be privileged to seek any remedy or maintain any proceeding, directly or indirectly, or to have any such remedy or proceeding sought on their behalf, in the courts of the United States,** or of its States, territories, and possessions, except under such regulations as the Attorney General, with the approval of the Secretary of War, may from time to time prescribe.

FRANKLIN D. ROOSEVELT

Source: Franklin D. Roosevelt, Proclamation 2561 – Denying Certain Enemies Access to the Courts, July 2, 1942. Online by Gerhard Peters and John T. Woolley, *The American Presidency Project.* http://www.presidency.ucsb.edu/ws/?pid=16281.

With this passage, Roosevelt denied the saboteurs the opportunity to have their case reviewed by civilian courts. Ultimate review authority resided with the president. Nonetheless, counsel for the defense sought review in civilian courts, seeking to petition for habeas relief and thereby challenging the constitutionality of the proclamation. The federal district court denied the petition in a brief decision and counsel for the accused saboteurs appealed to the U.S. Supreme Court for review of the district court decision. The court heard nine hours of oral arguments in the case within days of the lower court ruling, and rendered a per curiam decision, but did not prepare a full opinion until several months later. The per curiam upheld the jurisdiction of the tribunal to prosecute the accused saboteurs and denied their petition for habeas relief. Upon the completion of the tribunal's 19-day inquiry, six of the men were sentenced to death by hanging. When the court's decision in *Ex Parte Quirin* was released in late October, the court addressed the *Milligan* precedent by drawing distinctions between the saboteurs and Milligan. Milligan was a nonbelligerent U.S. citizen "not subject to the laws of war." The saboteurs, however, were deemed "unlawful enemy combatants," in that they were enemies who had entered the United States in civilian clothes and not as uniformed soldiers (who would be lawful combatants). Had the saboteurs been classified as lawful combatants, they would have received protections as prisoners of war under the Hague Conventions. However, as enemy belligerents, they were determined to have been rightfully subjected to trial by military tribunal, outside international and statutory protections. The court reasoned, "It is enough that petitioners here, upon the conceded facts, . . . were held in good faith for trial by military commission, charged with being enemies who, with the purpose of destroying war materials and utilities, entered or after entry remained in our territory without uniform—an offense against the law of war. We hold only that those particular acts constitute an offense against the law of war which the Constitution authorizes to be tried by military commission." The decision in *Ex Parte Quirin* would become an important precedent after September 11, 2001, as the president sought to use military tribunals to prosecute suspected terrorists.

Japanese Internment

Korematsu v. United States

December 18, 1944

INTRODUCTION

When the American Pacific Fleet was destroyed in the attack on Pearl Harbor on December 7, 1941, there was substantial fear that the Japanese would attack the West Coast military installations next, perhaps as a prelude to an invasion of the United States. The commanding officer of the Western Defense Command, General DeWitt, wrote, "The Japanese race is an enemy race." Even Japanese Americans who were citizens, he reasoned, retained their "undiluted racial strains" and offered military commanders "no ground for assuming that any Japanese . . . will not turn against this nation when the final test of loyalty comes." As a consequence, President Roosevelt issued Executive Order 9066, authorizing military authorities to establish exclusion zones, detention centers, and curfews for people of Japanese descent in the proximity of military installations on the West Coast. Congress expanded the executive action with legislation that imposed penalties for noncompliance with the order. The purpose was to forcibly remove a race of people from sensitive military areas in order to protect those areas from possible sabotage. That there was no evidence of such attempts did not matter. The curfews were imposed, the exclusions began, and the relocation centers were soon populated by U.S. citizens who were detained because they were Japanese Americans. Fred Korematsu refused to be removed from his home. As a result, he was detained under the authority of the congressional statute for violating the exclusion order.

Justice Black is referring here to the strict scrutiny standard that courts adopt when government imposes a classification of some type on citizens (typically on the basis of race). Some classification schemes that treat certain classes of people differently from others are justifiable (for example, when we require lawyers to pass exams to practice law or when we impose an age restriction for driving). But others, such as classifications based on race or alienage, are assumed to be unconstitutional. To survive that high standard, the unequal treatment must serve a compelling state interest and be narrowly tailored to meet that interest. The question before the court then is whether Executive Order 9066, which singles out all members of a particular race for internment, is justified by public necessity. Ironically, many historians have pointed out that Nazi Germany, which was at war with the United States by this point, used similar "public necessity" justifications for persecuting and eventually murdering millions of Jews across Europe.

MR. JUSTICE BLACK delivered the opinion of the Court.

The petitioner, an American citizen of Japanese descent, was convicted in a federal district court for remaining in San Leandro, California, a "Military Area," contrary to Civilian Exclusion Order No. 34 of the Commanding General of the Western Command, U.S. Army, which directed that, after May 9, 1942, all persons of Japanese ancestry should be excluded from that area.

It should be noted, to begin with, that all legal restrictions which curtail the civil rights of a single racial group are immediately suspect. That is not to say that all such restrictions are unconstitutional. It is to say that courts must subject them to the most rigid scrutiny. Pressing

public necessity may sometimes justify the existence of such restrictions; racial antagonism never can.

One of the series of orders and proclamations, a curfew order, which, like the exclusion order here, was promulgated pursuant to Executive Order 9066, subjected all persons of Japanese ancestry in prescribed West Coast military areas to remain in their residences from 8 p.m. to 6 a.m. As is the case with the exclusion order here, that prior curfew order was designed as a "protection against espionage and against sabotage." In *Hirabayashi v. United States,* we sustained a conviction obtained for violation of the curfew order. The Hirabayashi conviction and this one thus rest on the same 1942 Congressional Act and the same basic executive and military orders, all of which orders were aimed at the twin dangers of espionage and sabotage.

The 1942 Act was attacked in the *Hirabayashi* case as . . . a constitutionally prohibited discrimination solely on account of race. . . . We upheld the curfew order as an exercise of the power of the government to take steps necessary to prevent espionage and sabotage in an area threatened by Japanese attack.

In the *Hirabayashi* case, which dealt with the curfew order, the court suggested that "as a matter of policy it might have been wiser for the military to have dealt with these people on an individual basis and through the process of investigation and hearings separated those who were loyal from those who were not." However, the court, continued, "Peacetime procedures do not necessarily fit wartime needs." Keep this in mind as you review Justice Jackson's dissent below.

In the light of the principles we announced in the *Hirabayashi* case, we are unable to conclude that it was beyond the war power of Congress and the Executive to exclude those of Japanese ancestry from the West Coast war area at the time they did. . . . The military authorities, charged with the primary responsibility of defending our shores, concluded that curfew provided inadequate protection and ordered exclusion.

Like curfew, exclusion of those of Japanese origin was deemed necessary because of the presence of an unascertained number of disloyal members of the group, most of whom we have no doubt were loyal to this country. It was because we could not reject the finding of the military authorities that it was impossible to bring about an immediate segregation of the disloyal from the loyal that we sustained the validity of the curfew order as applying

The majority is drawing a connection between the *Hirabayashi* and *Korematsu* cases. In *Hirabayashi,* the curfew case, the court deferred to the military's judgment that separating loyal citizens from disloyal citizens would be cumbersome and likely impossible given the immediacy of the purported danger. The justification of military expediency in *Hirabayashi* appears to the court to be a satisfactory rationale for deference to the military leaders in *Korematsu* as well. The court reasons that the danger posed by the threat of sabotage to military installations justifies the detention of a class of individuals. Requiring the military or civilian courts to determine individual guilt or innocence, in the court's view, was not possible. Collective guilt had to be assumed.

to the whole group. In the instant case, temporary exclusion of the entire group was rested by the military on the same ground.

We uphold the exclusion order as of the time it was made and when the petitioner violated it. In doing so, we are not unmindful of the hardships imposed by it upon a large group of American citizens. But hardships are part of war, and war is an aggregation of hardships. All citizens alike, both in and out of uniform, feel the impact of war in greater or lesser measure. Citizenship has its responsibilities, as well as its privileges, and, in time of war, the burden is always heavier.

Compulsory exclusion of large groups of citizens from their homes, except under circumstances of direst emergency and peril, is inconsistent with our basic governmental institutions. But when, under conditions of modern warfare, our shores are threatened by hostile forces, the power to protect must be commensurate with the threatened danger.

It is said that we are dealing here with the case of imprisonment of a citizen in a concentration camp solely because of his ancestry, without evidence or inquiry concerning his loyalty and good disposition towards the United States.... Korematsu was not excluded from the Military Area because of hostility to him or his race. He was excluded because we are at war with the Japanese Empire, because the properly constituted military authorities feared an invasion of our West Coast and felt constrained to take proper security measures, because they decided that the military urgency of the situation demanded that all citizens of Japanese ancestry be segregated from the West Coast temporarily, and, finally, because Congress, reposing its confidence in this time of war in our military leaders—as inevitably it must—determined that they should have the power to do just this. There was evidence of disloyalty on the part of some, the military authorities considered that the need for action was great, and time was short. We cannot—by availing ourselves of the calm perspective of hindsight—now say that, at that time, these actions were unjustified.

Affirmed.

Mr. Justice Murphy, dissenting:

This exclusion of "all persons of Japanese ancestry, both alien and non-alien," from the Pacific Coast area on a plea of military necessity in the absence of martial law ought not to be approved. Such exclusion goes over "the very brink of constitutional power," and falls into the ugly abyss of racism.

No one denies, of course, that there were some disloyal persons of Japanese descent on the Pacific Coast who did all in their power to aid their ancestral land. **Similar disloyal activities have been engaged in by many persons of German, Italian and even more pioneer stock in our country. But to infer that examples of individual disloyalty prove group disloyalty and justify discriminatory action against the entire group is to deny that, under our system of law, individual guilt is the sole basis for deprivation of rights.** Moreover, this inference, which is at the very heart of the evacuation orders, has been used in support of the abhorrent and despicable treatment of minority groups by the dictatorial tyrannies which this nation is now pledged to destroy.

Justices Murphy, Roberts, and Jackson each wrote separate dissents. All of them pointed out in sharp terms the racial antagonism that appeared to characterize the court's decision in the case.

Any inconvenience that may have accompanied an attempt to conform to procedural due process cannot be said to justify violations of constitutional rights of individuals.... I dissent, therefore, from this legalization of racism.

Mr. Justice Jackson, dissenting:

Korematsu was born on our soil, of parents born in Japan. The Constitution makes him a citizen of the United States by nativity, and a citizen of California by residence. No claim is made that he is not loyal to this country. Korematsu, however, has been convicted of an act not commonly a crime. It consists merely of being present in the state whereof he is a citizen, near the place where he was born, and where all his life he has lived.

In addition to his objection to the legalization of racism, Jackson's dissent also revealed the likely consequences of the court's action for the future of executive power. This decision, he argued, has a "generative power" that will invite expansive use by others. Jackson suggested that because the court affirmed the action of the military, the decision would "lay around like a loaded weapon" available for use by future executives to use when conditions appear to justify its use.

A citizen's presence in the locality, however, was made a crime only if his parents were of Japanese birth. Had Korematsu been one of four—the others being, say, a German alien enemy, an Italian alien enemy, and a citizen of American-born ancestors, convicted of treason but out on parole—only Korematsu's presence would have violated the order. The difference between their innocence and his crime would result, not from anything he did, said, or thought, different than they, but only in that he was born of different racial stock.

Jackson begins by picking up on the theme of racial antagonism that was introduced by both Justices Murphy and Roberts in dissents, even as it was rejected by Justice Black. He then makes the point that at the heart of the court's decision is the assumption of inheritable guilt. That premise runs counter to the rule of law, Jackson reasons.

Now, if any fundamental assumption underlies our system, it is that guilt is personal and not inheritable. But here is an attempt to make an otherwise innocent act a crime merely because this prisoner is the son of parents as to whom he had no choice, and belongs to a race from which there is no way to resign. If Congress, in peacetime legislation, should enact such a criminal law, I should suppose this Court would refuse to enforce it.

Referring to the difficulty of determining individual guilt of the thousands of detainees, Jackson suggests that it is improper for the court to have sanctioned this executive order and subsequent congressional statute.

But if we cannot confine military expedients by the Constitution, neither would I distort the Constitution to approve all that the military may deem expedient.... Even if they were permissible military procedures, I deny that it follows that they are constitutional. If, as the Court holds, it does follow, then we may as well say that any military order will be constitutional, and have done with it.

Much is said of the danger to liberty from the Army program for deporting and detaining these citizens of Japanese extraction. But a judicial construction of the due process clause that will sustain this order is a far more subtle blow to liberty than the promulgation of the order itself. A military order, however unconstitutional, is not apt to last longer than the military emergency. But once a judicial opinion rationalizes such an order to show that it conforms to the Constitution, or rather rationalizes the Constitution to show that the Constitution sanctions such an order, the Court for all time has validated the principle. **The principle then lies about like a loaded weapon, ready for the hand of any authority** that can bring forward a plausible claim of an urgent need. Every repetition imbeds that principle more deeply in our law and thinking and expands it to new purposes. A military commander may overstep the bounds of constitutionality, and it is an incident. But if we review and approve, that passing incident becomes the doctrine of the Constitution. There it has a generative power of its own, and all that it creates will be in its own image.

Source: *Korematsu v. United States*, 323 U.S. 214 (1944).

Jackson's dissent would prove prophetic. Several subsequent actions by executives—and even Congress—in times of uncertainty and insecurity have been defended on similar grounds as the Executive Order 9066. Congressional investigations during the Red Scare of the 1950s, indefinite detention of suspected terrorists at Guantanamo Bay after 9/11, and other recent antiterrorism policies share something of this quality.

The court's decision in *Korematsu v. United States* has never been overturned. In 1988, however, Congress issued a formal apology to Japanese Americans who had been detained in the relocation centers. The legislation provided each of the 60,000 or so surviving detainees approximately $20,000 in reparations—a sum that was widely criticized as inadequate compensation for the loss of work, homes, relationships, and property as a result of the internment.

The Steel Seizure Case

Youngstown Sheet and Tube Co. v. Sawyer

June 2, 1952

INTRODUCTION

When North Korea invaded South Korea in 1950, the United States sent troops to defend South Korea under the legal authority of the United Nations Security Council. The North Koreans were supported by China and the USSR, while the United States led the defense of the South by the United Nations. Over the three years of the Korean conflict, more than 120,000 U.S. soldiers were killed or wounded. However, there was no declaration of war by the U.S. Congress as this was a *police action* of the United Nations. Nonetheless, President Truman and Congress placed the United States on war footing by initiating a series of economic measures meant to stabilize the wartime economy. One of the mechanisms employed by Truman to combat the dramatic economic inflation that occurred at the onset of the conflict was the establishment of the Wage Stabilization Board within the Economic Stabilization Agency. The board would make wage control recommendations to the president and have the authority to implement those controls once adopted.

A year into the Korean conflict, a labor dispute emerged in the steel industry. The steelworkers' union announced that it would strike unless a labor agreement could be reached with the steel companies. By April 1952, the strike seemed imminent as negotiations among the labor, the Wage Stabilization Board, and the steel industry faltered. Truman was in a bind. A work stoppage in the domestic steel industry would "immediately jeopardize and imperil . . . national defense" because steel was necessary for the manufacturing of weapons, tanks, and other military equipment. But to prevent the work stoppage, he would have to take action that appeared to have no statute, no precedent, nor any explicit constitutional language to support it.

Just hours before the strike was to begin, Truman issued Executive Order 10340 instructing Secretary of Commerce Charles Sawyer to nationalize the industry and insure the continued production of steel. That order cited no legal basis for the president's authority to seize the nation's steel mills. Indeed, there were statutes on the books that gave the president that authority for certain reasons, but none granted that authority for the purpose of resolving labor disputes. One in particular, the Taft-Hartley Act of 1947, actually gave the president the power to impose a moratorium on a strike through an 80-day *cooling-off period* in order to bring parties to the negotiating table. However, rather than take action pursuant to that statute, the president cited the inherent powers of the presidency as the legal basis for seizing the country's steel mills. The steel companies complied with the order but sought an injunction in federal court. The district court found for the steel companies, but the court of appeals reversed the injunction and the companies appealed to the U.S. Supreme Court. Justice Hugo Black wrote the opinion of the court, which struck Truman's actions. But the decision in *Youngstown Sheet and Tube Co. v. Sawyer* is remembered by most scholars and legal experts less for Black's opinion than for Justice Robert H. Jackson's concurrence.

MR. JUSTICE JACKSON, concurring in the judgment and opinion of the Court.

That comprehensive and undefined presidential powers hold both practical advantages and grave dangers for the country will impress anyone who has served as legal adviser to a President in time of transition and public anxiety.... The opinions of judges, no less than executives and publicists, often suffer the infirmity of confusing the issue of a power's validity with the cause it is invoked to promote, of confounding the permanent executive office with its temporary occupant. The tendency is strong to emphasize transient results upon policies—such as wages or stabilization—and lose sight of enduring consequences upon the balanced power structure of our Republic.

A judge, like an executive adviser, may be surprised at the poverty of really useful and unambiguous authority applicable to concrete problems of executive power as they actually present themselves. Just what our forefathers did envision, or would have envisioned had they foreseen modern conditions, must be divined from materials almost as enigmatic as the dreams Joseph was called upon to interpret for Pharaoh. A century and a half of partisan debate and scholarly speculation yields no net result, but only supplies more or less apt quotations from respected sources on each side of any question. They largely cancel each other. And court decisions are indecisive because of the judicial practice of dealing with the largest questions in the most narrow way.

The actual art of governing under our Constitution does not, and cannot, conform to judicial definitions of the power of any of its branches based on isolated clauses, or even single Articles torn from context. While the Constitution diffuses power the better to secure liberty, it also contemplates that practice will integrate the dispersed powers into a workable government. It enjoins upon its branches separateness but interdependence, autonomy but reciprocity. Presidential powers are not fixed but fluctuate depending upon their disjunction or conjunction with those of Congress. We may well

Prior to serving on the court, Justice Jackson had been the solicitor general and the attorney general under President Franklin Roosevelt. In addition, he was the principal legal architect of the International Military Tribunal in Nuremberg that prosecuted the Nazis after World War II. As a result of those experiences, he was—relative to his brethren on the court—uniquely qualified to reflect on the "concrete problems" of executive power. Ever mindful of the practical consequences of law, Jackson draws attention to three key elements that attend most separation of powers cases: the absence of determinative rules, the importance of political context in the resolution of specific cases, and the inadequacy of simply applying the case facts to the law.

begin by a somewhat over-simplified grouping of practical situations in which a President may doubt, or others may challenge, his powers, and by distinguishing roughly the legal consequences of this factor of relativity.

1. When the President acts pursuant to an express or implied authorization of Congress, his authority is at its maximum, for it includes all that he possesses in his own right plus all that Congress can delegate.

2. When the President acts in absence of either a congressional grant or denial of authority, he can only rely upon his own independent powers, but there is a zone of twilight in which he and Congress may have concurrent authority, or in which its distribution is uncertain. Therefore, congressional inertia, indifference or quiescence may sometimes, at least, as a practical matter, enable, if not invite, measures on independent presidential responsibility. In this area, any actual test of power is likely to depend on the imperatives of events and contemporary imponderables, rather than on abstract theories of law.

3. When the President takes measures incompatible with the expressed or implied will of Congress, his power is at its lowest ebb, for then he can rely only upon his own constitutional powers minus any constitutional powers of Congress over the matter. . . .

It is worth noting that these three categories match rather closely the theories of executive power discussed earlier in this book (and reflected in multiple chapters): the literalist theory, the stewardship theory, and the prerogative power. The framework that Justice Jackson develops gives a conceptual boundary to the scope of executive power in light of the authority that Congress concedes. That is, presidential power is to be understood in relation to Congress, not simply in relation to whether the president deems his or her actions warranted by an emergency.

Into which of these classifications does this executive seizure of the steel industry fit? It is eliminated from the first by admission, for it is conceded that no congressional authorization exists for this seizure.

Can it then be defended under flexible tests available to the second category? It seems clearly eliminated from that class, because Congress has not left seizure of private property an open field, but has covered it by three statutory policies inconsistent with this seizure.

This leaves the current seizure to be justified only by the severe tests under the third grouping, where it can be supported only by any remainder of executive power after subtraction of such powers as Congress may have over the subject. In short, we can sustain the President only by holding that seizure of such strike-bound industries is within his domain and beyond control by Congress. Thus, this Court's first review of such seizures occurs under circumstances which leave presidential power most vulnerable to attack and in the least favorable of possible constitutional postures.

Nothing in our Constitution is plainer than that declaration of a war is entrusted only to Congress. Of course, a state of war may, in fact, exist without a formal declaration. But no doctrine that the Court could promulgate would seem to me more sinister and alarming than that a President whose conduct of foreign affairs is so largely uncontrolled, and often even is unknown, can vastly enlarge his mastery over the internal affairs of the country by his own commitment of the Nation's armed forces to some foreign venture.

Assuming that we are in a war *de facto,* whether it is or is not a war *de jure,* does that empower the Commander in Chief to seize industries he thinks necessary to supply our army? . . .

That military powers of the Commander in Chief were not to supersede representative government of internal affairs seems obvious from the Constitution and from elementary American history.

. . . No penance would ever expiate the sin against free government of holding that a President can escape control of executive powers by law through assuming his military role. **What the power of command may include I do not try to envision, but I think it is not a military prerogative, without support of law, to seize persons or property because they are important or even essential for the military and naval establishment.**

Recall the *Korematsu* case. In *Korematsu*, the court upheld the detention of Japanese Americans because of national security concerns; here, the court strikes the temporary seizing of steel mills. With reference to "persons or property," Jackson seems to suggest that both actions (the internment of a class of individuals on the basis of race and the seizure of the steel industry) were unconstitutional and that military expediency must not endow the executive with illimitable powers.

. . . The appeal, however, that we declare the existence of inherent powers *ex necessitate* to meet an emergency asks us to do what many think would be wise, although it is something the forefathers omitted. . . . Aside from suspension of the privilege of the writ of habeas corpus in time of rebellion or invasion, when the public safety may require it, they made no express provision for exercise of extraordinary authority because of a crisis. I do not think we rightfully may so amend their work, and, if we could, I am not convinced it would be wise to do so, although many modern nations have forthrightly recognized that war and economic crises may upset the normal balance between liberty and authority....

[C]ontemporary foreign experience . . . suggests that emergency powers are consistent with free government only when their control is lodged elsewhere than in the Executive who exercises them. That is the safeguard that would be nullified by our adoption of the "inherent powers" formula....

In the practical working of our Government, we already have evolved a technique within the framework of the Constitution by which normal executive powers may be considerably expanded to meet an emergency. Congress may and has granted extraordinary authorities which lie dormant in normal times but may be called into play by the Executive in war or upon proclamation of a national emergency.

In view of the ease, expedition and safety with which Congress can grant and has granted large emergency powers, certainly ample to embrace this crisis, I am quite unimpressed with the argument that we should affirm possession of them without statute....

Justice Jackson again illustrates the limit of the positive law. We can read Article II's Take Care clause and its vestment of *the executive power* in the president, but those expressed provisions can only take us so far toward understanding what powers the president can be understood to possess. The modern presidency has "real powers" in addition to "paper powers." The literalist theory that Taft articulated is no longer a reasonable understanding. Again, it is worth recalling Jackson's admonition from his *Korematsu* dissent. He wrote, "[t]he principle . . . lies about like a loaded weapon, ready for the hand of any authority that can bring forward a plausible claim of an urgent need. Every repetition imbeds that principle more deeply in our law and thinking and expands it to new purposes."

As to whether there is imperative necessity for such powers, it is relevant to note the gap that exists between the President's paper powers and his real powers. The Constitution does not disclose the measure of the actual controls wielded by the modern presidential office. That instrument must be understood as an Eighteenth-Century sketch of a government hoped for, not as a blueprint of the Government that is. Vast accretions of federal power, eroded from that reserved by the States, have magnified the scope of presidential activity. Subtle shifts take place in the centers of real power that do not show on the face of the Constitution.

Executive power has the advantage of concentration in a single head in whose choice the whole Nation has a part, making him the focus of public hopes and expectations. . . .

I cannot be brought to believe that this country will suffer if the Court refuses further to aggrandize the presidential office, already so potent and so relatively immune from judicial review, at the expense of Congress.

But I have no illusion that any decision by this Court can keep power in the hands of Congress if it is not wise and timely in meeting its problems. We may say that power to legislate for emergencies belongs in the hands of Congress, but only Congress itself can prevent power from slipping through its fingers.

The executive action we have here originates in the individual will of the President, and represents an exercise of authority without law. No one, perhaps not even the President, knows the limits of the power he may seek to exert in this instance, and the parties affected cannot learn the limit of their rights. We do not know today what powers over labor or property would be claimed to flow from Government possession if we should legalize it, what rights to compensation would be claimed or recognized, or on what contingency it would end. With all its defects, delays and inconveniences, men have discovered no technique for long preserving free government except that the Executive be under the law, and that the law be made by parliamentary deliberations.

Such institutions may be destined to pass away. But it is the duty of the Court to be last, not first, to give them up.

Source: *Youngstown Sheet & Tube Co. v. Sawyer*, 343 U.S. 579 (1952).

Bay of Pigs Invasion

John F. Kennedy's Address
April 20, 1961

INTRODUCTION

In 1959, Fidel Castro led an armed insurrection in Cuba that led to the overthrow of Cuba's dictator Fulgencio Batista. The United States was very suspicious of Cuba's new leadership and, in particular, its relationship with the Soviet Union. Soon after Castro came to power, the Eisenhower administration put into place a CIA-led counterrevolutionary training program. That program was developed to prepare Cuban exiles for an invasion of their homeland. The program's premise was that significant numbers of Cuba's citizen population as well as key elements of the Cuban military would rise up in opposition to Castro and in support of the invasion. When President Kennedy took office in January 1961, this project—based in Guatemala—was well underway. On the advice of many in his new administration, President Kennedy authorized the invasion plans.

The plan that Kennedy authorized included at least two stages of an assault. The first stage, two days prior to the main invasion, included an air assault on the Cuban air defense systems by vintage U.S. World War II bombers from an airbase in Nicaragua. In an effort to disguise the involvement of the United States, the bombers were repainted to resemble Cuban aircraft. The bombings failed to destroy each of the key targets and left the Cuban air defenses mostly intact. Photos were released that revealed the real origins of the bombers, forcing Kennedy to discontinue the air attack. The second wave of the invasion came at dawn on April 17 as Brigade 2506, an assault team of about 1,400 Cuban exiles, disembarked from four supply ships and landed at the Bay of Pigs. There they came under heavy fire. Because President Kennedy had called off air support to limit U.S. exposure, the troops on the ground received no protection from above. Moreover, Cuban air force planes had destroyed their support ships moored in the harbor. The invasion force held out for two days. They found no support from among the Cuban population or the Cuban military. Over 100 died during the invasion. The remaining soldiers were taken prisoner where they remained for almost two years. It was a deeply embarrassing episode for the new president. On April 20, he gave the following address to the American Society of Newspaper Editors on the Bay of Pigs invasion.

The President of a great democracy such as ours, and the editors of great newspapers such as yours, owe a common obligation to the people: an obligation to present the facts, to present them with candor, and to present them in perspective. It is with that obligation in mind that I have decided in the last 24 hours to discuss briefly at this time the recent events in Cuba.

On that unhappy island, as in so many other arenas of the contest for freedom, the news has grown worse instead of better. I have emphasized before that this was a struggle of Cuban patriots against a Cuban dictator. While we could not be expected to hide our sympathies, we made it repeatedly clear that the armed forces of this country would not intervene in any way. **Any unilateral American intervention, in the absence of an external attack upon ourselves or an ally, would have been contrary to our traditions and to our international obligations.**

But let the record show that our restraint is not inexhaustible. Should it ever appear that the inter-American doctrine of non-interference merely conceals or excuses a policy of non-action—if the nations of this Hemisphere should fail to meet their commitments against outside Communist penetration—then I want it clearly understood that this Government will not hesitate in meeting its primary obligations which are to the security of our Nation!

Should that time ever come, we do not intend to be lectured on "intervention" by those whose character was stamped for all time on the bloody streets of Budapest! Nor would we expect or accept the same outcome which this small band of gallant Cuban refugees must have known that they were chancing, determined as they were against heavy odds to pursue their courageous attempts to regain their Island's freedom.

But Cuba is not an island unto itself; and our concern is not ended by mere expressions of nonintervention or regret. This is not the first time in either ancient or recent history that a small band of freedom fighters has engaged the armor of totalitarianism.

It is not the first time that Communist tanks have rolled over gallant men and women fighting to redeem the independence of their homeland. Nor is it by any means the final episode in the eternal struggle of liberty against tyranny, anywhere on the face of the globe, including Cuba itself.

President Kennedy is awkwardly trying to distance the United States from the invasion of Cuba by Cuban exiles while at the same time attempting to justify it. International perspectives on this were pretty clear—the United States had its fingerprints all over the action. As a result, Castro could credibly claim that the United States had violated Cuban sovereignty. In order to prevent further invasions, Castro requested substantial military assistance from the USSR. The shipment of missiles capable of reaching the U.S. mainland and the construction of multiple missile sites was soon underway. The construction of those bases would ultimately lead to the Cuban Missile Crisis of 1962.

Since this was not an official U.S. operation, the U.S. government could not intervene or negotiate the prisoners' release with Castro; it had to remain a private endeavor. After approximately 20 months (on Christmas Eve, 1962), the prisoners were released in exchange for medical equipment, medicine, and food. Their release was arranged through unofficial negotiations orchestrated on Robert Kennedy's behalf by private attorneys, James Donovan and John Nolan. While Donovan and Nolan made the overtures to Castro, a team of private attorneys oversaw the acquisition and transportation of goods onto a ship bound for Cuba to make the deal happen. Bobby Kennedy sent his longtime friend E. Barrett Prettyman Jr. to Cuba to oversee the exchange, negotiate with Castro, and escort prisoners back to the United States.

Meanwhile we will not accept Mr. Castro's attempts to blame this nation for the hatred which his onetime supporters now regard his repression. But there are from this sobering episode useful lessons for us all to learn. Some may be still obscure, and await further information. Some are clear today.

First, it is clear that the forces of communism are not to be underestimated, in Cuba or anywhere else in the world. The advantages of a police state—its use of mass terror and arrests to prevent the spread of free dissent—cannot be overlooked by those who expect the fall of every fanatic tyrant. If the self-discipline of the free cannot match the iron discipline of the mailed fist—in economic, political, scientific and all the other kinds of struggles as well as the military—then the peril to freedom will continue to rise.

Secondly, it is clear that this Nation, in concert with all the free nations of this hemisphere, must take an ever closer and more realistic look at the menace of external Communist intervention and domination in Cuba. The American people are not complacent about Iron Curtain tanks and planes less than 90 miles from their shore. But a nation of Cuba's size is less a threat to our survival than it is a base for subverting the survival of other free nations throughout the hemisphere. It is not primarily our interest or our security but theirs which is now, today, in the greater peril. It is for their sake as well as our own that we must show our will.

Third, and finally, it is clearer than ever that we face a relentless struggle in every corner of the globe that goes far beyond the clash of armies or even nuclear armaments. The armies are there, and in large number. The nuclear armaments are there. But they serve primarily as the shield behind which subversion, infiltration, and a host of other tactics steadily advance, picking off vulnerable areas one by one in situations which do not permit our own armed intervention.

Power is the hallmark of this offensive-power and discipline and deceit. The legitimate discontent of yearning people is exploited. The legitimate trappings of self-determination are employed. But once in power, all talk of discontent is repressed, all self-determination disappears, and the promise of a revolution of hope is betrayed, as in Cuba, into a reign of terror.

We dare not fail to see the insidious nature of this new and deeper struggle. We dare not fail to grasp the new concepts, the new tools, the new sense of urgency we will need to combat it—whether in Cuba or South Viet-Nam. And we dare not fail to realize that this struggle is taking place every day, without fanfare, in thousands of villages and markets—day and night—and in classrooms all over the globe.

No greater task faces this country or this administration. No other challenge is more deserving of our every effort and energy. **Too long we have fixed our eyes on traditional military needs, on armies prepared to cross borders, on missiles poised for flight. Now it should be clear that this is no longer enough—that our security may be lost piece by piece, country by country, without the firing of a single missile or the crossing of a single border.**

We intend to profit from this lesson. We intend to reexamine and reorient our forces of all kinds—our tactics and our institutions here in this community. We intend to intensify our efforts for a struggle in many ways more difficult than war, where disappointment will often accompany us.

For I am convinced that we in this country and in the free world possess the necessary resource, and the skill, and the added strength that comes from a belief in the freedom of man. And I am equally convinced that history will record the fact that this bitter struggle reached its climax in the late 1950's and the early 1960's. Let me then make clear as the President of the United States that I am determined upon our system's survival and success, regardless of the cost and regardless of the peril!

Source: John F. Kennedy, Address Before the American Society of Newspaper Editors, April 20, 1961. *Public Papers of the Presidents of the United States: John F. Kennedy, 1961.* Entry 138 (Washington, DC: GPO, 1962), 304–306.

There were other lessons President Kennedy learned as a result of this experience. For instance, after the Bay of Pigs, Kennedy approached his military and national security operations differently than he had in the first 90 days of his term. Ted Sorensen, Kennedy's confidant and speech writer, noted in an interview in 1964 that Kennedy "was more skeptical of the recommendations that came to him from the experts. He challenged their assumptions, their premises, even their facts. He made certain that everyone went on a written record of exactly where they stood so that they would be thoughtful in their recommendations. He inquired not only as to the results ... but the consequences which we could expect from those results, counter-consequences from those consequences, and so on. So that in every way ... he approached this kind of situation in a more precise and knowledgeable fashion and kept the control of the decision making more tightly within his own hands" (Sorensen, Theodore C. 1964. Recorded interview by Carl Kaysen, April 4 (p. 23). John F. Kennedy Library Oral History Program).

Watergate

Final Senate Report

February 7, 1973

INTRODUCTION

In early 1972, the Special Investigations Unit within the White House shifted its focus from the perceived threats to national security presented by Ellsberg and others to the reelection prospects of President Nixon. As the plumbers directed their efforts on the reelection of Nixon, their tactics did not shift, only their targets. In January of that year, Nixon was down in the polls and at one point was tied with Democratic Senator Edmund Muskie of Maine, the frontrunner for the Democratic nomination for president. In collaboration with the Committee to Reelect the President (CRP), the plumbers had three objectives with respect to the 1972 campaign: they sought to weaken Muskie, the Democratic frontrunner; divide the Democratic Party; and ultimately secure the nomination of George McGovern, someone the CRP considered the weakest Democratic candidate. There was nothing particularly illegal about those objectives, but the methods employed to achieve those political goals were often illegal and brazenly unethical. In particular, the activities of the plumbers were paid for by Nixon through CRP campaign funds in violation of federal law. The reference to Watergate has come to mean many things. But at the very least, it refers to two conspiracies that have their origins in the Nixon White House. The first conspiracy was the destabilization of the Democratic primaries in 1972. The illegality of the actions the plumbers took to achieve that goal eventually gave rise to a second conspiracy—that of a cover-up of those activities.

The Final Report of the Select Committee on Presidential Campaign Activities

United States Senate

Pursuant to S. Res. 60, February 7, 1973

Introduction

This report presents the findings and recommendations of the Senate Select Committee on Presidential Campaign Activities based on its investigation of the Watergate break-in and coverup, illegal and improper campaign practices and financing, and other wrongdoing during the Presidential campaign of 1972. Once termed "a cancer growing on the

Presidency" by a principle committee witness, Watergate is one of America's most tragic happenings. **This characterization of Watergate is not merely based on the fact that the Democratic National Committee headquarters at the Watergate was burglarized in the early morning hours of June 17, 1972. Rather, it is also an appraisal of the events that led to the burglary and its sordid aftermath, an aftermath characterized by corruption, fraud, and abuse of official power.**

The Select Committee is actually conscious that at the time it presents this report the issue of impeachment of the President on Watergate-related evidence is pending in the Judiciary Committee of the House of Representatives. The Select Committee also recognizes that there are pending indictments against numerous defendants, most of whom were witnesses before the committee, which charge crimes that, directly or indirectly relate to its inquiry. It thus must be stressed that the committee's hearings were not conducted, and this report not prepared, to determine the legal guilt or innocence of any person or whether the President should be impeached. In this regard, it is important to note that the committee, during its short lifespan, has not obtained all the information it sought or desired and thus certain of its findings are tentative, subject to reevaluation when the full facts emerge. **Moreover, the committee, in stating the facts as it sees them, has not applied the standard of proof applicable to a criminal proceeding—proof beyond a reasonable doubt. Its conclusions, therefore must not be interpreted as a final legal judgment that any individual has violated the criminal laws.**

Before turning to a recitation of the facts as the committee sees them, certain general observations based on the evidence before the committee are appropriate. The Watergate affair reflects an alarming indifference displayed by some in the high public office or position to concepts of morality and public responsibility and trust. Indeed, the conduct of many Watergate participants seems grounded on the belief that the ends justified the means, that the laws could be flaunted to maintain the present administration in office.

On June 17, 1972, a 24-year-old security guard named Frank Wills noticed tape on the latches of two doors to the Democratic National Committee's headquarters in Washington, DC's Watergate Hotel. Wills called the police to report a break-in and five men were arrested as they attempted to photograph documents and hide sophisticated electronic eavesdropping devices in the Democratic National Committee's offices. In the weeks and months following the arrests, investigative journalists from the *Washington Post,* Bob Woodward and Carl Bernstein, uncovered links between the burglary and Nixon's reelection campaign. Nixon and other White House officials denied any involvement in the affair. When Nixon won reelection in November, media continued to explore the connections among the White House, the CRP, and the illegal activities of the plumbers. Eventually, in February 1973, the Senate passed a resolution to establish an inquiry into the campaign activities of the Nixon White House. This is an excerpt from the final report of that committee's investigations.

The Senate Select Committee was granted the power to subpoena witnesses and take testimony to investigate illegal, unethical, and improper activities of the Nixon White House during the 1972 presidential campaign. Though Senator Edward Kennedy (D-MA) introduced the legislation, Kennedy was widely perceived to have presidential ambitions of his own, which would likely have presented a conflict of interest for the investigation. The 76-year-old Democratic Senator Sam Ervin of North Carolina, the Chairman of the Constitutional Rights Subcommittee of the Senate Judiciary Committee, was appointed Chair instead. The Select Committee was given a year to conduct its investigation. This report was released in June 1974, just a month before the first of three Articles of Impeachment were passed in the House of Representatives.

Unfortunately, the attitude that the law can be bent where expediency dictates was not confined to a few Government and campaign officials. The testimony respecting the campaign funding practices of some of the Nation's largest and most respectable corporations furnishes clear examples of the subjugation of legal and ethical standards to pragmatic considerations. Hopefully, after the flood of Watergate revelations the country has witnessed, the public can now expect, at least for some years to come, a higher standard of conduct from its public officials and its business and professional leaders. Also, it is hoped that the Watergate exposures have created what former Vice President Agnew has called a "post-Watergate mortality" where respect for law and mortality is paramount.

In approaching its task of recommending remedial legislation, the committee is mindful that revelations of past scandals have often failed to produce meaningful reform. Too frequently there is a tendency to overreact in the wake of a particular scandal and burden the penal code with ill-considered laws directed to the specific—perhaps aberrational—conduct exposed. This proliferation of criminal laws has tended to over-complicate the penal code and consequently, to impair the effectiveness of its administration. Moreover, legislation is, at best, a blunt weapon to combat immorality.

The "post-Watergate mentality" to which the report refers, and the subsequent recommendations that the Committee made and Congress pursued, marked an important opportunity for Congress to reassert itself in the face of corruption, personal vengeance, illegality, and conspiracy in the executive branch. How successful those attempts ultimately proved to be is something worth considering as you review subsequent chapters.

While this report does not make certain specific recommendations for new criminal legislation or for strengthening existing criminal laws, the committee has been careful to recommend only where the need is clear. **Its major legislation recommendations relate to the creation of new institutions necessary to safeguard the electoral process, to provide the requisite checks against the abuse of executive power and to insure the prompt and just enforcement of laws that already exist. Surely one of the most penetrating lessons of Watergate is that campaign practices must be effectively supervised and enforcement of the criminal laws vigorously pursued against all offenders—even those of high estate—if our free institutions are to survive.**

The committee's mandate was broad and its time to meet it brief. Nonetheless, the committee believes that, though its efforts and those of others, the basic facts of the Watergate scandal have been exposed to public view and, as a result, the American people have been reawakened to the task democracy imposes upon them—steadfast vigilance of the conduct of the public officials they chose to lead them. This public awareness, in turn, has provided the atmosphere necessary to support other essential governmental responses to Watergate such as the work of the Special Prosecutor and the activities of the House Judiciary Committee on impeachment. Because the Nation is now alert, because the processes of justice are now functioning and because the time is ripe for passage of new laws to safeguard the electoral process, the committee is hopeful that, despite the excesses of Watergate, the Nation will return to its democratic ideals established almost 200 years ago.

Source: Final Report of the Senate Select Committee on Presidential Campaign Activities (Washington, DC: Government Printing Office, 1974).

Presidential Impoundment of Funds

Richard Nixon's Veto of H.R. 3298

April 5, 1973

INTRODUCTION

In late March 1973, Congress passed H.R. 3298, a bill that was meant to revive a rural water and sewer program run by the Department of Agriculture that had been terminated three months earlier. The reason the earlier iteration of the program had ended was that the funds that Congress had appropriated for it in 1972 had been impounded by the president. That is, the president had refused to distribute the congressionally appropriated funds because of his fear that the disbursement of those funds would limit his ability to curtail rising inflation due to high federal budget deficits. He simply determined that while Congress had made the appropriation, it was within the president's constitutional authority to refuse to expend those funds. When the bill was passed, Nixon sent this message—along with his veto—back to Congress. In this veto message, not only does he object to the funding of such projects, but he vigorously defends his impoundment authority.

Nixon made the argument that this was a power exercised by presidents since the nation's founding. For example, in 1803, as events along the Mississippi took a "peaceable turn of affairs," Jefferson refused to expend funds for gunboats that Congress had appropriated. FDR also impounded funds during the Great Depression to shift appropriations to matters of greater priority. After World War II, Congress granted statutory authority to the president to establish reserves "to provide for contingencies." That act, the Omnibus Appropriations Act of 1951, became the principal statutory basis for presidential impoundments. However, the act also included explicit language that the establishment of financial reserves was not meant to authorize executive noncompliance with congressional intent. Nonetheless, presidents Eisenhower and Kennedy continued the impoundment practice—but most often under their authority as commander in chief, where appropriations exceeded military necessity. Johnson, however, began to use the impoundment of funds to fight inflation, a practice his successor expanded into an even wider set of policy areas.

To the House of Representatives:

I am returning today without my approval H.R. 3298, an act to restore the rural water and sewer grant program which was terminated earlier this year.

My recent budget proposals to the Congress reflect the results of an intensive effort to identify Federal programs that should be reformed, cut back or eliminated. In each case we asked one simple question: would this program justify an increase in taxes in order to pay for it?

For many years, local communities have proudly financed and built their own water and sewer facilities. They have recognized that these services are primarily local in nature and should be primarily a local responsibility—just as local communities pay for their own garbage services and fire protection.

Resurrection of the rural water and sewer program would serve only to undercut that tradition, shoving aside local authorities for the increasingly powerful Federal Government.

This program also enlarges the Federal responsibility in a particularly ineffective and insidious way. Experience has shown that water and sewer grants have been distributed in a totally scattershot fashion. Many rural communities, although qualified under the program, have built their own water and sewage systems without waiting for Federal help. They need no incentive from Washington. Yet, in other cases, the water and sewer grants actually delay construction, as communities which would ordinarily finance the facilities on their own, choose instead to wait in line for Federal subsidies. The result has been a very uneven pattern of distribution. It should also come as no surprise that over time the program has attained a distinct flavor of pork barrel.

In view of the many defects in this program, I am convinced that it should no longer be inflicted on the American taxpayer. Congressional restoration of water and sewer grants at the appropriated level of H.R. 3298 would increase Federal spending by at least $300 million during fiscal years 1973–1975. This would represent a dangerous crack in the fiscal dam that this Administration has constructed to hold back a further flood of inflation or higher taxes, or both.

A grave constitutional question is also raised by H.R. 3298, which purports to mandate the spending of the full amount appropriated by the Congress. The Attorney General has advised me that such a mandate conflicts with the allocation of executive power to the President

In all, Nixon impounded approximately $18 billion in 1972–1973 and $12 billion in the 1973–1974 budgets. When queried in a January 31, 1973, press conference, President Nixon defended his impoundment authority on at least two grounds. First, that it was within his Article II powers. Second, since Congress was most responsive to particular interests, the president was obliged to be attentive to the common interest. He responded to a reporter's question regarding his impoundment authority by saying, "[t]he constitutional right for the President of the United States to impound funds—and that is not to spend money, when the spending of money would mean either increasing prices or increasing taxes for all the people-that right is absolutely clear. The general interest of this country is don't break the family budget by raising the taxes or raising prices, and I am going to stand for that general interest. Therefore, I will not spend money if the Congress overspends. . . ."

made by Article II of the Constitution. Thus, H.R. 3298 is objectionable not only in its practical and economic aspects, but on basic legal grounds as well.

In reconsidering this bill, the Congress should bear in mind that my fiscal year 1974 budget already provides $345 million in Rural Development Act loan funds for water supply systems in rural areas which will help local communities borrow at favorable interest rates. In addition, the Environmental Protection Agency will be providing grants of $5 billion in fiscal years 1973 and 1974 for waste disposal facilities across the country. These grants will be awarded in accordance with State established needs, and may be used in rural areas for high priority projects.

I recognize that despite these programs, some rural communities in need of sewer assistance may still have financing difficulties because of their inability to borrow at reasonable rates. Fortunately, a solution to this problem exists.

If my veto of this bill is sustained, I will use my authority under the Rural Development Act to provide qualified rural communities with loans not only for water facilities but also for the development of sewage facilities. These loans for sewer services will be available in fiscal years 1973 and 1974. This step—taken at a fraction of the cost to the taxpayer required by H.R. 3298—will permit qualified small communities to compete for credit on reasonable terms.

Taken in conjunction with other measures already planned, this loan provision should provide sufficient Federal support to those communities which critically need water and sewage systems without shattering the limits of sound fiscal policy. **I therefore urge all thoughtful, responsible Members of the Congress to join with me in preventing this costly, unwise and probably unconstitutional measure from becoming law.**

In upholding my veto of the Vocational Rehabilitation Act earlier this week, the Congress demonstrated that it can set aside partisan political considerations in the interest of

In his 1972 reelection campaign, Nixon repeatedly admonished Congress to give him the authority to cut federal spending in order to keep the deficit down. The Democratic Congress, however, refused to give him that authority. Instead, Congress established a commission to study ways to assert congressional control over budgetary issues. That committee came up with a number of recommendations that ultimately were incorporated in the 1974 Congressional Budget and Impoundment Act. The act established standing budget committees in both the House and the Senate, founded the politically independent Congressional Budget Office (CBO), and, importantly, severely constrained the impoundment authority of the president. Curiously, Nixon signed that bill. By the time it came to his desk, Watergate had consumed his presidency and he was in a far weaker position politically than he had been at the time of his reelection. In fact, he signed the bill on July 12, 1974, just three weeks before resigning the presidency. He knew he would not have the votes in Congress to sustain a veto, as he had in the case of this measure, H.R. 3298.

America's economic well-being. I urge the Members of the Congress to hold to that same resolve in. reconsidering this second piece of inflationary, budget-breaking legislation.

Together, we can hold down taxes and inflation for all of the American people. Together, we can also create a climate in which local and State governments will have both the incentive and the means to meet their legitimate responsibilities without undue interference from Washington and without a proliferation of costly and unnecessary Federal programs such as the one which H.R. 3298 would re-establish.

Source: Richard Nixon, Veto of the Rural Water and Sewer Grant Program Bill, April 5, 1973. Online by Gerhard Peters and John T. Woolley, *The American Presidency Project*. http://www.presidency.ucsb.edu/ws/?pid=3795.

The Pentagon Papers

Richard Nixon's Statement

May 22, 1973

INTRODUCTION

Dr. Daniel Ellsberg was a former Marine lieutenant, Harvard-trained economist, and Rand Corporation analyst who worked on a 1967 top-secret study, commissioned by the U.S. government, on the origins of the Vietnam War since 1945. Ellsberg had earlier been in favor of the war but had become decidedly antiwar by 1969 while still at Rand. He began to secretly photocopy the report in hopes that he could ultimately make it public. In March 1971, after he left Rand, Dr. Ellsberg released the top-secret documents in his possession to the press. Those papers came to be known as the Pentagon Papers. Ellsberg was indicted with several counts of espionage, theft, and criminal conspiracy. In May 1973, after several months on trial, the District Court judge threw out the case once it was revealed that CIA operatives had burglarized the offices of Dr. Lewis Fielding, Ellsberg's psychiatrist, with the intention of finding information that would discredit Ellsberg.

After a swift legal battle over the power of government to exercise *prior restraint* and prevent the press from reporting on the Pentagon Papers, the U.S. Supreme Court ruled in favor of the *New York Times* and other news outlets that sought to release the documents they acquired from Ellsberg. In its decision, the court found that the release of the stolen documents, while damaging and embarrassing to the U.S. government, did not pose a threat to national security sufficient to justify the exercise of prior restraint.

On Sunday, June 13, 1971, the New York Times published the first installment of what came to be known as "The Pentagon Papers." Not until a few hours before publication did any responsible Government official know that they had been stolen. Most officials did not know they existed. No senior official of the Government had read them or knew with certainty what they contained.

All the Government knew, at first, was that the papers comprised 47 volumes and some 7,000 pages, which had been taken from the most sensitive files of the Departments of State and Defense and the CIA, covering military and diplomatic moves in a war that was still going on.

Moreover, a majority of the documents published with the first three installments in the Times had not been included in the 47-volume study—raising serious questions about what and how much else might have been taken.

There was every reason to believe this was a security leak of unprecedented proportions.

It created a situation in which the ability of the Government to carry on foreign relations even in the best of circumstances could have been severely compromised. Other governments no longer knew whether they could deal with the United States in confidence. Against the background of the delicate negotiations the United States was then involved in on a number of fronts—with regard to Vietnam, China, the Middle East, nuclear arms limitations, U.S.-Soviet relations, and others—in which the utmost degree of confidentiality was vital, it posed a threat so grave as to require extraordinary actions.

Therefore during the week following the Pentagon Papers publication, **I approved the creation of a Special Investigations Unit within the White House—which later came to be known as the "plumbers."** This was a small group at the White House whose principal purpose was to stop security leaks and to investigate other sensitive security matters. I looked to John Ehrlichman for the supervision of this group. Egil Krogh, Mr. Ehrlichman's assistant, was put in charge. David Young was added to this unit, as were E. Howard Hunt and G. Gordon Liddy.

The unit operated under extremely tight security rules. Its existence and functions were known only to a very few persons at the White House. These included Messrs. Haldeman, Ehrlichman, and Dean.

At about the time the unit was created, Daniel Ellsberg was identified as the person who had given the Pentagon Papers to the New York Times. I told Mr. Krogh that as a matter of first priority, the unit should find out all it could about Mr. Ellsberg's associates and his motives. Because of the extreme gravity of the situation, and not then knowing what additional national secrets Mr. Ellsberg might disclose, I did impress upon Mr. Krogh the vital importance to the national security of his assignment. I did not authorize and had no knowledge of any illegal means to be used to achieve this goal.

However, because of the emphasis I put on the crucial importance of protecting the national security, I can understand

The plumbers would become one of the most notorious groups in American presidential history. In addition to their break-in at the Los Angeles office, they were involved in covert actions on behalf of the Committee to Reelect the President, including the Watergate break-in. The plumbers were only one dimension, however, of Nixon's efforts to deal with the threat that he perceived from radicals, leftists, antiwar activists, journalists, and political opponents. Once legal means of dealing with those he deemed subversive were no longer available to him, Nixon authorized a private system of burglaries, wiretaps, political blackmail, and dirty tricks that collectively ultimately brought down his presidency.

how highly motivated individuals could have felt justified in engaging in specific activities that I would have disapproved had they been brought to my attention.

As was later discovered, Nixon did indeed have knowledge of these events. Forty years later, Dr. Ellsberg was interviewed by the *New York Times* about what lessons we might have learned from the Pentagon Papers case. He responded, "[i]t seems to me that what the Pentagon Papers really demonstrated 40 years ago was the price of . . . letting a small group of men in secret in the executive branch make these decisions—initiate them secretly, carry them out secretly and manipulate Congress, and lie to Congress and the public as to why they're doing it and what they're doing—is a recipe for, a guarantee of Vietnams and Iraqs and Libyas, and in general foolish, reckless, dangerous policies" (Daniel Ellsberg, NYT, June 7, 2011; Source: http://www.nytimes.com/2011/06/08/us/08pentagon.html?pagewanted=2, accessed February 4, 2015).

Consequently, as President, I must and do assume responsibility for such actions despite the fact that I at no time approved or had knowledge of them.

I also assigned the unit a number of other investigatory matters, dealing in part with compiling an accurate record of events related to the Vietnam war, on which the Government's records were inadequate (many previous records having been removed with the change of administrations) and which bore directly on the negotiations then in progress. Additional assignments included tracing down other national security leaks, including one that seriously compromised the U.S. negotiating position in the SALT talks.

The work of the unit tapered off around the end of 1971. The nature of its work was such that it involved matters that, from a national security standpoint, were highly sensitive then and remain so today.

These intelligence activities had no connection with the break-in of the Democratic headquarters, or the aftermath.

I considered it my responsibility to see that the Watergate investigation did not impinge adversely upon the national security area. For example, on April 18, 1973, when I learned that Mr. Hunt, a former member of the Special Investigations Unit at the White House, was to be questioned by the U.S. Attorney, I directed Assistant Attorney General Petersen to pursue every issue involving Watergate but to confine his investigation to Watergate and related matters and to stay out of national security matters. Subsequently, on April 25, 1973, Attorney General Kleindienst informed me that because the Government had clear evidence that Mr. Hunt was involved in the break-in of the office of the psychiatrist who had treated Mr. Ellsberg, he, the Attorney General, believed that despite the fact that no evidence had been obtained from Hunt's acts, a report should nevertheless be made to the court trying the Ellsberg case. I concurred, and directed that the information be transmitted to Judge Byrne immediately.

Source: Richard Nixon, Statements about the Watergate Investigations, May 22, 1973. Online by Gerhard Peters and John T. Woolley, *The American Presidency Project*. http://www.presidency.ucsb.edu/ws/?pid=3855.

War Powers Resolution

Richard Nixon's Veto

October 24, 1973

INTRODUCTION

Although Article I, Section 8, Clause 11 grants Congress the authority to declare war, Article II, Section 2, Clause 2 of the Constitution provides that "the President shall be Commander in Chief of the Army and Navy of the United States. . . ." As a result, only Congress can declare war, but is dependent on the executive branch to command the troops once war is declared. This is not a power Congress has exercised very often, however. In fact, Congress has declared war only five times in the nation's history. Meanwhile, presidents have exercised their war powers on hundreds of occasions without a formal congressional declaration of war. The nature of military conflicts has changed, too. The opportunity for a formal declaration of war prior to the onset of hostilities seems, in the modern context, to be unlikely. Instead, the swiftness and secrecy of covert operations or targeted airstrikes now characterizes the contemporary era. The evolution of military conflict then left Congress far less equipped to exercise its constitutional prerogative in determining when the United States should make war. But the decline in congressional authority over the exercise of military force was not simply a function of changes in the nature of the conflicts, or in advances in weapon systems and deployment methods that attended those changes; rather, as in many other contexts, Congress's willingness ceded that authority to the presidency. For instance, the 1964 Gulf of Tonkin Resolution authorized the president—at his discretion—to "take all necessary steps" to defend South Vietnam. The result was a significant escalation of the conflict in Southeast Asia and provided President Johnson with the *political cover* to continue that escalation. The only means by which Congress could ultimately bring U.S. involvement in the war to an end was by defunding the military appropriations for the war in Vietnam, which they eventually did in August 1973. In the aftermath of that episode, many in Congress sought to reassert congressional control over the power of the executive to engage U.S. forces in military conflicts. The result was the passage, just a few months later, of the War Powers Resolution of 1973. Citing constitutional and practical objections, Nixon vetoed the bill. On November 7, 1973, the House of Representatives and the Senate voted to override the President's veto. The Constitution prescribes that overrides of presidential vetoes require the approval of two-thirds of the members of both chambers. The override vote in the House overcame the two-thirds requirement by only four votes. The vote in the Senate was less uncertain.

To the House of Representatives:

I hereby return without my approval House Joint Resolution 542—the War Powers Resolution. While I am in accord with the desire of the Congress to assert its proper role in the conduct of our foreign affairs, the restrictions which this resolution would impose upon the authority of the President are both unconstitutional and dangerous to the best interests of our Nation.

The proper roles of the Congress and the Executive in the conduct of foreign affairs have been debated since the founding of our country. Only recently, however, has there been a serious challenge to the wisdom of the Founding Fathers in choosing not to draw a precise and detailed line of demarcation between the foreign policy powers of the two branches.

The Founding Fathers understood the impossibility of foreseeing every contingency that might arise in this complex area. They acknowledged the need for flexibility in responding to changing circumstances. They recognized that foreign policy decisions must be made through close cooperation between the two branches and not through rigidly codified procedures.

These principles remain as valid today as they were when our Constitution was written. Yet House Joint Resolution 542 would violate those principles by defining the President's powers in ways which would strictly limit his constitutional authority.

CLEARLY UNCONSTITUTIONAL

House Joint Resolution 542 would attempt to take away, by a mere legislative act, authorities which the President has properly exercised under the Constitution for almost 200 years. **One of its provisions would automatically cut off certain authorities after sixty days unless the Congress extended them. Another would allow the Congress to eliminate certain authorities merely by the passage of a concurrent resolution—an action which does not normally have the force of law, since it denies the President his constitutional role in approving legislation.**

I believe that both these provisions are unconstitutional. The only way in which the constitutional powers of a branch

The resolution was an attempt to force legislative and executive collaboration in coming to a collective judgment about the propriety of military action. In addition, the resolution sought to limit military actions by the president to those exercised pursuant to (1) a declaration of war, (2) under a statutory congressional authorization, or (3) a national emergency created by an attack on the United States. Specifically, the War Powers Resolution required the president to report to Congress within 48 hours of the onset of military action. After 60 days, the military action must end unless Congress declares war or specifically authorizes its continuance; Congress votes to extend the 60-day period (by up to 30 days); or Congress is physically unable to meet due to an invasion or attack. Congress is also given the authority to remove troops from military hostilities by a concurrent resolution. In this passage, Nixon raises the constitutional objections to both a congressional encroachment on the president's role as commander in chief and the authority that Congress has to recall troops by concurrent resolution would violate the presentment clauses of the Constitution.

of the Government can be altered is by amending the Constitution—and any attempt to make such alterations by legislation alone is clearly without force.

UNDERMINING OUR FOREIGN POLICY

While I firmly believe that a veto of House Joint Resolution 542 is warranted solely on constitutional grounds, I am also deeply disturbed by the practical consequences of this resolution. For it would seriously undermine this Nation's ability to act decisively and convincingly in times of international crisis. As a result, the confidence of our allies in our ability to assist them could be diminished and the respect of our adversaries for our deterrent posture could decline. A permanent and substantial element of unpredictability would be injected into the world's assessment of American behavior, further increasing the likelihood of miscalculation and war.

If this resolution had been in operation, America's effective response to a variety of challenges in recent years would have been vastly complicated or even made impossible. We may well have been unable to respond in the way we did during the Berlin crisis of 1961, the Cuban missile crisis of 1962, the Congo rescue operation in 1964, and the Jordanian crisis of 1970—to mention just a few examples. In addition, our recent actions to bring about a peaceful settlement of the hostilities in the Middle East would have been seriously impaired if this resolution had been in force.

While all the specific consequences of House Joint Resolution 542 cannot yet be predicted, it is clear that it would undercut the ability of the United States to act as an effective influence for peace. For example, the provision automatically cutting off certain authorities after 60 days unless they are extended by the Congress could work to prolong or intensify a crisis. Until the Congress suspended the deadline, there would be at least a chance of United States withdrawal and an adversary would be tempted therefore to postpone serious negotiations until the 60 days were up. Only after the Congress acted would there be a strong incentive for an adversary to negotiate. In addition, the very existence of a deadline could lead to an escalation of hostilities in order to achieve certain objectives before the 60 days expired.

The measure would jeopardize our role as a force for peace in other ways as well.

It would, for example, strike from the President's hand a wide range of important peace-keeping tools by eliminating his ability to exercise quiet diplomacy backed by subtle shifts in our military deployments. It would also cast into doubt authorities which Presidents have used to undertake certain humanitarian relief missions in conflict areas, to protect fishing boats from seizure, to deal with ship or aircraft hijackings, and to respond to threats of attack. Not the least of the adverse consequences of this resolution would be the prohibition contained in section 8 against fulfilling our obligations under the NATO treaty as ratified by the Senate.

Finally, since the bill is somewhat vague as to when the 60 day rule would apply, it could lead to extreme confusion and dangerous disagreements concerning the prerogatives of the two branches, seriously damaging our ability to respond to international crises.

The initial report, if delayed for whatever reason, would subsequently put off any attempt for congressional control. That is, if the president delayed reporting, the 60-day clock does not start until a report is made. What, exactly, would trigger the requisite reporting by the president to Congress was not specified in the resolution. That ambiguity has indeed led to confusion, and in some cases, resort to the federal judiciary. The courts, however, have generally refused to rule on those cases.

FAILURE TO REQUIRE POSITIVE CONGRESSIONAL ACTION

I am particularly disturbed by the fact that certain of the President's constitutional powers as Commander in Chief of the Armed Forces would terminate automatically under this resolution. 60 days after they were invoked. **No overt Congressional action would be required to cut off these powers—they would disappear automatically unless the Congress extended them. In effect, the Congress is here attempting to increase its policy-making role through a provision which requires it to take absolutely no action at all.**

It is not clear that Congress would likely be inclined to take the positive action Nixon demands. One can imagine that as the 60-day (or 90-day) deadline approaches, there is very little incentive for Congress to constrain or limit military actions. Two or three months (after the initial report, which itself may have been delayed) is sufficient time for initial hostilities to grow into major military emergencies and national security threats. At that point, one can imagine Congress being driven more by the powerful public impulse for decisive military action rather than investigation and deliberation on the propriety of that action. Once troops are in harm's way, a different dynamic is likely to take hold.

In my view, the proper way for the Congress to make known its will on such foreign policy questions is through a positive action, with full debate on the merits of the issue and with each member taking the responsibility of casting a yes or

Since Nixon, presidents' decisions to seek .... congressional authorization for military action abroad have largely turned on political calculations rather than a desire to comply with the terms of the War Powers Resolution. For instance, in February 2015, President Obama sought congressional authority to take military action against militants of the Islamic State (known as ISIS) in Syria and Iraq. Prior to seeking congressional approval under the War Powers Act, Obama had ordered targeted airstrikes against the terrorist group, but had done so with what the administration claimed was authority granted by a 2001 authorization for the use of force in the fight against al-Qaeda. The difficulty, however, was that ISIS and al-Qaeda were not connected groups. Nonetheless, the lack of a connection between the two groups did not matter, according to Obama. Though he sought the support from Congress, the president maintained that he did not need their explicit authorization to continue the fight against ISIS.

no vote after considering those merits. The authorization and appropriations process represents one of the ways in which such influence can be exercised. I do not, however, believe that the Congress can responsibly contribute its considered, collective judgment on such grave questions without full debate and without a yes or no vote. Yet this is precisely what the joint resolution would allow. **It would give every future Congress the ability to handcuff every future President merely by doing nothing and sitting still. In my view, one cannot become a responsible partner unless one is prepared to take responsible action.**

STRENGTHENING COOPERATION BETWEEN

THE CONGRESS AND THE EXECUTIVE BRANCHES

The responsible and effective exercise of the war powers requires the fullest cooperation between the Congress and the Executive and the prudent fulfillment by each branch of its constitutional responsibilities. House Joint Resolution 542 includes certain constructive measures which would foster this process by enhancing the flow of information from the executive branch to the Congress. Section 3, for example, calls for consultations with the Congress before and during the involvement of the United States forces in hostilities abroad. This provision is consistent with the desire of this Administration for regularized consultations with the Congress in an even wider range of circumstances.

I believe that full and cooperative participation in foreign policy matters by both the executive and the legislative branches could be enhanced by a careful and dispassionate study of their constitutional roles. Helpful proposals for such a study have already been made in the Congress. I would welcome the establishment of a non-partisan commission on the constitutional roles of the Congress and the President in the conduct of foreign affairs. This commission could make a thorough review of the principal constitutional issues in Executive-Congressional relations, including the war powers, the international agreement powers, and the question of Executive privilege, and then submit its recommendations to the President and the Congress. The members of such a commission could be drawn from both parties—and could represent many perspectives including those of the Congress, the executive branch, the legal profession, and the academic community.

This Administration is dedicated to strengthening co-operation between the Congress and the President in the conduct of foreign affairs and to preserving the constitutional prerogatives of both branches of our Government. I know that the Congress shares that goal. A commission on the constitutional roles of the Congress and the President would provide a useful opportunity for both branches to work together toward that common objective.

RICHARD NIXON

The White House,

October 24, 1973.

Source: Richard Nixon, Veto of the War Powers Resolution, October 24, 1973. Online by Gerhard Peters and John T. Woolley, *The American Presidency Project.* http://www.presidency.ucsb.edu/ws/?pid=4021.

Executive Privilege

United States v. Nixon

July 24, 1974

INTRODUCTION

During the course of its investigations into the Watergate break-in, its cover-up, and other wrong-doing during the 1972 presidential campaign, the Senate Select Committee learned from John Dean, former counsel to President Nixon, that he and the president had multiple conversations about obstructing the Watergate investigations. He also provided specific dates for those conversations. Later, the committee learned from a former White House aide, Alexander Butterfield, that the president had secretly installed a recording system in the Oval Office and had taped all conversations for—as Butterfield told the committee—"posterity, for the Nixon Library."

Upon learning of the existence of the recording mechanism, Archibald Cox, the special prosecutor for Watergate, subpoenaed the tapes. The president resisted the subpoena, claiming executive privilege. As Nixon reasoned, "[u]nless a President can protect the privacy of the advice he gets, he cannot get the advice he needs. This principle is recognized in the constitutional doctrine of executive privilege, which has been defended and maintained by every President since Washington and which has been recognized by the courts, whenever tested, as inherent in the Presidency. I consider it to be my constitutional responsibility to defend this principle." Federal District Court Judge John Sirica, however, upheld the constitutionality of the subpoena. After several attempts by Nixon to find compromise solutions to turning over the tapes, the district court ordered the administration to provide the tapes. That order to turn over evidence, a subpoena *duces tecum*, compelled both the prosecutor and the administration to seek review by the Supreme Court. Review was granted and the court issued its unanimous decision just eight weeks after oral arguments.

By the time the court heard this case, Archibald Cox had been replaced by Leon Jaworski as special prosecutor. Once Cox subpoenaed the tapes, Nixon demanded that Elliot Richardson, the new attorney general of the United States, fire the special prosecutor. At his Senate confirmation hearings, however, Richardson gave assurances to the senators that the special prosecutor for Watergate would not be subjected to political influence from the White House. Richardson could not honor that pledge if he fired Cox on Nixon's command. Instead, Richardson resigned. His deputy, William Ruckleshaus, was asked to fire Cox, but he too resigned rather than comply with Nixon's order. Ultimately, Acting Attorney General Robert Bork dismissed Cox (Bork would later be nominated by President Reagan for appointment to the Supreme Court). After a massive outcry for what came to be known as the Saturday Night Massacre,

MR. CHIEF JUSTICE BURGER delivered the opinion of the Court.

On March 1, 1974, a grand jury of the United States District Court for the District of Columbia returned an indictment charging seven named individuals 3 with various offenses, including conspiracy to defraud the United States and to obstruct justice. **Although he was not designated as such in the indictment, the grand jury named the President, among others, as an unindicted coconspirator.** On April 18, 1974, upon motion of the Special Prosecutor, a subpoena *duces tecum* was issued pursuant to Rule 17 (c) to the President by the United States District Court and made returnable on May 2, 1974. This subpoena required the production, in advance of the September 9 trial date, of certain tapes, memo-randa, papers, transcripts, or other writings relating to certain precisely identified meetings between the President and others. The Special Prosecutor was able to fix the time, place, and persons present at these discussions because the White House daily logs and appointment records had been delivered to him. On April 30, the President publicly released edited transcripts of 43 conversations; portions of 20 conversations subject to subpoena in the present case were included. On May 1, 1974, the President's counsel filed a "special appearance" and a motion to quash the subpoena under Rule 17 (c). This motion was accompanied by a formal claim of privilege. At a subsequent hearing, further motions to expunge the grand jury's action naming the President as an unindicted coconspirator and for protective orders against the disclosure of that information were filed or raised orally by counsel for the President.

On May 20, 1974, the District Court denied the motion to quash and the motions to expunge and for protective orders. It further ordered "the President or any subordinate officer, official, or employee with custody or control of the documents or objects subpoenaed," to deliver to the District Court, on or before May 31, 1974, the originals of all subpoenaed items, as well as an index and analysis of those items, together with tape copies of those portions of the subpoenaed recordings for which transcripts had been released to the public by the President on April 30.

The District Court held that the judiciary, not the President, was the final arbiter of a claim of executive privilege. The court concluded that, under the circumstances of this case, the presumptive privilege was overcome by the Special Prosecutor's prima facie "demonstration of need sufficiently compelling to warrant judicial examination in chambers . . . ."

THE CLAIM OF PRIVILEGE

A

... [W]e turn to the claim that the subpoena should be quashed because it demands "confidential conversations

Leon Jaworski was appointed special prosecutor. Unfortunately for Nixon, he too pressed the administration to turn over the tapes.

Interestingly, the federal grand jury voted to indict several individuals in the administration, including the president. However, Leon Jaworski was not certain that a sitting president could be indicted without first being impeached. As a result, Nixon was named as an unindicted coconspirator.

between a President and his close advisors that it would be inconsistent with the public interest to produce." The first contention is a broad claim that the separation of powers doctrine precludes judicial review of a President's claim of privilege. The second contention is that if he does not prevail on the claim of absolute privilege, the court should hold as a matter of constitutional law that the privilege prevails over the subpoena *duces tecum*.

In the performance of assigned constitutional duties each branch of the Government must initially interpret the Constitution, and the interpretation of its powers by any branch is due great respect from the others. The President's counsel, as we have noted, reads the Constitution as providing an absolute privilege of confidentiality for all Presidential communications.

Our system of government "requires that federal courts on occasion interpret the Constitution in a manner at variance with the construction given the document by another branch." *Powell v. McCormack*, supra, at 549. And in *Baker v. Carr, 369 U.S., at 211*, the Court stated:

"Deciding whether a matter has in any measure been committed by the Constitution to another branch of government, or whether the action of that branch exceeds whatever authority has been committed, is itself a delicate exercise in constitutional interpretation, and is a responsibility of this Court as ultimate interpreter of the Constitution."

B

In support of his claim of absolute privilege, the President's counsel urges two grounds, one of which is common to all governments and one of which is peculiar to our system of separation of powers. The first ground is the valid need for protection of communications between high Government officials and those who advise and assist them in the performance of their manifold duties; the importance of this confidentiality is too plain to require further discussion. Human experience teaches that those who expect public dissemination of their remarks may well temper candor with a concern for appearances and for their own interests to the detriment of the decisionmaking process.

The second ground asserted by the President's counsel in support of the claim of absolute privilege rests on the doctrine of separation of powers. Here it is argued that the independence of the Executive Branch within its own sphere, insulates a President from a judicial subpoena in an ongoing criminal prosecution, and thereby protects confidential Presidential communications.

However, neither the doctrine of separation of powers, nor the need for confidentiality of high-level communications, without more, can sustain an absolute, unqualified Presidential privilege of immunity from judicial process under all circumstances. The President's need for complete candor and objectivity from advisers calls for great deference from the courts. However, when the privilege depends solely on the broad, undifferentiated claim of public interest in the confidentiality of such conversations, a confrontation with other values arises. Absent a claim of need to protect military, diplomatic, or sensitive national security secrets, we find it difficult to accept the argument that even the very important interest in confidentiality of Presidential communications is significantly diminished by production of such material for in camera inspection with all the protection that a district court will be obliged to provide.

The impediment that an absolute, unqualified privilege would place in the way of the primary constitutional duty of the Judicial Branch to do justice in criminal prosecutions would plainly conflict with the function of the courts under Art. III. In designing the structure of our Government and dividing and allocating the sovereign power among three co-equal branches, the Framers of the Constitution sought to provide a comprehensive system, but the separate powers were not intended to operate with absolute independence.

"While the Constitution diffuses power the better to secure liberty, it also contemplates that practice will integrate the dispersed powers into a workable government. It enjoins upon its branches separateness but interdependence, autonomy but reciprocity." *Youngstown Sheet & Tube Co. v. Sawyer, 343 U.S., at 635* (Jackson, J., concurring).

To read the Art. II powers of the President as providing an absolute privilege as against a subpoena essential to enforcement of criminal statutes on no more than a generalized claim of the public interest in confidentiality of nonmilitary and nondiplomatic discussions would upset the constitutional balance of "a workable government" and gravely impair the role of the courts under Art. III.

C

Since we conclude that the legitimate needs of the judicial process may outweigh Presidential privilege, it is necessary to resolve those competing interests in a manner that preserves the essential functions of each branch. The right and indeed the duty to resolve that question does not free the Judiciary from according high respect to the representations made on behalf of the President.

The expectation of a President to the confidentiality of his conversations and correspondence, like the claim of confidentiality of judicial deliberations, for example, has all the values to which we accord deference for the privacy of all citizens and, added to those values, is the necessity for protection of the public interest in candid, objective, and even blunt or harsh opinions in Presidential decision-making. A President and those who assist him must be free to explore alternatives in the process of shaping policies and making decisions and to do so in a way many would be unwilling to express except privately. These are the considerations justifying a presumptive privilege for Presidential communications. The privilege is fundamental to the operation of Government and inextricably rooted in the separation of powers under the Constitution.

But this presumptive privilege must be considered in light of our historic commitment to the rule of law. We have elected to employ an adversary system of criminal justice in which the parties contest all issues before a court of law. The need to develop all relevant facts in the adversary system is both fundamental and comprehensive. The ends of criminal justice would be defeated if judgments were to be founded on a partial or speculative presentation of the facts. The very integrity of the judicial system and public confidence in the system depend on full disclosure of all the facts, within the framework of the rules of evidence. To ensure that justice is done, it is imperative to the function of courts that compulsory process be available for the production of evidence needed either by the prosecution or by the defense.

In this case the President challenges a subpoena served on him as a third party requiring the production of materials for use in a criminal prosecution; he does so on the claim that he has a privilege against disclosure of confidential communications. He does not place his claim of privilege on the ground they are military or diplomatic secrets. As to these areas of Art. II duties the courts have traditionally shown the utmost deference to Presidential responsibilities.

In this case we must weigh the importance of the general privilege of confidentiality of Presidential communications in performance of the President's responsibilities against the inroads of such a privilege on the fair administration of criminal justice. The interest in preserving confidentiality is weighty indeed and entitled to great respect. However, we cannot conclude that advisers will be moved to temper the candor of their remarks by the infrequent occasions of disclosure because of the possibility that such conversations will be called for in the context of a criminal prosecution.

On the other hand, the allowance of the privilege to withhold evidence that is demonstrably relevant in a criminal trial would cut deeply into the guarantee of due process of law and gravely impair the basic function of the courts. **A President's acknowledged need for confidentiality in the communications of his office is general in nature, whereas the constitutional need for production of relevant evidence in a criminal proceeding is specific and**

With this decision rejecting the president's claim of executive privilege and requiring the release of the tapes, Nixon's choices were quite stark. He could either comply with the decision to release the tapes that provided clear evidence of his complicity in the cover-up or refuse to obey the order of the Supreme Court. Either road led to impeachment. In fact, the House was prepared to vote on three articles of impeachment. Within days of the court's decision, Nixon resigned the office of the president. Once he resigned, impeachment proceedings were halted. A month later, President Gerald Ford pardoned Nixon of "all crimes he committed or may have committed" as president.

Though this was obviously a tremendous blow to the Nixon administration, it may ironically have further extended executive power. The effect of the decision is to treat executive privilege as a presumptive privilege—something that presidents have by virtue of their position atop the executive branch. That is, in this passage, the court is quite clearly emphasizing the deference with which it will give the executive claiming executive privilege of materials that require absolute secrecy, such as national security communications.

central to the fair adjudication of a particular criminal case in the administration of justice. Without access to specific facts a criminal prosecution may be totally frustrated. The President's broad interest in confidentiality of communications will not be vitiated by disclosure of a limited number of conversations preliminarily shown to have some bearing on the pending criminal cases.

We conclude that when the ground for asserting privilege as to subpoenaed materials sought for use in a criminal trial is based only on the generalized interest in confidentiality, it cannot prevail over the fundamental demands of due process of law in the fair administration of criminal justice. The generalized assertion of privilege must yield to the demonstrated, specific need for evidence in a pending criminal trial.

We have earlier determined that the District Court did not err in authorizing the issuance of the subpoena. Accordingly we affirm the order of the District Court that subpoenaed materials be transmitted to that court.

Affirmed.

Source: *United States v. Nixon*, 418 U.S. 683 (1974).

The Church Committee Hearings and FISA

Final Report
April 26, 1976

INTRODUCTION

In the aftermath of the Watergate investigations and Nixon's resignation, the executive branch's abuse of intelligence gathering took center stage. Revelations of the existence of secret NSA, CIA, and FBI domestic surveillance programs spurred Congress to take action. Senator Frank Church (D-ID) was appointed chair of the Senate Select Committee to Study Governmental Operations with Respect to Intelligence Activities. This is the committee's final report on their investigation into, among other things, the use of the nation's surveillance apparatus by presidents for political rather than national security purposes. In addition to violating core principles of separation of powers and openness in a democratic society, the use of the surveillance programs to target U.S. citizens appeared to violate the 4th Amendment protections against unreasonable searches and seizures and other expectations of privacy and personal and associative liberty.

FINAL REPORT

PREFACE

In January 1975, the Senate resolved to establish a Committee to conduct an investigation and study of governmental operations with respect to intelligence activities and the extent, if any, to which illegal, improper, or unethical activities were engaged in by any agency of the Federal Government. This Committee was organized shortly thereafter and has conducted a year-long investigation into the intelligence activities of the United States Government, the first substantial inquiry into the intelligence community since World War II. **The inquiry arose out of allegations of substantial wrongdoing by intelligence agencies on behalf of the administrations which they served.** A deeper concern underlying the investigation was whether this Government's intelligence activities were governed and controlled consistently with the fundamental principles of American constitutional government—that power must be checked and balanced and that the preservation of liberty

On March 18, 1971, several activists broke into an FBI office in Media, Pennsylvania. The members of the group stole, photocopied, and mailed all the documents they could find to the *Washington Post*. Among the documents was one marked "COINTELPRO." COINTELPRO turned out to be a secret counterintelligence program run by the FBI to monitor, discredit, and destabilize key political movements such as the Civil Rights Movement, Black Power Movement, and the Antiwar Movement. That program dovetailed with another covert surveillance program that the National Security Administration ran, called Project Shamrock. The initial purpose of Shamrock was to collect information from international communications that implicated certain foreign targets whose names were provided by the CIA. Over the course of its 30-year existence, however, Shamrock expanded to include the electronic surveillance of domestic targets as well, including Vietnam War protesters and civil rights leaders such as Dr. Martin Luther King Jr. With the assistance of large telecommunications corporations, federal intelligence agencies were able to sift through massive amounts of communications involving U.S. citizens.

requires the restraint of laws, and not simply the good intentions of men.

The Committee's investigation has confirmed substantial wrongdoing. And it has demonstrated that intelligence activities have not generally been governed and controlled in accord with the fundamental principles of our constitutional system of government. . . . In the course of its investigation, the Committee has sought to answer three broad questions: First, whether domestic intelligence activities have been consistent with law and with the individual liberties guaranteed to American citizens by the Constitution. Second, whether America's foreign intelligence activities have served the national interest in a manner consistent with the nation's ideals and with national purposes. Third, whether the institutional procedures for directing and controlling intelligence agencies have adequately ensured their compliance with policy and law, and whether those procedures have been based upon the system of checks and balances among the branches of government required by our Constitution.

IV. CONCLUSIONS AND RECOMMENDATIONS

The findings which have emerged from our investigation convince us that the Government's domestic intelligence policies and practices require fundamental reform. . . . The Committee's fundamental conclusion is that intelligence activities have undermined the constitutional rights of citizens and that they have done so primarily because checks and balances designed by the framers of the Constitution to assure accountability have not been applied. Before examining that conclusion, we make the following observations.

The crescendo of improper intelligence activity in the latter part of the 1960s and the early 1970s shows what we must watch out for: In time of crisis, the Government will exercise its power to conduct domestic intelligence activities to the fullest extent. The distinction between legal dissent and criminal conduct is easily forgotten. Our job is to recommend means to help ensure that the distinction will always be observed.

In an era where the technological capability of Government relentlessly increases, we must be wary about the drift toward "big brother government." **The potential for abuse is awesome and requires special attention to fashioning restraints which not only cure past problems but anticipate and prevent the future misuse of technology.**

We cannot dismiss what we have found as isolated acts which were limited in time and confined to a few willful men. The failures to obey the law and, in the words of the oath of office, to "preserve, protect, and defend" the Constitution, have occurred repeatedly throughout administrations of both political parties going back four decades.

Our findings ... set forth a massive record of intelligence abuses over the years. Through a vast network of informants, and through the uncontrolled or illegal use of intrusive techniques—ranging from simple theft to sophisticated electronic surveillance—the Government has collected, and then used improperly, huge amounts of information about the private lives, political beliefs and associations of numerous Americans.

That these abuses have adversely affected the constitutional rights of particular Americans is beyond question.... Since the end of World War II, governmental power has been increasingly exercised through a proliferation of federal intelligence programs. The very size of this intelligence system, multiplies the opportunities for misuse. Exposure of the excesses of this huge structure has been necessary. Americans are now aware of the capability and proven willingness of their Government to collect intelligence about their lawful activities and associations. What some suspected and others feared has turned out to be largely true—vigorous expression of unpopular views, association with dissenting groups, participation in peaceful protest activities, have provoked both government surveillance and retaliation.

The natural tendency of Government is toward abuse of power. Men entrusted with power, even those aware of its dangers, tend, particularly when pressured, to slight liberty.

The "special attention" the Congress fashioned included enhanced oversight and statutory controls on executive intelligence gathering. In particular, Congress passed and President Carter signed the Foreign Intelligence Surveillance Act (FISA) of 1978 in response to this report. FISA created a new court, the Foreign Intelligence Surveillance Court, to hear requests for warrants for domestic electronic surveillance. The court meets in secret; its proceedings are closed to all because of the national security implications of its work. Seven judges, each appointed by the chief justice of the U.S. Supreme Court, comprise the FISA court. As it has developed over time, its role as a check on domestic surveillance activities appears to be rather limited, though. Since 1979, the court has granted the requested warrant in almost every case. Nonetheless, in the wake of September 11, 2001, President George W. Bush chose to circumvent the FISA court, instructing the intelligence community to initiate a practice of warrantless wiretapping—an issue considered in a later chapter.

Our constitutional system guards against this tendency.... In the field of intelligence those restraints have too often been ignored.

In a sense the growth of domestic intelligence activities mirrored the growth of presidential power generally. But more than any other activity, more even than exercise of the war power, intelligence activities have been left to the control of the Executive. For decades Congress and the courts as well as the press and the public have accepted the notion that the control of intelligence activities was the exclusive prerogative of the Chief Executive and his surrogates. The exercise of this power was not questioned or even inquired into by outsiders. Indeed, at times the power was seen as flowing not from the law but as inherent in the Presidency. Whatever the theory, the fact was that intelligence activities were essentially exempted from the normal system of checks and balances. Such Executive power, not founded in law or checked by Congress or the courts, contained the seeds of abuse and its growth was to be expected.... Each of us, from presidents to the most disadvantaged citizen, must obey the

While the committee clearly articulated the importance of intelligence gathering for the purpose of national security, Senator Church was insistent that national security ought not be used as an excuse for what really amounted to surveillance for the purpose of disrupting political dissent.

law. **As intelligence operations developed, however, rationalizations were fashioned to immunize them from the restraints of the Bill of Rights and the specific prohibitions of the criminal code. The experience of our investigation leads us to conclude that such rationalizations are a dangerous delusion.**

Although our recommendations are numerous and detailed, they flow naturally from our basic conclusion. Excessive intelligence activity which undermines individual rights must end. The system for controlling intelligence must be brought back within the constitutional scheme....

Accordingly, ... intelligence agencies must be made subject to the rule of law. In addition, ... no theory of "inherent constitutional authority" or otherwise, can justify the violation of any statute.

Source: Senate Select Committee to Study Governmental Operations with Respect to Intelligence Activities, 1975–76 (Church Committee). Final Report, S. Rep. No. 94-755 (1976). http://www.intelligence.senate.gov/sites/default/files/94755_I.pdf.

The Legislative Veto

INS v. Chadha

June 23, 1983

INTRODUCTION

Since the 1930s, Congress had written legislative veto provisions into more than 200 statutes. The legislative veto was a mechanism by which Congress could control executive branch implementation of the statute without having to pass new laws. The legislative veto provisions allowed Congress to delegate broad discretionary authority to executive agencies with the assurance that if the agencies began to stray from congressional preferences, the veto provision would enable Congress to withdraw that discretionary power. By a vote of one or both chambers (or sometimes even just a committee), Congress could invoke the legislative veto to constrain executive action on the statute. The effect of these provisions was to afford Congress the ability to delegate broadly with the benefit of maintaining control over the policy upon its implementation. The difficulty, according to the U.S. Supreme Court, was that the legislative veto violated the principle of the separation of powers. In particular, the court ruled, the provisions (in this case, Section 244(c)(2) of the Immigration and Nationality Act) violated the presentment clauses of Article 1.

Chief Justice Burger delivered the opinion of the Court.

... We turn now to the question whether action of one House of Congress under 244(c)(2) violates strictures of the Constitution. We begin, of course, with the presumption that the challenged statute is valid. Its wisdom is not the concern of the courts; if a challenged action does not violate the Constitution, it must be sustained.... By the same token, the fact that a given law or procedure is efficient, convenient, and useful in facilitating functions of government, standing alone, will not save it if it is contrary to the Constitution. Convenience and efficiency are not the primary objectives —or the hallmarks—of democratic government and our inquiry is sharpened rather than blunted by the fact that **congressional veto provisions are appearing with increasing frequency in statutes which delegate authority to executive and independent agencies.**

Since the 1930s, Congress had included legislative veto provisions in its delegations of legislative power to the executive branch. Congress has many incentives to delegate power to the president. For instance, when policies are highly complex and public attention is low, there is little value for Congress to exercise strict control over the policy, and delegation is an attractive option. So long as Congress gives the implementing authority a standard, or in the language of the court, "an intelligible principle" by which to implement the statute, the broad delegations have been permitted as extensions of Congress's own legislative power.

Explicit and unambiguous provisions of the Constitution prescribe and define the respective functions of the Congress and of the Executive in the legislative process.

Article I provides:

"All legislative Powers herein granted shall be vested in a Congress of the United States, which shall consist of a Senate and House of Representatives." Art. I, 1.

"Every Bill which shall have passed the House of Representatives and the Senate, shall, before it becomes a law, be presented to the President of the United States . . . ." Art. I, 7, cl. 2.

"Every Order, Resolution, or Vote to which the Concurrence of the Senate and House of Representatives may be necessary (except on a question of Adjournment) shall be presented to the President of the United States; and before the Same shall take Effect, shall be approved by him, or being disapproved by him, shall be repassed by two thirds of the Senate and House of Representatives, according to the Rules and Limitations prescribed in the Case of a Bill." Art. I, 7, cl. 3.

The records of the Constitutional Convention reveal that the requirement that all legislation be presented to the President before becoming law was uniformly accepted by the Framers. Presentment to the President and the Presidential veto were considered so imperative that the draftsmen took special pains to assure that these requirements could not be circumvented.

The decision to provide the President with a limited and qualified power to nullify proposed legislation by veto was based on the profound conviction of the Framers that the powers conferred on Congress were the powers to be most carefully circumscribed. It is beyond doubt that lawmaking was a power to be shared by both Houses and the President.

The bicameral requirement of Art. I, 1, 7, was of scarcely less concern to the Framers than was the Presidential veto and indeed the two concepts are interdependent. **By providing that no law could take effect without the concurrence of the prescribed majority of the Members of both Houses, the Framers reemphasized their belief that legislation should not be enacted unless it has been carefully and fully considered by the Nation's elected officials.**

Here, the court finds that because the vetoes would take effect without the president's signature or without an override of his veto, they violate the presentment clauses. In the court's view, the presentment clauses serve several important purposes, including guaranteeing presidential (and bicameral) participation in lawmaking. A mechanism that bypasses the president (and, in some cases, at least one chamber of Congress) would violate at least that important principle.

[T]he Framers were acutely conscious that the bicameral requirement and the Presentment Clauses would serve essential constitutional functions. The President's participation in the legislative process was to protect the Executive Branch from Congress and to protect the whole people from improvident laws. The division of the Congress into two distinctive bodies assures that the legislative power would be exercised only after opportunity for full study and debate in separate settings.

The Constitution sought to divide the delegated powers of the new Federal Government into three defined categories, Legislative, Executive, and Judicial, to assure, as nearly as possible, that each branch of government would confine itself to its assigned responsibility. The hydraulic pressure inherent within each of the separate Branches to exceed the outer limits of its power, even to accomplish desirable objectives, must be resisted.

The veto authorized by 244(c)(2) doubtless has been in many respects a convenient shortcut; the "sharing" with the Executive by Congress of its authority over aliens in this manner is, on its face, an appealing compromise. In purely practical terms, it is obviously easier for action to be taken by one House without submission to the President; but it is crystal clear from the records of the Convention, contemporaneous writings and debates, that the Framers ranked other values higher than efficiency.... The choices we discern as having been made in the Constitutional Convention impose burdens on governmental processes that often seem clumsy, inefficient, even unworkable, but those hard choices were consciously made by men who had lived under a form of government that permitted arbitrary governmental acts to go unchecked.... With all the obvious flaws of delay, untidiness, and potential for abuse, we have not yet found a better way to preserve freedom than by making the exercise of power subject to the carefully crafted restraints spelled out in the Constitution.

JUSTICE WHITE, dissenting.

Today the Court not only invalidates 244(c)(2) of the Immigration and Nationality Act, but also sounds the death knell for nearly 200 other statutory provisions in which Congress has reserved a "legislative veto." For this reason, the Court's decision is of surpassing importance.

[... The legislative veto] has become a central means by which Congress secures the accountability of executive and independent agencies. Without the legislative veto, Congress is faced with a Hobson's choice: either to refrain from delegating the necessary authority, leaving itself with a hopeless task of writing laws with the requisite specificity to cover endless special circumstances across the entire policy landscape, or in the alternative, to abdicate its law-making function to the Executive Branch and independent agencies. To choose the former leaves major national problems unresolved; to opt for the latter risks unaccountable policymaking by those not elected to fill that role. **Accordingly, over the past five decades, the legislative veto has been placed in nearly 200 statutes.**

Even this brief review suffices to demonstrate that the legislative veto is more than "efficient, convenient, and useful." It is an important if not indispensable political invention that allows the President and Congress to resolve major constitutional and policy differences, assures the accountability of independent regulatory agencies, and preserves Congress' control over lawmaking.

[T]he wisdom of the Framers was to anticipate that the Nation would grow and new problems of governance would require different solutions. Accordingly, our Federal Government was intentionally chartered with the flexibility

White challenges the majority's view of the legislative veto as simply a "useful" policy device. In an era of increasingly complex economic, technological, and social policies, congressional control over delegated discretion could be really important. In White's view, the legislative veto is a necessary democratic control of executive power—a way for Congress to maintain legislative authority.

to respond to contemporary needs without losing sight of fundamental democratic principles.

The power to exercise a legislative veto is not the power to write new law without bicameral approval or Presidential consideration. The veto must be authorized by statute and may only negative what an Executive department or independent agency has proposed.

The Court's holding today that all legislative-type action must be enacted through the lawmaking process ignores that legislative authority is routinely delegated to the Executive Branch, to the independent regulatory agencies, and to private individuals and groups.

This Court's decisions sanctioning such delegations make clear that Art. I does not require all action with the effect of legislation to be passed as a law.

... [B]y virtue of congressional delegation, legislative power can be exercised by independent agencies and Executive departments without the passage of new legislation. There is no question but that agency rulemaking is lawmaking in any functional or realistic sense of the term. When agencies are authorized to prescribe law through substantive rulemaking, the administrator's regulation is not only due deference, but is accorded "legislative effect."

Absent the veto, the agencies receiving delegations of legislative or quasi-legislative power may issue regulations having the force of law without bicameral approval and without the President's signature. It is thus not apparent why the reservation of a veto over the exercise of that legislative power must be subject to a more exacting test. In both cases, it is enough that the initial statutory authorizations comply with the Art. I requirements.

If the effective functioning of a complex modern government requires the delegation of vast authority which, by virtue of its breadth, is legislative or "quasi-legislative" in character,

Here, Justice White makes two important points. First, that the delegations which include the veto provisions are themselves legislative actions that follow typical legislative procedures (including bicameralism and presentment). And second, that the rulemaking activity of executive and independent agencies carries the full weight of law without following the prescriptions of the presentment clauses. Surely, he seems to suggest, the majority wouldn't strike rule making as a violation of the separation of powers or of the nondelegation doctrine.

I cannot accept that Art. I should forbid Congress to qualify that grant with a legislative veto.

Congressional control over agency discretionary authority did not end with the decision in *Chadha*. In fact, some scholars view the legislative veto as a relatively weak instrument of control when compared to mechanisms such as appropriations, hearings, reporting requirements, and other formal and informal powers held by congressional committees.

[T]he legislative veto device here—and in many other settings—is far from an instance of legislative tyranny over the Executive. **It is a necessary check on the unavoidably expanding power of the agencies, both Executive and independent, as they engage in exercising authority delegated by Congress.**

Source: *INS v. Chadha*, 462 U.S. 919 (1983).

The Chevron Two-Step

Chevron v. NRDC

June 25, 1984

INTRODUCTION

Congress amended the Clean Air Act in the late 1970s, during the Carter administration. The amendments were meant to bring states that had not met the National Ambient Air Quality Standards into compliance. To ensure compliance, the states that had yet to reach their goals were required to set up a permit program to "regulate new or modified major stationary sources of air pollution." Under Carter, the Environmental Protection Agency understood "source" to mean any particular device (i.e., smokestack) at a particular plant. During the Reagan administration, regulations were promulgated that interpreted the word "source" to include a plant as a whole and any adjacent or contiguous entity, not just a single point source, like a smokestack. That meant that under the new regulations, a permit would not be required so long as the total air pollution emitting from an entire plant did not increase. The court refers to this as the "bubble" concept. The National Resources Defense Council (NRDC) challenged the new regulation, arguing that while Congress was not clear what they meant by the word "source," what was clear was that the new regulations allowed polluters to circumvent the purpose of the Clean Air Act. The "bubble" conception of "source" was, in their view, completely at odds with the goals of the Clean Air Act. Chevron appealed the ruling of the D.C. Circuit Court which found for the NRDC.

The case, *Chevron v. NRDC*, is important to a study of presidential power in that it is the case from which the idea of *administrative deference* is derived. Administrative deference is the idea that judges should generally defer to agencies' understandings of delegated authority when the statutes that grant that authority meet certain requirements. Those requirements have come to be known as the Chevron Two-Step.

JUSTICE STEVENS delivered the opinion of the Court.

In the Clean Air Act Amendments of 1977, Congress enacted certain requirements applicable to States that had not achieved the national air quality standards established by the Environmental Protection Agency (EPA) pursuant to earlier legislation. The amended Clean Air Act required these "nonattainment" States to establish a permit program regulating "new or modified major stationary sources" of air pollution. Generally, a permit may not be issued for a new or modified major stationary source unless several stringent conditions are met. The EPA regulation promulgated to implement this permit requirement allows a State to adopt a plantwide definition of the term "stationary source." Under this definition, an existing plant that contains several pollution-emitting devices may install or modify one piece of equipment without meeting the permit conditions if the alteration will not increase the total emissions from the plant. The question presented by these cases is whether EPA's decision to allow States to treat all of the pollution-emitting devices within the same industrial grouping as though they were encased within a single "bubble" is based on a reasonable construction of the statutory term "stationary source."

When a court reviews an agency's construction of the statute which it administers, it is confronted with two questions. **First, always, is the question whether Congress has directly spoken to the precise question at issue. If the intent of Congress is clear, that is the end of the matter; for the court, as well as the agency, must give effect to the unambiguously expressed intent of Congress.**

If, however, the court determines Congress has not directly addressed the precise question at issue, the court does not simply impose its own construction on the statute, as would be necessary in the absence of an administrative interpretation. **Rather, if the statute is silent or ambiguous with respect to the specific issue, the question for the court is whether the agency's answer is based on a permissible construction of the statute.**

The power of an administrative agency to administer a congressionally created . . . program necessarily requires the formulation of policy and the making of rules to fill any gap left, implicitly or explicitly, by Congress. If Congress has explicitly left a gap for the agency to fill, there is an express delegation of authority to the agency to elucidate a specific provision of the statute by regulation. Such legislative regulations are given controlling weight unless they are arbitrary, capricious, or manifestly contrary to the statute. Sometimes the legislative delegation to an agency on a particular question is implicit, rather than explicit. In such a case, a court may not substitute its own construction of a statutory

Here, the court articulates the first step of the two-prong deference doctrine. When the statute is clear, the plain meaning of the statute guides agency action. For example, if the statute does not permit emissions of sulfur dioxide in excess of 9 million tons, then clearly the EPA may not promulgate regulations that permit greater emissions than 9 million tons of sulfur dioxide.

And here, the court takes up the second prong. In this second step, the issue is what to do when Congress has not "spoken" clearly. In this case, the specific concern is whether the EPA's interpretation of what constitutes a "source" is reasonable. The idea that a reasonable or "permissible" interpretation of the statute will prevail is consequential. The deference for executive-level agency interpretation means that judicial review of agency regulations, while not thwarted, is at least tempered. What is important is that the tempering effect could lead agencies (as agents of the sitting president) to drift from congressional preferences.

provision for a reasonable interpretation made by the administrator of an agency.

We have long recognized that considerable weight should be accorded to an executive department's construction of a statutory scheme it is entrusted to administer, and the principle of deference to administrative interpretations has been consistently followed by this Court whenever decision as to the meaning or reach of a statute has involved reconciling conflicting policies, and a full understanding of the force of the statutory policy in the given situation has depended upon more than ordinary knowledge respecting the matters subjected to agency regulations.

In light of these well-settled principles, it is clear that the Court of Appeals misconceived the nature of its role in reviewing the regulations at issue. Once it determined, after its own examination of the legislation, that Congress did not actually have an intent regarding the applicability of the bubble concept to the permit program, the question before it was not whether, in its view, the concept is "inappropriate" in the general context of a program designed to improve air quality, but whether the Administrator's view that it is appropriate in the context of this particular program is a reasonable one. Based on the examination of the legislation and its history which follows, we agree with the Court of Appeals that Congress did not have a specific intention on the applicability of the bubble concept in these cases, and conclude that the EPA's use of that concept here is a reasonable policy choice for the agency to make.

... Judges are not experts in the field, and are not part of either political branch of the Government. Courts must, in some cases, reconcile competing political interests, but not on the basis of the judges' personal policy preferences. In contrast, an agency to which Congress has delegated policymaking responsibilities may, within the limits of that delegation, properly rely upon the incumbent administration's views of wise policy to inform its judgments. While agencies are not directly accountable to the people, the Chief Executive is, and it is entirely

In this and a preceding passage, the court appears to admonish the lower federal court for its ruling. The court suggests that rather than impute judicial preferences for a regulatory scheme, the courts ought to defer to reasonable interpretation by agencies of congressional statutes. Interestingly, that judge was Circuit Judge Ruth Bader Ginsburg, who would be appointed to the Supreme Court by President Clinton in 1993.

appropriate for this political branch of the Government to make such policy choices—resolving the competing interests which Congress itself either inadvertently did not resolve, or intentionally left to be resolved by the agency charged with the administration of the statute in light of everyday realities.

When a challenge to an agency construction of a statutory provision, fairly conceptualized, really centers on the wisdom of the agency's policy, rather than whether it is a reasonable choice within a gap left open by Congress, the challenge must fail. In such a case, federal judges—who have no constituency—have a duty to respect legitimate policy choices made by those who do. The responsibilities for assessing the wisdom of such policy choices and resolving the struggle between competing views of the public interest are not judicial ones . . . .

The judgment of the Court of Appeals is reversed.

Source: *Chevron U.S.A., Inc. v. Natural Resources Defense Council, Inc.*, 467 U.S. 837 (1984).

Signing Statements as Policy Devices

Samuel Alito's Memo

February 5, 1986

INTRODUCTION

One of the tools available to presidents as they seek to shape policy outcomes is the presidential signing statement. A signing statement is a written presidential pronouncement regarding a piece of legislation that is issued at the time the president signs the bill into law. The statements are publicly available and provide opportunities for presidents to articulate their view of specific provisions of the bill. The specific comments may raise, among other issues, policy and funding concerns, suggestions for future legislative activity, guidelines for the implementation of the law by bureaucratic agents, or constitutional objections. Signing statements have a long history and have been used by most presidents since the founding. However, during the Reagan administration, the president's legal advisers began to push for the use of signing statements as a means to achieve both policy goals and to insert the president's view of legislation into the legislative history of a statute, presumably to influence courts and other political actors. The ultimate goal, of course, was to reposition and strengthen the executive branch's role in shaping important policies and in construing constitutional meaning—thereby securing the unitary executive.

February 5, 1986

Office of the Deputy Assistant Attorney General

TO: The Litigation Strategy Working Group

FROM: Samuel A. Alito, Jr. Deputy Assistant Attorney General Office of Legal Counsel

SUBJ: Using Presidential Signing Statement to Make Fuller Use of the President's Constitutionally Assigned Role in the Process of Enacting Law.

At our last meeting, I was asked to draft a preliminary proposal for implementing the idea of making fuller use of

Presidential signing statements. This memorandum is a rough first effort in that direction.

Objectives

Our primary objective is to ensure that Presidential signing statements assume their rightful place in the interpretation of legislation. In the past, Presidents have issued signing statements when presented with bills raising constitutional problems. OLC (*Office of Legal Counsel*) has played a role in this process, and the present proposal would not substantively alter that process. **The novelty of the proposal previously discussed by this Group is the suggestion that Presidential signing statements be used to address questions of interpretation.**

Under the Constitution, a bill becomes law only when passed by both houses of Congress and signed by the President (or enacted over his veto). Since the President's approval is just as important as that of the House or Senate, it seems to follow that the President's understanding of the bill should be just as important as that of Congress. **Yet in interpreting statutes, both courts and litigants (including lawyers in the Executive branch) invariably speak of "legislative" or "congressional" intent. Rarely if ever do courts or litigants inquire into the President's intent. Why is this so?**

Part of the reason undoubtedly is that Presidents, unlike Congress, do not customarily comment on their understanding of bills. Congress churns out great masses of legislative history bearing on its intent—committee reports, floor debates, hearings. Presidents have traditionally created nothing comparable. Presidents have seldom explained in any depth or detail how they interpreted the bills they have signed. Presidential approval is usually accompanied by a statement that is often little more than a press release. **From the perspective of the Executive Branch, the issuance of interpretive signing statements would have two chief advantages. First, it would increase the power of the Executive to shape the law. Second, by forcing some rethinking by courts, scholars, and litigants, it may**

There is the clear recognition that what Alito is proposing is new. Historically, the role of the signing statement was rhetorical—praising or chastising members of Congress for their positions on the legislation, commenting on its value and purpose, and so forth. To find a way to use those rather anodyne statements to reconceive a role for the president in the statute's interpretation was indeed novel and signaled what could become an important shift in presidential–congressional relations.

As Congress and the president struggle for control over policy, they are engaged in a dynamic and fluid decision-making process. And, in many cases, courts become involved. When courts interpret statutes, some judges refer to the legislative history to discern what it was that Congress intended the statute to accomplish. This memo reflects the Reagan administration's strategy to have the presidential signing statement included in that history, so courts could review presidential preferences regarding the statute as well. Within days of this memo from Alito, Attorney General Edwin Meese announced that the administration had arranged with West Publishing Company (the principal legal research service for lawyers and judges) to have the signing statements included in the company's published accounts of the legislative history of statutes. It is worth noting that the author of this memo, Samuel Alito Jr., would later be appointed to the U.S. Supreme Court by President George W. Bush, himself a firm advocate of the unitary executive perspective.

help to curb some of the prevalent abuses of legislative history.

The purpose of referring to the legislative history of a bill is to sift through the hearings, committee reports, amendments, floor debate, and so on that characterized the bill's history in the legislative context in order to understand how the bill ought to be interpreted. There are many difficulties in doing so, however. For one thing, "Congress is a 'they,' not an 'it,'" as political scientist Ken Shepsle once quipped. There may be multiple intents and purposes for any number of a bill's provisions, especially since most bills are referred to multiple committees and proceed through both chambers of Congress on their way to the president's desk. Moreover, given the power of specific members of Congress—agenda-setters, such as committee chairs and leaders in both chambers—particular individuals are able to manufacture a specific "intent" that really only reflects a specific preference, rather than some general understanding of a provision. The expectation we gather from this passage is that a presidential signing statement may help judges and attorneys cut through those difficulties by positing the president's view of legislative intent. But that surely brings with it its own problems.

Problems

I see five primary obstacles to the enhanced use of Presidential signing statements.

1. Resources. The most important problem is the manpower that will be required. One need only consider the size of the congressional staffs responsible for creating legislative history to appreciate the dimensions of the potential commitment that may be required if the Executive Branch were to undertake to issue interpretive statements regarding all important legislation touching on matters of federal concern. In all likelihood, it would be necessary to create a new office with a substantial staff to serve as a clearinghouse for statements furnished by the various departments and agencies. Each department and agency would also have to devote significant resources to the project.

2. Timing. Under the Constitution (Art. I, sec. 7), if Congress is in session, a bill must be signed or vetoed within 10 days after its presentation to the President. Since presidential signing statements have traditionally been issued at the time of the signing of legislation, very little time has been available for the preparation and review of such statements. These time constraints will become much more troublesome if presidential signing statements become longer, more substantive, and more detailed.

3. Congressional Relations. It seems likely that our new type of signing statement will not be warmly welcomed by Congress. The novelty of the procedure and the potential increase of presidential power are two factors that may account for this anticipated reaction. In addition, and perhaps most important, Congress is likely to resent the fact that the President will get in the last word on questions of interpretation. Because of the anticipated reaction of Congress, it seems likely that some Executive Branch officers concerned about congressional relations may likewise oppose this effort. In the past, signing statements prepared by OLC have

The Reagan administration's success in promoting signing statements might cut both ways. Yes, it may reposition the president in the struggle over policy. But, in some important respects, it may hamper the president's ability to control implementation of the statute. The issuance of a signing statement that raises constitutional objections may signal to Congress that the president is not going to comply with the bill. Once Congress has been alerted to possible noncompliance, they have many effective means to monitor the agencies responsible for implementing the law, including drafting new statutes, limiting appropriation and reauthorizations, and dragging officials up to Capitol Hill for oversight hearings.

sometimes been substantially changed by the White House or OMB (*Office of Management and Budget*) due to such concerns. **As signing statements become more and more controversial, this problem is likely to get worse.**

4. Acceptance by Executive Departments and Agencies. Once a clearinghouse unit is established or designated, it seems likely that there will be friction between that unit and the various departments and agencies wishing to insert interpretive statements into presidential signing statements. If the lines of authority are not clear, this inevitable friction may be magnified.

5. Theoretical problems. Because presidential intent has been all but ignored in interpreting the meaning of statutes, the theoretical problems have not been explored. For example:

- In general, is presidential intent entitled to the same weight as legislative intent or is it of much less significance? As previously noted, presidential approval of legislation is generally just as important as congressional approval. Moreover, the President frequently proposes legislation. On the other hand, Congress has the opportunity to shape the bills that are presented to the President, and the President's role at that point is limited to approving or disapproving. For this reason, some may argue that only Congressional intent matters for purposes of interpretation. If our project is to succeed, we must be fully prepared to answer this argument.

- What happens when there is a clear conflict between the congressional and presidential understanding? Whose intent controls? Is the law totally void? Is it inoperative only to the extent that there is disagreement?

- If presidential intent is of little or no significance when inconsistent with congressional intent, what role is there for presidential intent? Is it entitled to the deference comparable to that customarily given to administrative interpretations?

Source: Samuel A. Alito, Jr., Deputy Assistant Attorney General. Memo to the Litigation Strategy Working Group, Using Presidential Signing Statement to Make Fuller Use of the President's Constitutionally Assigned Role in the Process of Enacting Law, February 5, 1986. U.S. National Archives. http://www.archives.gov/news/samuel-alito/accession-060-89-269/Acc060-89-269-box6-SG-LSWG-AlitotoLSWG-Feb1986.pdf.

The Iran/Contra Affair

Ronald Reagan's Address to the Nation
March 4, 1987

INTRODUCTION

Through the 1980s, the Sandinistas controlled the government of Nicaragua following the broadly based insurrection in 1979 that ended the dictatorship of Anastasio Somoza. As the Sandinistas enacted leftist policies that ran afoul of U.S. interests, the Reagan administration began to provide support for the opposition group, the Contras. In October 1984, however, Congress passed an appropriations bill that included a section known as the Boland Amendment. That amendment prohibited any funding "that would have the effect of supporting... military or paramilitary operations in Nicaragua by any nation, organization, movement, or individual." On October 5, 1986, a plane carrying military supplies for the Contras crashed in Nicaragua after being shot down by Sandinista forces. Its pilot, Eugene Hasenfus, was able to parachute to safety but was captured by the Sandinistas. During his detention, he made public statements that the military supply flights he was running for the Contras were being orchestrated by the Central Intelligence Agency through its contacts in El Salvador. A little black book of phone numbers and contacts' names recovered from the crash site provided additional evidence of that arrangement, as did phone records that revealed multiple calls to the White House from the contacts in El Salvador. These revelations prompted a series of investigations. If the Reagan administration was indeed providing support for the Contra rebels, they were doing so in direct violation of the Boland Amendment. In the ensuing weeks, a wave of news stories emerged, revealing a vast private operation of mercenaries, terrorists, and spies under the direct control of the Reagan White House in an orchestrated effort to circumvent U.S. law.

Meanwhile, on October 8—just three days after the plane crash—the FBI announced it was investigating the company that owned the supply plane. The FBI learned that in addition to the supply of weapons to the Contras, Southern Air Transport was involved in a series of secret shipments of arms to Iran. As the investigation revealed, the Reagan administration had, in a secret and ultimately unsuccessful attempt to free hostages being held in Lebanon, used the profits from the sale of weapons to Iran to fund the Contras in Nicaragua. It became clear that throughout these operations, Congress and the American people had been purposefully deceived by the president's staff, if not by Reagan himself.

March 4, 1987

My fellow Americans:

I've spoken to you from this historic office on many occasions and about many things. The power of the Presidency

is often thought to reside within this Oval Office. Yet it doesn't rest here; it rests in you, the American people, and in your trust. Your trust is what gives a President his powers of leadership and his personal strength, and it's what I want to talk to you about this evening.

For the past 3 months, I've been silent on the revelations about Iran. And you must have been thinking: "Well, why doesn't he tell us what's happening? Why doesn't he just speak to us as he has in the past when we've faced troubles or tragedies?" Others of you, I guess, were thinking: "What's he doing hiding out in the White House?" Well, the reason I haven't spoken to you before now is this: You deserve the truth. And as frustrating as the waiting has been, I felt it was improper to come to you with sketchy reports, or possibly even erroneous statements, which would then have to be corrected, creating even more doubt and confusion. There's been enough of that. I've paid a price for my silence in terms of your trust and confidence. But I've had to wait, as you have, for the complete story. **That's why . . . I appointed a Special Review Board, the Tower board, which took on the chore of pulling the truth together for me and getting to the bottom of things. It has now issued its findings.**

On December 1, 1986, Reagan appointed this three-person panel to investigate the matter. That panel was known as the Tower Commission. Two weeks later, the Justice Department appointed Lawrence Walsh as independent counsel to run a separate investigation. And on January 6, 1987, the Senate and the House created special investigatory committees. By May 5, Congress began its public hearings on the matter.

I'm often accused of being an optimist, and it's true I had to hunt pretty hard to find any good news in the Board's report. . . . Its findings are honest, convincing, and highly critical; and I accept them. And tonight I want to share with you my thoughts on these findings and report to you on the actions I'm taking to implement the Board's recommendations. First, let me say I take full responsibility for my own actions and for those of my administration. As angry as I may be about activities undertaken without my knowledge, I am still accountable for those activities. As disappointed as I may be in some who served me, I'm still the one who must answer to the American people for this behavior. And as personally distasteful as I find secret bank accounts and diverted funds—well, as the Navy would say, this happened on my watch.

Let's start with the part that is the most controversial. A few months ago I told the American people I did not trade arms for hostages. My heart and my best intentions still tell me that's true, but the facts and the evidence tell me it is not. As the Tower board reported, what began as a strategic opening to Iran deteriorated, in its implementation, into trading arms for hostages. This runs counter to my own beliefs, to administration policy, and to the original strategy we had in mind. There are reasons why it happened, but no excuses. It was a mistake. I undertook the original Iran initiative in order to develop relations with those who might assume leadership in a post-Khomeini government.

The Tower Commission discovered that the U.S. sales of arms to Iran had been happening since at least early 1984 and continued through late October 1986. The Reagan administration had hoped to use the sale of arms to Iran as a mechanism for bringing Iranian influence to bear on negotiations with Hezbollah over the release of U.S. hostages being held in Lebanon. This became known as the "arms for hostages deal" and when revealed, came under intense criticism because it violated the stated U.S. policy of not negotiating with terrorists. It may also have violated arms export control laws. Among other critiques, the Tower Commission's report stated that "[the arms for hostages trade] could not help but create an incentive for future hostage taking."

It's clear from the Board's report, however, that I let my personal concern for the hostages spill over into the geopolitical strategy of reaching out to Iran. I asked so many questions about the hostages welfare that I didn't ask enough about the specifics of the total Iran plan. Let me say to the hostage families: We have not given up. We never will. And I promise you we'll use every legitimate means to free your loved ones from captivity. But I must also caution that those Americans who freely remain in such dangerous areas must know that they're responsible for their own safety.

Now, another major aspect of the Board's findings regards the transfer of funds to the Nicaraguan contras. The Tower board wasn't able to find out what happened to this money, so the facts here will be left to the continuing investigations of the court appointed Independent Counsel and the two congressional investigating committees. I'm confident the truth will come out about this matter, as well. As I told the Tower board, I didn't know about any diversion of funds to the contras. But as President, I cannot escape responsibility.

Much has been said about my management style, a style that's worked successfully for me during 8 years as Governor of California and for most of my Presidency. The way I work is to identify the problem, find the right individuals to do the job, and then let them go to it. I've found this invariably brings out the best in people. They seem to rise to their full capability, and in the long run you get more done. When it came to managing the NSC staff, let's face it, my style didn't match its previous track record. I've already begun correcting this. As a start, yesterday I met with the entire professional staff of the National Security Council. I defined for them the values I want to guide the national security policies of this country. I told them that I wanted a policy that was as justifiable and understandable in public as it was in secret. I wanted a policy that reflected the will of the Congress as well as of the White House. And I told them that there'll be no more freelancing by individuals when it comes to our national security.

You've heard a lot about the staff of the National Security Council in recent months. Well, I can tell you, they are good and dedicated government employees, who put in long hours for the Nation's benefit. They are eager and anxious to serve their country. **One thing still upsetting me, however, is that no one kept proper records of meetings or decisions. This led to my failure to recollect whether I approved an arms shipment before or after the fact. I did approve it; I just can't say specifically when.** Well, rest assured, there's plenty of record-keeping now going on at 1600 Pennsylvania Avenue.

For nearly a week now, I've been studying the Board's report. I want the American people to know that this wrenching ordeal of recent months has not been in vain. I endorse every one of the Tower board's recommendations. In fact, I'm going beyond its recommendations so as to put the house in even better order. I'm taking action in three basic areas: personnel, national security policy, and the process for making sure that the system works.

First, personnel—I've brought in an accomplished and highly respected new team here at the White House. They bring new blood, new energy, and new credibility and experience.... Already, almost half the NSC professional staff is comprised of new people.

Yesterday I nominated William Webster, a man of sterling reputation, to be Director of the Central Intelligence Agency.

In 1986, after several unsuccessful attempts to secure the release of the hostages through the sale of weapons to Iran (brokered by the Israelis), and a secret trip by the National Security Adviser Robert McFarlane on behalf of the president, one hostage was released on July 26. At that point, a key member of the National Security Council, Oliver North, recommended that President Reagan approve the shipment of more arms to Iran in order to secure the release of more hostages. Reagan did so on July 30. The October 29 shipment of arms for hostages that resulted from this approval by Reagan resulted in the release of one additional hostage on November 2. The multiple investigations of Iran/Contra uncovered conflicting accounts of what the president knew about the arms for hostages deal and the use of those funds to circumvent U.S. law. When questioned, Reagan was not particularly forthcoming. In a letter to the Tower Commission just days prior to this public statement, the president wrote: "In trying to recall events that happened eighteen months ago ... I have no personal notes or records to help my recollection on this matter. The only honest answer is to state that try as I might, I cannot recall anything whatsoever about whether I approved an Israeli sale in advance or whether I approved replenishment of Israeli stocks around August of 1985. My answer therefore and the simple truth is, 'I don't remember—period.'" Key advisors to the president differed in their recollections. One highly placed advisor told the commission that Reagan was "quite enthusiastic and perhaps excessively enthusiastic, given the uncertainties involved." Another advisor reported that he believed that the president certainly would have approved of the arms for hostages deal and the diversion of the funds to support the Contras in Nicaragua. And because he knew that the president would approve, he reasoned, he did not seek the president's formal approval so as to insulate Reagan from any wrongdoing.

Mr. Webster has served as Director of the FBI and as a U.S. District Court judge. He understands the meaning of "rule of law." So that his knowledge of national security matters can be available to me on a continuing basis, I will also appoint John Tower to serve as a member of my Foreign Intelligence Advisory Board. I am considering other changes in personnel, and I'll move more furniture, as I see fit, in the weeks and months ahead.

Second, in the area of national security policy, I have ordered the NSC to begin a comprehensive review of all covert operations. I have also directed that any covert activity be in support of clear policy objectives and in compliance with American values. I expect a covert policy that, if Americans saw it on the front page of their newspaper, they'd say, "That makes sense." I have had issued a directive prohibiting the NSC staff itself from undertaking covert operations—no ifs, ands, or buts. I have asked Vice President Bush to reconvene his task force on terrorism to review our terrorist policy in light of the events that have occurred.

Third, in terms of the process of reaching national security decisions, I am adopting in total the Tower report's model of how the NSC process and staff should work. . . . I've created the post of NSC legal adviser to assure a greater sensitivity to matters of law. I am also determined to make the congressional oversight process work. Proper procedures for consultation with the Congress will be followed, not only in letter but in spirit. Before the end of March, I will report to the Congress on all the steps I've taken in line with the Tower board's conclusions.

Now, what should happen when you make a mistake is this: You take your knocks, you learn your lessons, and then you move on. That's the healthiest way to deal with a problem. This in no way diminishes the importance of the other continuing investigations, but the business of our country and our people must proceed. I've gotten this message from Republicans and Democrats in Congress, from allies around the world, and—if we're reading the signals right—even from the Soviets. And of course, I've heard the message from you, the American people. You know, by the time you reach my age, you've made plenty of mistakes. And if you've lived your life properly—so, you learn. You put things in perspective. You pull your energies together. You change. You go forward.

My fellow Americans, I have a great deal that I want to accomplish with you and for you over the next 2 years. And the Lord willing, that's exactly what I intend to do. Good night, and God bless you.

Source: Ronald Reagan, Address to the Nation on the Iran Arms and Contra Aid Controversy, March 4, 1987. *Public Papers of the President: Ronald Reagan (Book 1)* (Washington DC: Government Printing Office, 1987), 208–211.

Appointment and Removal Power

Morrison v. Olson

June 29, 1988

INTRODUCTION

In the fall of 1973, President Nixon ordered Attorney General Elliot Richardson to fire Watergate Special Prosecutor Archibald Cox who had subpoenaed the White House tapes that ultimately implicated the president in the cover-up of the Watergate affair. Ordinarily, as an executive officer, Cox could have been removed at the president's request. However, the attorney general had promised the Senate that he would not interfere in Cox's investigations and would only act to remove Cox "for extraordinary improprieties." When Richardson resigned rather than comply with the president's demand, his Deputy Attorney General William Ruckelshaus was instructed to do so. He too resigned rather than comply with what he thought was inappropriate political influence from the White House. Ultimately, Nixon's instructions to fire Cox were followed by then acting Attorney General Robert Bork. Upon review, a federal district court ruled that Cox's removal by Bork was illegal. That episode became known as the Saturday Night Massacre and led to the passage of legislation that established a mechanism for the appointment of a special prosecutor to investigate executive branch officials. The establishment of an independent counsel free from White House and Justice Department political control was, in light of Watergate, an important step in cleaning up politics. However, in 1992, the legislation that created the independent counsel was not reauthorized. At that time, President George H.W. Bush, who had been vice president during independent counsel's investigations of Iran-Contra and other suspected improprieties, was opposed to its continuance. So too were most congressional Republicans. Ironically, many of those who were opposed to the office of independent counsel during the Walsh investigation, in particular, sought to reinstate the legislation when a Democratic president, Bill Clinton, came into office.

The Saturday Night Massacre and the special prosecutor legislation it provoked reveal important principles with respect to the separation of powers. On one hand, presidents have the constitutional obligation to "take care" that the laws are "faithfully executed." That means that they presumably should have control over those who are taking actions on their behalf. But, on the other hand, too much political control by the administration over subordinates would certainly limit the subordinates' independence and perhaps limit their investigative autonomy, as we'll see in this case dealing with independent special prosecutors. The difficulty in balancing these two perspectives emerged in this 1988 U.S. Supreme Court case, *Morrison v. Olson*. The case dealt with the constitutionality of the independent counsel provisions of the Ethics in Government Act of 1978.

CHIEF JUSTICE REHNQUIST delivered the opinion of the Court.

Briefly stated, Title VI of the Ethics in Government Act allows for the appointment of an "independent counsel" to investigate and, if appropriate, prosecute certain high-ranking Government officials for violations of federal criminal laws. The Act requires the Attorney General, upon receipt of information that he determines is "sufficient to constitute grounds to investigate whether any person [covered by the Act] may have violated any Federal criminal law," to conduct a preliminary investigation of the matter. When the Attorney General has completed this investigation, or 90 days has elapsed, he is required to report to a special court (the Special Division) created by the Act "for the purpose of appointing independent counsels." If the Attorney General has determined that there are "reasonable grounds to believe that further investigation or prosecution is warranted," then he "shall apply to the division of the court for the appointment of an independent counsel."

With respect to all matters within the independent counsel's jurisdiction, the Act grants the counsel "full power and independent authority to exercise all investigative and prosecutorial functions and powers of the Department of Justice, the Attorney General, and any other officer or employee of the Department of Justice."

The impeachment provisions are the only constitutional reference to the removal of executive branch officials. For most of the country's history, however, means short of impeachment have been assumed to be appropriate routes for subordinates' removal within the executive branch. But who has that authority to remove those subordinate officials is an important question. Is that power solely vested in the president, or may Congress limit presidential removal authority?

Two statutory provisions govern the length of an independent counsel's tenure in office. The first defines the procedure for removing an independent counsel:

"An independent counsel appointed under this chapter may be removed from office, other than by impeachment and conviction, only by the personal action of the Attorney General and only for good cause, physical disability, mental incapacity, or any other condition that substantially impairs the performance of such independent counsel's duties."

If an independent counsel is removed pursuant to this section, the Attorney General is required to submit a report to both the Special Division and the Judiciary Committees of the Senate and the House "specifying the facts found and the ultimate grounds for such removal."

The other provision governing the tenure of the independent counsel defines the procedures for "terminating" the counsel's office. Under 596(b)(1), the office of an independent counsel terminates when he or she notifies the Attorney General that he or she has completed or substantially completed any investigations or prosecutions undertaken pursuant to the Act. In addition, the Special Division, acting either on its own or on the suggestion of the Attorney General, may terminate the office of an independent counsel at any time if it finds that "the investigation of all matters within the prosecutorial jurisdiction of such independent counsel . . . have been completed or so substantially completed that it would be appropriate for the Department of Justice to complete such investigations and prosecutions."

Finally, . . . [t]he "appropriate committees of the Congress" are given oversight jurisdiction in regard to the official conduct of an independent counsel, and the counsel is required by the Act to cooperate with Congress in the exercise of this jurisdiction.

. . .

We turn to consider the merits of appellees' constitutional claims.

III

The Appointments Clause of Article II reads as follows:

"[The President] shall nominate, and by and with the Advice and Consent of the Senate, shall appoint Ambassadors, other public Ministers and Consuls, Judges of the supreme Court, and all other Officers of the United States, whose Appointments are not herein otherwise provided for, and which shall be established by Law: but the Congress may by Law vest the Appointment of such inferior Officers, as they think proper, in the President alone, in the Courts of Law, or in the Heads of Departments." U.S. Const., Art. II, 2, cl. 2.

The initial question is . . . whether appellant is an "inferior" or a "principal" officer. If she is the latter, as the Court of Appeals concluded, then the Act is in violation of the Appointments Clause.

In previous cases involving the appointment authority of the president, the court viewed officials as being of two types, either an inferior officer or a principal. In its 1976 decision in *Buckley v. Valeo*, the court determined that if the official is a principal officer, that person must be appointed consistent with the Appointments clause requirements of advice and consent of the Senate. But, if the officer is deemed to be an inferior officer, the president has the power to appoint that individual independent of congressional approval.

The line between "inferior" and "principal" officers is one that is far from clear, and the Framers provided little guidance into where it should be drawn. We need not attempt here to decide exactly where the line falls between the two types of officers, because in our view appellant clearly falls on the "inferior officer" side of that line. Several factors lead to this conclusion.

First, appellant is subject to removal by a higher Executive Branch official. . . . Second, appellant is empowered by the Act to perform only certain, limited duties. . . . Third, appellant's office is limited in jurisdiction. . . . Finally, appellant's office is limited in tenure. . . . [T]he office of independent counsel is "temporary" in the sense that an independent counsel is appointed essentially to accomplish a single task, and when that task is over the office is terminated. In our view, these factors . . . are sufficient to establish that appellant is an "inferior" officer in the constitutional sense.

Here, the court addresses whether the independent character of the independent counsel position reflects responsibilities that are "purely executive," or are indeed, independent. If the position is purely executive, the court reasons, the court will apply the standard established in the *Myers v. United States* (1926) case and affirmed in *Bowsher v. Synar* (1986) that acknowledges "the unrestricted power of the President to remove purely executive officers." In its view, however, the removal provisions of the statute more accurately reflect the case *Humphrey's Executor v. United States* (1935). In that case, the court found that "the Constitution did not give the President 'illimitable power of removal' over the officers of independent agencies."

We now turn to consider whether the Act is invalid under the constitutional principle of separation of powers. Two related issues must be addressed: The first is whether the provision of the Act restricting the Attorney General's power to remove the independent counsel to only those instances in which he can show "good cause," taken by itself, impermissibly interferes with the President's exercise of his constitutionally appointed functions. The second is whether, taken as a whole, the Act violates the separation of powers by reducing the President's ability to control the prosecutorial powers wielded by the independent counsel.

Unlike both Bowsher and Myers, this case does not involve an attempt by Congress itself to gain a role in the removal of executive officials other than its established powers of impeachment and conviction. The Act instead puts the removal power squarely in the hands of the Executive Branch; an independent counsel may be removed from office, "only by the personal action of the Attorney General, and only for good cause." In our view, the removal provisions of the Act make this case more analogous to Humphrey's Executor v. United States (1935) than to Myers or Bowsher.

... There is no real dispute that the functions performed by the independent counsel are "executive" in the sense that they are law enforcement functions that typically have been undertaken by officials within the Executive Branch. As we noted above, however, the independent counsel is an inferior officer under the Appointments Clause, with limited jurisdiction and tenure and lacking policymaking or significant administrative authority. Although the counsel exercises no small amount of discretion and judgment in deciding how to carry out his or her duties under the Act, we simply do not see how the President's need to control the exercise of that discretion is so central to the functioning of the Executive Branch as to require as a matter of constitutional law that the counsel be terminable at will by the President.

... This is not a case in which the power to remove an executive official has been completely stripped from the President, thus providing no means for the President to ensure the "faithful execution" of the laws. Rather, because the independent counsel may be terminated for "good cause," the Executive, through the Attorney General, retains ample authority to assure that the counsel is competently performing his or her statutory responsibilities in a manner that comports with the provisions of the Act. Here, ... the congressional determination to limit the removal power of the Attorney General was essential, in the view of Congress, to establish the necessary independence of the office. **We do not think that this limitation as it presently stands sufficiently deprives the President of control over the independent counsel to interfere impermissibly with his constitutional obligation to ensure the faithful execution of the laws.**

In this passage, the court appears to recognize that balance that must be struck between the autonomy necessary to fulfill a president's obligation to "faithfully execute" the law and the independence that must be maintained by a special prosecutor investigating potential wrongdoing within the executive branch.

The final question to be addressed is whether the Act, taken as a whole, violates the principle of separation of powers by unduly interfering with the role of the Executive Branch. Time and again we have reaffirmed the importance in our constitutional scheme of the separation of governmental powers into the three coordinate branches. We have not hesitated to invalidate provisions of law which violate this principle. On the other hand, we have never held that the

Constitution requires that the three branches of Government "operate with absolute independence."

This is a clear reference to the case *INS v.* .... *Chadha* (1983) in which the court ruled the legislative veto an unconstitutional violation of the presentment clauses.

Unlike some of our previous cases, this case simply does not pose a "dange[r] of congressional usurpation of Executive Branch functions." Indeed, with the exception of the power of impeachment, Congress retained for itself no powers of control or supervision over an independent counsel. Congress' role under the Act is limited to receiving reports or other information and oversight of the independent counsel's activities, functions that we have recognized generally as being incidental to the legislative function of Congress.

Similarly, we do not think that the Act works any judicial usurpation of properly executive functions. As should be apparent from our discussion of the Appointments Clause above, the power to appoint inferior officers such as independent counsel is not in itself an "executive" function in the constitutional sense .... In addition, once the court has appointed a counsel and defined his or her jurisdiction, it has no power to supervise or control the activities of the counsel.

Finally, we do not think that the Act "impermissibly undermine[s]" the powers of the Executive Branch, or "disrupts the proper balance between the coordinate branches [by] prevent[ing] the Executive Branch from accomplishing its constitutionally assigned functions." ... It is undeniable that the Act reduces the amount of control or supervision that the Attorney General and, through him, the President exercises over the investigation and prosecution of a certain class of alleged criminal activity. The Attorney General is not allowed to appoint the individual of his choice; he does not determine the counsel's jurisdiction; and his power to remove a counsel is limited. Nonetheless, the Act does give the Attorney General several means of supervising or controlling the prosecutorial powers that may be wielded by an independent counsel. Most importantly, the Attorney General retains the power to remove the counsel for "good cause," a power that we have already concluded provides the Executive with substantial ability to ensure that the laws are "faithfully executed" by an independent counsel. . . . **Notwithstanding the fact that the counsel is to some degree "independent" and free from executive supervision to a greater extent than other federal prosecutors, in our view these features of the Act give the Executive Branch sufficient control over the independent counsel to ensure that the President is able to perform his constitutionally assigned duties.**

In sum, we conclude today that it does not violate the Appointments Clause for Congress to vest the appointment of independent counsel in the Special Division; that the powers exercised by the Special Division under the Act do not violate Article III; and that the Act does not violate the separation-of-powers principle by impermissibly interfering with the functions of the Executive Branch. The decision of the Court of Appeals is therefore

Reversed.

Source: *Morrison v. Olson*, 487 U.S. 654 (1988).

Justice Scalia dissented in this case. He began by asserting a broad view of executive power, reminding the majority that the language of Article II—"The executive Power shall be vested in a President of the United States"—"... does not mean some of the executive power, but all of the executive power." He develops an argument in support of the "unitary executive," a view of executive power that, in his judgment, "was precisely what the Founders had in mind when they provided that all executive powers would be exercised by a single Chief Executive. . . . The President is directly dependent on the people, and since there is only one president, he is responsible. The people know whom to blame." In Scalia's view, the "[g]overnmental investigation and prosecution of crimes is quintessentially executive function." The president has ultimate control over any prosecutorial abuse that the independent counsel may exhibit and is the sole organ with the authority to remove that official. Any objection to any particular exercise of that power can be expressed politically, through the ballot box. As a curious historical irony, just a few years later, many liberal defenders of President Clinton turned to the conservative Justice Scalia's dissent in *Morrison v. Olson* when the Starr investigation became, in their judgment, a "political fishing expedition."

The Iran/Contra Affair

Final Report of the Independent Counsel Investigation

August 4, 1993

INTRODUCTION

Just a few years after Watergate, President Carter signed a package of reform measures known as the Ethics in Government Act. Among its "good government" provisions were financial disclosure requirements and lobbying restrictions. In addition, the act included provisions for the appointment of an independent special prosecutor to investigate high ranking officials in the executive branch. Under the act, the attorney general is obligated to recommend the appointment of a special prosecutor (later called an independent counsel) by a three-judge panel in the D.C. Circuit Court of Appeals when he or she has "reasonable grounds to believe" that further investigation into misconduct by public officials is warranted.

Recall that the Iran/Contra affair dealt with the arms sales to Iran in exchange for the release of hostages being held in Lebanon by Hezbollah, in violation of U.S. policy and possibly in violation of arms export control laws. The funds from those weapons sales were then diverted, illegally, to fund the Contras in Nicaragua. As the facts of Iran/Contra began to emerge in the fall of 1986, Lawrence Walsh, a lifelong Republican and prominent federal judge in "semi-retirement," was appointed independent counsel by the D.C. Circuit and charged with further investigating the growing scandal. This is an excerpt from his final report, issued in August 1993.

Volume I: Part XI

Concluding Observations

The underlying facts of Iran/contra are that, regardless of criminality, President Reagan, the secretary of state, the secretary of defense, and the director of central intelligence and their necessary assistants committed themselves, however reluctantly, to two programs contrary to congressional policy and contrary to national policy. They skirted the law, some of them broke the law, and almost all of them tried to cover up the President's willful activities.

What protection do the people of the United States have against such a concerted action by such powerful officers? The Constitution provides for congressional oversight and congressional control of appropriations, but if false information is given to Congress, these checks and balances are of lessened value. Further, in the give and take of the political community, congressional oversight is often overtaken and subordinated by the need to keep Government functioning, by the need to anticipate the future, and by the ever-present requirement of maintaining consensus among the elected officials who are the Government.

The disrespect for Congress by a popular and powerful President and his appointees was obscured when Congress accepted the tendered concept of a runaway conspiracy of subordinate officers and avoided the unpleasant confrontation with a powerful President and his Cabinet. **In haste to display and conclude its investigation of this unwelcome issue, Congress destroyed the most effective lines of inquiry by giving immunity to Oliver L. North and John M. Poindexter so that they could exculpate and eliminate the need for the testimony of President Reagan and Vice President Bush.**

In the summer of 1987, Congress had initiated its own investigations into Iran/Contra. As part of those investigations, Congress granted immunity from prosecution to both North and Poindexter, which, in the judgment of Walsh, was a key mistake. During North's testimony, which was broadcast live on national television that summer, the 43-year-old National Security Council deputy director for political and military affairs was hardly contrite. He did not implicate others in the illegal diversion of funds; rather, he lectured the investigatory committee on duty, honor, and patriotism and became a deeply polarizing figure in the whole affair.

Immunity is ordinarily given by a prosecutor to a witness who will incriminate someone more important than himself. Congress gave immunity to North and Poindexter, who incriminated only themselves and who largely exculpated those responsible for the initiation, supervision and support of their activities. This delayed and infinitely complicated the effort to prosecute North and Poindexter, and it largely destroyed the likelihood that their prompt conviction and appropriate sentence would induce meaningful cooperation.

These important political decisions were properly the responsibility of Congress. It was for the Committees to decide whether the welfare of the nation was served or endangered by a continuation of its investigation, a more deliberate effort to test the self-serving denials presented by Cabinet officers and to search for the full ramifications of the activities in question. Having made this decision, however, no one could gainsay the added difficulties thrust upon Independent Counsel. These difficulties could be dealt with only by the investment of large amounts of additional time and large amounts of expense.

... The investigation into Iran/contra nevertheless demonstrates that the rule of law upon which our democratic system of government depends can be applied to the highest officials even when they are operating in the secret areas of diplomacy and national security.

Despite extraordinary difficulties imposed by the destruction and withholding of records, the need to protect classified information, and the congressional grants of immunity to some of the principals involved, Independent Counsel was able to bring criminal charges against nine government officers and five private citizens involved in illegal activities growing out of the Iran/contra affair.

When, in 1984, Congress strengthened the Boland Amendment to prohibit any funding of the Contras in Nicaragua, Reagan told National Security Adviser Robert McFarlane, "I want you to do whatever you have to do to help these people (the Contras) keep body and soul together." In response to the president's admonition, North, along with a number of other key advisers, established a Contra supply network in violation of U.S. law. A secret web of private individual funders and shadowy financial systems emerged. Several key pieces of evidence were uncovered that directly linked the arms sales to Iran and the funding of the Contras. One was a memo prepared for the president in 1986. The memo said that the $12 million received from the sale of the weapons "will be used to purchase critically needed supplies for the Nicaraguan Democratic Resistance Forces." It was the "smoking gun" of the investigation. However, Walsh and others could not find evidence that North's memo was actually seen by the president, even though it was attached to a document the president signed. The shadowy network of private financing had been approved by Reagan, and in fact, letters soliciting private financing for the Contras were sent on White House letterhead.

More importantly, **the investigation and the prosecutions arising out of it have provided a much more accurate picture of how two secret Administration policies—keeping the contras alive "body and soul" during the Boland cut-off period and seeking the release of Americans held hostage by selling arms to Iran—veered off into criminality.**

Evidence obtained by Independent Counsel establishes that the Iran/contra affair was not an aberrational scheme carried out by a "cabal of zealots" on the National Security Council staff, as the congressional Select Committees concluded in their majority report. Instead, it was the product of two foreign policy directives by President Reagan which skirted the law and which were executed by the NSC staff with the knowledge and support of high officials in the CIA, State and Defense departments, and to a lesser extent, officials in other agencies.

Independent Counsel found no evidence of dissent among his Cabinet officers from the President's determination to support the contras after federal law banned the use of appropriated funds for that purpose in the Boland Amendment in October 1984. Even the two Cabinet officers who opposed the sale of arms to Iran on the grounds that it was illegal and bad policy—Defense Secretary Caspar W. Weinberger and Secretary of State George P. Shultz—either cooperated with the decision once made, as in the case of Weinberger, or stood aloof from it while being kept informed of its progress, as was the case of Shultz.

In its report section titled "Who Was Responsible," the Select Committees named CIA Director William Casey, National Security Advisers Robert C. McFarlane and John M. Poindexter, along with NSC staff member Oliver L. North, and private sector operatives Richard V. Secord and Albert Hakim. With the exception of Casey who died before he could be questioned by the OIC, Independent Counsel charged and obtained criminal convictions of each of the men named by Congress. There is little doubt that, operationally, these men were central players.

But the investigation and prosecutions have shown that these six were not out-of-control mavericks who acted alone without the knowledge or assistance of others. The evidence establishes that the central NSC operatives kept their superiors—including Reagan, Bush, Shultz, Weinberger and other high officials—informed of their efforts generally, if not in detail, and their superiors either condoned or turned a blind eye to them. When it was required, the NSC principals and their private sector operatives received the assistance of high-ranking officers in the CIA, the Defense Department, and the Department of State.

Of the 14 persons charged criminally during the investigation, four were convicted of felony charges after trial by jury, seven pleaded guilty either to felonies or misdemeanors, and one had his case dismissed because the Administration refused to declassify information deemed necessary to the defendant by the trial judge. Two cases that were awaiting trial were aborted by pardons granted by President Bush. As this report explained earlier, many persons who committed crimes were not charged. Some minor crimes were never investigated and some that were investigated were not solved. But Independent Counsel believes that to the extent possible, the central Iran/contra crimes were vigorously prosecuted and the significant acts of obstruction were fully charged.

Like the Tower Commission, the Walsh investigation found that the Reagan administration was involved in a determined effort to keep the Contras financed during a time when Congress had explicitly cut off military aid. As North's immunized testimony suggests, this was a fight against communism and the White House was not going to let Congress tell them how to wage that fight. If it meant deceiving Congress, "so be it," they seemed to feel. Between March and June 1986, at least nine arms shipments were delivered to the Contras in direct violation of the Boland Amendment. In a message on May 15, 1986, National Security Adviser John Poindexter instructed North to lie to Congress: "From now on," he wrote, "I don't want you to talk to anybody else... about your operational roles. In fact, you need to generate a cover story that I have insisted that you stop." Right after receiving that memo, North appeared before the House Intelligence Committee and denied any involvement in military operations or fundraising for the Contras. Then, once the Hasenfus plane went down that fall, North began the cover-up by destroying documents that would implicate the White House.

When former National Security Adviser Robert McFarlane testified before Congress, he said that as soon as the link between the White House and the supply plane was discovered, he and other in the White House began to erect a "firewall" to insulate the administration and in particular the president from being implicated. North testified that CIA director William Casey (who died during the investigations into Iran/Contra) instructed him to destroy all evidence of the arms deal. Consequently, the destruction of evidence began as key documents were altered or shredded. According to McFarlane, the objective was to rewrite the events in an effort to "distance the President from the initial approval of the arms sale." For his part, Reagan remained unable to recall his awareness of the events. As the Walsh Report concludes (in Chapter 27): "[b]y July 1992, when Reagan agreed to a final, extensive interview with Independent Counsel, it was obvious that the former President truly lacked specific recollection of even the major Iran/contra events which took place in 1984–1987."

Fundamentally, the Iran/contra affair was the first known criminal assault on the post-Watergate rules governing the activities of national security officials. Reagan Administration officials rendered these rules ineffective by creating private operations, supported with privately generated funds that successfully evaded executive and legislative oversight and control. Congress was defrauded. Its appropriations restrictions having been circumvented, Congress was led to believe that the Administration was following the law. Numerous congressional inquiries were thwarted through false testimony and the destruction and concealment of government records.

The destruction and concealment of records and information, beginning at the twilight of Iran/contra and continuing throughout subsequent investigations, should be of particular concern.... In the course of his work, Independent Counsel located large caches of handwritten notes and other documents maintained by high officials that were never relinquished to investigators. Major aspects of Iran/contra would never have been uncovered had all of the officials who attempted to destroy or withhold their records of the affair succeeded.

. . .

All of this conduct—the evasions of the Executive branch and the Congress, the lies, the conspiracies, the acts of obstruction—had to be addressed by the criminal justice system.

The path Independent Counsel embarked upon in late 1986 has been a long and arduous one. When he hired 10 attorneys in early 1987, Independent Counsel's conception of the operational conspiracy—with its array of Government officials and private contractors, its web of secret foreign accounts, and its world-wide breadth—was extremely hazy. Outlining an investigation of a runaway conspiracy disavowed by the President was quite different from the ultimate investigation of the President and three major agencies, each with the power to frustrate an investigation by persisting in the classification of non-secret but embarrassing information. Completing the factual mosaic required examining pieces spread worldwide in activities that occurred over a three-year period by officials from the largest agencies of government and a host of private operatives who, by necessity, design and training, worked secretly and deceptively.

Source: Walsh, Lawrence E. *Final Report of the Independent Counsel for Iran-Contra Matters*, Vol. 1 (Washington, DC: GPO, 1993).

The Paula Jones Case

Clinton v. Jones

May 27, 1997

INTRODUCTION

William Jefferson Clinton was elected president in 1992. Prior to his election, Clinton was governor of the State of Arkansas. On May 8, 1991, Governor Clinton delivered a speech at a conference in Little Rock. On that day, Paula Jones was working at the registration desk of the hotel where the governor spoke. Ms. Jones alleged that a security officer for the governor took her to visit Clinton in a private room in the hotel, where he made sexual advances that she rejected. Upon rejecting his overtures, she claimed that her supervisors at the hotel punished her for spurning the governor. When Clinton was elected president, Ms. Jones claimed that she was further harmed by public statements made by Clinton's former staffer that mischaracterized her involvement in the incident. She sought almost $200,000 in civil damages from the president. The question before the court in this case was whether a sitting president could be sued for civil damages for actions taken either before the person became president or for conduct that was unrelated to the individual's official responsibilities. Clinton had argued that due to the many obligations and responsibilities of the office of the president, the courts should grant a deferral of the litigation until the end of his term in office. Justice Stevens, writing for a unanimous court, disagreed.

STEVENS, J., Opinion of the Court

This case raises a constitutional and a prudential question concerning the Office of the President of the United States. Respondent, a private citizen, seeks to recover damages from the current occupant of that office based on actions allegedly taken before his term began. The President submits that in all but the most exceptional cases the Constitution requires federal courts to defer such litigation until his term ends and that, in any event, respect for the office warrants such a stay. Despite the force of the arguments supporting the President's submissions, we conclude that they must be rejected.

. . .

While our decision to grant the petition expressed no judgment concerning the merits of the case, it does reflect our appraisal of its importance. The representations made

on behalf of the Executive Branch as to the potential impact
of the precedent established by the Court of Appeals merit
our respectful and deliberate consideration.

Petitioner's (Clinton's) principal submission—that "in all but
the most exceptional cases," the Constitution affords the
President temporary immunity from civil damages litigation
arising out of events that occurred before he took office—
cannot be sustained on the basis of precedent.

Only three sitting Presidents have been defendants in
civil litigation involving their actions prior to taking office.
Complaints against Theodore Roosevelt and Harry Truman
had been dismissed before they took office; the dismissals
were affirmed after their respective inaugurations. Two
companion cases arising out of an automobile accident were
filed against John F. Kennedy in 1960 during the Presidential
campaign. . . . The motion for a stay was denied by the District Court, and the matter was settled out of court. **Thus,
none of those cases sheds any light on the constitutional
issue before us.**

The reason the Paula Jones civil suit is different, the court reasons, is because (1) the
actions occurred prior to Clinton taking
office and (2) were outside of his official
capacity as president. Insofar as those conditions hold, the president enjoys no special
immunity from suit in civil litigation. The
court, therefore, establishes an important
principle in this case: immunity from civil
suits is "grounded in 'the nature of the function performed, not the identity of the actor
who performed it.' "

The principal rationale for affording certain public servants
immunity from suits for money damages arising out of their
official acts is inapplicable to unofficial conduct. In cases
involving prosecutors, legislators, and judges we have repeatedly explained that the immunity serves the public interest in
enabling such officials to perform their designated functions
effectively without fear that a particular decision may give rise
to personal liability. https://www.law.cornell.edu/supreme
court/text/520/681 - ZO-520_US_681n18.

That rationale provided the principal basis for our holding
that a former President of the United States was "entitled to
absolute immunity from damages liability predicated on his
official acts," (in Nixon v. Fitzgerald). Our central concern
was to avoid rendering the President "unduly cautious in
the discharge of his official duties."

This reasoning provides no support for an immunity for unofficial conduct. As we explained in Fitzgerald, "the sphere of

protected action must be related closely to the immunity's justifying purposes." Because of the President's broad responsibilities, we recognized in that case an immunity from damages claims arising out of official acts extending to the "outer perimeter of his authority." But we have never suggested that the President, or any other official, has an immunity that extends beyond the scope of any action taken in an official capacity. Moreover, when defining the scope of an immunity for acts clearly taken within an official capacity, we have applied a functional approach. "Frequently our decisions have held that an official's absolute immunity should extend only to acts in performance of particular functions of his office.". . .

Petitioner's effort to construct an immunity from suit for unofficial acts grounded purely in the identity of his office is unsupported by precedent.

With respect to acts taken in his "public character"—that is official acts—the President may be disciplined principally by impeachment, not by private lawsuits for damages. But he is otherwise subject to the laws for his purely private acts.

Petitioner's strongest argument supporting his immunity claim is based on the text and structure of the Constitution. He does not contend that the occupant of the Office of the President is "above the law," in the sense that his conduct is entirely immune from judicial scrutiny. The President argues merely for a postponement of the judicial proceedings that will determine whether he violated any law. His argument is grounded in the character of the office that was created by Article II of the Constitution, and relies on separation of powers principles that have structured our constitutional arrangement since the founding.

As a starting premise, petitioner contends that he occupies a unique office with powers and responsibilities so vast and important that the public interest demands that he devote his undivided time and attention to his public duties. He submits that—given the nature of the office—the doctrine of separation of powers places limits on the authority of the

Federal Judiciary to interfere with the Executive Branch that
would be transgressed by allowing this action to proceed.

. . .

As a factual matter, petitioner contends that this particular
case—as well as the potential additional litigation that
an affirmance of the Court of Appeals judgment might
spawn—may impose an unacceptable burden on the President's time and energy, and thereby impair the effective
performance of his office.

Petitioner's predictive judgment finds little support in either
history or the relatively narrow compass of the issues raised
in this particular case. As we have already noted, in the more
than 200 year history of the Republic, only three sitting Presidents have been subjected to suits for their private actions.
**If the past is any indicator, it seems unlikely that a deluge
of such litigation will ever engulf the Presidency. As for
the case at hand, if properly managed by the District
Court, it appears to us highly unlikely to occupy any substantial amount of petitioner's time.**

. . .

In sum, "[i]t is settled law that the separation of powers
doctrine does not bar every exercise of jurisdiction over
the President of the United States." Fitzgerald, 457 U. S., at
753-754. If the Judiciary may severely burden the Executive
Branch by reviewing the legality of the President's official conduct, and if it may direct appropriate process to the President
himself, it must follow that the federal courts have power to
determine the legality of his unofficial conduct. The burden
on the President's time and energy that is a mere by product
of such review surely cannot be considered as onerous as the
direct burden imposed by judicial review and the occasional
invalidation of his official actions. We therefore hold that
the doctrine of separation of powers does not require federal
courts to stay all private actions against the President until he
leaves office.

One might be inclined to say that the court
got it wrong on this point; that Justice Stevens and the others completely misjudged
the consequences of their ruling in this case.
To be fair, however, the court could hardly
have envisioned Clinton's actions that followed its ruling. As a direct result of this
decision, the civil suit against Clinton (in
the case of *Jones v. Clinton*) was allowed to
proceed. The federal judge in that case dismissed the sexual harassment lawsuit against
Clinton. However, prior to its dismissal, one
of the witnesses in *Jones v. Clinton*, Monica
Lewinsky, denied having a sexual relationship with Clinton. It was later revealed that
she had indeed been intimate with Clinton.
Those revelations led the independent counsel Ken Starr, who had been investigating a
series of other allegations against the Clintons, to pursue perjury and obstruction of
justice charges for Clinton's deposition in
the Paula Jones case. Those charges led to
House impeachment proceedings.

. . .

A similar concern was levied against the reauthorization of the independent counsel law, which was allowed to expire in 1999, after the Clinton impeachment proceedings.

We add a final comment on two matters that are discussed at length in the briefs: **the risk that our decision will generate a large volume of politically motivated harassing and frivolous litigation,** and the danger that national security concerns might prevent the President from explaining a legitimate need for a continuance.

We are not persuaded that either of these risks is serious. Most frivolous and vexatious litigation is terminated at the pleading stage or on summary judgment, with little if any personal involvement by the defendant. Moreover, the availability of sanctions provides a significant deterrent to litigation directed at the President in his unofficial capacity for purposes of political gain or harassment. History indicates that the likelihood that a significant number of such cases will be filed is remote. [And, as to the second risk] [s]everal Presidents, including petitioner, have given testimony without jeopardizing the Nation's security. In short, we have confidence in the ability of our federal judges to deal with both of these concerns.

If Congress deems it appropriate to afford the President stronger protection, it may respond with appropriate legislation.

Accordingly, the judgment of the Court of Appeals is affirmed.

It is so ordered.

Source: *Clinton v. Jones*, 520 U.S. 681 (1997).

The Line Item Veto

Clinton v. City of New York

June 25, 1998

INTRODUCTION

As we've seen in *Morrison v. Olson, INS v. Chadha, Bowsher v. Synar,* and other similar cases, balancing the tension between preserving a clear separation of powers among the branches of government while at the same time recognizing that the branches must often share powers has been difficult. This case, *Clinton v. City of New York* (1998), in which the court struck down the Line Item Veto Act provides yet another perspective on the court's attempt to strike that balance, even as one of the institutions (Congress) ceded qualified budgetary authority to the president.

In *Bowsher v. Synar* (1986), the court ruled that giving the comptroller general budget-cutting authority violated the separation of powers. In that case, Chief Justice Burger reasoned that because the comptroller general took actions that were executive in nature (implementing budget cuts under the Gramm-Rudman-Hollings Deficit Control Act), and because only Congress could remove that official, Gramm-Rudman-Hollings gave Congress a congressional veto of executive action in violation of the principle established in *Chadha* (the legislative veto case). As an alternative budget-cutting measure, the new Republican majority in Congress passed and President Clinton signed the Line Item Veto Act. Under the act, the president could strike specific lines from appropriations bills passed by Congress without having to veto the whole bill. Specifically, the act gave the president the power to strike three types of provisions: "any dollar amount of discretionary budget authority; any item of new direct spending; or any limited tax benefit." Just weeks after it went into effect, President Clinton used the line item veto to strike lines from two pieces of legislation: one line item veto struck new direct spending for New York and the other vetoed a limited tax benefit for the Snake River Potato Growers cooperative.

JUSTICE STEVENS delivered the opinion of the Court.

The Line Item Veto Act . . . requires the President to adhere to precise procedures whenever he exercises his cancellation authority. In identifying items for cancellation he must consider the legislative history, the purposes, and other relevant information about the items. He must determine, with respect to each cancellation, that it will "(i) reduce the Federal budget deficit; (ii) not impair any essential Government functions; and (iii) not harm the national interest." Moreover, he must transmit a special message to Congress notifying it of each cancellation within five calendar days (excluding Sundays) after the enactment of the canceled provision. It is undisputed that the President meticulously followed these procedures in these cases.

In both legal and practical effect, the President has amended two Acts of Congress by repealing a portion of each. "[R]epeal of statutes, no less than enactment, must conform with Art. I." INS v. Chadha (1983). There is no provision in the Constitution that authorizes the President to enact, to amend, or to repeal statutes. Both Article I and Article II assign responsibilities to the President that directly relate to the lawmaking process, but neither addresses the issue presented by these cases. The President "shall from time to time give to the Congress Information on the State of the Union, and recommend to their Consideration such Measures as he shall judge necessary and expedient . . . ." Art. II, Sect. 3. Thus, he may initiate and influence legislative proposals. Moreover, after a bill has passed both Houses of Congress, but "before it become[s] a Law," it must be presented to the President. If he approves it, "he shall sign it, but if not he shall return it, with his Objections to that House in which it shall have originated, who shall enter the Objections at large on their Journal, and proceed to reconsider it." Art. I, Sect. 7, cl. 2.

His "return" of a bill, which is usually described as a "veto," is subject to being overridden by a two-thirds vote in each House.

There are important differences between the President's "return" of a bill pursuant to Article I, and the exercise of the President's cancellation authority pursuant to the Line Item Veto Act. The constitutional return takes place before the bill becomes law; the statutory cancellation occurs after the bill becomes law. The constitutional return is of the entire bill; the statutory cancellation is of only a part. Although the Constitution expressly authorizes the President to play a role in the process of enacting statutes, it is silent on the subject of unilateral Presidential action that either repeals or amends parts of duly enacted statutes.

There are powerful reasons for construing constitutional silence on this profoundly important issue as equivalent to an express prohibition. The procedures governing the enactment of statutes set forth in the text of Article I were the product of the great debates and compromises that produced the Constitution itself. Familiar historical materials provide abundant support for the conclusion that the power to enact statutes may only "be exercised in accord with a single, finely wrought and exhaustively considered, procedure." Chadha, 462 U.S., at 951.

What has emerged in these cases from the President's exercise of his statutory cancellation powers, however, are truncated versions of two bills that passed both Houses of Congress. They are not the product of the "finely wrought" procedure that the Framers designed.

. . .

The Line Item Veto Act authorizes the President himself to effect the repeal of laws, for his own policy reasons, without observing the procedures set out in Article I, Sect. 7. The fact that Congress intended such a result is of no moment. Although Congress presumably anticipated that the President might cancel some of the items in the Balanced Budget Act and in the Taxpayer Relief Act, Congress cannot alter the procedures set out in Article I, Sect. 7, without amending the Constitution.

Neither are we persuaded by the Government's contention that the President's authority to cancel new direct spending and tax benefit items is no greater than his traditional authority to decline to spend appropriated funds. The Government has reviewed in some detail the series of statutes in which Congress has given the Executive broad discretion over the expenditure of appropriated funds. . . . **In those statutes, as in later years, the President was given wide discretion with respect to both the amounts to be spent and how the money would be allocated among different functions. It is argued that the Line Item Veto Act merely confers comparable discretionary authority over the expenditure of appropriated funds.** The critical difference between this

It is useful to compare the court's view of the constitutionality of the line item veto with the actions that presidents since James Monroe have taken with respect to presidential signing statements. Does the "constitutional silence" Stevens describes with respect to the line item veto then mean that constitutional objections in signing statements are similarly prohibited? Like the line item veto, signing statements appear to strike specific provisions of statutes; however, they are qualitatively different. Though they are compiled in the legislative history, signing statements reflect presidential preference and interpretation rather than explicit vetoes of those offending provisions. The court has never taken up the issue of the constitutionality of signing statements.

This was a key point raised in the dissent in this case. Justice Breyer, O'Connor, and Scalia wrote that there is "not a dime's worth of difference between Congress authorizing the President to cancel a spending item, and Congress's authorizing money to be spent on a particular item at the President's discretion." They point to the *J. W. Hampton & Co. v. United States* case, in which the court determined that delegations of discretion by Congress to the executive are permissible so long as Congress lays down an "intelligible principle" to which the president is expected to conform in taking discretionary actions. By their reasoning, the Lime Item Veto Act was far more clear in its guidelines than many other grants of discretion that the court has upheld since the *J. W. Hampton* case.

statute and all of its predecessors, however, is that unlike any of them, this Act gives the President the unilateral power to change the text of duly enacted statutes. None of the Act's predecessors could even arguably have been construed to authorize such a change.

. . .

[O]ur decision rests on the narrow ground that the procedures authorized by the Line Item Veto Act are not authorized by the Constitution. The Balanced Budget Act of 1997 is a 500-page document that became "Public Law 105-33" after three procedural steps were taken: (1) a bill containing its exact text was approved by a majority of the Members of the House of Representatives; (2) the Senate approved precisely the same text; and (3) that text was signed into law by the President. The Constitution explicitly requires that each of those three steps be taken before a bill may "become a law." Art. I, Sect. 7. If one paragraph of that text had been omitted at any one of those three stages, Public Law 105-33 would not have been validly enacted. If the Line Item Veto Act were valid, it would authorize the President to create a different law—one whose text was not voted on by either House of Congress or presented to the President for signature. Something that might be known as "Public Law 105-33 as modified by the President" may or may not be desirable, but it is surely not a document that may "become a law" pursuant to the procedures designed by the Framers of Article I, Sect. 7, of the Constitution.

If there is to be a new procedure in which the President will play a different role in determining the final text of what may "become a law," such change must come not by legislation but through the amendment procedures set forth in Article V of the Constitution. The judgment of the District Court is affirmed.

Source: *Clinton v. City of New York*, 524 U.S. 417 (1998).

Impeachment of President Clinton

House of Representatives Trial Memorandum

January 11, 1999

INTRODUCTION

In December 1998, the House of Representatives passed two articles of impeachment against President Clinton, one for perjury and the other for obstruction of justice. The adoption of those articles of impeachment was the culmination of a series of investigations related to, but extending beyond, the Paula Jones case. In fact, the president and Mrs. Clinton had been under investigation by an independent counsel for most of his presidency. The first federal investigations began in the summer of 1993, soon after Clinton took office. Travelgate involved a series of inquiries into allegations that Clinton had fired long-serving employees in the White House travel office in order to replace them with friends of the Clintons from their days in Arkansas. That ethics investigation was quickly followed by another inquiry into the death of deputy White House counsel and Clinton's close friend, Vince Foster. Within hours of Foster's death, and before federal investigators were admitted, White House staffers entered his office. Speculation arose that the staffers had illegally removed documents from his office that had bearing on the Clintons' role in Whitewater. In the late 1970s, Bill and Clinton cofounded Whitewater Development Corporation. Their partner in that venture, James McDougal, subsequently founded a small savings and loan company. That company struggled and came under the scrutiny of federal regulators for financial improprieties, including providing funding to pay off the debt from one of Bill Clinton's campaigns for governor. McDougal turned to Hillary Clinton's law firm for assistance. When the savings and loan was shut down by the federal government in 1989, federal investigators discovered that the Clintons may have been beneficiaries of the company's illegal financial practices. After growing concern over the Clintons' involvement in the affair, Attorney General Janet Reno authorized an investigation into Whitewater. Soon after the investigation began, a high-ranking Department of Justice official with ties to Hillary Clinton's old Arkansas law firm, Webster Hubbell, abruptly resigned amid speculation that he was involved in the growing scandal. Another friend of the Clintons, Vernon Jordan, helped provide financial support for Hubbell while he was under investigation. Vernon Jordan would later become the linchpin to the full investigation that ultimately led to the impeachment of President Clinton.

During the Whitewater investigation, Republicans in Congress became dismayed with the pace and vigor of the investigation under the moderate Republican special counsel assigned to the matter by Reno. In response, they renewed the Independent Counsel law and appointed Kenneth Starr to take over the investigation. His investigation expanded beyond Whitewater upon revelations of Monica Lewinsky's suspected perjury in the Paula Jones case. Starr petitioned for his inquiry into Whitewater to include the possibility that the president committed perjury and obstructed justice once it was learned that Vernon Jordan provided Ms. Lewinsky (who had been an unpaid intern) assistance in finding a job outside of the White House. Starr suspected that the arrangement was brokered by Jordan on the president's behalf in exchange for Lewinsky's false testimony in the Paula Jones case. The broader investigation eventually led to the two articles of impeachment—neither of which had anything to do with Travelgate, Vince Foster, or Whitewater.

IN THE SENATE OF THE UNITED STATES

Sitting as a Court of Impeachment

In Re Impeachment of President William Jefferson Clinton

TRIAL MEMORANDUM OF THE

UNITED STATES HOUSE OF REPRESENTATIVES

> **Now comes the United States House of Representatives, by and through its duly authorized Managers, and respectfully submits to the United States Senate its Brief in connection with the Impeachment Trial of William Jefferson Clinton, President of the United States.**

SUMMARY

The President is charged in two Articles with: 1) Perjury and false and misleading testimony and statements under oath before a federal grand jury (Article I), and 2) engaging in a course of conduct or scheme to delay and obstruct justice (Article II).

The evidence contained in the record, when viewed as a unified whole, overwhelmingly supports both charges.

Perjury and False Statements Under Oath

President Clinton deliberately and willfully testified falsely under oath when he appeared before a federal grand jury on August 17, 1998. Although what follows is not exhaustive, some of the more overt examples will serve to illustrate.

At the very outset, the President read a prepared statement, which itself contained totally false assertions and other clearly misleading information.

The President relied on his statement nineteen times in his testimony when questioned about his relationship with Ms. Lewinsky.

The Constitution requires that presidents and other officials can only be impeached for "treason, bribery, and other high crimes and misdemeanors." But it is for Congress to determine what actions amount to impeachable offenses in particular cases. Impeachment proceedings begin when the House of Representatives votes to adopt article(s) of impeachment. At that stage, all that is required is a simple majority. Once the House votes to impeach the president, the Senate hears the case, with the chief justice of the Supreme Court presiding over the trial. Two-thirds of the Senate must vote "guilty" in order to convict.

President Clinton falsely testified that he was not paying attention when his lawyer employed Ms. Lewinsky's false affidavit at the Jones deposition.

He falsely claimed that his actions with Ms. Lewinsky did not fall within the definition of "sexual relations" that was given at his deposition.

He falsely testified that he answered questions truthfully at his deposition concerning, among other subjects, whether he had been alone with Ms. Lewinsky.

He falsely testified that he instructed Ms. Lewinsky to turn over the gifts if she were subpoenaed.

He falsely denied trying to influence Ms. Currie after his deposition.

Betty Currie was Clinton's personal secretary.

He falsely testified that he was truthful to his aides when he gave accounts of his relationship, which accounts were subsequently disseminated to the media and the grand jury.

Obstruction of Justice

The President engaged in an ongoing scheme to obstruct both the Jones civil case and the grand jury. Further, he undertook a continuing and concerted plan to tamper with witnesses and prospective witnesses for the purpose of causing those witnesses to provide false and misleading testimony. Examples abound:

The President and Ms. Lewinsky concocted a cover story to conceal their relationship, and the President suggested that she employ that story if subpoenaed in the Jones case.

The President suggested that Ms. Lewinsky provide an affidavit to avoid testifying in the Jones case, when he knew that the affidavit would need to be false to accomplish its purpose.

The President knowingly and willfully allowed his attorney to file Ms. Lewinsky's false affidavit and to use it for the purpose of obstructing justice in the Jones case.

The President suggested to Ms. Lewinsky that she provide a false account of how she received her job at the Pentagon.

The President attempted to influence the expected testimony of his secretary, Ms. Currie, by providing her with a false account of his meetings with Ms. Lewinsky.

The President provided several of his top aides with elaborate lies about his relationship with Ms. Lewinsky, so that those aides would convey the false information to the public and to the grand jury. When he did this, he knew that those aides would likely be called to testify, while he was declining several invitations to testify. By this action, he obstructed and delayed the operation of the grand jury.

The President conspired with Ms. Lewinsky and Ms. Currie to conceal evidence that he had been subpoenaed in the Jones case, and thereby delayed and obstructed justice.

The President and his representatives orchestrated a campaign to discredit Ms. Lewinsky in order to affect adversely her credibility as a witness, and thereby attempted to obstruct justice both in the Jones case and the grand jury.

The President lied repeatedly under oath in his deposition in the Jones case, and thereby obstructed justice in that case.

The President's lies and misleading statements under oath at the grand jury were calculated to, and did obstruct, delay and prevent the due administration of justice by that body.

The President employed the power of his office to procure a job for Ms. Lewinsky after she signed the false affidavit by causing his friend to exert extraordinary efforts for that purpose.

The foregoing are merely accusations of an ongoing pattern of obstruction of justice, and witness tampering extending over a period of several months, and having the effect of seriously compromising the integrity of the entire judicial system.

The effect of the President's misconduct has been devastating in several respects.

1) He violated repeatedly his oath to "preserve, protect and defend the Constitution of the United States."

2) He ignored his constitutional duty as chief law enforcement officer to "take care that the laws be faithfully executed."

3) He deliberately and unlawfully obstructed Paula Jones's rights as a citizen to due process and the equal protection of the laws, though he had sworn to protect those rights.

4) By his pattern of lies under oath, misleading statements and deceit, he has seriously undermined the integrity and credibility of the Office of President and thereby the honor and integrity of the United States.

5) His pattern of perjuries, obstruction of justice, and witness tampering has affected the truth seeking process which is the foundation of our legal system.

6) By mounting an assault in the truth seeking process, he has attacked the entire Judicial Branch of government.

The Articles of Impeachment that the House has preferred state offenses that warrant, if proved, the conviction and removal from office of President William Jefferson Clinton. The Articles charge that the President has committed perjury before a federal grand jury and that he obstructed justice in a federal civil rights action. **The Senate's own precedents establish beyond doubt that perjury warrants conviction and removal. During the 1980s, the Senate convicted and removed three federal**

Judge Harry Claiborne was impeached and removed in 1986 for income tax evasion; Judge Walter Nixon was convicted of lying to a federal grand jury and removed in 1989; and Judge Alcee Hastings, though acquitted of criminal charges, was impeached and removed in 1989. Each was a federal district judge.

> **judges for committing perjury. Obstruction of justice undermines the judicial system in the same fashion that perjury does, and it also warrants conviction and removal.**

Under our Constitution, judges are impeached under the same standard as Presidents—treason, bribery, or other high crimes and misdemeanors. Thus, these judicial impeachments for perjury set the standard here. Finally, the Senate's own precedents further establish that the President's crimes need not arise directly out of his official duties. Two of the three judges removed in the 1980s were removed for perjury that had nothing to do with their official duties.

INTRODUCTION

This Brief is intended solely to advise the Senate generally of the evidence that the Managers intend to produce, if permitted, and of the applicable legal principles. It is not intended to discuss exhaustively all of the evidence, nor does it necessarily include each and every witness and document that the Managers would produce in the course of the trial. This Brief, then, is merely an outline for the use of the Senate in reviewing and assessing the evidence as it is set forth at trial—it is not, and is not intended to be a substitute for a trial at which all of the relevant facts will be developed.

H. RES. 611, 105th Cong. 2nd Sess. (1998).

The House Impeachment Resolution charges the President with high crimes and misdemeanors in two Articles. Article One alleges that President Clinton "willfully corrupted and manipulated the judicial process of the United States for his personal gain and exoneration, impeding the administration of justice" in that he willfully provided perjurious, false and misleading testimony to a federal grand jury on August 17, 1998. Article Two asserts that the President "has prevented, obstructed, and impeded the administration of justice and engaged in a course of conduct or scheme designed to delay, impede, cover up, and conceal the existence of evidence and testimony related to a federal civil rights action brought against him." **Both Articles are now before the Senate of the United States for trial as provided by the Constitution of the United States.**

The Office of President represents to the American people and to the world, the strength, the philosophy and most of all, the honor and integrity that makes us a great nation and an example for the world. Because all eyes are focused upon that high office, the character and credibility of any temporary occupant of the Oval Office is vital to the domestic and foreign welfare of the citizens. Consequently, serious breaches of integrity and duty of necessity adversely influence the reputation of the United States.

This case is not about sex or private conduct. It is about multiple obstructions of justice, perjury, false and misleading statements, and witness tampering—all committed or orchestrated by the President of the United States.

Source: U.S. House of Representatives, Trial Memorandum, January 11, 1999. In Congressional Record, January 14, 1999 (Washington, DC: Government Printing Office), S63.

Until the 1930s, voting on impeachment in the Senate proceeded in two stages. First, Senators would vote "guilty" or "not guilty" on each of the charges. Then, at the second stage, the Senate would vote whether or not to remove the official from office. That two-stage process would permit the Senate to determine that the person was guilty, but decline to remove the person from office. After the 1930s, however, the two-step process was consolidated into only one step. That shift in procedural rules meant that Senators who may have thought that Clinton was guilty of perjury or obstruction of justice—but also thought that he should not be removed from office—were forced to vote "not guilty." On February 12, 1998, the Senate voted on these two articles of impeachment brought by the House and acquitted the president on both, falling well short of the two-thirds requirement.

Responding to 9/11

Authorization for Use of Military Force
September 18, 2001

INTRODUCTION

On September 11, 2001, terrorists connected to al-Qaeda flew planes into the World Trade Center in New York City and the Pentagon in Alexandria, VA. Within days, President George W. Bush declared a "war on terror." This was an important step toward consolidating presidential power in a time of threats to the nation's security. Other nations where similar terrorist attacks had occurred, such as Great Britain and Spain, had labeled terrorists' attacks as crimes, punishable under existing criminal law. By labeling the attacks on New York and the Pentagon as acts of war, President Bush was able to draw upon broad emergency powers in order to defend the country in the Global War on Terror. Many of the subsequent chapters in this volume trace their origins to this moment. The decision to engage terrorism militarily (and for an unlimited amount of time) rather than through the existing criminal codes gave rise to an expansive array of presidential powers that remains with us today. Many have argued that President Bush's actions in this war on terror violated fundamental principles of the rule of law in both the international and domestic contexts—in addition to violations of the separation of powers and individual liberty guaranteed by the U.S. Constitution. By relying on a vast reserve of inherent powers in addition to his role as commander in chief, Bush was able to centralize and insulate executive authority—outside the reach of Congress—consistent with the unitary executive thesis described earlier. And when Congress did act, it was generally in deference to the will of the president. Three days after 9/11, Congress passed—without substantive review—legislation drafted by the White House giving the president broad powers. The Authorization for Use of Military Force (AUMF) passed the House by a vote of 420-1 and 98-0 in the Senate. President Bush signed the legislation on September 18.

Joint Resolution

To authorize the use of United States Armed Forces against those responsible for the recent attacks launched against the United States.

Whereas, on September 11, 2001, acts of treacherous violence were committed against the United States and its citizens; and

Whereas, such acts render it both necessary and appropriate that the United States exercise its rights to self-defense and to protect United States citizens both at home and abroad; and

Whereas, in light of the threat to the national security and foreign policy of the United States posed by these grave acts of violence; and

Whereas, such acts continue to pose an unusual and extraordinary threat to the national security and foreign policy of the United States; and

Whereas, the President has authority under the Constitution to take action to deter and prevent acts of international terrorism against the United States: Now, therefore, be it

Resolved by the Senate and House of Representatives of the United States of America in Congress assembled,

SECTION 1. SHORT TITLE. This joint resolution may be cited as the "Authorization for Use of Military Force".

SEC. 2. AUTHORIZATION FOR USE OF UNITED STATES ARMED FORCES.

(a) IN GENERAL.—**That the President is authorized to use all necessary and appropriate force against those nations, organizations, or persons he determines planned, authorized, committed, or aided the terrorist attacks that occurred on September 11, 2001, or harbored such organizations or persons, in order to prevent any future acts of international terrorism against the United States by such nations, organizations or persons.**

This resolution grants the president broad discretion to take powers typically reserved for chief executives during wartime. You will note that there are two important dimensions to this broad grant of authority. First, it gives the president the authority "to use all necessary and appropriate force" against those who he determines participated in the attacks on 9/11. In a rare instance of congressional pushback, Congress rejected language drafted by Bush's staff that added "in the United States" to that sentence. Had Congress acquiesced on that, they would have authorized military action in the domestic context as well. The second dimension authorizes the president to take actions "in order to prevent any future acts" of terrorism. Given that the war on terror was of an unknown duration, these two prongs of the AUMF give exceptional discretionary power to the president. Congressional passage of the AUMF, along with Bush's view of his constitutional authority and inherent power in the fight against global terrorism, were subsequently employed quite broadly to justify the harnessing of executive powers that followed September 11.

(b) WAR POWERS RESOLUTION REQUIREMENTS.—

(1) SPECIFIC STATUTORY AUTHORIZATION.—Consistent with section 8(a)(1) of the War Powers Resolution, the Congress declares that this section is intended to constitute specific statutory authorization within the meaning of section 5(b) of the War Powers Resolution.

(2) APPLICABILITY OF OTHER REQUIREMENTS.—
Nothing in this resolution supercedes any requirement of
the War Powers Resolution.

Approved September 18, 2001.

Source: Public Law 107-40, September 18, 2001. 115 Stat. 224. http://
www.gpo.gov/fdsys/pkg/PLAW-107publ40/pdf/PLAW-107publ40.pdf.

War in Afghanistan: Operation Enduring Freedom

George W. Bush's Speech Announcing Air Strikes in Afghanistan

October 7, 2001

INTRODUCTION

Within a month of the attacks on the World Trade Center and Pentagon, President Bush announced the beginning of U.S. combat operations in Afghanistan, code-named Operation Enduring Freedom. Afghanistan became the focus of U.S. attention because the Taliban regime that ruled the country had provided safe haven to al-Qaeda, the terrorist organization known to have been responsible for the September 11 attacks. The Taliban had ruled the country since 1996 adhering to a fundamentalist view of Islamic law. Under the Taliban's rule, women could not hold jobs or receive education, no music, dancing, or sports were permitted, and public executions and amputations were commonplace. An alliance between al-Qaeda and the Taliban emerged when Osama bin Laden, the leader of al-Qaeda, moved there in 1996, and established al-Qaeda terrorist training camps. When the Taliban refused to hand over bin Laden after 9/11, the U.S. initiated military operations against the Taliban in Afghanistan. U.S. forces were joined by an opposition group in Afghanistan, known as the Northern Alliance. One of the principal targets of the operations was Tora Bora, a cave complex high in the mountains of Afghanistan, close to the Pakistan border, where military intelligence believed bin Laden was headquartered.

Good afternoon. On my orders, the United States military has begun strikes against Al Qaida terrorist training camps and military installations of the Taliban regime in Afghanistan. These carefully targeted actions are designed to disrupt the use of Afghanistan as a terrorist base of operations and to attack the military capability of the Taliban regime.

We are joined in this operation by our staunch friend Great Britain. Other close friends, including Canada, Australia, Germany, and France, have pledged forces as the operation unfolds. **More than 40 countries in the Middle East, Africa, Europe, and across Asia have granted air transit or landing rights. Many more have shared intelligence. We are supported by the collective will of the world.**

On September 22, several countries in the Middle East withdrew their recognition of the Taliban as the legal government of Afghanistan. Only Pakistan maintained diplomatic ties to the regime.

More than 2 weeks ago, I gave Taliban leaders a series of clear and specific demands: Close terrorist training camps; hand over leaders of the Al Qaida network; and return all foreign nationals, including American citizens, unjustly detained in your country. None of these demands were met. And now the Taliban will pay a price. By destroying camps and disrupting communications, we will make it more difficult for the terror network to train new recruits and coordinate their evil plans.

Initially, the terrorists may burrow deeper into caves and other entrenched hiding places. Our military action is also designed to clear the way for sustained, comprehensive, and relentless operations to drive them out and bring them to justice.

At the same time, the oppressed people of Afghanistan will know the generosity of America and our allies. As we strike military targets, we'll also drop food, medicine, and supplies to the starving and suffering men and women and children of Afghanistan.

The United States of America is a friend to the Afghan people, and we are the friends of almost a billion worldwide who practice the Islamic faith. The United States of America is an enemy of those who aid terrorists and of the barbaric criminals who profane a great religion by committing murder in its name.

This military action is a part of our campaign against terrorism, another front in a war that has already been joined through diplomacy, intelligence, the freezing of financial assets, and the arrests of known terrorists by law enforcement agents in 38 countries. Given the nature and reach of our enemies, we will win this conflict by the patient accumulation of successes, by meeting a series of challenges with determination and will and purpose.

Today we focus on Afghanistan, but the battle is broader. Every nation has a choice to make. In this conflict, there is no neutral ground. If any government sponsors the outlaws and killers of innocents, they have become outlaws and murderers, themselves. And they will take that lonely path at their own peril.

I'm speaking to you today from the Treaty Room of the White House, a place where American Presidents have worked for peace. We're a peaceful nation. Yet, as we have learned so suddenly and so tragically, there can be no peace in a world of sudden terror. In the face of today's new threat, the only way to pursue peace is to pursue those who threaten it.

We did not ask for this mission, but we will fulfill it. The name of today's military operation is Enduring Freedom. We defend not only our precious freedoms but also the freedom of people everywhere to live and raise their children free from fear.

I know many Americans feel fear today, and our Government is taking strong precautions. All law enforcement and intelligence agencies are working aggressively around America, around the world, and around the clock. At my request, many Governors have activated the National Guard to strengthen airport security. We have called up Reserves to reinforce our military capability and strengthen the protection of our homeland.

In the months ahead, our patience will be one of our strengths: patience with the long waits that will result from tighter security; patience and understanding that it will take time to achieve our goals; patience in all the sacrifices that may come.

By the end of the year, the Taliban was out of power and al-Qaeda's strength in Afghanistan was greatly diminished. But bin Laden was not found. Many suspected he had escaped into Pakistan during the early days of the military operations.

Today those sacrifices are being made by members of our Armed Forces who now defend us so far from home, and by their proud and worried families. A Commander in Chief sends America's sons and daughters into a battle in a foreign land only after the greatest care and a lot of prayer. We ask a lot of those who wear our uniform. We ask them to leave their loved ones, to travel great distances, to risk injury, even to be prepared to make the ultimate sacrifice of their lives.

They are dedicated; they are honorable; they represent the best of our country. And we are grateful.

To all the men and women in our military—every sailor, every soldier, every airman, every coastguardsman, every marine—I say this: Your mission is defined; your objectives are clear; your goal is just; you have my full confidence; and you will have every tool you need to carry out your duty.

I recently received a touching letter that says a lot about the state of America in these difficult times, a letter from a fourthgrade girl with a father in the military: "As much as I don't want my dad to fight," she wrote, "I'm willing to give him to you."

This is a precious gift, the greatest she could give. This young girl knows what America is all about. Since September 11, an entire generation of young Americans has gained new understanding of the value of freedom and its cost in duty and in sacrifice.

In June 2002, Hamid Karzai was named interim president of the transitional government in Afghanistan (he was subsequently elected president in 2004). The reforms he initiated were rather limited, however, as his government's control over regions outside the capital city of Kabul was tenuous. It was an uneasy peace that reigned in the country as threats of Taliban resurgence remained. Nonetheless, the Bush administration began to turn its attention to another deployment of troops, this time against Saddam Hussein in Iraq.

The battle is now joined on many fronts. We will not waver; we will not tire; we will not falter; and we will not fail. Peace and freedom will prevail.

Thank you. May God continue to bless America.

Source: George W. Bush, Address to the Nation Announcing Strikes Against Al Qaida Training Camps and Taliban Military Installations in Afghanistan, October 7, 2001. *Public Papers of the Presidents of the United States: George W. Bush* (Book II) (Washington, DC: Government Printing Office, 2001), 1201–1202.

USA PATRIOT Act

George W. Bush's Signing Statement
October 26, 2001

INTRODUCTION

In the days following the September 11, 2001, terror attacks on the World Trade Center and the Pentagon, Congress passed, with overwhelming majorities in both chambers, the USA PATRIOT Act of 2001. Like the AUMF before it, the PATRIOT Act was principally authored by the Bush administration. In fact, on the day the House voted, the Republican House leadership accepted the administration's substitute bill in place of its own version. Congress held very little debate and no hearings on the measure. The legislation passed 357-66 in the House and 98-1 in the Senate, where Democratic Senator Russ Feingold of Wisconsin cast the lone "nay" vote.

Good morning and welcome to the White House. Today we take an essential step in defeating terrorism, while protecting the constitutional rights of all Americans. **With my signature, this law will give intelligence and law enforcement officials important new tools to fight a present danger.**

I commend the House and Senate for the hard work they put into this legislation. Members of Congress and their staffs spent long nights and weekends to get this important bill to my desk. I appreciate their efforts and bipartisanship in passing this new law.

I want to thank the Vice President and his staff for working hard to make sure this law was passed. I want to thank the Secretary of State and the Secretary of Treasury for being here, both of whom lead important parts of our war against terrorism. I want to thank Attorney General John Ashcroft for spending a lot of time on the Hill to make the case for a balanced piece of legislation. I want to thank the Director of the FBI and the Director of the CIA for waging an incredibly important part on the two-front war, one overseas and a front here at home. **I want to thank Governor Tom Ridge for his leadership.**

The law expanded the electronic surveillance powers of government, appropriated money for new antiterror initiatives and money laundering investigations, substantially altered immigration laws and strengthened border protections, monitored resident aliens more closely, and increased intelligence gathering and communication capacities of government.

Within a year, Governor Ridge (R-PA) would become the first secretary of the newly established U.S. Department of Homeland Security, leading the largest reorganization of the federal bureaucracy since 1947. Homeland Security was responsible for coordinating the vast national security infrastructure that emerged following 9/11.

. . .

The changes, effective today, will help counter a threat like no other our Nation has ever faced. We've seen the enemy and the murder of thousands of innocent, unsuspecting people. They recognize no barrier of morality. They have no conscience. The terrorists cannot be reasoned with.

. . .

But one thing is for certain: These terrorists must be pursued; they must be defeated; and they must be brought to justice. And that is the purpose of this legislation. Since the 11th of September, the men and women of our intelligence and law enforcement agencies have been relentless in their response to new and sudden challenges.

We have seen the horrors terrorists can inflict. We may never know what horrors our country was spared by the diligent and determined work of our police forces, the FBI, ATF agents, Federal marshals, custom officers, Secret Service, intelligence professionals, and local law enforcement officials. Under the most trying conditions, they are serving this country with excellence and often with bravery.

They deserve our full support and every means of help that we can provide. We're dealing with terrorists who operate by highly sophisticated methods and technologies, some of which were not even available when our existing laws were written. **The bill before me takes account of the new realities and dangers posed by modern terrorists. It will help law enforcement to identify, to dismantle, to disrupt, and to punish terrorists before they strike.**

Three elements proved to be very controversial: (1) the expansion of electronic surveillance activities; (2) provisions authorizing the attorney general to detain noncitizens believed to be national security risks; and (3) Section 215—that authorized, "[t]he Director of the FBI . . . or his designee . . . [to] make an application for an order requiring the production of any tangible things (books, records, papers, etc.) for an investigation to protect against terrorism." Among other things, that provision authorized the government to require phone companies, Internet providers, and libraries to reveal to government investigators how their customers were using their services. Section 215 also had a "gag order," which prohibited the service provider from revealing to anyone else that there was an investigation.

For example, this legislation gives law enforcement officials better tools to put an end to financial counterfeiting, smuggling, and money laundering. Secondly, it gives intelligence operations and criminal operations the chance to operate not on separate tracks but to share vital information so necessary to disrupt a terrorist attack before it occurs.

As of today, we're changing the laws governing information sharing. And as importantly, we're changing the culture of our various agencies that fight terrorism. Countering and investigating terrorist activity is the number one priority for both law enforcement and intelligence agencies.

Surveillance of communications is another essential tool to pursue and stop terrorists. **The existing law was written in the era of rotary telephones. This new law that I sign today will allow surveillance of all communications used by terrorists, including e-mails, the Internet, and cell phones. As of today, we'll be able to better meet the technological challenges posed by this proliferation of communications technology.**

Investigations are often slowed by limit on the reach of Federal search warrants. Law enforcement agencies have to get a new warrant for each new district they investigate, even when they're after the same suspect. Under this new law, warrants are valid across all districts and across all States.

And finally, the new legislation greatly enhances the penalties that will fall on terrorists or anyone who helps them. Current statutes deal more severely with drug traffickers than with terrorists. That changes today. We are enacting new and harsh penalties for possession of biological weapons. We're making it easier to seize the assets of groups and individuals involved in terrorism. The Government will have wider latitude in deporting known terrorists and their supporters. The statute of limitations on terrorist acts will be lengthened, as will prison sentences for terrorists.

This bill was carefully drafted and considered. Led by the Members of Congress on this stage and those seated in the audience, it was crafted with skill and care, determination and a spirit of bipartisanship for which the entire Nation is grateful. **This bill met with an overwhelming—overwhelming—agreement in Congress because it upholds and respects the civil liberties guaranteed by our Constitution.**

Following the Nixon administration's use of the intelligence services such as the CIA and NSA for domestic political purposes, Congress took steps to ensure that the historical division between domestic (i.e., FBI) and foreign intelligence gathering services (i.e., CIA and NSA) was reinforced. The PATRIOT Act blurred that division. For example, in 2005, the National Security Administration's massive "data mining" program was revealed to have been targeting both foreign and domestic targets. The Edward Snowden leaks discussed in a later chapter on the Obama administration demonstrate the program's scale and longevity.

The new law broadened in significant ways the electronic surveillance capacities of both law enforcement and counterterrorism authorities. Both terrorism and "computer abuse and fraud" would be sufficient bases for securing a wiretap. The law allowed the government to track Internet communications and, importantly, allowed government investigators to conduct "roving wiretaps" so that the tap followed the suspect regardless of the phones used by the suspect. Under the new law, officials could obtain a wiretap without giving judges information regarding the target of the wiretap or the location of the wiretap. Essentially, the PATRIOT Act granted investigators a nationwide warrant at their discretion; it permitted law enforcement to obtain information about individuals' private behaviors without individualized suspicion or meaningful judicial oversight. It delegated broad powers to law enforcement that did not necessarily have anything to do with counterterrorism. In this respect, the act changed in rather fundamental ways the Foreign Intelligence Surveillance Act (FISA) of 1978, discussed in an earlier chapter.

As criticism of the act emerged in the months following its passage, the nation's top law enforcement official, Attorney General John Ashcroft, appeared in December 2001 before the Senate Judiciary Committee. Responding to the critics' concerns about the difficult balance to be struck between national security and individual liberty, he indicated neither he nor the president would be swayed by such appeals: "[t]errorist operatives infiltrate our communities—plotting, planning and waiting to kill again. They enjoy the benefits of our free society even as they commit themselves to our destruction. They exploit our openness... by deliberate, premeditated design.... [T]o those who scare peace-loving people with phantoms of lost liberty; my message is this: 'Your tactics only aid terrorists—for they erode our national unity and diminish our resolve. They give ammunition to America's enemies, and pause to America's friends.'"

This legislation is essential not only to pursuing and punishing terrorists but also preventing more atrocities in the hands of the evil ones. This Government will enforce this law with all the urgency of a nation at war. The elected branches of our Government and both political parties are united in our resolve to find and stop and punish those who would do harm to the American people.

It is now my honor to sign into law the USA PATRIOT ACT of 2001.

Source: George W. Bush, Remarks on Signing the USA PATRIOT ACT of 2001, October 26, 2001. *Public Papers of the Presidents of the United States: George W. Bush (Book II)* (Washington, DC: Government Printing Office, 2001), 1306–1307.

Habeas Corpus and Guantanamo Bay

George W. Bush's Military Order

November 13, 2001

INTRODUCTION

One of the consequences of the war on terror was the dilemma of what to do with those Taliban fighters and suspected terrorists who were captured in Afghanistan and elsewhere. As we've seen, international law distinguishes between those who are lawful combatants and those who are unlawful combatants. Lawful combatants are due legal protections afforded to prisoners of war. Unlawful combatants, however, could be subject to the laws of the detaining authority. As in the case of the Nazi saboteurs, they could be tried, convicted, and sentenced to death. But first, presumably, there had to be some means to determine that the individuals being detained were combatants at all, rather than innocent civilians. In such cases, Article 4 of the Geneva Convention provides that a "competent tribunal" determine their status. Of course, one option would be to try their cases in the civil justice system, which had been used successfully in the past and was used in many cases after 2001. However, the Bush administration determined that a system of military detention would be used for the vast majority of cases. The system would be established under the authority of the Secretary of Defense, and any review of the status of a detainee would be conducted according to processes determined by the executive branch.

This volume contains multiple references to the dozens of legal memoranda that circulated around the Bush White House in the weeks following September 11, 2001. Generally, those memos reflected key assumptions and claims with respect to executive power and the legal status of captured prisoners during the undeclared war on terror. Among them was the view that the president had plenary (complete) authority to abrogate (limit or override) international and domestic laws, agreements, or treaties. Congress and the courts had no role to play in constraining the commander in chief and the legal apparatus for detainees would be coordinated and overseen by the Pentagon. Agents of the executive branch (i.e., military personnel) would be absolved from criminal actions taken in interrogating detainees in that war on terror. Moreover, because the detention facility in Guantanamo Bay, Cuba, was not a U.S. territory and its prisoners were not "lawful combatants" due certain basic protections under the Geneva Conventions, the entire detainee program stood outside of federal and international law. Each of these assertions was reflected in a key memo, again from the Office of Legal Counsel, by Deputy Assistant Attorney General Patrick Philbin. That November 6, 2001, memo was drafted to justify the exclusive authority of the president to detain individuals captured in the war on terror. The Philbin memo provided the legal argument for the entire military detention program, which was established in this military order issued by President Bush a week later. This is the military order the president issued.

Detention, Treatment, and Trial of Certain Non-Citizens in the War against Terrorism

By the authority vested in me as President and as Commander in Chief of the Armed Forces of the United States by the Constitution and the laws of the United States of America, including the Authorization for Use of Military Force Joint Resolution (Public Law 107-40, 115 Stat. 224) and sections 821 and 836 of title 10, United States Code, it is hereby ordered as follows:

Section 1. Findings.

(a) International terrorists, including members of al Qaida, have carried out attacks on United States diplomatic and military personnel and facilities abroad and on citizens and property within the United States on a scale that has created a state of armed conflict that requires the use of the United States Armed Forces.

(b) In light of grave acts of terrorism and threats of terrorism, including the terrorist attacks on September 11, 2001, on the headquarters of the United States Department of Defense in the national capital region, on the World Trade Center in New York, and on civilian aircraft such as in Pennsylvania, I proclaimed a national emergency on September 14, 2001 (Proc. 7463, Declaration of National Emergency by Reason of Certain Terrorist Attacks).

(c) Individuals acting alone and in concert involved in international terrorism possess both the capability and the intention to undertake further terrorist attacks against the United States that, if not detected and prevented, will cause mass deaths, mass injuries, and massive destruction of property, and may place at risk the continuity of the operations of the United States Government.

(d) The ability of the United States to protect the United States and its citizens, and to help its allies and other cooperating nations protect their nations and their citizens, from such further terrorist attacks depends in significant part upon using the United States Armed Forces to identify terrorists and those who support them, to disrupt their activities, and to eliminate their ability to conduct or support such attacks.

(e) To protect the United States and its citizens, and for the effective conduct of military operations and prevention of terrorist attacks, it is necessary for individuals subject to this order pursuant to section 2 hereof to be detained, and, when tried, to be tried for violations of the laws of war and other applicable laws by military tribunals.

(f) Given the danger to the safety of the United States and the nature of international terrorism, and to the extent provided by and under this order, I find consistent with section 836 of title 10, United States Code, that **it is not practicable to apply in military commissions under this order the principles of law and the rules of evidence generally recognized in the trial of criminal cases in the United States district courts.**

> Among the detainees were many who may have been innocent. U.S. forces often relied upon informants to reveal to them whom to capture. Those informants may have made mistakes, misidentified particular people, or simply had grudges or debts that would no longer be a worry if the person were to disappear into U.S. custody. Because the rules of evidence mentioned here did not conform to civilian procedures, those individuals who may have been hapless innocents had no means by which to challenge their detentions. In fact, they had no means to learn what charges were levied against them or by whom.

(g) Having fully considered the magnitude of the potential deaths, injuries, and property destruction that would result from potential acts of terrorism against the United States, and the probability that such acts will occur, I have determined that an extraordinary emergency exists for national defense purposes, that this emergency constitutes an urgent and compelling government interest, and that issuance of this order is necessary to meet the emergency.

Sec. 2. Definition and Policy.

(a) The term "individual subject to this order" shall mean any individual who is not a United States citizen with respect to whom I determine from time to time in writing that:

(1) there is reason to believe that such individual, at the relevant times, (i) is or was a member of the organization known as al Qaida; (ii) has engaged in, aided or abetted, or conspired to commit, acts of international terrorism, or acts in preparation therefore, that have caused, threaten to cause, or have as their aim to cause, injury to or adverse effects on the United States, its citizens, national security, foreign policy, or economy; or (iii) has knowingly harbored one or more individuals described in subparagraphs (i) or (ii) of subsection 2(a)(1) of this order; and

(2) it is in the interest of the United States that such individual be subject to this order.

(b) It is the policy of the United States that the Secretary of Defense shall take all necessary measures to ensure that any individual subject to this order is detained in accordance with section 3, and, if the individual is to be tried, that such individual is tried only in accordance with section 4.

Sec. 3. Detention Authority of the Secretary of Defense. Any individual subject to this order shall be -

A consistent theme through the OLC memos, including the one from Philbin, was the administration's argument that suspected terrorists held at the detention facilities at Guantanamo Bay were outside of U.S. sovereignty; therefore, the detainees had no recourse to U.S. courts. Under a lease brokered between Cuba and the United States in 1903, Cuba retains sovereignty over the military base, but the United States has "complete jurisdiction and control." In a 2002 Federal District Court decision consistent with this view, the judge ruled that detainees at Guantanamo could not seek habeas relief in U.S. courts. A separate case, in the 9th Circuit, however, identified the jurisdictional control that the U.S. exercises over the base as sufficient to grant petitions for writ of habeas corpus in U.S. courts. Ultimately, the U.S. Supreme Court granted review and decided in *Rasul v. Bush* (2004) that federal courts did have the authority to hear challenges to the detention of suspected terrorists held at Guantanamo.

(a) detained at an appropriate location designated by the Secretary of Defense outside or within the United States;

(b) treated humanely, without any adverse distinction based on race, color, religion, gender, birth, wealth, or any similar criteria;

(c) afforded adequate food, drinking water, shelter, clothing, and medical treatment;

(d) allowed the free exercise of religion consistent with the requirements of such detention; and

(e) detained in accordance with such other conditions as the Secretary of Defense may prescribe.

Sec. 4. Authority of the Secretary of Defense Regarding Trials of Individuals Subject to this Order.

(a) Any individual subject to this order shall, when tried, be tried by military commission for any and all offenses triable by military commission that such individual is alleged to have committed, and may be punished in accordance with the penalties provided under applicable law, including life imprisonment or death.

(b) As a military function and in light of the findings in section 1, including subsection (f) thereof, the Secretary of Defense shall issue such orders and regulations, including orders for the appointment of one or more military commissions, as may be necessary to carry out subsection (a) of this section.

(c) Orders and regulations issued under subsection (b) of this section shall include, but not be limited to, rules for the conduct of the proceedings of military commissions, including pretrial, trial, and post-trial procedures, modes of proof, issuance of process, and qualifications of attorneys, which shall at a minimum provide for -

(1) military commissions to sit at any time and any place, consistent with such guidance regarding time and place as the Secretary of Defense may provide;

(2) a full and fair trial, with the military commission sitting as the triers of both fact and law;

(3) admission of such evidence as would, in the opinion of the presiding officer of the military commission (or instead, if any other member of the commission so requests at the time the presiding officer renders that opinion, the opinion of the commission rendered at that time by a majority of the commission), have probative value to a reasonable person;

The OLC conceded that U.S. courts might have some role in reviewing the determinations made by the military commission regarding whether the detainee was an enemy combatant. However, that review would only include evidence provided by the military authorities and would not provide the detainee or his counsel the opportunity to challenge the evidence or the determination of its "probative value."

(4) in a manner consistent with the protection of information classified or classifiable under Executive Order 12958 of April 17, 1995, as amended, or any successor Executive Order, protected by statute or rule from unauthorized disclosure, or otherwise protected by law, (A) the handling of, admission into evidence of, and access to materials and information, and (B) the conduct, closure of, and access to proceedings;

(5) conduct of the prosecution by one or more attorneys designated by the Secretary of Defense and conduct of the defense by attorneys for the individual subject to this order;

(6) conviction only upon the concurrence of two-thirds of the members of the commission present at the time of the vote, a majority being present;

(7) sentencing only upon the concurrence of two-thirds of the members of the commission present at the time of the vote, a majority being present; and

(8) submission of the record of the trial, including any conviction or sentence, for review and final decision by me or by the Secretary of Defense if so designated by me for that purpose.

. . .

Sec. 7. Relationship to Other Law and Forums.

(a) Nothing in this order shall be construed to -

(1) authorize the disclosure of state secrets to any person not otherwise authorized to have access to them;

(2) limit the authority of the President as Commander in Chief of the Armed Forces or the power of the President to grant reprieves and pardons; or

(3) limit the lawful authority of the Secretary of Defense, any military commander, or any other officer or agent of the United States or of any State to detain or try any person who is not an individual subject to this order.

(b) With respect to any individual subject to this order -

The reference here to "exclusive jurisdiction" explicitly means that the military authorities have total control over the tribunals, with no recourse (save the limited review role mentioned above) to the U.S. federal courts.

(1) military tribunals shall have exclusive jurisdiction with respect to offenses by the individual; and

(2) the individual shall not be privileged to seek any remedy or maintain any proceeding, directly or indirectly, or to have any such remedy or proceeding sought on the individual's behalf, in

(i) any court of the United States, or any State thereof, (ii) any court of any foreign nation, or (iii) any international tribunal.

(c) This order is not intended to and does not create any right, benefit, or privilege, substantive or procedural, enforceable at law or equity by any party, against the United States, its departments, agencies, or other entities, its officers or employees, or any other person.

(d) For purposes of this order, the term "State" includes any State, district, territory, or possession of the United States.

(e) I reserve the authority to direct the Secretary of Defense, at any time hereafter, to transfer to a governmental authority control of any individual subject to this order. Nothing in this order shall be construed to limit the authority of any such governmental authority to prosecute any individual for whom control is transferred.

George W. Bush

The White House

November 13, 2001

Source: George W. Bush, Military Order – Detention, Treatment, and Trial of Certain Non-Citizens in the War against Terrorism, November 13, 2001. Online by Gerhard Peters and John T. Woolley, *The American Presidency Project.* http://www.presidency.ucsb.edu/ws/?pid=63124.

The Axis of Evil

George W. Bush's State of the Union Address
January 29, 2002

INTRODUCTION

Officials who had been at initial national security briefings when President Bush took office in early 2001 reported that the removal of Saddam Hussein from Iraq was one of his top objectives. That perspective was shared by his closest advisers, including Dick Cheney, Donald Rumsfeld, and Paul Wolfowitz. In fact, even when, on September 21, the administration received confirmation that Iraq did not have any hand in the attacks, Wolfowitz and others still pressed the case to attack Iraq. Though Bush insisted their efforts remain focused on bin Laden and the al-Qaeda terror network, on November 21, 2001, Bush instructed Rumsfeld to develop plans for an invasion of Iraq. Without evidence of a connection to 9/11, the AUMF would not be sufficient to justify the deployment of U.S. troops to Iraq. The administration explored the legal implications of a policy of pre-emptive war. To take such preemptive action against a state (in this case, Iraq), the Bush administration had to demonstrate two things: (1) that there was solid evidence that Iraq had the means to wage war against the United States and (2) that there was solid evidence that Iraq had the intention of doing so imminently. Thus began the administration's multipronged approach to making the case for an invasion of Iraq.

Thank you very much. Mr. Speaker, Vice President Cheney, Members of Congress, distinguished guests, fellow citizens: As we gather tonight, our Nation is at war; our economy is in recession; and the civilized world faces unprecedented dangers. Yet, the state of our Union has never been stronger.

We last met in an hour of shock and suffering. In 4 short months, our Nation has comforted the victims, begun to rebuild New York and the Pentagon, rallied a great coalition, captured, arrested, and rid the world of thousands of terrorists, destroyed Afghanistan's terrorist training camps, saved a people from starvation, and freed a country from brutal oppression.

The decision by the Bush administration to hold detainees at Guantanamo Bay is covered in another chapter in this volume.

The American flag flies again over our Embassy in Kabul. **Terrorists who once occupied Afghanistan now occupy cells at Guantanamo Bay. And terrorist leaders who urged followers to sacrifice their lives are running for their own.**

251

America and Afghanistan are now allies against terror. We'll be partners in rebuilding that country. And this evening we welcomed the distinguished interim leader of a liberated Afghanistan, Chairman Hamid Karzai.

... When I called our troops into action, I did so with complete confidence in their courage and skill. And tonight, thanks to them, we are winning the war on terror. The men and women of our Armed Forces have delivered a message now clear to every enemy of the United States: Even 7,000 miles away, across oceans and continents, on mountaintops and in caves, you will not escape the justice of this Nation.

Our cause is just, and it continues. Our discoveries in Afghanistan confirmed our worst fears and showed us the true scope of the task ahead. We have seen the depth of our enemies' hatred in videos where they laugh about the loss of innocent life. And the depth of their hatred is equaled by the madness of the destruction they design. We have found diagrams of American nuclear powerplants and public water facilities, detailed instructions for making chemical weapons, surveillance maps of American cities, and thorough descriptions of landmarks in America and throughout the world.

What we have found in Afghanistan confirms that, far from ending there, our war against terror is only beginning. Most of the 19 men who hijacked planes on September the 11th were trained in Afghanistan's camps, and so were tens of thousands of others. Thousands of dangerous killers, schooled in the methods of murder, often supported by outlaw regimes, are now spread throughout the world like ticking timebombs, set to go off without warning.

This State of the Union address given by President Bush after the Taliban had been removed from power in Afghanistan reveals one of the first public indications that the administration was preparing to broaden the war on terror to include action against Saddam Hussein, the dictator in power in Iraq. Just a month prior, Vice President Cheney appeared on the news show *Meet the Press,* and claimed that there was "pretty conclusive" evidence that Iraq had been harboring terrorists. The public learned later that the claims were incorrect. Iraq neither harbored terrorists nor controlled weapons of mass destruction, nor did Iraq pose an imminent threat to the national security of the United States.

... Our Nation will continue to be steadfast and patient and persistent in the pursuit of two great objectives. First, we will shut down terrorist camps, disrupt terrorist plans, and bring terrorists to justice. And second, we must prevent the terrorists and regimes who seek chemical, biological, or nuclear weapons from threatening the United States and the world.

. . . Our second goal is to prevent regimes that sponsor terror from threatening America or our friends and allies with weapons of mass destruction. Some of these regimes have been pretty quiet since September the 11th, but we know their true nature.

North Korea is a regime arming with missiles and weapons of mass destruction, while starving its citizens.

Iran aggressively pursues these weapons and exports terror, while an unelected few repress the Iranian people's hope for freedom.

Two views of the role played by national security intelligence emerged following the deployment of troops to Iraq after the vote by Congress in 2002 to grant the president that authority. One view is that the intelligence was flawed and the president and his advisers were its victims, making the best decisions they could with faulty information. Thus, by that account, the decision to invade Iraq was the right decision given the information at their disposal at the time. CIA Director George Tenet, for example, resigned in large part due to his role in presenting the faulty intelligence. In retrospect, after it was discovered that there were no weapons of mass destruction, nor any Iraqi connection to 9/11, many suggested that perhaps the United States ought not have gone in. The other perspective is far more critical of the president and his staff. It conceives of them as relying upon false and misleading information to manufacture support for a position they long held. On that account, the Bush-Cheney team was committed to regime change in Iraq and used what they knew to be faulty intelligence to make the case to support a preemptive war. Statements made by administration officials that were known at the time to be false (or misused or misrepresented) are mustered as evidence in support of this perspective; among the examples often mentioned are Cheney's continuing (even though it had been refuted by the CIA) claim that one of the 9/11 attackers met with an Iraqi spy in Prague, National Security Adviser Rice's remark that "we don't want the 'smoking gun' (evidence of WMDs) to be a mushroom cloud," Donald Rumsfeld's assertions that he had "bullet-proof" evidence connecting Hussein and bin Laden, and his claim that "we all know that; even a trained ape knows that" Iraq has WMD. The second view has become the dominant perspective—politics, not faulty intelligence, drove the decision to invade Iraq.

Iraq continues to flaunt its hostility toward America and to support terror. The Iraqi regime has plotted to develop anthrax and nerve gas and nuclear weapons for over a decade. This is a regime that has already used poison gas to murder thousands of its own citizens, leaving the bodies of mothers huddled over their dead children. This is a regime that agreed to international inspections, then kicked out the inspectors. This is a regime that has something to hide from the civilized world.

States like these and their terrorist allies constitute an axis of evil, arming to threaten the peace of the world. By seeking weapons of mass destruction, these regimes pose a grave and growing danger. They could provide these arms to terrorists, giving them the means to match their hatred. They could attack our allies or attempt to blackmail the United States. In any of these cases, the price of indifference would be catastrophic.

We will work closely with our coalition to deny terrorists and their state sponsors the materials, technology, and expertise to make and deliver weapons of mass destruction. We will develop and deploy effective missile defenses to protect America and our allies from sudden attack. And all nations should know: America will do what is necessary to ensure our Nation's security.

We'll be deliberate; yet, time is not on our side. I will not wait on events while dangers gather. I will not stand by as peril draws closer and closer. The United States of America will not permit the world's most dangerous regimes to threaten us with the world's most destructive weapons.

U.S. forces invaded Iraq in March 2003 and quickly ousted Saddam Hussein. After the initial invasion, an insurgency emerged to oppose the U.S. and coalition forces in place in Iraq. A surge in new troops in 2007 reduced the unrest and was followed by a withdrawal of troops in 2011. Iraq remained a very unstable place, however, and by 2014, the Islamic State (also known as ISIS or ISIL) emerged as a dangerous regional threat. American forces were once again engaged in combat operations in Iraq.

. . . In a single instant, we realized that this will be a decisive decade in the history of liberty, that we've been called to a unique role in human events. Rarely has the world faced a choice more clear or consequential.

Our enemies send other people's children on missions of suicide and murder. They embrace tyranny and death as a cause and a creed. We stand for a different choice, made long ago on the day of our founding. We affirm it again today. We choose freedom and the dignity of every life.

Steadfast in our purpose, we now press on. We have known freedom's price. We have shown freedom's power. And in this great conflict, my fellow Americans, we will see freedom's victory.

Thank you all. May God bless.

Source: George W. Bush, Address before a Joint Session of the Congress on the State of the Union, January 29, 2002. *Public Papers of the Presidents of the United States: George W. Bush (Book I)* (Washington, DC: Government Printing Office, 2002), 129–136.

Enemy Combatants

George W. Bush's Memorandum on Detainees
February 7, 2002

INTRODUCTION

The Constitution prescribes that Congress and the president share the power to make war. Specifically, Congress is granted the power to declare war and raise armies, while the executive shall be the commander in chief of the armed forces once war has been declared. That sharing of the war powers, as we've seen, has not always been so neatly applied. In fact, in the modern era, Congress has largely abandoned its role in war-making. Prior Congresses, such as those before the *Youngstown Sheet and Tube* case, saw an active role for legislators in the conduct of war. Contemporary Congresses, though, largely defer to presidential war powers. Part of that has to do with the way armed conflicts tend to be waged in the contemporary era, relative to the battlefields of World War I, for example. The swiftness of targeted air strikes, special forces operations, and the like have shifted the terms of congressional engagement in war-making to privilege president-initiated combat activities. In addition, the press, the public, and even the courts have tended to share (and reinforce) this perspective. At this point, even if legislators were inclined to circumscribe presidential military power, constituent demand and the "rally 'round the president" effect would render such attempts electorally difficult. Many expressions of executive power that are couched as militarily necessary, then, tend to be insulated from congressional (and judicial) scrutiny by both contemporary practice and electoral politics, if not the secrecy that often attends such claims.

Once President Bush declared the terrorist attacks of 9/11 acts of war rather than criminal conduct, and Congress passed the Authorization for Use of Military Force—which gave the president broad discretion to "use all necessary and appropriate force"—national security concerns were invoked to override due process requirements, separation of powers principles, privacy protection, international law, and other legal obligations that typically restrain executive action. This memo reflects the new dynamic, or as Bush called it, the "new paradigm" in the Global War on Terror. It sets out for key executive branch officials the administration's policy for how to deal with those whom the armed forces detain in prosecuting that war on terror. Ultimately, several other key legal documents, including the infamous Torture Memo, provide further clarification regarding the legal status of detainees (and, by extension, how they can be treated while in detention). The abuses of detainees uncovered at Abu Ghraib and elsewhere have their origins in the policy established by this 2002 memo from the president.

THE WHITE HOUSE

February 7, 2002

MEMORANDUM FOR:

THE VICE PRESIDENT

THE SECRETARY OF STATE

THE SECRETARY OF DEFENSE

THE ATTORNEY GENERAL

CHIEF OF STAFF TO THE PRESIDENT

DIRECTOR OF CENTRAL INTELLIGENCE

ASSISTANT TO THE PRESIDENT FOR NATIONAL
SECURITY AFFAIRS

CHAIRMAN OF THE JOINT CHIEFS OF STAFF

SUBJECT: Humane Treatment of Taliban and al Qaeda
Detainees

1. Our recent extensive discussions regarding the status of al
Qaeda and Taliban detainees confirm that the application of
Geneva Convention Relative to the Treatment of Prisoners
of War of August 12, 1949, (Geneva) to the conflict with al
Qaeda and the Taliban involves complex legal questions.
By its terms, Geneva applies to conflicts involving "High Contracting Parties," which can only be states. Moreover, it
assumes the existence of "regular" armed forces fighting on
behalf of states. However, the war against terrorism ushers in
a new paradigm, one in which groups with broad, international
reach commit horrific acts against innocent civilians, sometimes with the direct support of states. **Our nation recognizes
that this new paradigm—ushered in not by us, but by
terrorists—requires new thinking in the law of war, but
thinking that should nevertheless be consistent with the
principles of Geneva.**

2. Pursuant to my authority as commander in chief and chief
executive of the United States, and relying on the opinion of

The Civil War, World War I, and World War II
demanded broad, unilateral presidential
powers. But in each case, the accrual of executive powers ebbed as the conflicts were
resolved. Those wars were waged against
identifiable enemies in uniform, on known
battlefields, for a discrete period of time.
The war against international terror networks
that began after September 11 had none of
those qualities. The Geneva Conventions were
established in 1949, in the context of the post–
World War II era, and require the humane
treatment of prisoners of war. In the view of
the administration attorneys, the Geneva Conventions, while laudable, were to be viewed as
anachronistic—appropriate for another time,
and another war, but not this one.

the Department of Justice dated January 22, 2002, and on the legal opinion rendered by the attorney general in his letter of February 1, 2002, I hereby determine as follows:

Bush's legal team decided that the Geneva protections afforded prisoners of war would not apply to the present conflict because those who are detained in the war on terror are nonstate actors, and therefore not parties to the terms of the Conventions. In a memo dated one week prior to this memo, Attorney General John Ashcroft suggested that either of two arguments would suffice to deny detainees protections under the Geneva Conventions: (1) Afghanistan was a failed state and could not have been a party to the treaty or its protections or (2) Afghanistan was a party to the treaty, but al-Qaeda and Taliban detainees acted as unlawful combatants, not soldiers, and were therefore not protected by Art. 3 of the Geneva Conventions. The administration went with option 1, in large part because it was presumed to provide more protection for U.S. personnel were they to be captured by enemy forces.

a. I accept the legal conclusion of the Department of Justice and determine that none of the provisions of Geneva apply to our conflict with al Qaeda in Afghanistan or elsewhere throughout the world because, among other reasons, al Qaeda is not a High Contracting Party to Geneva.

b. I accept the legal conclusion of the attorney general and the Department of Justice that I have the authority under the Constitution to suspend Geneva as between the United States and Afghanistan, but I decline to exercise that authority at this time. Accordingly, I determine that the provisions of Geneva will apply to our present conflict with the Taliban. I reserve the right to exercise the authority in this or future conflicts.

c. I also accept the legal conclusion of the Department of Justice and determine that common Article 3 of Geneva does not apply to either al Qaeda or Taliban detainees, because, among other reasons, the relevant conflicts are international in scope and common Article 3 applies only to "armed conflict not of an international character."

Because of the inapplicability of the Geneva Conventions, detainees would not be afforded protections consistent with those accords. Rather, they had a separate legal status, that of "enemy combatants." Under the Geneva Convention, "lawful" combatants are soldiers in the conventional sense and are considered prisoners of war due legal protections under the laws of war. But "unlawful" combatants are spies or saboteurs and are afforded only those legal remedies provided by the detaining authority. However, it became immediately clear that the legal remedies afforded detainees did not match the "law on the books" in the United States. They had no chance for habeas relief, and therefore no way to challenge their detention. And, as we learned, they were also subjected to torture during their interrogations, because the domestic and international laws that prohibited torture were construed to be not applicable to them.

d. Based on the facts supplied by the Department of Defense and the recommendation of the Department of Justice, I determine that the Taliban detainees are unlawful combatants and, therefore, do not qualify as prisoners of war under Article 4 of Geneva. **I note that, because Geneva does not apply to our conflict with al Qaeda, al Qaeda detainees also do not qualify as prisoners of war.**

3. Of course, our values as a nation, values that we share with many nations in the world, call for us to treat detainees humanely, including those who are not legally entitled to such treatment. Our nation has been and will continue to be a strong supporter of Geneva and its principles. As a matter of policy, the United States Armed Forces shall continue to

treat detainees humanely and, to the extent appropriate and consistent with military necessity, in a manner consistent with the principles of Geneva.

4. The United States will hold states, organizations, and individuals who gain control of United States personnel responsible for treating such personnel humanely and consistent with applicable law.

5. I hereby reaffirm the order previously issued by the secretary of defense to the United States Armed Forces **requiring that the detainees be treated humanely and, to the extent appropriate and consistent with military necessity, in a manner consistent with the principles of Geneva.**

The key phrase here is "to the extent appropriate and consistent with military necessity." Consider that phrase in the context of the president's view of his authority as commander in chief. Under his "new paradigm," his actions pursuant to his war-making powers were completely insulated from review by Congress or the courts. This legal argument regarding the inapplicability of Geneva Conventions specifically and U.S. constitutional and statutory law (by implication) was reinforced in later memos and policies dealing with enemy combatants.

6. I hereby direct the secretary of state to communicate my determinations in an appropriate manner to our allies, and other countries and international organizations cooperating in the war against terrorism of global reach.

George W. Bush

Source: George W. Bush, Humane Treatment of al Qaeda and Taliban Detainees, Memorandum for the Vice President, the Secretary of State, the Secretary of Defense, the Attorney General, Chief of Staff to the President, Director of Central Intelligence, Assistant to the President for National Security Affairs, and Chairman of the Joint Chiefs of Staff, February 7, 2002. http://nsarchive.gwu.edu/NSAEBB/NSAEBB127/02.02.07.pdf.

The Torture Memos

The Office of Legal Counsel's Memo on Interrogation Standards
August 1, 2002

INTRODUCTION

The Torture Memos were a series of legal memoranda developed by the Office of Legal Counsel that gave interrogators wide latitude in their treatment of detainees and provided a means to absolve those interrogators of criminal liability if they tortured prisoners. John Yoo, deputy assistant attorney general, constructed much of the legal argument for the new policies. Jay Bybee, assistant attorney general, signed off on this memo, which was sent to White House counsel Alberto Gonzalez, who would later become attorney general. The legal argument presented in this memo, and reflected in the dozens of similar memos that were drafted by OLC at this time, was accepted by the president as the correct interpretation of international law, constitutional law, and U.S. statutory law regarding the treatment of enemy combatants. As a result, military authorities took actions during interrogations that reflected the Department of Justice's novel interpretation of applicable law described here. That approach was put into place immediately and continued until 2004, when the memo became public and was roundly criticized by legal scholars, policy makers, and military personnel.

August 1, 2002

Memorandum for Alberto Gonzalez, Counsel to the President

Re: Standards of Conduct for Interrogation under 18 U.S.C. §§ 2340-2340A

The September 11, 2001 terrorist attacks marked a state of international armed conflict between the United States and the al Qaeda terrorist organization. Pursuant to his Commander-in-Chief power, as supported by an act of Congress, the President has ordered the Armed Forces to carry out military operations against al Qaeda, which includes the power both to kill and to capturemembers of the enemy. **Interrogation arises as a necessary and legitimate element of the detention of al Qaeda and Taliban members during an armed conflict.**

The memo makes the case that because the president has unlimited authority in a time of war to take actions necessary to defend the country, international and domestic law cannot infringe upon that power. Moreover, any attempt by Congress to regulate the president's conduct of interrogation of detainees would violate his authority as commander in chief.

259

. . .

Section 2340 defines the act of torture as an: act committed by a person acting under the color of law specifically intended to inflict severe physical or mental pain or suffering (other than pain or suffering incidental to lawful sanctions) upon another person within his custody or physical control.

Section 2340's definition of torture must be read as a sum of these component parts. Each component of the definition emphasizes that torture is not the mere infliction of pain or suffering on another, but is instead a step well removed. The victim must experience intense pain or suffering of the kind that is equivalent to the pain that would be associated with serious physical injury so severe that death, organ failure, or permanent damage resulting in a loss of significant body function will likely result. If that pain or suffering is psychological, that suffering must result from one of the acts set forth in the statute. In addition, these acts must cause long-term mental harm. Indeed, this view of the criminal act of torture is consistent with the term's common meaning. Torture is generally understood to involve "intense pain" or "excruciating pain," or put another way, "extreme anguish of body or mind." **In short, reading the definition of torture as a whole, it is plain that the term encompasses only extreme acts.**

. . .

Thus, the United States is within its international law obligations even if it uses interrogation methods that might constitute cruel, inhuman, or degrading treatment or punishment, so long as their use is justified by self-defense or necessity. . . .

In the current conflict, we believe that a defendant accused of violating the criminal prohibitions described above might, in certain circumstances, have grounds to properly claim the defense of another. The threat of an impending terrorist attack threatens the lives of hundreds if not thousands of American citizens. Whether such a defense will be upheld depends on the specific context within which

As a result of this reasoning, "enhanced interrogation techniques," such as waterboarding, sleep deprivation, forced stress positions, and so on, which—until this point—would have met the definition of torture, would now be permitted because they did not rise to this new threshold for torture established by the OLC attorneys. Consequently, military authorities had Bush administration approval for inflicting great pain, so long as it did not constitute an "extreme act" that led to organ failure or death.

One of the aims of the memo is to protect U.S. interrogators from criminal liability as they employ techniques that traditionally have been understood to amount to torture. In this passage, Yoo and Bybee reason that even otherwise unlawful activity, such as torture, could be justified if it was in self-defense or in the defense of another. Even though the detainees pose no risk, they could be harmed in order to prevent future attacks.

the interrogation decision is made. If an attack appears increasingly certain, but our intelligence services and armed forces cannot prevent it without the information from the interrogation of a specific individual, then the more likely it will appear that the conduct in question will be seen as necessary. The increasing certainty of an attack will also satisfy the imminence requirement. Finally, the fact that previous al Qaeda attacks have had as their aim the deaths of American citizens, and that evidence of other plots have had a similar goal in mind, would justify proportionality of interrogation methods designed to elicit information to prevent such deaths.

To be sure, this situation is different from the usual self-defense justification, and, indeed, it overlaps with elements of the necessity defense. Self-defense as usually discussed involves using force against an individual who is about to conduct the attack. In the current circumstances, however, an enemy combatant in detention does not himself present a threat of harm. He is not actually carrying out the attack; rather, he has participated in the planning and preparation for the attack, or merely has knowledge of the attack through his membership in the terrorist organization. Nonetheless, some leading scholarly commentators believe that interrogation of such individuals using methods that might violate section 2340A would be justified under the doctrine of self-defense, because the combatant by aiding and promoting the terrorist plot "has culpably caused the situation where someone might get hurt. If hurting him is the only means to prevent the death or injury of others put at risk by his actions, such torture should be permissible, and on the same basis that self-defense is permissible. . . .

Under the present circumstances, therefore, even though a detained enemy combatant may not be the exact attacker—he is not planting the bomb, or piloting a hijacked plane to kill civilians—he still may be harmed in self-defense if he has knowledge of future attacks because he has assisted in their planning and execution.

There can be little doubt that the nation's right to self-defense has been triggered under our law. . . . The President has a particular responsibility and power to take steps to defend the nation, and its people. As Commander-in-Chief and Chief Executive, he may use the armed forces to protect the nation and its people. And he may employ secret agents to aid in his work as Commander-in-Chief. As the Supreme Court observed in The Prize Cases (1862), in response to an armed attack on the United States "the President is not only authorized but bound to resist force by force . . . without waiting for any special legislative authority." The September 11 events were a direct attack on the United States that triggered its right to use force under domestic and international law in self-defense, and as we have explained above, the President has authorized the use of military force with the support of Congress. **As we have made clear in other opinions involving the war against al Qaeda, the Nation's right to self-defense has been triggered by the events of September 11.**

If a government defendant were to harm an enemy combatant during an interrogation in a manner that might arguably violate a criminal prohibition, he would be doing so in order to prevent further attacks on the United States by the al Qaeda terrorist network. In that case, we believe that he could argue that the executive branch's constitutional authority to protect the nation from attack justified his actions. This national and international version of the right to self-defense could supplement and bolster the government defendant's individual right.

. . . [E]ven if the criminal prohibitions outlined above applied, and an interrogation method might violate those prohibitions, necessity or self-defense could provide justifications for any criminal liability.

Please let us know if we can be of further assistance.

Jay S. Bybee

Assistant Attorney General

Source: Office of Legal Counsel, Memorandum for Alberto R. Gonzales, Counsel to the President, re: Standards of Conduct for Interrogation under 18 U.S.C. §§ 2340-2340A, August 1, 2002. https://www2.gwu.edu/~nsarchiv/NSAEBB/NSAEBB127/02.08.01.pdf.

The legal reasoning presented in this memo was rejected by Bybee's replacement, Jack Goldsmith, after Bybee took a federal judgeship. Goldsmith was forced to resign due to his criticism of the memos and Attorney General Ashcroft reinstituted the policy. The existence of the memo and its authorization of torture in interrogations leaked when the Abu Ghraib scandal revealed severe prisoner abuse in detention facilities in Iraq. By the end of the Bush administration, the new head of OLC repudiated this memo specifically, writing: "The federal prohibition on torture, 18 U.S.C. §§ 2340-2340A, is constitutional, and . . . [t]he President, like all officers of the Government, is not above the law." Within days of taking office, President Obama rescinded all Bush-era OLC memos that gave legal guidance to interrogators. Finally, in 2014, the Senate Intelligence Committee released its 6,000-page report on torture and detainees. The report found that "the harsh interrogation methods did not succeed in exacting useful intelligence."

Cheney and the Energy Task Force

Cheney v. United States District Court

June 24, 2004

INTRODUCTION

In support of their claims of executive privilege, presidents generally argue that public disclosure of communications between high-level officials and their advisers compromises the quality and breadth of the information and perspectives the high ranking official receive. That is, those who may reasonably expect that their communications will be disseminated are likely to "temper candor with a concern for appearances and for their own interests to the detriment of the decision making process" (*U.S. v. Nixon*, 1974). In recognition of this difficulty, the U.S. Supreme Court noted that executive privilege is a presumptive constitutional privilege for executive communications. However, in *U.S. v. Nixon*, the court rejected that executive privilege claim in the context of criminal prosecutions. Chief Justice Burger wrote, "... [n]either the doctrine of separation of powers, nor the need for confidentiality of high level communications, without more, can sustain an absolute, unqualified executive privilege of immunity from judicial processes under all circumstances." Since then, the court has drawn distinctions between two types of executive privilege: communicative privilege of the sort at issue in *U.S. v. Nixon* and the deliberative process privilege at issue in this case, *Cheney v. U.S. District Court for D.C.* (2004).

This case arose when a Task Force (NEPDG), convened by Vice President Dick Cheney within days of George W. Bush taking office, began to hold a series of closed meetings to discuss U.S. energy policy under the new administration. When the Task Force completed its work in May 2001, it issued a series of policy recommendations. Those policies largely reflected President Bush's views as he had articulated them during the 2000 campaign. However, the Task Force did not include in the report the names and affiliations of those with whom it had met to develop the report. Citizen watchdog organizations and environmental organizations suspected that the groups and individuals who met with the Task Force were overwhelmingly from oil and gas industries and trade associations representing energy providers such as Enron, BP, and Duke Energy. The critics' suspicions were heightened due to the fact that prior to taking his position as vice president, Cheney was the CEO of Halliburton, one of the world's largest providers of oil extraction products and services. In addition, the secrecy that shrouded the process suggested that the policies that emerged were a result of the interests of those in the room with the Task Force rather than the public good. Later, in 2002, the *New York Times* reported that of the 25 largest energy producers who contributed to the Bush-Cheney campaign, 18 met with the energy Task Force to develop policy. Public interest groups and environmental organizations brought suit against Cheney under the Freedom of Information Act (FOIA) to gain access to the records of the secret meetings. They also sued under the Federal Advisory Committee Act (FACA), which requires open meetings and the disclosure of names and affiliations of members of consultative bodies. Lower federal courts split on the question of whether the Task Force was required under FACA to release the names. The U.S. Supreme Court ruled in 2004 that this situation was not a criminal inquiry like the one in *U.S. v. Nixon*; therefore, Cheney was not obligated to do so.

Justice Kennedy delivered the opinion of the Court.

. . .

[T]he Vice President and his co-members on the NEPDG are
the subjects of the discovery orders. The mandamus petition
alleges that the orders threaten "substantial intrusions on the
process by which those in closest operational proximity to
the President advise the President." . . . **It is well established
that "a President's communications and activities encompass a vastly wider range of sensitive material than would
be true of any 'ordinary individual.' "**

Remember that in the *Clinton v. Jones* case,
for example, the court expressed a similar
concern for the special character of the executive that may limit the propriety of civil
actions against the president: "We have, in
short, long recognized the 'unique position
in the constitutional scheme' that [the Office
of the President] occupies."

. . . As *United States* v. *Nixon* explained, these principles do
not mean that the "President is above the law." Rather, they
simply acknowledge that the public interest requires that a
coequal branch of Government "afford Presidential confidentiality the greatest protection consistent with the fair
administration of justice," and give recognition to the paramount necessity of protecting the Executive Branch from
vexatious litigation that might distract it from the energetic
performance of its constitutional duties.

These separation-of-powers considerations should inform a
court of appeals' evaluation of a mandamus petition involving the President or the Vice President. Accepted mandamus
standards are broad enough to allow a court of appeals to prevent a lower court from interfering with a coequal branch's
ability to discharge its constitutional responsibilities. . . .

The Court of Appeals dismissed these separation-of-powers
concerns. Relying on *United States* v. *Nixon*, it held that even
though respondents' discovery requests are overbroad and
"go well beyond FACA's requirements," the Vice President
and his former colleagues on the NEPDG "shall bear the burden" of invoking privilege with narrow specificity and
objecting to the discovery requests with "detailed precision."
In its view, this result was required by *Nixon*'s rejection of an
"absolute, unqualified Presidential privilege of immunity
from judicial process under all circumstances." If *Nixon*
refused to recognize broad claims of confidentiality where

the President had asserted executive privilege, the majority reasoned, *Nixon* must have rejected, *a fortiori*, petitioners' claim of discovery immunity where the privilege has not even been invoked. According to the majority, because the Executive Branch can invoke executive privilege to maintain the separation of powers, mandamus relief is premature.

Here, the court points to what it sees as the critical distinction between the obligation of executive branch officials in criminal proceedings (*U.S. v. Nixon*) versus the obligations they have in civil proceedings, such as the case with the litigation over the Cheney Task Force. Remember, as a result of the *Nixon* case, the executive's interest in confidentiality is presumed, unless it can be overcome by the need to protect national security, diplomatic, military secrets, or criminal inquiries. In the court's judgment, the desire to learn the names of those attending the closed meetings did not meet that standard.

This analysis, however, overlooks fundamental differences in the two cases. *Nixon* **cannot bear the weight the Court of Appeals puts upon it. First, unlike this case, which concerns respondents' requests for information for use in a civil suit,** *Nixon* **involves the proper balance between the Executive's interest in the confidentiality of its communications and the "constitutional need for production of relevant evidence in a criminal proceeding."** The Court's decision was explicit that it was "not . . . concerned with the balance between the President's generalized interest in confidentiality and the need for relevant evidence in civil litigation . . . . We address only the conflict between the President's assertion of a generalized privilege of confidentiality and the constitutional need for relevant evidence in criminal trials."

The distinction *Nixon* drew between criminal and civil proceedings is not just a matter of formalism. As the Court explained, the need for information in the criminal context is much weightier because "our historic[al] commitment to the rule of law . . . is nowhere more profoundly manifest than in our view that 'the twofold aim [of criminal justice] is that guilt shall not escape or innocence suffer.' " In light of the "fundamental" and "comprehensive" need for "every man's evidence" in the criminal justice system, not only must the Executive Branch first assert privilege to resist disclosure, but privilege claims that shield information from a grand jury proceeding or a criminal trial are not to be "expansively construed, for they are in derogation of the search for truth." The need for information for use in civil cases, while far from negligible, does not share the urgency or significance of the criminal subpoena requests in *Nixon*. As *Nixon* recognized, the right to production of relevant evidence in civil proceedings does not have the same "constitutional dimensions."

The Court also observed in *Nixon* that a "primary constitutional duty of the Judicial Branch [is] to do justice in criminal prosecutions." Withholding materials from a tribunal in an ongoing criminal case when the information is necessary to the court in carrying out its tasks "conflict[s] with the function of the courts under Art. III." Such an impairment of the "essential functions of [another] branch," is impermissible. Withholding the information in this case, however, does not hamper another branch's ability to perform its "essential functions" in quite the same way. The District Court ordered discovery here, not to remedy known statutory violations, but to ascertain whether FACA's disclosure requirements even apply to the NEPDG in the first place. Even if FACA embodies important congressional objectives, the only consequence from respondents' inability to obtain the discovery they seek is that it would be more difficult for private complainants to vindicate Congress' policy objectives under FACA.... The situation here cannot, in fairness, be compared to *Nixon,* where a court's ability to fulfill its constitutional responsibility to resolve cases and controversies within its jurisdiction hinges on the availability of certain indispensable information.

A party's need for information is only one facet of the problem. An important factor weighing in the opposite direction is the burden imposed by the discovery orders. This is not a routine discovery dispute. The discovery requests are directed to the Vice President and other senior Government officials who served on the NEPDG to give advice and make recommendations to the President. The Executive Branch, at its highest level, is seeking the aid of the courts to protect its constitutional prerogatives. As we have already noted, special considerations control when the Executive Branch's interests in maintaining the autonomy of its office and safeguarding the confidentiality of its communications are implicated.

... Even when compared against *United States* v. *Nixon*'s criminal subpoenas, which did involve the President, the civil discovery here militates against respondents' position. The observation in *Nixon* that production of confidential information would not disrupt the functioning of the Executive Branch cannot be applied in a mechanistic fashion to civil litigation. In the criminal justice system, there are various constraints, albeit imperfect, to filter out insubstantial legal claims. The decision to prosecute a criminal case, for example, is made by a publicly accountable prosecutor subject to budgetary considerations and under an ethical obligation, not only to win and zealously to advocate for his client but also to serve the cause of justice.... **In contrast, there are no analogous checks in the civil discovery process here....**

Finally, the narrow subpoena orders in *United States* v. *Nixon* stand on an altogether different footing from the overly broad discovery requests approved by the District Court in this case. The criminal subpoenas in *Nixon* were required to satisfy exacting standards of "(1) relevancy; (2) admissibility; (3) specificity." They were "not intended to provide a means of discovery." ... The very specificity of the subpoena requests serves as an important safeguard against unnecessary intrusion into the operation of the Office of the President.

In contrast to *Nixon*'s subpoena orders that "precisely identi-fied" and "specific[ally] ... enumerated" the relevant materials, the discovery requests here, as the panel majority acknowledged, ask for everything under the sky....

Given the breadth of the discovery requests in this case compared to the narrow subpoena orders in *United States* v. *Nixon*, our precedent provides no support for the proposition that the Executive Branch "shall bear the burden" of invoking executive privilege with sufficient specificity and of making particularized objections. To be sure, *Nixon* held that the President cannot, through the assertion of a "broad [and] undifferentiated" need for confidentiality and the invocation of an "absolute, unqualified" executive privilege, withhold information in the face of subpoena orders. It did so, however, only after the party requesting the information—the special prosecutor—had satisfied his burden of showing the propriety of the requests. Here, as the Court of Appeals

The majority is of the opinion that if they issue the mandamus (a legal order compelling an official to exercise some nondiscretionary act, like releasing the names), the executive would be inundated with requests —some perhaps frivolous—for the release of records regarding privileged information and deliberative processes, greatly interfering with the "functioning of the Executive Branch."

acknowledged, the discovery requests are anything but appropriate. They provide respondents all the disclosure to which they would be entitled in the event they prevail on the merits, and much more besides. In these circumstances, *Nixon* does not require the Executive Branch to bear the onus of critiquing the unacceptable discovery requests line by line.

. . .

Contrary to the District Court's and the Court of Appeals' conclusions, *Nixon* does not leave them the sole option of inviting the Executive Branch to invoke executive privilege while remaining otherwise powerless to modify a party's overly broad discovery requests. Executive privilege is an extraordinary assertion of power "not to be lightly invoked." Once executive privilege is asserted, coequal branches of the Government are set on a collision course. The Judiciary is forced into the difficult task of balancing the need for information in a judicial proceeding and the Executive's Article II prerogatives. This inquiry places courts in the awkward position of evaluating the Executive's claims of confidentiality and autonomy, and pushes to the fore difficult questions of separation of powers and checks and balances. These "occasion[s] for constitutional confrontation between the two branches" should be avoided whenever possible.

V

. . . [W]e decline petitioners' invitation to direct the Court of Appeals to issue the writ against the District Court. . . . We note only that all courts should be mindful of the burdens imposed on the Executive Branch in any future proceedings. . . .

The judgment of the Court of Appeals for the District of Columbia is vacated, and the case is remanded for further proceedings consistent with this opinion.

Source: *Cheney v. United States District Court*, 542 U.S. 367 (2004).

U.S. Citizens as Enemy Combatants

Hamdi v. Rumsfeld

June 28, 2004

INTRODUCTION

On June 28, 2004, the U.S. Supreme Court handed down three rulings pertaining to detainees in the war on terror. The *Rasul* case was one of them. In *Rasul,* the court decided that Guantanamo was within the jurisdictional authority of the United States, and as a consequence, prisoners held at the detention facility there could petition U.S. courts for habeas relief. That meant that the detaining authority could not simply hold them indefinitely; they would have to justify the detentions on some grounds. The other two cases involved two remaining questions, not decided in *Rasul.* First, is the "some evidence" standard advocated by the Bush administration sufficient to hold the prisoners? And second, what processes are due the prisoners—a full blown criminal trial or something short of that, like a military commission?

The two other cases decided on the same day as Rasul were *Hamdi v. Rumsfeld* and *Rumsfeld v. Padilla.* The cases dealt with the procedural protections the military authorities were obligated to provide Hamdi and Padilla, both U.S. citizens. The court determined that Padilla's habeas petition was improperly submitted and declined review (though took up separate legal issues in a later version of the case). But the court decided the *Hamdi* case on the merits, even though no single opinion captured a majority of the justices' votes.

The case, excerpted here, involved Yaser Hamdi, a U.S. citizen born in Louisiana and captured in Afghanistan after being turned over to U.S. forces by the Northern Alliance in exchange for financial compensation. Like many detainees, Hamdi was held at Guantanamo. However, once it was determined that he was a U.S. citizen, he was transferred to the naval brig in South Carolina. In the *Hamdi* case, the court had to determine what processes are due someone who is a U.S. citizen on U.S. soil but deemed an "enemy combatant."

The Authorization for Use of Military Force (AUMF) was passed within days of September 11, 2001. It authorized the president to use "all necessary and appropriate force" against "nations, organizations, or persons" associated with the terrorist attacks. That designation included both al-Qaeda terrorists and members of the Taliban in Afghanistan who supported al-Qaeda. In addition, the use of "all necessary and appropriate force" would include the detention of individuals who are either Taliban fighters or members of al-Qaeda. According to the court, detention is "fundamental and accepted an incident to war" and thereby "a proper exercise of the 'necessary and appropriate force' Congress authorized the President to use."

Justice O'Connor announced the judgment of the Court.

. . . The threshold question before us is whether the Executive has the authority to detain citizens who qualify as "enemy combatants." . . . The Government maintains that no explicit congressional authorization is required, because the Executive possesses plenary authority to detain pursuant to Article II of the Constitution. We do not reach the question whether Article II provides such authority, however, because **we agree with the Government's alternative position, that Congress has in fact authorized Hamdi's detention, through the AUMF.**

269

. . .

Hamdi objects, nevertheless, that Congress has not authorized the *indefinite* detention to which he is now subject. . . .
We take Hamdi's objection to be not to the lack of certainty
regarding the date on which the conflict will end, but to the
substantial prospect of perpetual detention. We recognize
that the national security underpinnings of the "war on terror," although crucially important, are broad and malleable.
As the Government concedes, "given its unconventional
nature, the current conflict is unlikely to end with a formal
cease-fire agreement." The prospect Hamdi raises is therefore not far-fetched. . . . Hamdi's detention could last for the
rest of his life.

. . . Hamdi contends that the AUMF does not authorize indefinite or perpetual detention. Certainly, we agree that indefinite
detention for the purpose of interrogation is not authorized.
Further, we understand Congress' grant of authority for the
use of "necessary and appropriate force" to include the authority to detain for the duration of the relevant conflict, and . . . [a]
ctive combat operations against Taliban fighters apparently are
ongoing in Afghanistan. . . . The United States may detain, for
the duration of these hostilities, individuals legitimately determined to be Taliban combatants who "engaged in an armed
conflict against the United States." If the record establishes that
United States troops are still involved in active combat in
Afghanistan, those detentions are part of the exercise of "necessary and appropriate force," and therefore are authorized by
the AUMF.

. . .

Even in cases in which the detention of enemy combatants is
legally authorized, there remains the question of what process is constitutionally due to a citizen who disputes his
enemy-combatant status. **Hamdi argues that he is owed a
meaningful and timely hearing and that "extra-judicial
detention [that] begins and ends with the submission of
an affidavit based on third-hand hearsay" does not com-
port with the Fifth and Fourteenth Amendments.** . . .

The "third-hand hearsay" refers to the so-
called Mobbs Declaration. Michael Mobbs
was a Department of Defense official who
compiled the accounts of Hamdi's movements and affiliations that led to his capture.
According to Mobbs, Hamdi was not simply
an aid worker traveling in Afghanistan when
he was kidnapped by the Northern Alliance,
as Hamdi's father claimed was the case.
Rather, Mobbs indicated that Hamdi had
joined the Taliban and remained with them
after September 11. At the time, the administration's procedures (per the Military Order
signed by Bush) for determining whether a
detainee was a combatant included a showing of "some evidence" that the prisoner
was not an innocent civilian. Under the
existing rules of procedure, the detainee
was not permitted to challenge the evidence
or know its source. Those representing Hamdi's challenge argued this violated fundamental due process rights of the accused
guaranteed by the 5th and 14th Amendments
to the Constitution.

Though they reach radically different conclusions on the process that ought to attend the present proceeding, the parties begin on common ground. All agree that, absent suspension, the writ of habeas corpus remains available to every individual detained within the United States. Only in the rarest of circumstances has Congress seen fit to suspend the writ. At all other times, it has remained a critical check on the Executive, ensuring that it does not detain individuals except in accordance with law. All agree suspension of the writ has not occurred here. Thus, it is undisputed that Hamdi was properly before an Article III court to challenge his detention . . .

The Government's . . . argument . . . that further factual exploration is unwarranted and inappropriate in light of the extraordinary constitutional interests at stake. Under the Government's most extreme rendition of this argument, "[r]espect for separation of powers and the limited institutional capabilities of courts in matters of military decision-making in connection with an ongoing conflict" ought to eliminate entirely any individual process, restricting the courts to investigating only whether legal authorization exists for the broader detention scheme. At most, the Government argues, courts should review its determination that a citizen is an enemy combatant under a very deferential "some evidence" standard. . . . Under this review, a court would assume the accuracy of the Government's articulated basis for Hamdi's detention, . . . and assess only whether that articulated basis was a legitimate one. . . .

In response, Hamdi emphasizes that this Court consistently has recognized that an individual challenging his detention may not be held at the will of the Executive without recourse to some proceeding before a neutral tribunal to determine whether the Executive's asserted justifications for that detention have basis in fact and warrant in law. He argues that the Fourth Circuit inappropriately "ceded power to the Executive during wartime to define the conduct for which a citizen may be detained, judge whether that citizen has engaged in the proscribed conduct, and imprison that citizen indefinitely," and that due process demands that he receive a hearing in which he may challenge the [the evidence against him] and adduce his own counter evidence.

. . .

Striking the proper constitutional balance here is of great importance to the Nation during this period of ongoing combat. But it is equally vital that our calculus not give short shrift to the values that this country holds dear or to the privilege that is American citizenship. It is during our most challenging and uncertain moments that our Nation's commitment to due process is most severely tested; and it is in those times that we must preserve our commitment at home to the principles for which we fight abroad.

. . .

With due recognition of these competing concerns, we believe that neither the process proposed by the Government nor the process apparently envisioned by the District Court below strikes the proper constitutional balance when a United States citizen is detained in the United States as an enemy combatant. That is, "the risk of erroneous deprivation" of a detainee's liberty interest is unacceptably high under the Government's proposed rule, while some of the "additional or substitute procedural safeguards" suggested by the District Court are unwarranted in light of their limited "probable value" and the burdens they may impose on the military in such cases.

We therefore hold that a citizen-detainee seeking to challenge his classification as an enemy combatant must receive notice of the factual basis for his classification, and a fair opportunity to rebut the Government's factual assertions before a neutral decisionmaker.... These essential constitutional promises may not be eroded.

. . .

In sum, while the full protections that accompany challenges to detentions in other settings may prove unworkable and inappropriate in the enemy-combatant setting, the threats to military operations posed by a basic system of independent review are not so weighty as to trump a citizen's core rights to challenge meaningfully the Government's case and to be heard by an impartial adjudicator.

In so holding, we necessarily reject the Government's assertion that separation of powers principles mandate a heavily circumscribed role for the courts in such circumstances. Indeed, the position that the courts must forgo any examination of the individual case and focus exclusively on the legality of the broader detention scheme cannot be mandated by any reasonable view of separation of powers, as this approach serves only to *condense* power into a single branch of government. We have long since made clear that a state of war is not a blank check for the President when it comes to the rights of the Nation's citizens. *Youngstown Sheet & Tube*, 343 U.S., at 587. Whatever power the United States Constitution envisions for the Executive in its exchanges with other nations or with enemy organizations in times of conflict, it most assuredly envisions a role for all three branches when individual liberties are at stake.... Likewise, we have made clear that, unless Congress acts to suspend it, the Great Writ of habeas corpus allows the Judicial Branch to play a necessary role in maintaining this delicate balance of governance, serving as an important judicial check on the Executive's discretion in the realm of detentions.... **Absent suspension of the writ by Congress, a citizen detained as an enemy combatant is entitled to this process.**

Because we conclude that due process demands some system for a citizen detainee to refute his classification, the proposed "some evidence" standard is inadequate. Any process in which the Executive's factual assertions go wholly unchallenged or are simply presumed correct without any opportunity for the alleged combatant to demonstrate otherwise falls constitutionally short.

. . .

It was a fractured decision—no majority coalesced around any opinion—including this from O'Connor. But this was a key holding, as eight of the nine Justices agreed that the president does not have the authority to hold indefinitely a U.S. citizen in violation of the due process protections of the 5th and 14th Amendments. The lone holdout was Justice Thomas, who argued that the president's broad authority as commander in chief circumscribes judicial review of executive decision-making during wartime.

The judgment of the United States Court of Appeals for the Fourth Circuit is vacated, and the case is remanded for further proceedings.

It is so ordered.

Source: *Hamdi v. Rumsfeld*, 542 U.S. 507 (2004).

Combatant Status Review Tribunals (CSRTs)

U.S. Department of Defense Factsheet
July 7, 2004

INTRODUCTION

Together with *Rasul,* the *Hamdi* decision appeared to limit the power of the executive branch to hold prisoners indefinitely without an opportunity to challenge their detention. *Hamdi,* in particular, obligated the administration to afford prisoners some hearing—including an opportunity to rebut evidence against them—to determine whether they were indeed combatants. However, the court's ruling in *Hamdi* did not specify the particular mechanism for this review procedure, nor did the court suggest that military authorities had to provide all the procedural protections of the U.S. civil justice system. On July 7, 2004, a week after the court's decisions, the Department of Defense established Combatant Status Review Tribunals to meet the legal obligations set forth in the court's opinion in *Hamdi.*

The rules of evidence that CSRTs employ are not those of the civilian justice system. Rather, they reflect "existing military regulations," such as Army Regulation 190-8, that are designed to comply with Article 5 of the Third Geneva convention. That article affords prisoners whose status as belligerents is in question access to a "competent tribunal." Language in the court's decision in *Hamdi* indicated that such a process might be sufficient to meet both the due process requirements and military necessity.

In response to last week's decisions by the Supreme Court, the Deputy Secretary of Defense today issued an order creating procedures for a Combatant Status Review Tribunal to provide detainees at Guantanamo Bay Naval Base with notice of the basis for their detention and review of their detention as enemy combatants. Each of these individuals has been determined to be an enemy combatant through multiple levels of review by the Department of Defense. **The procedures for the Review Tribunal are intended to reflect the guidance the Supreme Court provided in its decisions last week.**

The Supreme Court's Decisions

The Supreme Court held that the federal courts have jurisdiction to hear challenges to the legality of the detention of enemy combatants held at Guantanamo Bay [*Rasul*]. In a separate decision—involving an American citizen held in the United States—the Court also held that due process would be satisfied by notice and an opportunity to be heard, and indicated that such process could properly be provided in the context of a hearing before a tribunal of military officers [*Hamdi*].

The Court specifically cited certain existing military regulations, Army Regulation 190-8, which it suggested might be sufficient to meet the standards it articulated. The tribunals established under those regulations are relatively informal and occur without counsel or a personal representative. The process is a streamlined process designed to allow for expeditious determinations; in citing it, the Court recognized the military's need for flexibility and indicated that the process might provide all that was needed even for a citizen. Even in a traditional conflict, such a hearing is not provided to everyone who is detained, but only in cases of doubt as to the basis for detention.

The Process

The order issued today creates tribunals very much like those cited favorably by the Court to meet the unique circumstances of the Guantanamo detainees, and will provide an expeditious opportunity for non-citizen detainees to receive notice and an opportunity to be heard. It will not preclude them from seeking additional review in federal court.

Many critics of the CSRT process argue that the tribunals simply confirmed the military's predetermined status. Keep in mind that not all detainees at Guantanamo were given CSRT hearings, only those whose status as a combatant was in question. The degree to which their status was in question was at the discretion of the military authorities, and the presumption was that each of the detainees appearing before the CSRTs was indeed a combatant.

Notice

By July 17, each detainee will be notified of the review of his detention as an enemy combatant, of the opportunity to consult with a personal representative, and of the right to seek review in U.S. courts.

Personal Representative

Each detainee will be assigned a military officer as a personal representative to assist in connection with the Tribunal process. This person is not a lawyer but provides assistance to the detainee that is not normally offered in the process cited favorably by the Supreme Court or required by the Geneva Conventions.

Tribunals

Detainees will be afforded an opportunity to appear before and present evidence to a Tribunal composed of three neutral commissioned military officers, none of whom was involved in the apprehension, detention, interrogation, or previous determination of status of the detainee.

Hearings

The detainee will be allowed to attend all proceedings of the Tribunal except for those involving deliberation and voting or which would compromise national security if held in the presence of the detainee.

The detainee will be provided with an interpreter and his personal representative will be available to assist at the hearing.

The detainee will be allowed to present evidence, to call witnesses if reasonably available, and to question witnesses called by the Tribunal.

The detainee will have the right to testify or otherwise address the Tribunal in oral or written form, but may not be compelled to testify.

Decision

The Tribunal will decide whether a preponderance of evidence supports the detention of the individual as an enemy combatant, and there will be a rebuttable presumption in favor of the Government's evidence.

Non-Enemy Combatant Determination

If the Tribunal determines that the detainee should no longer be classified as an enemy combatant, the Secretary of Defense will advise the Secretary of State, who will coordinate the transfer of the detainee for release to the detainee's country of citizenship or other disposition consistent with domestic and international obligations and U.S. foreign policy.

Source: U.S. Department of Defense. Factsheet: Combatant Status Review Tribunals. http://www.defense.gov/news/Jul2004/d20040707factsheet.pdf.

In U.S. criminal courts, the defendant has the protection of a presumption of innocence. In these tribunals, however, the prisoner was assumed to be guilty. To overcome the presumption that the prisoner was indeed a combatant, the detainee bore the responsibility of disputing the government's account of their involvement. To do so, they were allowed access to some of the evidence against them (but not if that information was classified) and provided a representative (but not necessarily an attorney). Moreover, evidence that was obtained during interrogations (including evidence that was acquired through the use of "enhanced interrogation techniques") could be used against them. They also had the ability to call witnesses on their behalf (but only those who were reasonably available). It is not clear who might be "reasonably available"—even by phone —to a CSRT hearing in Guantanamo Bay, well away from the field of battle. According to the Department of Defense, 520 detainees had been processed by the CSRTs through March 2005. Of which, 38 were determined to be nonenemy combatants. Those who remained in custody were then given annual reviews by an Administrative Review Board to determine if they continued to present a threat to the United States.

Warrantless Wiretapping

George W. Bush's Press Conference
December 19, 2005

INTRODUCTION

On December 16, 2005, the *New York Times* ran a front-page story revealing that soon after the September 11 attacks, President Bush "secretly authorized the National Security Agency to eavesdrop on Americans and others inside the United States in order to investigate suspected terrorist activity"—without the warrants that are required for domestic wiretaps. It was the largest surveillance operation in American history. The revelation that the NSA, whose mission is to conduct foreign surveillance, was authorized by the president to spy domestically in contravention of the 1978 Foreign Intelligence Surveillance Act (explored in an earlier chapter in this volume) raised serious questions about executive power in the fight against terrorism. In fact, the *New York Times* sat on the story for over a year at the request of the Bush administration. Government officials were concerned that its publication would jeopardize ongoing terrorism investigations. Ultimately, the story ran with key pieces of information excised due to national security concerns. In this press conference, the president responds to the report of warrantless domestic surveillance by the NSA by justifying the program as a necessary tool in the fight against global terrorism.

The President. Welcome. Please be seated. Thanks.

Our mission in Iraq is critical to victory in the global war on terror. After our country was attacked on September the 11th and nearly 3,000 lives were lost, I vowed to do everything within my power to bring justice to those who were responsible. I also pledged to the American people to do everything within my power to prevent this from happening again. What we quickly learned was that Al Qaida was not a conventional enemy. Some lived in our cities and communities and communicated from here in America to plot and plan with bin Laden's lieutenants in Afghanistan, Pakistan, and elsewhere. Then they boarded our airplanes and launched the worst attack on our country in our Nation's history.

This new threat required us to think and act differently. And as the 9/11 Commission pointed out, to prevent this from happening again, we need to connect the dots before the

The president makes a connection between the global war on terror and military operations in Iraq. There was no evidence supporting the connection between Iraq and the 9/11 attacks, nor was there evidence of Iraqi weapons of mass destruction, nor did Iraq pose an imminent threat to the national security of the United States or its allies. Nonetheless, the administration was insistent in making the link in its public statements.

This statement suggests that the blurring of lines of authority—domestic and foreign operations for the FBI domestically and the CIA and NSA in the foreign context—was justified given the global war on terror. Those limits were put into place after Watergate to constrain government's ability to use the CIA and NSA for domestic spying purposes.

By passing the Authorization for Use of Military Force (AUMF), Congress granted the president broad discretion to use "all necessary and appropriate force" against those, who in his judgment "planned, authorized, committed or aided" the terrorist attacks of September 11, 2001. The president buttresses the authority he derives from the AUMF with reference to his Article II powers as commander in chief. Together, he says, they grant him the power to direct the NSA to conduct the surveillance, even if it violates the 1978 statute. However, there were reports that elements of the program, specifically those relating to the request of records from telephone service providers, had begun well before 9/11. If that was the case, there was no statutory basis for his actions, and its authority at that time could only be derived from some claim of inherent presidential power.

In 2009, government investigators issued a report on the NSA program, which was code-named Stellarwind. That report, which was declassified in 2015, revealed that in 2006 (prior to its authorization by Congress in 2007), the FBI examined each of the leads derived from the warrantless wiretapping program in Stellarwind from 2004 through January 2006. The FBI investigation determined that none provided any information of use (though, it should be noted, there were redactions). Of the leads generated prior to 2004, 1.2% of them were determined to have provided useful information about terrorists.

enemy attacks, not after. **And we need to recognize that dealing with Al Qaida is not simply a matter of law enforcement; it requires defending the country against an enemy that declared war against the United States of America.**

As President and Commander in Chief, I have the constitutional responsibility and the constitutional authority to protect our country. Article II of the Constitution gives me that responsibility and the authority necessary to fulfill it. **And after September the 11th, the United States Congress also granted me additional authority to use military force against Al Qaida.**

After September the 11th, one question my administration had to answer was how, using the authorities I have, how do we effectively detect enemies hiding in our midst and prevent them from striking us again? We know that a 2-minute phone conversation between somebody linked to Al Qaida here and an operative overseas could lead directly to the loss of thousands of lives. To save American lives, we must be able to act fast and to detect these conversations so we can prevent new attacks.

So, consistent with U.S. law and the Constitution, I authorized the interception of international communications of people with known links to Al Qaida and related terrorist organizations. This program is carefully reviewed approximately every 45 days to ensure it is being used properly. Leaders in the United States Congress have been briefed more than a dozen times on this program. **And it has been effective in disrupting the enemy while safeguarding our civil liberties.**

This program has targeted those with known links to Al Qaida. I've reauthorized this program more than 30 times since the September the 11th attacks, and I intend to do so for so long as our Nation is—for so long as the Nation faces the continuing threat of an enemy that wants to kill American citizens.

. . .

I'll be glad to answer some questions.

Q. Are you going to order a leaks investigation into the disclosure of the NSA surveillance program? And why did you skip the basic safeguard of asking courts for permission for these intercepts?

The President. Let me start with the first question. . . . The fact that we're discussing this program is helping the enemy.

You've got to understand—and I hope the American people understand—there is still an enemy that would like to strike the United States of America, and they're very dangerous. And the discussion about how we try to find them will enable them to adjust. Now, I can understand you asking these questions, and if I were you, I'd be asking me these questions too. But it is a shameful act by somebody who has got secrets of the United States Government and feels like they need to disclose them publicly. . . . We're at war, and we must protect America's secrets.

Q. [W]hy did you skip the basic safeguards of asking courts for permission for the intercepts?

The President. First of all, I—right after September the 11th, I knew we were fighting a different kind of war. And so I asked people in my administration to analyze how best for me and our Government to do the job people expect us to do, which is to detect and prevent a possible attack. That's what the American people want. We looked at the possible scenarios. And the people responsible for helping us protect and defend came forth with the current program, because it enables us to move faster and quicker. And that's important. We've got to be fast on our feet, quick to detect and prevent.

We use FISA still—you're referring to the FISA court in your question—of course we use FISAs. **But FISA is for long-term monitoring. What is needed in order to protect the American people is the ability to move quickly to detect.**

Remember the Church Committee's report that emerged after Watergate. In that report, the committee wrote: "[i]n an era where the technological capability of Government relentlessly increases, we must be wary about the drift toward 'big brother government.' The potential for abuse is awesome and requires special attention to fashioning restraints which not only cure past problems but anticipate and prevent the future misuse of technology." That admonition, made in light of the use of intelligence agencies to monitor Vietnam War protesters and civil rights activists, gave rise to the FISA law and the establishment of the Foreign Intelligence Surveillance Court in 1978. The president's concern here is that the FISA procedures are anachronistic in the new context—they do not match the rapidity of the changing conditions that mark counterterror operations and surveillance. Long-term monitoring permission might not catch disposable cell phone use, for example.

Now, having suggested this idea, I then, obviously, went to the question, is it legal to do so? I am—I swore to uphold the laws. Do I have the legal authority to do this? And the answer is, absolutely. As I mentioned in my remarks, the legal authority is derived from the Constitution as well as the authorization of force by the United States Congress.

. . .

Q. Democrats have said that you have acted beyond the law and that you have even broken the law. There are some Republicans who are calling for congressional hearings and even an independent investigation. Are you willing to go before Members of Congress and explain this eavesdropping program? And do you support an independent investigation?

The President. We have been talking to Members of the United States Congress. We have met with them over 12 times. And it's important for them to be brought into this process. Again, I repeat, I understand people's concerns. But I also want to assure the American people that I am doing what you expect me to do, which is to safeguard civil liberties and, at the same time, protect the United States of America. And we've explained the authorities under which I'm making our decisions and will continue to do so. Secondly, . . . [t]his is a war. Of course we consult with Congress and have been consulting with Congress and will continue to do so.

Q. Thank you, Mr. President. . . . According to FISA's own records, it's received nearly 19,000 requests for wiretaps or search warrants since 1979, rejected just five of them. It also operates in secret, so security shouldn't be a concern, and it can be applied retroactively. Given such a powerful tool of law enforcement is at your disposal, sir, why did you see fit to sidetrack that process?

The President. We used the process to monitor. But also, this is a different era, a different war. So what we're—people are changing phone numbers and phone calls, and they're moving quick[ly]. And we've got to be able to detect and prevent.

And without revealing the operating details of our program, I just want to assure the American people that, one, I've got the authority to do this; two, it is a necessary part of my job to protect you; and three, we're guarding your civil liberties. And we're guarding the civil liberties by monitoring the program on a regular basis, by having the folks at NSA, the legal team, as well as the Inspector General, monitor the program, and we're briefing Congress. This is a part of our effort to protect the American people. . . .

Q. Thank you, Mr. President. I wonder if you can tell us today, sir, what, if any, limits you believe there are or should be on the powers of a President during a war, at wartime? And if the global war on terror is going to last for decades, as has been forecast, does that mean that we're going to see, therefore, a more or less permanent expansion of the unchecked power of the Executive in American society?

The President. First of all, I disagree with your assertion of "unchecked power."

Q. Well——

The President. Hold on for a second, please. There is the check of people being sworn to uphold the law, for starters. There is oversight. We're talking to Congress all the time, and on this program, to suggest there's unchecked power is not listening to what I'm telling you. **I'm telling you, we have briefed the United States Congress on this program a dozen times.**

It is relevant to note that briefing Congress on unilateral executive action during wartime is rather different than reporting to Congress pursuant to a statute. The latter is under congressional authority; the former is premised on a rejection of a role for Congress in constraining the unitary executive.

This is an awesome responsibility, to make decisions on behalf of the American people, and I understand that. And we'll continue to work with the Congress, as well as people within our own administration, to constantly monitor programs such as the one I described to you, to make sure that we're protecting the civil liberties of the United States. To say "unchecked power" basically is ascribing some kind of dictatorial position to the President, which I strongly reject.

Source: George W. Bush, The President's News Conference, December 19, 2005. *Public Papers of the Presidents of the United States: George W. Bush (Book II)* (Washington, DC: Government Printing Office, 2005), 1875–1888.

Suspension of Habeas Corpus

Boumediene v. Bush

June 12, 2008

INTRODUCTION

After *Hamdi v. Rumsfeld* (2004), the deputy secretary of defense established Combatant Status Review Tribunals (CSRTs) to determine whether certain individuals detained at Guantanamo were "enemy combatants." Lakhdar Boumediene and others appeared before CSRT panels, and each of the detainees was determined to be an enemy combatant. Subsequent to their designation, the detainees petitioned the District Court for the District of Columbia for habeas relief. While this was happening, Congress passed the Detainee Treatment Act of 2005 (DTA). A provision of the DTA explicitly denied habeas relief for Guantanamo detainees. In addition, the DTA also provided that the Court of Appeals for the District of Columbia Circuit shall have "exclusive" jurisdiction to review decisions of the CSRTs. Those detainees, like Boumediene, who were deemed enemy combatants by the CSRT faced subsequent trial in military tribunals—a military justice structure implemented by executive order in the early days after 9/11. In *Hamdan v. Rumsfeld* (2006), decided before the DTA was enacted, the court held that the military tribunal system was inconsistent with the standards provided for in the Uniform Code of Military Justice (UCMJ) and violated international law. In response to the *Hamdan* ruling, Congress passed the Military Commissions Act of 2006 (MCA). The MCA gave statutory authority to many of the processes and rules that had been established by the Department of Defense and, in particular, structured the commissions in ways that explicitly departed from the UCMJ requirements. In addition, the MCA stripped the authority of all federal courts to hear habeas petitions from detainees. One of the key questions before the court in the Boumediene case, then, was whether Congress, through the specific provision (§7) of the MCA, suspended the writ of habeas corpus without following constitutional obligations under the Suspension Clause. The Suspension Clause (Art. I,§9, cl. 2) reads as follows: "The Privilege of the Writ of Habeas Corpus shall not be suspended, unless when in Cases of Rebellion or Invasion the public Safety may require it." As you will see, the court found that Congress had unconstitutionally denied meaningful habeas relief without suspending the writ under the Suspension Clause.

Justice Kennedy delivered the opinion of the Court.

Petitioners are aliens designated as enemy combatants and detained at the United States Naval Station at Guantanamo Bay, Cuba. There are others detained there, also aliens, who are not parties to this suit.

Petitioners present a question not resolved by our earlier cases relating to the detention of aliens at Guantanamo: whether they have the constitutional privilege of habeas corpus, a privilege not to be withdrawn except in conformance with the Suspension Clause. We hold these petitioners do have the habeas corpus privilege. Congress has enacted a statute, the Detainee Treatment Act of 2005 (DTA), that provides certain procedures for review of the detainees' status. We hold that those procedures are not an adequate and effective substitute for habeas corpus.

In deciding the constitutional questions now presented we must determine whether petitioners are barred from seeking the writ or invoking the protections of the Suspension Clause either because of their status, *i.e.*, petitioners' designation by the Executive Branch as enemy combatants, or their physical location, *i.e.*, their presence at Guantanamo Bay. The Government contends that noncitizens designated as enemy combatants and detained in territory located outside our Nation's borders have no constitutional rights and no privilege of habeas corpus.

Guantanamo Bay is not formally part of the United States. And under the terms of the lease between the United States and Cuba, Cuba retains "ultimate sovereignty" over the territory while the United States exercises "complete jurisdiction and control." ... [F]or purposes of our analysis, we accept the Government's position that Cuba, and not the United States, retains *de jure* sovereignty over Guantanamo Bay. As we did in *Rasul*, however, we take notice of the obvious and uncontested fact that the United States, by virtue of its complete jurisdiction and control over the base, maintains *de facto* sovereignty over this territory.

The Court has discussed the issue of the Constitution's extra-territorial application on many occasions. These decisions undermine the Government's argument that, at least as applied to noncitizens, the Constitution necessarily stops where *de jure* sovereignty ends. ... **In every practical sense Guantanamo is not abroad; it is within the constant jurisdiction of the United States. ...**

As in *Rasul*, the court determines that just because they are held at Guantanamo, the detainees (and executive authority) do not exist outside the rule of law. The court suggests that if Congress or the president had absolute discretion over whether constitutional guarantees apply within the jurisdiction of the United States, it would completely rework the constitutional order. Kennedy writes, for example, "To hold the political branches have the power to switch the Constitution on or off at will...would [lead] to a regime in which Congress and the President, not this Court, say 'what the law is' Marbury v. Madison (1803)."

These concerns have particular bearing upon the Suspension Clause question in the cases now before us, for the writ of habeas corpus is itself an indispensable mechanism for monitoring the separation of powers. The test for determining the scope of this provision must not be subject to manipulation by those whose power it is designed to restrain.

... [T]he procedural protections afforded to the detainees in the CSRT hearings ... fall well short of the procedures and adversarial mechanisms that would eliminate the need for habeas corpus review. Although the detainee is assigned a "Personal Representative" to assist him during CSRT proceedings, the Secretary of the Navy's memorandum makes clear that person is not the detainee's lawyer or even his "advocate." The Government's evidence is accorded a presumption of validity. The detainee is allowed to present "reasonably available" evidence, but his ability to rebut the Government's evidence against him is limited by the circumstances of his confinement and his lack of counsel at this stage. And although the detainee can seek review of his status determination in the Court of Appeals, that review process cannot cure all defects in the earlier proceedings.

. . .

We hold that Art. I, §9, cl. 2, of the Constitution has full effect at Guantanamo Bay. If the privilege of habeas corpus is to be denied to the detainees now before us, Congress must act in accordance with the requirements of the Suspension Clause. Petitioners, therefore, are entitled to the privilege of habeas corpus to challenge the legality of their detention. **In light of this holding the question becomes whether the statute stripping jurisdiction to issue the writ avoids the Suspension Clause mandate because Congress has provided adequate substitute procedures for habeas corpus.**

. . .

The Court of Appeals has jurisdiction not to inquire into the legality of the detention generally but only to assess whether the CSRT complied with the "standards and procedures

The referent for the "statue stripping jurisdiction" is §7 of the MCA. The Bush administration argued that Congress met the obligations under the Suspension Clause because the review process allowed under the DTA of 2005 provides an adequate substitute in the DC Court of Appeals. Under that provision, Congress granted that court jurisdiction to consider "(i) whether the status determination of the [CSRT] ... was consistent with the standards and procedures specified by the Secretary of Defense ... and (ii) ... whether the use of such standards and procedures to make the determination is consistent with the Constitution and laws of the United States." But that, says the court, is not the same thing as challenging the legality of one's detention—the principal protection afforded by the writ of habeas corpus. Therefore, Kennedy reasons, it is an inadequate substitute for habeas relief.

specified by the Secretary of Defense" and whether those standards and procedures are lawful. If Congress had envisioned DTA review as coextensive with traditional habeas corpus, it would not have drafted the statute in this manner.

By granting the Court of Appeals "exclusive" jurisdiction over petitioners' cases, Congress . . . intended the Court of Appeals to have a more limited role in enemy combatant status determinations than a district court has in habeas corpus proceedings. To the extent any doubt remains about Congress' intent, the legislative history confirms what the plain text strongly suggests: In passing the DTA Congress did not intend to create a process that differs from traditional habeas corpus process in name only. It intended to create a more limited procedure. . . . It is against this background that we must interpret the DTA and assess its adequacy as a substitute for habeas corpus. . . .

[H]ere the detention is by executive order. Where a person is detained by executive order, rather than, say, after being tried and convicted in a court, the need for collateral review is most pressing. A criminal conviction in the usual course occurs after a judicial hearing before a tribunal disinterested in the outcome and committed to procedures designed to ensure its own independence. These dynamics are not inherent in executive detention orders or executive review procedures. In this context the need for habeas corpus is more urgent. The intended duration of the detention and the reasons for it bear upon the precise scope of the inquiry. Habeas corpus proceedings need not resemble a criminal trial, even when the detention is by executive order. But the writ must be effective. **The habeas court must have sufficient authority to conduct a meaningful review of both the cause for detention and the Executive's power to detain.**

To determine the necessary scope of habeas corpus review, therefore, we must assess the CSRT process, the mechanism through which petitioners' designation as enemy combatants became final. Whether one characterizes the CSRT process as direct review of the Executive's battlefield determination that the detainee is an enemy combatant . . . or as the first step

Because Congress did not formally suspend the writ of habeas corpus, due process guarantees the detainees a meaningful alternative to habeas. The two challenges permitted by the DTA of 2005 upon review in the Court of Appeals fall far short of an opportunity to "meaningfully review" a detention of an enemy combatant. Insofar as the review is not meaningful, it does not meet the guarantees of habeas relief. And insofar as Congress, through §7 of the MCA, further strips jurisdiction of courts, habeas has been suspended without adhering to the obligations under the Suspension Clause.

in the collateral review of a battlefield determination makes no difference in a proper analysis of whether the procedures Congress put in place are an adequate substitute for habeas corpus. What matters is the sum total of procedural protections afforded to the detainee at all stages, direct and collateral.

Petitioners identify what they see as myriad deficiencies in the CSRTs. The most relevant for our purposes are the constraints upon the detainee's ability to rebut the factual basis for the Government's assertion that he is an enemy combatant. As already noted, at the CSRT stage the detainee has limited means to find or present evidence to challenge the Government's case against him. [T]he detainee's opportunity to question witnesses is likely to be more theoretical than real.

. . . Habeas corpus is a collateral process that exists, in Justice Holmes' words, to "cu[t] through all forms and g[o] to the very tissue of the structure. It comes in from the outside, not in subordination to the proceedings, and although every form may have been preserved opens the inquiry whether they have been more than an empty shell." *Frank* v. *Mangum* (1915) (dissenting opinion). Even when the procedures authorizing detention are structurally sound, the Suspension Clause remains applicable and the writ relevant.

. . .

For the writ of habeas corpus, or its substitute, to function as an effective and proper remedy in this context, the court that conducts the habeas proceeding must have the means to correct errors that occurred during the CSRT proceedings. This includes some authority to assess the sufficiency of the Government's evidence against the detainee. It also must have the authority to admit and consider relevant exculpatory evidence that was not introduced during the earlier proceeding. [T]hat opportunity is constitutionally required.

We . . . hold that when the judicial power to issue habeas corpus properly is invoked the judicial officer must have adequate authority to make a determination in light of the relevant law and facts and to formulate and issue appropriate orders for relief, including, if necessary, an order directing the prisoner's release.

The DTA does not explicitly empower the Court of Appeals to order the applicant in a DTA review proceeding released should the court find that the standards and procedures used at his CSRT hearing were insufficient to justify detention. This is troubling.

To hold that the detainees at Guantanamo may, under the DTA, challenge the President's legal authority to detain them, contest the CSRT's findings of fact, supplement the record on review with exculpatory evidence, and request an order of release would come close to reinstating the habeas corpus process Congress sought to deny them. The language of the statute, read in light of Congress' reasons for enacting it, cannot bear this interpretation. Petitioners have met their burden of establishing that the DTA review process is, on its face, an inadequate substitute for habeas corpus.

. . . [T]he Government has not established that the detainees' access to the statutory review provisions at issue is an adequate substitute for the writ of habeas corpus. MCA §7 thus effects an unconstitutional suspension of the writ.

In light of our conclusion that there is no jurisdictional bar to the District Court's entertaining petitioners' claims the question remains whether there are prudential barriers to habeas corpus review under these circumstances. . . . Here, as is true with detainees apprehended abroad, a relevant consideration in determining the courts' role is whether there are suitable alternative processes in place to protect against the arbitrary exercise of governmental power.

. . .

Our decision today holds only that the petitioners before us are entitled to seek the writ; that the DTA review procedures are an inadequate substitute for habeas corpus; and that the

In reviewing the legislative history of the DTA, the court determined that Congress had not envisioned the review process to be full habeas proceedings, with the potential outcome being the release of the person being detained. In fact, comments entered into the record (though, curiously, not actually a part of the debate on the floor) by Senators Graham and Kyl, reflect their clear preference for the absence of full habeas review. In fact, Congress sought to remove jurisdiction from all federal courts (other than the limited review mentioned above through the DC Court of Appeals) for all pending habeas petitions. The consequence of that, clearly, was very little review of the administration's determination of a detainee's status, and no opportunity for release upon a finding that the procedures ran afoul of the Secretary of Defense's requirements or constitutional or statutory protections.

petitioners in these cases need not exhaust the review procedures in the Court of Appeals before proceeding with their habeas actions in the District Court. The only law we identify as unconstitutional is MCA §7. Accordingly, both the DTA and the CSRT process remain intact. Our holding with regard to exhaustion should not be read to imply that a habeas court should intervene the moment an enemy combatant steps foot in a territory where the writ runs. The Executive is entitled to a reasonable period of time to determine a detainee's status before a court entertains that detainee's habeas corpus petition. The CSRT process is the mechanism Congress and the President set up to deal with these issues. Except in cases of undue delay, federal courts should refrain from entertaining an enemy combatant's habeas corpus petition at least until after the Department, acting via the CSRT, has had a chance to review his status.

Security subsists, too, in fidelity to freedom's first principles. Chief among these are freedom from arbitrary and unlawful restraint and the personal liberty that is secured by adherence to the separation of powers. It is from these principles that the judicial authority to consider petitions for habeas corpus relief derives. . . . The laws and Constitution are designed to survive, and remain in force, in extraordinary times. Liberty and security can be reconciled; and in our system they are reconciled within the framework of the law. The Framers decided that habeas corpus, a right of first importance, must be a part of that framework, a part of that law.

Source: *Boumediene v. Bush*, 553 U.S. 723 (2008).

Limits on Signing Statements

Barack Obama's Memorandum to Agency Heads

March 9, 2009

INTRODUCTION

Though they have been used by almost every president, signing statements came to popular attention following a story by Charles Savage of the *Boston Globe* about a signing statement by President Bush in which he appeared to nullify an important provision of the Detainee Treatment Act of 2005, a measure Bush had previously vowed to veto. In 2008, amid the uproar over presidential unilateralism, then candidate Barack Obama pledged to "not use signing statements to nullify or undermine congressional instructions as enacted into law." His Republican opponent in that race, Senator John McCain, also decried the use of signing statements in no small part because he had introduced the Detainee Treatment Act in the Senate.

Consistent with his campaign pledge, President Obama issued this memorandum on March 9, just a few weeks after taking office. Though the memorandum was directed to the heads of executive departments and agencies in his administration, the audience was rather broader than that. This was understood at the time to be a very public repudiation of the unitary executive perspective that characterized the Bush presidency. However, in many important respects, Obama's subsequent use of signing statements reflected the Bush, Clinton, and Reagan view of its efficacy as a policy device.

Subject: Presidential Signing Statements

For nearly two centuries, Presidents have issued statements addressing constitutional or other legal questions upon signing bills into law (signing statements). **Particularly since omnibus bills have become prevalent, signing statements have often been used to ensure that concerns about the constitutionality of discrete statutory provisions do not require a veto of the entire bill.**

In recent years, there has been considerable public discussion and criticism of the use of signing statements to raise constitutional objections to statutory provisions. There is no doubt that the practice of issuing such statements can be abused. Constitutional signing statements should not be used to suggest that the President will disregard statutory requirements on the basis of policy disagreements. At the same

Omnibus bills are pieces of legislation that combine several different policies into one package. Because they are conglomerations of many specific and unrelated provisions, congressional debate and deliberation over specific measures of the omnibus package is somewhat limited. It also makes it harder for a president to veto, since a veto would strike the entire package—not just the specific provision to which the president objects. They are, then, multidimensional legislative products. Here, the president indicates that the use of a signing statement to express concerns about the constitutionality of one of those dimensions would be appropriate.

time, such signing statements serve a legitimate function in our system, at least when based on well-founded constitutional objections. In appropriately limited circumstances, they represent an exercise of the President's constitutional obligation to take care that the laws be faithfully executed, and they promote a healthy dialogue between the executive branch and the Congress.

With these considerations in mind and based upon advice of the Department of Justice, I will issue signing statements to address constitutional concerns only when it is appropriate to do so as a means of discharging my constitutional responsibilities. In issuing signing statements, I shall adhere to the following principles:

1. The executive branch will take appropriate and timely steps, whenever practicable, to inform the Congress of its constitutional concerns about pending legislation. Such communication should facilitate the efforts of the executive branch and the Congress to work together to address these concerns during the legislative process, thus minimizing the number of occasions on which I am presented with an enrolled bill that may require a signing statement.

2. Because legislation enacted by the Congress comes with a presumption of constitutionality, I will strive to avoid the conclusion that any part of an enrolled bill is unconstitutional. In exercising my responsibility to determine whether a provision of an enrolled bill is unconstitutional, I will act with caution and restraint, based only on interpretations of the Constitution that are well-founded.

3. To promote transparency and accountability, I will ensure that signing statements identify my constitutional concerns about a statutory provision with sufficient specificity to make clear the nature and basis of the constitutional objection.

4. I will announce in signing statements that I will construe a statutory provision in a manner that avoids a constitutional problem only if that construction is a legitimate one.

Presidents are constantly communicating to Congress about pending legislation—through both formal and informal mechanisms. Among other means of communication, presidents use Statements of Administrative Policy (SAPs) to convey provision-specific information to Congress as it deliberates on a measure. SAPs express the president's position on pending legislation, representing the culmination of several levels of review and comment. The White House gathers comments from the agencies that would be affected by the pending policy, makes sure those views are consistent with presidential preferences, and turns them into a draft SAP. The draft SAP is then distributed to policy advisors before being finalized and sent to congressional committee members. Obama suggests that presidential communications—such as the SAPs—can serve to prevent legislation that would otherwise warrant a signing statement. Nonetheless, presidents have sometimes issued signing statements that identified problems with provisions that were never addressed in SAPs.

To ensure that all signing statements previously issued are followed only when consistent with these principles, executive branch departments and agencies are directed to seek the advice of the Attorney General before relying on signing statements issued prior to the date of this memorandum as the basis for disregarding, or otherwise refusing to comply with, any provision of a statute.

This memorandum is not intended to, and does not, create any right or benefit, substantive or procedural, enforceable at law or in equity by any party against the United States, its departments, agencies, or entities, its officers, employees, or agents, or any other person.

This memorandum shall be published in the *Federal Register.*

BARACK OBAMA

Source: Barack Obama, Memorandum on Presidential Signing Statements, March 9, 2009. 74 Federal Register 10669-10670. Document number E9-5442.

Here is the passage that presents a direct rebuke of the Bush era signing statements that had generated such controversy. Obama is directing all agency heads to disregard earlier constitutional objections and seek guidance before implementing regulations predicated on those signing statements. It is not clear, however, that while implementing laws, agencies had been following the objections identified in signing statements. In fact, one study discovered that most of the time the implementing agency was executing the provision of law that had generated a signing statement consistent with congressional (rather than presidential) preference. That raises an important question about the value of signing statements as presidential policy devices: if presidents issue signing statements, and agencies don't seem to implement laws consistent with the president's view of the offending provisions, then do signing statements even matter? Some have reasoned that the continued use of signing statements is a way for presidents to skew the bargaining with Congress in their favor, creating the impression that presidential power overrides congressional authority in a particular area or procedure. Also, issuing signing statements might enable the executive to be the *last mover* in the bargaining game with Congress. But that view doesn't account for congressional oversight and budgetary authority over implementing agencies. In addition, the Alito memo discussed earlier in this volume suggests that even if policy implementation isn't the goal, future court decisions may be influenced by the signing statements. So it should not be a surprise to discover that contrary to his campaign pledge, Obama has continued to issue signing statements, even if his pace (and the number of constitutional objections have diminished) has ebbed, relative to his predecessor.

Detainee Policy under Obama

Barack Obama's Statement on Military Commissions

May 15, 2009

INTRODUCTION

In *Boumediene,* the court held that the detainees in Guantanamo have a constitutional right to habeas relief and that the review process provided by Congress in the Detainee Treatment Act was not an adequate substitute for full habeas review. That decision meant that habeas petitions from prisoners held at Guantanamo could proceed. But these were the final days of the Bush administration. Two weeks after Barack Obama was elected president, a federal judge ordered the release of five of the six petitioners in the *Boumediene* case, ruling that the government did not have sufficient justification to continue to detain the prisoners. When Obama took office, almost 800 detainees had been held at Guantanamo. Of that number, approximately 500 had been removed either by being returned to their home country or by transferring to a third country. Roughly 230 detainees remained at the Guantanamo detention facility when Obama took office. One of the new president's first actions was to sign Executive Order 13493 establishing a Task Force "to conduct a comprehensive review of the lawful options available to the Federal Government with respect to the apprehension, detention, trial, transfer, release, or other disposition of individuals captured or apprehended in connection with armed conflicts and counterterrorism operations, and to identify such options as are consistent with the national security and foreign policy interests of the United States and the interests of justice." The executive order was then followed by a new set of guidelines for the military commissions, which had been halted pending the report of the Task Force.

---

§7 of the MCA of 2006 was the key provision that, in the court's judgment in *Boumediene,* suspended the writ of habeas corpus without following constitutionally prescribed procedures.

Military commissions have a long tradition in the United States. They are appropriate for trying enemies who violate the laws of war, provided that they are properly structured and administered. In the past, I have supported the use of military commissions as one avenue to try detainees, in addition to prosecution in Article III courts. In 2006, I voted in favor of the use of military commissions. **But I objected strongly to the Military Commissions Act that was drafted by the Bush administration and passed by Congress because it failed to establish a legitimate legal framework and undermined our capability to ensure swift and certain justice against those detainees that we were holding at the time. Indeed, the system of military commissions at Guantanamo Bay had only succeeded in prosecuting three suspected terrorists in more than 7 years.**

Today the Department of Defense will be seeking additional continuances in several pending military commission proceedings. We will seek more time to allow us time to reform the military commission process. The Secretary of Defense will notify the Congress of several changes to the rules governing the commissions. The rule changes will ensure that: **First, statements that have been obtained from detainees using cruel, inhuman, and degrading interrogation methods will no longer be admitted as evidence at trial; second, the use of hearsay will be limited, so that the burden will no longer be on the party who objects to hearsay to disprove its reliability; third, the accused will have greater latitude in selecting their counsel; fourth, basic protections will be provided for those who refuse to testify; and fifth, military commission judges may establish the jurisdiction of their own courts.**

These reforms will begin to restore the commissions as a legitimate forum for prosecution, while bringing them in line with the rule of law. **In addition, we will work with the Congress on additional reforms that will permit commissions to prosecute terrorists effectively and be an avenue, along with Federal prosecutions in Article III courts, for administering justice.** This is the best way to protect our country, while upholding our deeply held values.

Source: Barack Obama, Statement on Military Commissions, May 15, 2009. *Public Papers of the Presidents of the United States: Barack Obama (Book 1)* (Washington, DC: Government Printing Office, 2009), 655.

Part of the charge to the new Task Force included figuring out a way to process the remaining 230 detainees either through military commissions with the new procedural protections or through the civilian criminal justice system, with the ultimate goal of closing the Guantanamo detention facility within the year. During the review period, however, all military commissions were suspended (note the reference to "seeking additional continuances"). They were reinstated with new rules of procedure by executive order in March 2011. The 120 who remained in custody at Guantanamo were sorted into three categories. In the first category were 48 detainees, who, by virtue of having been subjected to torture and other coercive interrogation techniques, posed *evidentiary problems* for adjudication through the new military commissions or, certainly, civilian courts. Consequently, they remained in *legal limbo*, likely to be held indefinitely. The 2011 Executive Order provides for a process of periodic review for this category of detainees to determine if their continued detention is justified. The second category was composed of about 36 detainees who were likely to face trial in U.S. criminal courts. That left 121 detainees awaiting transfer to another country willing to take them.

The prospect of trying detainees in U.S. courts did not sit well with many members of Congress, who feared that the higher evidentiary standards and presumption of innocence that attends civilian trials would mean that former detainees could potentially be released in the United States. In particular, Republicans in Congress were concerned that the president was soft on terrorists by letting them *lawyer up*. As a result, Congress voted to prohibit the transfer or release of Guantanamo prisoners into the United States, thus preventing the administration from using civilian courts for detainee trials and ensuring that military tribunals would be the only politically viable option.

The Continuation of the State Secrets Privilege

Department of Justice Press Release

September 23, 2009

INTRODUCTION

As a presidential candidate, Barack Obama was highly critical of President Bush's use of the state secrets privilege to shield his administration from lawsuits challenging counterterrorism policies, including extraordinary rendition, torture, and warrantless wiretapping. The day after his inauguration, President Obama issued a memorandum to agency and department heads establishing systematic transparency in the executive branch: "[m]y Administration is committed to creating an unprecedented level of openness in Government. We will work together to ensure the public trust and establish a system of transparency, public participation, and collaboration." It was not long, however, before the Obama administration continued the practice of its predecessor in asserting the state secrets privilege to block lawsuits that might require the disclosure of national security secrets —including cases dealing with governmental surveillance and the torture of suspected terrorists.

The purpose of the privilege is to protect critical national security information from disclosure in civil litigation, even litigation in which the government is not involved. That purpose, however, places the judiciary's responsibility for uncovering truth through discovery procedures at odds with government's national security interests. And when courts generally defer to government's claims of national security, the judicial function is thereby circumscribed. The state secret privilege was first recognized by the U.S. Supreme Court in a 1953 case, *U.S. v. Reynolds*, in which the widows of the crew of a downed U.S. Air Force B-29 bomber sought details about the flight's crash. In that case, the government declined to turn over the accident report, arguing—successfully—that disclosure of the documents would endanger national security. Many years later, the report was released revealing that the U.S. Air Force was negligent in the deaths of the nine crewmembers. So the case that gave rise to assertions of privileged military and intelligence information also reveals just how problematic the assertion of the state secrets privilege can be—as an effective means for government to shield its own misconduct.

Attorney General Establishes New State Secrets Policies and Procedures

Attorney General Eric Holder today issued a memorandum instituting new Department of Justice policies and procedures in order to ensure greater accountability in the government's assertion of the state secrets privilege in litigation.

"This policy is an important step toward rebuilding the public's trust in the government's use of this privilege while recognizing the imperative need to protect national security," Holder said. "It sets out clear procedures that will provide greater accountability and ensure the state secrets privilege is invoked only when necessary and in the narrowest way possible."

Earlier this year, Attorney General Holder ordered senior Justice officials to conduct a review of the Department's existing state secrets policies and procedures, including an internal evaluation of the pending cases in which the privilege had been invoked. The results of that internal review were shared with an interagency group comprised of officials from the Department and the intelligence community, which provided input into the formulation of the new policies and procedures. The new policy and procedures take effect October 1, 2009.

The Attorney General's memorandum outlines several aspects of the new administrative process that increases accountability and oversight, including:

Facilitation of Court Review—**The policy ensures that before approving invocation of the state secrets privilege in court, the Department must be satisfied that there is strong evidentiary support for it. In order to facilitate meaningful judicial scrutiny of the privilege assertions, the Department will submit evidence to the court for review.**

When Obama came into office, his administration inherited a series of pending lawsuits from those who alleged that they had been illegally wiretapped or tortured. In each of those cases, the Bush administration had asserted the state secrets privilege, and in each of the pending appeals, the Obama administration continued those assertions. In response, many Democrats in Congress began the process of drafting legislation to rein in the president's use of the privilege. This policy, announced by Attorney General Holder, was the administration's attempt to thwart legislative momentum against the actions of the president.

Significant Harm Standard—The policy adopts a more rigorous standard to govern when the Department will defend assertions of the state secrets privilege in new cases. **Under the new policy, the Department will now defend the assertion of the privilege only to the extent necessary to protect against the risk of significant harm to national security.**

The previous "reasonable danger" standard was established in the *U.S. v. Reynolds* case and permits government to withhold information when there is a "reasonable danger" of revealing information that would jeopardize national security. The new standard that the attorney general adopted here would replace the "reasonable danger" standard with a more rigorous "significant harm" standard, thereby limiting the scope of cases in which the government could make the assertion of state secrets.

Narrow Tailoring of Privilege Assertions—Under this policy, the Department will narrowly tailor the use of the states secrets privilege whenever possible to allow cases to move forward in the event that the sensitive information at issue is not critical to

Under this new policy, a process of review of NSA or CIA requests for the invocation of the privilege is required. That review process includes high-level Department of Justice officials, including the attorney general. This provision of the policy explicitly states that the review team will reject petitions for assertions of the privilege if the motivation for asserting the privilege is to hide official misconduct. This formalized process was in sharp contrast to the more informal procedures adopted by the Bush administration, procedures that did not require the attorney general to sign off on the requests for the assertion of the state secrets privilege. It is important to note at least two things: first, the new procedures did not foreclose governmental assertions of state secrets, only established a means by which certain claims would proceed; and second, while the procedures establish a means for judges to review the government's claims for the assertion of the privilege, it was not uncommon for judges to accept the government's assertions without reviewing the basis for them.

the case. **As part of this policy, the Department also commits not to invoke the privilege for the purpose of concealing government wrongdoing or avoiding embarrassment to government agencies or officials.**

State Secrets Review Committee—A State Secrets Review Committee will be formed consisting of senior Department officials designated by the Attorney General who will evaluate any recommendation by the Assistant Attorney General of the relevant Division to invoke the privilege. The Committee would make its recommendation to the Associate Attorney General, who would review and refer to the Deputy Attorney General for a final recommendation to the Attorney General or his designee.

Approval by the Attorney General—The policy requires the approval of the Attorney General prior to the invocation of the states secret privilege, except when the Attorney General is recused or unavailable. Previously, the invocation of the state secrets privilege could be approved by the appropriate Assistant Attorney General.

Referral to Inspectors General. The policy implements a referral process to relevant Offices of Inspector General whenever there are credible allegations of government wrongdoing in a case, but the assertion of state secrets privilege might preclude the case from moving forward.

Under the policy, the Department also commits to provide periodic reports on all cases in which the privilege is asserted to the appropriate oversight Committees in Congress.

Source: Department of Justice, Press Release: Attorney General Establishes New State Secrets Policies and Procedures, September 23, 2009. http://www.justice.gov/opa/pr/attorney-general-establishes-new-state-secrets-policies-and-procedures.

Drone Strikes and Targeted Killings of U.S. Citizens

Memorandum for the Attorney General

July 16, 2010

INTRODUCTION

In September 2011, Anwar al-Aulaqi, an American citizen and member of the al-Qaeda in the Arabian Peninsula (AQAP) terrorist network, was killed by a U.S. drone strike in Yemen. The targeted killing of alleged terrorists by drone strikes became a frequently employed, but highly controversial, element of the counterterror efforts of the Obama administration. The ability of unmanned drones (and special operation raids like the one that killed bin Laden in 2011) to kill specific individuals with limited "collateral damage" provides the CIA and the Department of Defense a low-cost means to fight terror networks in the face of defense-related budget cuts and ebbing public support for protracted troop deployments. As efficient—and politically palatable—as they may be, they remain extrajudicial executions of individuals by U.S. military and intelligence services. The drone program began during the Bush administration and became a key component of the Obama administration's antiterror efforts. A New America Foundation report found that in Obama's first two years in office, he authorized four times the number of drone strikes that Bush did in his two terms in office. The Obama strikes were estimated to have killed between 1,299 and 2,264 suspected terrorists. But even as surgical as the strikes can be, it was clear they also resulted in civilian casualties. The growing frequency of these targeted killings under President Obama alarmed many international human rights organizations, foreign leaders, and many members of Congress. The critics of the drone program argue that the targeted killings violate international law and, in the case of the targeted killing of U.S. citizens like al-Aulaqi, U.S. Constitutional law. "Imagine," the critics might have argued, "if China or Russia decided to grant themselves the authority to start unilaterally killing people anywhere in the world." The legality of the drone program was addressed in this internal memo prepared for Attorney General Holder. The memo was leaked in February 2013 and drew a great deal of criticism from those who were opposed to the administration's reliance on targeted killings. In response to the rising concerns over the policy, Attorney General Holder noted that "... [w]e only take these kinds of actions when there's an imminent threat, when capture is not feasible and when we are confident that we're doing so in a way that's consistent with federal and international law."

Office of the Assistant Attorney General U.S. Department of
Justice Office of Legal Counsel

July 16, 2010

MEMORANDUM FOR THE ATTORNEY GENERAL

Re: Applicability of Federal Criminal Laws and the Constitution to Contemplated Lethal Operations Against Shaykh Anwar al-Aulaqi

We begin with the contemplated DoD operation. We need not attempt here to identify the minimum conditions that might establish a public authority justification for that operation. In light of the combination of circumstances that we understand would be present, and which we describe below, we conclude that the justification would be available because the operation would constitute the "lawful conduct of war"—a well-established variant of the public authority justification.

This is a reference to Justice Jackson's concurrence in *Youngstown Sheet & Tube Co. v. Sawyer* (1952) that we explored in an earlier chapter in this volume. Jackson wrote, "[w]hen the President acts pursuant to an express or implied authorization of Congress, his authority is at its maximum, for it includes all that he possesses in his own right plus all that Congress can delegate."

In applying this variant of the public authority justification to the contemplated DoD operation, we note as an initial matter that DoD would undertake the operation pursuant to Executive war powers that Congress has expressly authorized.

The Authorization for Use of Military Force (AUMF) passed following the September 11 attacks granted the president the authority to "use all necessary and appropriate force against those nations, organizations, or persons he determines planned, authorized, committed or aided the terrorist attacks that occurred on September 11, 2001, or harbored such organizations or persons, in order to prevent any future acts of international terrorism against the United States by such nations, organizations, or persons." Many have expressed concern that the initial AUMF, passed 10 years prior to al-Aulaqi's killing in Yemen, is insufficient legal basis for operations against individuals with only tenuous connections to those who committed the 9/11 attacks and who are located in regions—such as Yemen, Pakistan, and Somalia—outside of the recognized war zones of Afghanistan, Iraq, and Libya.

By authorizing the use of force against "organizations" that planned, authorized, and committed the September 11th attacks, **Congress clearly authorized the President's use of "necessary and appropriate" force against al-Qaida forces, because al-Qaida carried out the September 11th attacks.**

Based upon the facts represented to us, the target of the contemplated operation has engaged in conduct as part of that organization that brings him within the scope of the AUMF. High-level government officials have concluded, on the basis of al-Aulaqi's activities in Yemen, that al-Aulaqi is a leader of AQAP whose activities in Yemen pose a "continued and imminent threat" of violence to United States persons and interests. Indeed, the facts represented to us indicate that al-Aulaqi has been involved, through his operational and leadership roles within AQAP, in an abortive attack within the United States and continues to plot attacks intended to kill Americans from his base of operations in Yemen. The contemplated DoD operation, therefore, would be carried out against someone who is within the core of individuals against whom Congress has authorized the use of necessary and appropriate force.

Al-Aulaqi is a United States citizen, however, and so we must also consider whether his citizenship precludes the AUMF from serving as the source of lawful authority for the contemplated DoD operation. There is no precedent directly addressing the question in circumstances such as those present here; but the Supreme Court has recognized that, because military detention of enemy forces is "by 'universal agreement and practice,' [an] 'important incident of war,'" Hamdi v. Rumsfeld (2004), the AUMF authorized the President to detain a member of Taliban forces who was captured abroad in an armed conflict against the United States on a traditional battlefield.

In light of these precedents, we believe the AUMF's authority to use lethal force abroad also may apply in appropriate circumstances to a United States citizen who is part of the forces of an enemy organization within the scope of the force authorization. The use of lethal force against such enemy forces, like military detention, is an "important incident of war."

And thus, just as the AUMF authorizes the military detention of a U.S. citizen captured abroad who is part of an armed force within the scope of the AUMF, it also authorizes the use of "necessary and appropriate" lethal force against a U.S. citizen who has joined such an armed force. Moreover, DoD would conduct the operation in a manner that would not violate any possible constitutional protections that al-Aulaqi enjoys by reason of his citizenship. **Accordingly, we do not believe al-Aulaqi's citizenship provides a basis for concluding that he is immune from a use of force abroad that the AUMF otherwise authorizes.**

We believe similar reasoning supports the constitutionality of the contemplated operations here. As explained above, on the facts represented to us, a decision-maker could reasonably decide that the threat posed by al-Aulaqi's activities to United States persons is "continued" and "imminent."

The remainder of this memo reveals that the decision to deploy a drone strike against an individual follows a decision-making process high-ranking members of the executive branch counterterror apparatus employ to consider whether or not to target a suspected terrorist with lethal force, even if that terrorist is a U.S. citizen. The legal arguments of this memorandum generated deep concern among many in the Senate, including Senator Ron Wyden (D-OR), who released a statement arguing that "every American has the right to know when their government believes it is allowed to kill them." He continued: "The Justice Department memo...touches on a number of important issues, but it leaves many of the most important questions about the President's lethal authorities unanswered. Questions like 'how much evidence does the President need to decide that a particular American is part of a terrorist group?,' 'does the President have to provide individual Americans with the opportunity to surrender?' and 'can the President order intelligence agencies or the military to kill an American who is inside the United States?' need to be asked and answered in a way that is consistent with American laws and American values. This memo does not answer these questions."

In addition to the nature of the threat posed by al-Aulaqi's activities, both agencies here have represented that they intend to capture rather than target al-Aulaqi if feasible; yet we also understand that an operation by either agency to capture al-Aulaqi in Yemen would be infeasible at this time.

In the present circumstances, as we understand the facts, the U.S. citizen in question has gone overseas and become part of the forces of an enemy with which the United States is engaged in an armed conflict; that person is engaged in continual planning and direction of attacks upon U.S. persons from one of the enemy's overseas bases of operations; the U.S. government does not know precisely when such attacks will occur; and a capture operation would be infeasible. At least where high-level government officials have determined that a capture operation overseas is infeasible and that the targeted person is part of a dangerous enemy force and is engaged in activities that pose a continued and imminent threat to U.S. persons or interests the use of lethal force would not violate the Fourth Amendment. And thus that the intrusion on any Fourth Amendment interests would be outweighed by "the importance of the governmental interests [that] justify the intrusion," based on the facts that have been represented to us.

Please let us know if we can be of further assistance.

David J. Barron

Acting Assistant Attorney General

Source: Office of Legal Council, Memorandum for the Attorney General re: Applicability of Federal Criminal Laws and the Constitution to Contemplated Lethal Operations Against Shaykh Anwar al-Aulaqi, July 16, 2010. https://www.aclu.org/sites/default/files/field_document/2014-06-23_barron-memorandum.pdf.

Obama, Libya, and the War Powers Resolution
John Boehner's Letter to the President
June 14, 2011

INTRODUCTION

In 2011, as the Libyan dictator Colonel Muammar Qaddafi waged a vicious war against rebels and violently repressed antigovernment protests in Libya, President Obama warned: "If Qaddafi does not comply with the resolution, the international community will impose consequences, and the resolution will be enforced through military action." The attacks by militants continued and the United States took military action on March 18, 2011. The U.S. military involvement began with the destruction of Libyan air defenses and then participated in a NATO-led bombing campaign of Qaddafi-controlled positions. Consistent with the requirements of the War Powers Act of 1973, the president informed Congress of the military actions within 48 hours. That started the clock—President Obama had 60 days to seek approval from Congress for continuation of the hostilities or 30 days to stop the hostilities in Libya. However, as this letter from Speaker of the House John Boehner shows, the president neither sought congressional approval nor halted the hostilities by the time the 60-day window had closed, in violation of the War Powers Act.

The Department of Justice's Office of Legal Counsel (OLC) plays a prominent role in shaping the parameters of executive power. For instance, the flurry of memos authorizing torture of terror suspects, and the memo justifying the targeted killing of U.S. citizens engaged in hostilities against the United States are key examples explored in this volume. Since the 1930s, the OLC's determinations have been the last word on the constitutional and statutory authority of executive actions. Even during the Bush administration, when the Bybee and Yoo memos provided dubious legal authority for otherwise illegal activity, Bush followed the OLC guidance. However, in this case, OLC's determination that President Obama was obligated, under the War Powers Act, to seek approval for the continuation of hostilities was ignored. Instead, the president determined—contrary to the views of the OLC—that the United States was only playing a supporting role in a NATO action against Qaddafi, and therefore not engaged in hostilities. In this sense, the precedent Obama established to circumvent the Department of Justice's legal guidance would grant future presidents the basis to undermine what had for several decades been a key limit on the exercise of executive power.

June 14, 2011

The President

The White House

1600 Pennsylvania Avenue, Northwest

Washington, DC 20500

Dear Mr. President:

Five days from now, our country will reach the 90-day mark from the notification to Congress regarding the commencement of the military operation in Libya, which began on March 18, 2011. On June 3, 2011, the House passed a resolution which, among other provisions, made clear that the Administration has not asked for, nor received, Congressional authorization of the mission in Libya. Therefore, it would appear that in five days, the Administration will be in violation of the War Powers Resolution unless it asks for and receives authorization from Congress or withdraws all U.S. troops and resources from the mission.

Since the mission began, the Administration has provided tactical operational briefings to the House of Representatives, but the White House has systematically avoided requesting a formal authorization for its action. It has simultaneously sought, however, to portray that its actions are consistent with the War Powers Resolution. The combination of these actions has left many Members of Congress, as well as the American people, frustrated by the lack of clarity over the Administration's strategic policies, by a refusal to acknowledge and respect the role of the Congress, and by a refusal to comply with the basic tenets of the War Powers Resolution.

You took an oath before the American people on January 20, 2009 in which you swore to "faithfully execute the Office of President" and to "preserve, protect and defend the Constitution of the United States." The Constitution requires the President to "take Care that the Laws be faithfully executed," and one of those laws is the War Powers Resolution, which requires an approving action by Congress or withdrawal within 90 days from the notification of a military operation. **Given the mission you have ordered to the U.S. Armed Forces with respect to Libya and the text of the War Powers Resolution, the House is left to conclude that you have made one of two determinations: either you have concluded the War Powers Resolution does not apply to the mission in Libya, or you have determined the War Powers**

A key legal advisor to the State Department appeared before a congressional committee and argued that the NATO bombing campaign in which the United States was participating did not constitute a war, as it involved no ground troops, posed no grave danger to American forces, and was not likely to escalate. In response to his testimony, Democratic Senator (and veteran) Jim Webb argued: "[w]hen you have an operation that goes on for months, costs billions of dollars, where the United States is providing two-thirds of the troops, even under the NATO fig leaf, where they're dropping bombs that are killing people, . . . I would say that's hostilities."

Resolution is contrary to the Constitution. The House, and the American people whom we represent, deserve to know the determination you have made.

Therefore, on behalf of the institution and the American people, I must ask you the following questions: Have you or your Administration conducted the legal analysis to justify your position as to whether your Administration views itself to be in compliance with the War Powers Resolution so that it may continue current operations, absent formal Congressional support or authorization, once the 90-day mark is reached? **Assuming you conducted that analysis, was it with the consensus view of all stakeholders of the relevant Departments in the Executive branch?** In addition, has there been an introduction of a new set of facts or circumstances which would have changed the legal analysis the Office of Legal Counsel released on April 1, 2011? Given the gravity of the constitutional and statutory questions involved, I request your answer by Friday, June 17, 2011.

From the beginning, the House of Representatives has sought to balance two equal imperatives regarding Libya which have been in direct contradiction: the House of Representatives takes seriously America's leadership role in the world; our country's interests in the region; and the commitments to and from its steadfast allies. At the same time, strong concern and opposition exists to the use of military force when the military mission, by design, cannot secure a U.S. strategic policy objective. The ongoing, deeply divisive debate originated with a lack of genuine consultation prior to commencement of operations and has been further exacerbated by the lack of visibility and leadership from you and your Administration.

I respect your authority as Commander-in-Chief, though I remain deeply concerned the Congress has not been provided answers from the Executive branch to fundamental questions regarding the Libya mission necessary for us to fulfill our equally important Constitutional responsibilities. I believe in the moral leadership our country can and should exhibit, especially during such a transformational time in the

Boehner is clearly concerned that Obama has disregarded the Office of Legal Counsel's judgment regarding the applicability of the War Powers Act and is seeking a justification for abandoning a practice that has long stood for restraining executive authority. On June 24, the House voted overwhelmingly to reject President Obama's authority to continue what they considered to be "hostilities" in Libya but did not succeed in defunding military support. The actions ended in October, upon the death of Colonel Qaddafi.

Middle East. I sincerely hope the Administration will faithfully comply with the War Powers Resolution and the requests made by the House of Representatives, and that you will use your unique authority as our President to engage the American people regarding our mission in Libya.

Respectfully,

John A. Boehner

Speaker of the House

Source: Office of the Speaker of the House, Press release, June 14, 2011. http://www.speaker.gov/sites/speaker.house.gov/files/UploadedFiles/Letter_to_POTUS_Libya_061411.PDF.

Syria and an Expanding View of War Powers
Barack Obama's Address to the Nation
September 10, 2013

INTRODUCTION

For two years, the Obama administration had called for President Bashar al-Assad to step down as president of Syria, but did not taken direct action against Assad except to offer humanitarian assistance and support to the opposition working to rid Syria of Assad and his "horrific use of violence against the Syrian people" (Letter from Miguel E. Rodriguez, Assistant to the President and Director of the Office of Legislative Affairs, The White House, April 25, 2013, http://www.seattletimes.com/seattle-news/politics/text-of-white-house-letter-on-syria-to-senators/). Within weeks of his reelection, Obama was asked about the Assad regime's possible use of chemical weapons against the Syrian people. The president's response was "I want to make it absolutely clear to Assad and those under his command: The world is watching. The use of chemical weapons is and would be totally unacceptable. If you make the tragic mistake of using these weapons, there will be consequences and you will be held accountable." On August 21, 2013, it became clear that Assad's government forces gassed over 1,000 Syrian people in a brutal civil war that by that time had claimed over 100,000 lives. President Obama decided that the humanitarian aid and support for the opposition was insufficient and sought authorization from Congress to take military action against Assad.

THE PRESIDENT: My fellow Americans, tonight I want to talk to you about Syria—why it matters, and where we go from here.

Over the past two years, what began as a series of peaceful protests against the repressive regime of Bashar al-Assad has turned into a brutal civil war. Over 100,000 people have been killed. Millions have fled the country. In that time, America has worked with allies to provide humanitarian support, to help the moderate opposition, and to shape a political settlement. But I have resisted calls for military action, because we cannot resolve someone else's civil war through force, particularly after a decade of war in Iraq and Afghanistan.

The situation profoundly changed, though, on August 21st, when Assad's government gassed to death over a thousand people, including hundreds of children. The images from this massacre are sickening: Men, women, children lying in rows, killed by poison gas. Others foaming at the mouth, gasping for breath. A father clutching his dead children, imploring them to get up and walk. **On that terrible night, the world saw in gruesome detail the terrible nature of chemical weapons, and why the overwhelming majority of humanity has declared them off-limits—a crime against humanity, and a violation of the laws of war.**

. . .

On August 21st, these basic rules were violated, along with our sense of common humanity. No one disputes that chemical weapons were used in Syria. The world saw thousands of videos, cell phone pictures, and social media accounts from the attack, and humanitarian organizations told stories of hospitals packed with people who had symptoms of poison gas.

Moreover, we know the Assad regime was responsible. In the days leading up to August 21st, we know that Assad's chemical weapons personnel prepared for an attack near an area where they mix sarin gas. They distributed gasmasks to their troops. Then they fired rockets from a regime-controlled area into 11 neighborhoods that the regime has been trying to wipe clear of opposition forces. Shortly after those rockets landed, the gas spread, and hospitals filled with the dying and the wounded. We know senior figures in Assad's military machine reviewed the results of the attack, and the regime increased their shelling of the same neighborhoods in the days that followed. We've also studied samples of blood and hair from people at the site that tested positive for sarin.

When dictators commit atrocities, they depend upon the world to look the other way until those horrifying pictures fade from memory. But these things happened. The facts cannot be denied. The question now is what the United States of America, and the international community, is prepared to do about it. Because what happened to those people—to those children—is not only a violation of international law, it's also a danger to our security.

The proposed military intervention in Syria presented difficult legal questions for the president. Obama was proposing military action against a sovereign state for the purposes of punishing an alleged war crime, stabilizing a region, and enforcing international chemical weapons agreements, rather than preventing an imminent attack on the United States or its allies. Moreover, the action would be taken without authorization from the UN Security Council and without support from other international institutions, such as NATO. It would, very plainly, be unprecedented. As a result of the uncertainty regarding the legality of its actions, the Obama administration sought approval from Congress before initiating a limited military intervention in Syria. He faced an uphill battle in getting authorization from Congress, however. Indeed, his prospects were dim in the Senate and even more unlikely in the House.

Let me explain why. If we fail to act, the Assad regime will see no reason to stop using chemical weapons. As the ban against these weapons erodes, other tyrants will have no reason to think twice about acquiring poison gas, and using them. Over time, our troops would again face the prospect of chemical warfare on the battlefield. And it could be easier for terrorist organizations to obtain these weapons, and to use them to attack civilians.

If fighting spills beyond Syria's borders, these weapons could threaten allies like Turkey, Jordan, and Israel. And a failure to stand against the use of chemical weapons would weaken prohibitions against other weapons of mass destruction, and embolden Assad's ally, Iran—which must decide whether to ignore international law by building a nuclear weapon, or to take a more peaceful path.

This is not a world we should accept. This is what's at stake. And that is why, after careful deliberation, I determined that it is in the national security interests of the United States to respond to the Assad regime's use of chemical weapons through a targeted military strike. The purpose of this strike would be to deter Assad from using chemical weapons, to degrade his regime's ability to use them, and to make clear to the world that we will not tolerate their use.

That's my judgment as Commander-in-Chief. But I'm also the President of the world's oldest constitutional democracy. So even though I possess the authority to order military strikes, I believed it was right, in the absence of a direct or imminent threat to our security, to take this debate to Congress. I believe our democracy is stronger when the President acts with the support of Congress. And I believe that America acts more effectively abroad when we stand together.

This is especially true after a decade that put more and more war-making power in the hands of the President, and more and more burdens on the shoulders of our troops, while sidelining the people's representatives from the critical decisions about when we use force.

. . .

[O]ver the last few days, we've seen some encouraging signs. In part because of the credible threat of U.S. military action, as well as constructive talks that I had with President Putin, the Russian government has indicated a willingness to join with the international community in pushing Assad to give up his chemical weapons. The Assad regime has now admitted that it has these weapons, and even said they'd join the Chemical Weapons Convention, which prohibits their use.

Ultimately, an agreement was brokered with Russia whereby Assad agreed to turn over his chemical weapons cache. The air strikes were called off and Obama asked Congress to postpone a vote on the authorization for military action against Assad.

It's too early to tell whether this offer will succeed, and any agreement must verify that the Assad regime keeps its commitments. But this initiative has the potential to remove the threat of chemical weapons without the use of force, particularly because Russia is one of Assad's strongest allies.

I have, therefore, asked the leaders of Congress to postpone a vote to authorize the use of force while we pursue this diplomatic path. I'm sending Secretary of State John Kerry to meet his Russian counterpart on Thursday, and I will continue my own discussions with President Putin.

. . .

Meanwhile, I've ordered our military to maintain their current posture to keep the pressure on Assad, and to be in a position to respond if diplomacy fails. And tonight, I give thanks again to our military and their families for their incredible strength and sacrifices.

My fellow Americans, for nearly seven decades, the United States has been the anchor of global security. This has meant doing more than forging international agreements—it has meant enforcing them. The burdens of leadership are often heavy, but the world is a better place because we have borne them.

And so, to my friends on the right, I ask you to reconcile your commitment to America's military might with a failure to act when a cause is so plainly just. To my friends on the left, I ask you to reconcile your belief in freedom and dignity for all people with those images of children writhing in pain, and going still on a cold hospital floor. **For sometimes resolutions and statements of condemnation are simply not enough.**

. . .

America is not the world's policeman. Terrible things happen across the globe, and it is beyond our means to right every wrong. But when, with modest effort and risk, we can stop children from being gassed to death, and thereby make our own children safer over the long run, I believe we should act. That's what makes America different. That's what makes us exceptional. With humility, but with resolve, let us never lose sight of that essential truth.

Thank you. God bless you. And God bless the United States of America.

Source: Barack Obama, Remarks by the President in Address to the Nation on Syria, September 10, 2013. https://www.whitehouse.gov/the-press-office/2013/09/10/remarks-president-address-nation-syria.

Even though the strikes were averted, the principle that a president may take military action against another country to uphold international norms and in the interest of preventing (and punishing) human rights abusers is likely to live beyond this particular case. That is, even in the absence of its exercise in the Syria case, unilateral executive war power gained broader potential applicability.

Obama's Recess Appointments

NLRB v. Noel Canning

June 26, 2014

INTRODUCTION

The president's power to appoint officials with the authority to execute law is a critical part of executive power. The Constitution delegates to the president the authority to appoint inferior governmental officers (those who have a superior other than the president). However, in the case of principal officers (agency heads, federal judges, ambassadors, and the like), the Constitution specifies that the appointment power is to be shared with Congress. Article II, §2, cl. 2 of the Constitution specifies that the president "... shall nominate, and by and with the Advice and Consent of the Senate, shall appoint Ambassadors, other public Ministers and Consuls, Judges of the supreme Court, and all other Officers of the United States...." Typically, that has meant that the president must first nominate individuals for these high-level positions, then they face a Senate confirmation vote before they can be appointed to their posts. Sometimes, however, the Senate is not in session when a vacancy arises that the president must fill in order to "faithfully execute the law." In such a case, Article II, §2, cl. 3 prescribes that "[t]he President shall have Power to fill up all Vacancies that may happen during the Recess of the Senate, by granting Commissions which shall expire at the End of their next Session." Pursuant to that provision, then, presidents may make recess appointments without Senate approval. On one hand, this is a useful means to ensure continuity in governmental operations by granting the president the power to appoint individuals to key positions while the Senate is not in session. On the other, it allows presidents to appoint individuals to office who might not otherwise be confirmed by the Senate—allowing the president to circumvent a key congressional check on the executive branch. According to a 2015 study by the Congressional Research Service, President Clinton made 139 recess appointments, President George W. Bush made 171, and President Reagan made 232. By the spring of 2015, President Obama had made 32. This case deals with three of Obama's recess appointments to the National Labor Relations Board. The appointments were made in 2012 during a very brief (three-day) intrasession recess of the Senate rather than during the intersession. An intersession recess is the break after the first year of the two one-year session of a particular Congress. Until this case, the Supreme Court had never interpreted the recess appointment clause, so a set of three novel legal questions had to be addressed. First, whether Article II, §2, cl. 3 permits recess appointments during intrasession recesses or just during the intersession. Second, whether a recess appointment can be made to fill a vacancy that remains vacant during a recess, or whether the recess appointment can only be made for vacancies that occur while the Senate is in recess. And third, whether the Senate can prevent the president from making recess appointments by holding *pro forma* sessions (without doing any Senate work) during their recess.

Justice Breyer delivered the opinion of the Court.

Respondent Noel Canning, a Pepsi-Cola distributor, asked the D. C. Circuit to set aside an order of the National Labor Relations Board, claiming that the Board lacked a quorum because three of the five Board members had been invalidly appointed. The nominations of the three members in question were pending in the Senate when it passed a December 17, 2011, resolution providing for a series of "*pro forma* session [s]," with "no business . . . transacted," every Tuesday and Friday through January 20, 2012. Invoking the Recess Appointments Clause—which gives the President the power "to fill up all Vacancies that may happen during the Recess of the Senate," Art. II, §2, cl. 3—the President appointed the three members in question between the January 3 and January 6 *pro forma* sessions. Noel Canning argued primarily that the appointments were invalid because the 3-day adjournment between those two sessions was not long enough to trigger the Recess Appointments Clause. The D. C. Circuit agreed that the appointments fell outside the scope of the Clause, but on different grounds. It held that the phrase "the recess," as used in the Clause, does not include intra-session recesses, and that the phrase "vacancies that may happen during the recess" applies only to vacancies that first come into existence during a recess.

Held:

1. The Recess Appointments Clause empowers the President to fill any existing vacancy during any recess—intra-session or inter-session—of sufficient length.

(a) Two background considerations are relevant to the questions here. First, the Recess Appointments Clause is a subsidiary method for appointing officers of the United States. The Founders intended the norm to be the method of appointment in Article II,§2, cl. 2, which requires Senate approval of Presidential nominations, at least for principal officers. The Recess Appointments Clause reflects the tension between the President's continuous need for "the assistance of subordinates," and the Senate's early practice of meeting for a single brief session each year. The Clause should be interpreted as granting the President the power to make appointments during a recess but not offering the President the authority routinely to avoid the need for Senate confirmation.

Second, in interpreting the Clause, the Court puts significant weight upon historical practice. The longstanding "practice of the government," can inform this Court's determination of "what the law is" in a separation-of-powers case. There is a great deal of history to consider here, for Presidents have made recess appointments since the beginning of the Republic. Their frequency suggests that the Senate and President have recognized that such appointments can be both necessary and appropriate in certain circumstances. The Court, in interpreting the Clause for the first time, must hesitate to upset the compromises and working arrangements that the elected branches of Government themselves have reached.

Here, the court takes up the first question—of whether an intrasession break constitutes a recess sufficient to trigger the recess appointment power of the president. In addressing the question for the first time, the court cannot draw upon legal precedent; rather, they look to the framers' understanding of what they meant by "recess," and the patterns of historical practice. The court concludes that intrasession recess appointments have occurred for over 150 years without Senate disapproval. As a result, this broad interpretation is a boon to presidents seeking to circumvent Senate approval of appointees. However, the court goes on to note that there is a limit to that power.

(b) The phrase "the recess of the Senate" applies to both inter-session recess (*i.e.*, breaks between formal sessions of the Senate) and intra-session recesses (*i.e.*, breaks in the midst of a formal session) of substantial length. The constitutional text is ambiguous. Founding-era dictionaries and usages show that the phrase "the recess" can encompass intra-session breaks. And this broader interpretation is demanded by the purpose of the Clause, which is to allow the President to make appointments so as to ensure the continued functioning of the Government while the Senate is away. The Senate is equally away and unavailable to participate in the appointments process during both an inter-session and an intra-session recess. History offers further support for this interpretation. From the founding until the Great Depression, every time the Senate took a substantial, non-holiday intra-session recess, the President made recess appointments. President Andrew Johnson made the first documented intra-session recess appointments in 1867 and 1868, and Presidents made similar appointments in 1921 and 1929. Since 1929, and particularly since the end of World War II, Congress has shortened its inter-session breaks and taken longer and more frequent intra-session breaks; Presidents accordingly have made more intra-session recess appointments. Meanwhile, the Senate has never taken any formal action to deny the validity of intra-session recess appointments. In 1905, the Senate Judiciary Committee defined "the recess" as "the period of time when the Senate" is absent and cannot "participate as a body in making appointments," and that functional definition encompasses both intra-session and inter-session recesses. A 1940 law regulating the payment of recess appointees has also been interpreted functionally by the Comptroller General (an officer of the Legislative Branch). In sum, Presidents have made intra-session recess appointments for a century and a half, and the Senate has never taken formal action to oppose them. That practice is long enough to entitle it to "great weight in a proper interpretation" of the constitutional provision.

The Clause does not say how long a recess must be in order to fall within the Clause, but even the Solicitor General concedes that a 3-day recess would be too short. The Adjournments Clause, Art. I, §5, cl. 4, reflects the fact that a 3-day break is not a significant interruption of legislative business. A Senate recess that is so short that it does not require the consent of the House under that Clause is not long enough to trigger the President's recess-appointment power. Moreover, the Court has not found a single example of a recess appointment made during an intra-session recess that was shorter than 10 days. There are a few examples of inter-session recess appointments made during recesses of less than 10 days, but these are anomalies. In light of historical practice, a recess of more than 3 days but less than 10 days is presumptively too short to fall within the Clause. The word "presumptively" leaves open the possibility that a very unusual circumstance could demand the exercise of the recess-appointment power during a shorter break.

(c) The phrase "vacancies that may happen during the recess of the Senate," Art. II, §2, cl. 3, applies both to vacancies that first come into existence during a recess and to vacancies that initially occur before a recess but continue to exist during the recess. Again, the text is ambiguous. As Thomas Jefferson observed, the Clause is

Once the court has established that intrasession recess appointments are permissible, they now turn to the question of how long must those breaks be in order to qualify as recesses. Here, the court finds that three days is insufficient (in the full opinion, Breyer explains that a national catastrophe, for example, would be an exception). The three-day break the court refers to was a result of the Republican-controlled Senate voting to meet for *pro forma* sessions every three days in order to deny Obama the authority to make the recess appointments.

Now the court turns to the second question posed in the case—whether vacancies that arise prior to a recess fall under the recess appointment authority of the president, or whether recess appointments can only be made for vacancies that occur during the recess itself. Again, there is no legal precedent to guide the court's interpretation. The court draws upon a review of historical practice and some *practical wisdom* to derive its judgment that prerecess vacancies can be covered by the recess appointments clause.

"certainly susceptible of [two] constructions." It "may mean 'vacancies that may happen to be' or 'may happen to fall'" during a recess. And, as Attorney General Wirt wrote in 1821, the broader reading is more consonant with the "reason and spirit" of the Clause. The purpose of the Clause is to permit the President, who is always acting to execute the law, to obtain the assistance of subordinate officers while the Senate, which acts only in intervals, is unavailable to confirm them. If a vacancy arises too late in the session for the President and Senate to have an opportunity to select a replacement, the narrower reading could paralyze important functions of the Federal Government, particularly at the time of the founding. The broader interpretation ensures that offices needing to be filled can be filled. It does raise a danger that the President may attempt to use the recess-appointment power to circumvent the Senate's advice and consent role. But the narrower interpretation risks undermining constitutionally conferred powers more seriously and more often. It would prevent a President from making any recess appointment to fill a vacancy that arose before a recess, no matter who the official, how dire the need, how uncontroversial the appointment, and how late in the session the office fell vacant.

Historical practice also strongly favors the broader interpretation. The tradition of applying the Clause to pre-recess vacancies dates at least to President Madison. Nearly every Attorney General to consider the question has approved the practice, and every President since James Buchanan has made recess appointments to pre-existing vacancies. It is a fair inference from the historical data that a large proportion of recess appointments over our Nation's history have filled pre-recess vacancies. The Senate Judiciary Committee in 1863 did issue a report disagreeing with the broader interpretation, and Congress passed a law known as the Pay Act prohibiting payment of recess appointments to pre-recess vacancies soon after. However, the Senate subsequently abandoned its hostility. In 1940, the Senate amended the Pay Act to permit payment of recess appointees in circumstances that would be unconstitutional under the narrower interpretation. In short, Presidents have made recess appointments to preexisting vacancies for two centuries, and the Senate as a body has not countered this practice for nearly three-quarters of a century, perhaps longer. The Court is reluctant to upset this traditional practice where doing so would seriously shrink the authority that Presidents have believed existed and have exercised for so long.

2. For purposes of the Recess Appointments Clause, the Senate is in session when it says that it is, provided that, under its own rules, it retains the capacity to transact Senate business.

This standard is consistent with the Constitution's broad delegation of authority to the Senate to determine how and when to conduct its business, as recognized by this Court's precedents. Although the Senate's own determination of when it is and is not in session should be given great weight, the Court's deference cannot be absolute. When the Senate is without the capacity to act, under its own rules, it is not in session even if it so declares.

Under the standard set forth here, the Senate was in session during the *pro forma* sessions at issue. It said it was in session, and Senate rules make clear that the Senate retained the power to conduct business. The Senate could have conducted business simply by passing a unanimous consent agreement. In fact, it did so; it passed a bill by unanimous consent during its *pro forma* session on December 23, 2011. The Court will not, as the Solicitor General urges, engage in an in-depth factual appraisal of what the Senate actually did during its *pro forma* sessions in order to determine whether it was in recess or in session for purposes of the Recess Appointments Clause.

Because the Senate was in session during its *pro forma* sessions, the President made the recess appointments at issue during a 3-day recess. Three days is too short a time to bring a recess within the scope of the Clause, so the President lacked the authority to make those appointments.

Source: *National Labor Relations Board v. Noel Canning*, 573 U.S. ___ (2014).

Finally, the court takes up the question of whether the pro forma sessions are actually sessions sufficient to disrupt what would otherwise be a recess—even if the Senate does no Senate business during those sessions. The court rules that the Senate retains the capacity to do business, even if it chooses not to conduct business. Therefore, the Senate was officially in session during those *pro forma* days, effectively limiting the longer recess period to a series of three-day intrasession recesses. And, as noted above, three days is insufficient to trigger the Recess Appointments Clause.

A New AUMF to Confront ISIS

Barack Obama's Request to Congress
February 11, 2015

INTRODUCTION

From the fall of 2014 through February 2015, the U.S. military carried out over 2,000 airstrikes in Syria and Iraq, targeting the terrorist organization known as the Islamic State of Iraq and the Levant (ISIL or ISIS). Though the airstrikes were executed without explicit congressional authorization, the Obama administration viewed the military campaign against ISIS as falling within the president's power under two existing grants of authority—the 2001 AUMF and the 2002 Iraq War Resolution. Nonetheless, the Obama administration sought congressional approval for military action against ISIS to—as Secretary of State Kerry put it—"dispel doubts that might exist anywhere that Americans are united in this effort." So, in this request to Congress for new authorization, Obama was simply seeking congressional approval of what he determined was his preexisting authority to take military action. Curiously, the president took the unprecedented step of seeking an authorization from Congress for military action that appeared to limit—rather than expand—presidential war powers. His proposal would limit the military action to three years and would preclude large-scale engagement by ground troops (though it did retain the authority to deploy special operation forces). The administration's position was that the president had the authority under existing statutes to take direct military action, so if the new legislation failed (which appeared likely, given its specific provisions and the initial response from Congress), the president was no worse off. And, even as the proposal appeared to limit executive war power, it included a provision that retained the president's authority under the 2001 AUMF to take all necessary action to combat terrorism. Republican Senator Rand Paul (KY) bristled at the president's request for a new authorization: "[i]t's disdainful to say, 'Well, you know, we want y'all to pass something, but it doesn't really matter because we'll just use 2001,' which is just absurd . . . and it just means that Congress is inconsequential."

February 11, 2015

To the Congress of the United States:

The so-called Islamic State of Iraq and the Levant (ISIL) poses a threat to the people and stability of Iraq, Syria, and the broader Middle East, and to U.S. national security. It threatens American personnel and facilities located in the region and is responsible for the deaths of U.S. citizens James Foley, Steven Sotloff, Abdul-Rahman Peter Kassig, and Kayla Mueller.

If left unchecked, ISIL will pose a threat beyond the Middle East, including to the United States homeland.

I have directed a comprehensive and sustained strategy to degrade and defeat ISIL. As part of this strategy, U.S. military forces are conducting a systematic campaign of airstrikes against ISIL in Iraq and Syria. Although existing statutes provide me with the authority I need to take these actions, I have repeatedly expressed my commitment to working with the Congress to pass a bipartisan authorization for the use of military force (AUMF) against ISIL. Consistent with this commitment, I am submitting a draft AUMF that would authorize the continued use of military force to degrade and defeat ISIL.

On multiple previous occasions, President Obama declared that the existing 2001 AUMF and the 2002 Iraq War resolution granted him the authority he needed to take action against ISIS. In September 2014, he stated, "I have the authority to address the threat from ISIS." The problem with that claim, though, was that the 2001 AUMF authorized the president to take military action against al-Qaeda and its affiliates that had a hand in the September 11 attacks—not ISIS, which did not exist at the time. And the 2002 resolution, which gave President Bush the authority to use military force against Iraq, would not apply either, as the military strikes were targeting ISIS, not Iraqi forces.

My Administration's draft AUMF would not authorize long-term, large-scale ground combat operations like those our Nation conducted in Iraq and Afghanistan. Local forces, rather than U.S. military forces, should be deployed to conduct such operations. The authorization I propose would provide the flexibility to conduct ground combat operations in other, more limited circumstances, such as rescue operations involving U.S. or coalition personnel or the use of special operations forces to take military action against ISIL leadership. It would also authorize the use of U.S. forces in situations where ground combat operations are not expected or intended, such as intelligence collection and sharing, missions to enable kinetic strikes, or the provision of operational planning and other forms of advice and assistance to partner forces.

Although my proposed AUMF does not address the 2001 AUMF, I remain committed to working with the Congress and the American people to refine, and ultimately repeal, the 2001 AUMF. Enacting an AUMF that is specific to the threat posed by ISIL could serve as a model for how we can work together to tailor the authorities granted by the 2001 AUMF.

Even as the proposal appeared to limit the president in important respects (such as by rescinding the 2002 authorization for military force against Iraq), it did nothing to revoke or limit the expansive 2001 AUMF. As a result, Congress was stymied and the measure failed. Large majorities supported military action against ISIS, but had different perspectives on the basis of the president's power to execute those strikes. Republicans felt that the draft legislation was too restrictive on presidential authority to combat ISIS, while Democrats perceived the retention of the 2001 AUMF as granting the president unfettered authority to wage war. The U.S. military strikes against ISIS continued without the new authorization —relying instead on the AUMF of 2001, even as the president recognized the need to refine or repeal the measure to accommodate the threat posed by ISIS.

I can think of no better way for the Congress to join me in supporting our Nation's security than by enacting this legislation, which would show the world we are united in our resolve to counter the threat posed by ISIL.

BARACK OBAMA

The White House

February 11, 2015.

Source: Barack Obama, Message to the Congress on Submitting Proposed Legislation to Authorize the Use of Military Force against the Islamic State of Iraq and the Levant (ISIL) Terrorist Organization, February 11, 2015. Online by Gerhard Peters and John T. Woolley, *The American Presidency Project.* http://www.presidency.ucsb.edu/ws/?pid=109409.

Snowden Leaks and a Revision of FISA

Barack Obama's Statement of Administration Policy

May 12, 2015

INTRODUCTION

In 2013, an NSA contractor named Edward Snowden leaked sensitive files documenting the existence and broad scale of a secret governmental electronic surveillance program that collected bulk phone records of Americans. The bulk data collection did not include the content of the calls themselves, only the record of the calls from which patterns of communication could presumably be discerned by counterterror investigators. That program began in October 2001, when, in the aftermath of the September 11 attacks, President Bush secretly authorized the NSA to begin a series of surveillance and data-collection programs, outside of the 1978 Foreign Intelligence Surveillance Act's limits on domestic spying (recall the discussion of FISA in an earlier chapter in this volume). The program was adopted in order to allow greater freedom for government antiterror investigators as they sought to uncover terrorist cells in the United States. In 2006, the Bush administration sought to establish a legal basis for the bulk collection of telecommunication data by bringing a request to the Foreign Intelligence Surveillance Court. At that time, the FISA court issued a secret ruling that interpreted Section 215 of the PATRIOT Act as permitting the bulk collection of phone records. A plain reading of the statute suggests that Section 215 only permits the collection of records that are determined to be *relevant* to a national security investigation. The Bush administration and the FISA court determined that Section 215 could be read broadly to permit the collection of all phone records, as long as only those that were deemed to be relevant were analyzed by the NSA. When the Snowden leaks revealed the existence of the bulk collection program, several suits were brought challenging its legality. As the deadline for Section 215's renewal approached in June 2015, several federal courts had ruled the bulk collection program illegal. Congress had to act to rewrite Section 215 to permit the bulk data collection, revise its scope, or explicitly end the program. In May, while Congress debated a compromise measure, called the USA FREEDOM Act, President Obama sent this Statement of Administration Policy to the House reflecting his view of the legislation. A few weeks later, the act was passed by both chambers and was signed by the president.

The Administration strongly supports House passage of H.R. 2048, the USA FREEDOM Act. The President has called on Congress to enact important changes to the Foreign Intelligence Surveillance Act (FISA) that enhance privacy and better safeguard our civil liberties, while keeping our Nation safe. The Administration applauds and appreciates the strong bipartisan and bicameral effort that led to the formulation of this bill, which strikes an appropriate balance between significant reform and preservation of important national security tools.

The bill strengthens the FISA's privacy and civil liberties protections, while preserving essential authorities our intelligence and law enforcement professionals need to protect the Nation. **The bill would implement various reforms, including prohibiting bulk collection through the use of Section 215, FISA pen registers, and National Security Letters, while maintaining authorities to conduct more targeted collection. It also enhances transparency by expanding the amount of information providers can disclose and requiring the government to increase its public reporting as well.**

As passed, the USA FREEDOM Act required the NSA and federal investigators to submit a warrant with their phone record requests on a case-by-case basis to telecommunication companies for specific counterterror investigations. This was a revision of Section 215 of the PATRIOT Act, which had been interpreted by the FISA court as permitting the NSA to hold indefinitely the telephone records of millions of Americans, in the absence of any individualized suspicion. The measure passed the Senate by a wide margin, even as key Republicans expressed concerns that the compromise bill would be too restrictive on antiterror investigators. Though the indiscriminant collection of phone data was tempered by the new legislation, other key investigative tools remained, many of which continued to cause concerns to civil libertarians.

The USA FREEDOM Act's significant reforms would provide the public greater trust and confidence in our national security programs and the checks and balances that form an integral part of their operation. Without passage of this bill, critical authorities that this legislation would reform could expire on June 1. The Administration supports swift House passage of the USA FREEDOM Act, and urges the Senate to follow suit.

Source: Barack Obama, Statement of Administration Policy: H.R. 2048 – USA FREEDOM Act, May 12, 2015. Online by Gerhard Peters and John T. Woolley, *The American Presidency Project.* http://www.presidency.ucsb.edu/ws/?pid=110143.

Timeline

Washington's Declaration of Neutrality, 1793
President Washington's declaration of neutrality in the war between France and Great Britain presented an early test of the executive's prerogative to interpret and execute the nation's treaty obligations.

Alien and Sedition Acts, 1798
The Alien and Sedition Acts of 1798 were passed by Federalists in Congress and signed by President Adams to weaken the political opposition posed by the Jeffersonian Republicans.

Jefferson and the Louisiana Purchase, 1803
The Louisiana Purchase was among the most consequential act of Jefferson's presidency, though its constitutional basis was questioned—even by Jefferson himself.

Jackson ignores USSC Decision in Cherokee Indian case, 1832
The court's decision in *Worcester v. Georgia* was ignored by President Andrew Jackson. The forced removal of Native Americans from the Southeast continued in the face of the court's ruling and resulted in the death of thousands of Cherokee on the Trail of Tears.

Polk sends troops to U.S.-Mexico Border, 1846
When American forces moved into a disputed boundary territory between Texas and Mexico, the Mexican military retaliated, killing several. President Polk sought a declaration of war from Congress.

Blockade of Southern Ports, 1861
When Fort Sumter, the federal garrison in the Charleston Harbor, South Carolina, fell to the Confederacy, President Lincoln initiated a naval blockade of Southern

ports to deny the Confederacy critical supplies. The court's decision in the Prize Cases reflects the principle that the president can use exceptional means to defend against an attack in the absence of congressional action.

The Arrest of John Merryman, 1861

John Merryman was arrested on the suspicion that he was a member of armed secessionist organization. He successfully petitioned for a writ of habeas corpus challenging his detention. The military official to whom the writ was given, however, refused to abide by the court's decision, citing presidential authority to suspend habeas relief in times of insurrection or rebellion.

Emancipation Proclamation, 1863

The Emancipation Proclamation declared all slaves in regions of the country that were in rebellion to be free. President Lincoln felt that the South could only be defeated with the abolition of slavery. Therefore, it was justified as a war measure to save the union.

Lincoln's Defense of the Suspension of Habeas, 1863

Lincoln argued that the enforcement of certain constitutional protections, such as free speech, free press, and habeas relief, would unduly limit the president in the face of a crisis.

Ex Parte Milligan, 1866

In a case resolved after the Civil War ended, the court ruled that the president has no constitutional authority to detain and try a civilian by military commission in areas where the civil courts of the United States are open and functioning.

Impeachment of Andrew Johnson, 1868

When the Congress overrode President Johnson's veto of a Civil Rights bill, a series of very public disputes between Johnson and the Radical Republicans in Congress ensued and ultimately led to impeachment proceedings.

William McKinley and the Spanish-American War, 1898

Under the terms of a treaty that ended a three-month war with Spain, the United States acquired Puerto Rico, Guam, and the Philippines. In addition, Cuba became a protectorate of the United States. Through his actions protecting U.S. interests abroad, President McKinley dramatically expanded the foreign policy-making role of the president.

Teddy Roosevelt's Square Deal, 1903

Teddy Roosevelt came into office with the goal of using the power of government to address the grave economic and social ills facing the nation. The reforms Roosevelt enacted included antimonopoly regulations, food and drug safety legislation, and the creation of environmental conservation measures—comprising a *square deal* for all.

Teddy Roosevelt's "New Nationalism," 1910

Roosevelt viewed the presidency as a *bully pulpit* that granted the occupant significant political authority for leadership on consequential issues facing the country. In this address, President Roosevelt defends his efforts to combat growing economic inequalities and the political influence of corporate interests.

Wilson's "New Freedom" Approach, 1913

Like Roosevelt, President Wilson's view of executive power was a dramatic departure from the literalist perspective of Taft. Wilson would oversee massive policy changes, many of which were the result of Roosevelt's New Nationalism and square deal initiatives years prior.

The Espionage Act, 1917

When Congress declared war on Germany and the United States entered World War I, President Wilson called for legal measures by which dissent could be silenced in a time of national emergency.

Nondelegation Doctrine, 1928

The principle of nondelegation means that *a power once delegated cannot be redelegated*. That is, citizens have delegated legislative authority to the Congress, no other branch. Therefore, Congress must not then redelegate that legislative authority. However, over time, Congress has been permitted to redelegate, resulting in broad discretion for the executive branch.

FDR's First 100 Days, 1933

Armed with overwhelming Democratic majorities in both chambers of Congress, President Franklin Delano Roosevelt set the federal government on a course of aggressive engagement with the economy in order to pull the country out of the Great Depression. He initiated a plan for a New Deal, several measures of which were introduced and enacted within the president's first 100 days in office.

Presidents and Foreign Affairs, 1936

In a case called *U.S. v. Curtiss-Wright Export Co.*, the court held that Congress has wide authority to delegate power to the president in foreign affairs.

The Four Horsemen, 1936

As soon as FDR's New Deal measures were implemented, the business interests opposed to the laws brought legal challenges, and the appeals were heard by a sympathetic core of four conservative justices known to their critics as the four horsemen. Many of the measures were struck.

The Court Packing Plan, 1937

Frustrated by the action of the four horsemen, FDR proposed that Congress pass legislation creating one new seat on the U.S. Supreme Court for every current justice over the age of 70. The proposed measure would bring the total number of justices on the court to 15 and effectively dilute the vote strength of the conservative core of the court. Congress did not pass the plan.

Four Freedoms, 1941
As U.S. involvement in another world war loomed, Roosevelt gave an important State of the Union Address, which came to be known as the Four Freedoms speech. It was primarily a speech about international affairs, but linked the themes of political democracy and economic democracy together. New Deal interventionism in the marketplace and the Allies' fight against fascism in Europe were now joined.

Pearl Harbor and a Declaration of War, 1941
On December 7, 1941, hundreds of Japanese fighter planes attacked the American Naval Base at Pearl Harbor destroying 18 U.S. warships, 300 airplanes, and leaving over 2,500 dead and 1,000 injured. The next day, Congress voted to declare war on Japan.

Operation Pastorius: The Nazi Saboteurs, 1942
Two groups of Nazi saboteurs came ashore in New York and Florida in June 1942. Their objectives included destroying key infrastructure and industrial sites. When they were captured, questions regarding their status as enemy combatants emerged.

Ex Parte Quirin, 1942
The capture of the saboteurs presented a dilemma for the Roosevelt administration: whether to try them in civilian court or by military tribunal. President Roosevelt chose to establish a military tribunal with the discretion to depart from standard court-martial practices when necessary.

Korematsu v. United States, 1944
After the attack on Pearl Harbor, there was substantial fear that the Japanese would continue the offensive against military targets on the West Coast. As a consequence, President Roosevelt issued an executive order authorizing military authorities to establish exclusion zones, detention centers, and curfews for people of Japanese descent in the proximity of military installations on the region.

The Steel Seizure Case: *Youngstown Sheet and Tube v. Sawyer*, 1952
Concerned that a steel workers' strike would pose a national security concern during the Korean War, President Truman issued an executive order nationalizing the steel industry to insure its continued production.

Bay of Pigs Invasion, 1961
When Fidel Castro came to power in Cuba, President Eisenhower authorized a secret training program for Cuban exiles for the purposes of invading the island to overthrow the new leader. Shortly upon his arrival in the White House, President Kennedy authorized the ill-fated invasion. It was a deeply embarrassing episode for the new president; scores died during the invasion and the remaining others were held prisoner for almost two years.

The Pentagon Papers, 1971

Dr. Daniel Ellsberg was an analyst who worked on a top-secret study of the Vietnam War. Ellsberg shared the secret documents in his possession to the *New York Times* and other outlets. Those papers came to be known as the Pentagon Papers. The Nixon administration sought to exercise *prior restraint* and prevent the press from reporting on the Pentagon Papers, but the U.S. Supreme Court ruled in favor of the *New York Times*.

Watergate, 1972

Watergate refers to two conspiracies that have their origins in the Nixon White House. The first conspiracy was to reach into *a bag of dirty tricks* to destabilize the Democratic primaries in 1972. The illegality of the actions the Nixon administration operatives took to achieve that goal eventually gave rise to a second conspiracy—the cover-up. In 1974, after multiple investigations, the House passed three articles of impeachment against President Nixon.

Impoundment of Funds, 1973

President Nixon refused to spend money that Congress had appropriated on multiple occasions (roughly $30 billion over two years). He determined that it was within the president's constitutional authority to refuse to expend funds if, in his view, Congress overappropriates. Congress responded by passing the 1974 Congressional Budget and Impoundment Act, which constrained the impoundment authority of the president.

War Powers Resolution of 1973

In the aftermath of Vietnam, Congress sought to reassert congressional control over the power of the executive to engage U.S. forces in military conflicts. The result was the War Powers Resolution of 1973.

U.S. v. Nixon, 1974

During the investigations into Watergate, the Senate Select Committee learned that the president had multiple conversations with his staff about obstructing the investigations and had recorded those conversations. The special prosecutor for Watergate subpoenaed the tape recordings, but the president resisted, claiming executive privilege. The court rejected the president's claims and required the release of the tapes. Nixon resigned just days later.

Church Committee and Creation of FISA, 1975

Revelations of the existence of secret NSA, CIA, and FBI domestic surveillance programs under the Nixon administration spurred Congress to establish the Senate Select Committee to Study Governmental Operations with Respect to Intelligence Activities. Its charge was to investigate the use of the nation's surveillance apparatus by presidents for political rather than national security purposes. Congress passed the Foreign Intelligence Surveillance Act (FISA) of 1978 in response to the committee's report.

Legislative Veto, 1983

The legislative veto was a mechanism by which Congress could control executive branch implementation of a statute without having to pass a new law. By a vote of one or both chambers, Congress could constrain the executive's implementation of the statute. In *INS v. Chadha*, the court ruled the legislative veto unconstitutional.

Chevron Doctrine, 1984

Chevron deference is the idea that judges should generally defer to agencies' understandings of their delegated authority when the statutes that grant that authority meet certain requirements. The deferential quality of the Chevron Doctrine grants the executive branch broad discretion in interpreting what can often be vague statutes passed by Congress.

Iran-Contra Affair, 1986

Federal investigations revealed that the Reagan administration had, in an attempt to free hostages being held in Lebanon, used the profits from the sale of weapons to Iran to illegally fund the Contras in Nicaragua.

Independent Counsel and Iran-Contra, 1986

Just a few years after Watergate, Congress passed a package of reform measures known as the Ethics in Government Act. The act included provisions for the appointment of an independent special prosecutor to investigate high-ranking officials in the executive branch. Lawrence Walsh was appointed to investigate Iran-Contra.

Presidential Signing Statements as Policy Devices, 1986

A signing statement is a written presidential pronouncement regarding a piece of legislation that is issued at the time the president signs the bill into law. During the Reagan administration, the president's legal advisers began to push for the use of signing statements to reposition and strengthen the executive branch's role in shaping important policies and in construing constitutional meaning.

Appointment and Removal Power, 1988

Presidents probably ought to have some control over those who are taking actions on their behalf. But too much political control by the administration over subordinates would limit the subordinates' independence and—in the case of independent special prosecutors—limit investigative autonomy. In *Morrison v. Olson*, the court considered the constitutionality of the independent counsel provisions of the Ethics in Government Act of 1978 in light of these competing perspectives.

Paula Jones Case, 1997

Alleging sexual harassment by President Clinton prior to his taking office, Paula Jones sought almost $200,000 in civil damages. The court decided that a sitting president could be sued for civil damages for actions taken either before the person became president or for conduct that was unrelated to the individual's official responsibilities. The civil suit against President Clinton was allowed to proceed.

House Impeachment Proceedings, 1998
In December 1998, the House of Representatives passed two articles of impeachment against President Clinton, one for perjury and the other for obstruction of justice. The adoption of those articles of impeachment was the culmination of a series of investigations related to, but extending beyond, the Paula Jones civil suit.

The Line Item Veto, 1998
Under the Line Item Veto Act, the president could strike specific lines from appropriations bills passed by Congress without having to veto the whole bill. The Line Item Veto was struck by the court in the case, *Clinton v. City of New York*.

Cheney and the Energy Task Force, 2001
Within days of George W. Bush taking office, his vice president, Dick Cheney, convened a series of secret meetings to discuss the future of U.S. energy policy. Concerned that the meetings included only oil and gas interests, public interest groups and environmental organizations brought suit to gain access to the records of the meetings. The U.S. Supreme Court ruled that since this was not a criminal inquiry, Cheney was not obligated to release the names of those with whom he met.

Authorization for the Use of Military Force (AUMF), 2001
On September 11, 2001, terrorists connected to al-Qaeda flew planes into the World Trade Center in New York City and the Pentagon in Alexandria, VA. Three days after 9/11, Congress passed legislation drafted by the White House giving the president broad powers.

War in Afghanistan, 2001
Within a month of the attacks on the World Trade Center and Pentagon, President Bush announced the beginning of U.S. combat operations in Afghanistan where Taliban regime had harbored al-Qaeda, the terrorist organization known to have been responsible for the September 11 attacks.

Passage of the PATRIOT Act, 2001
With very little debate and no hearings on a bill drafted largely by the Bush administration, Congress passed the PATRIOT Act, which among other things broadened the electronic surveillance capacities of both law enforcement and counterterrorism authorities.

Habeas Corpus and Guantanamo Bay, 2001
The Bush administration determined that a system of military detention would be used for the Taliban fighters and suspected terrorists who were captured in Afghanistan and elsewhere. Any review of the status of a detainee would be

conducted according to processes determined by the executive branch. According to administration lawyers, the entire detainee structure could remain outside the reach of federal and international law.

Axis of Evil, 2002

During his January 2002 State of the Union address, President Bush indicated that the administration was preparing to broaden the war on terror to include action against Saddam Hussein, the dictator in power in Iraq. However, without evidence of a connection to 9/11, the 2001 AUMF would not be sufficient to justify the deployment of U.S. troops to Iraq. The Axis of Evil was the beginning of the administration's public, multipronged approach to making the case for an invasion of Iraq.

Enemy Combatants, 2002

As several administration memos reveal, the legal remedies available to detainees were limited. As a result, many detainees were subjected to "enhanced interrogation techniques," because the domestic and international laws that prohibited torture were construed to be not applicable to them.

The Torture Memos, 2002

The Torture Memos were a series of legal memoranda developed by Office of Legal Counsel attorneys that gave U.S. military authorities broad discretion in their treatment of detainees and absolved those interrogators of criminal liability if they tortured prisoners.

Hamdi v. Rumsfeld, 2004

In *Hamdi*, the court had to determine what processes are due someone who is a U.S. citizen on U.S. soil but deemed an "enemy combatant." In its decision, the court ruled that the president does not have the authority to hold a U.S. citizen indefinitely.

Combatant Status Review Tribunals, 2004

A week after the court's decision in *Hamdi*, the Department of Defense established Combatant Status Review Tribunals (CSRTs) to meet the legal obligations set forth in the court's opinion.

Warrantless Wiretapping, 2005

The *New York Times* ran a front-page story about the Bush administration's use of domestic warrantless wiretapping in violation of the 1978 FISA. When the scale of its use became clear, it was revealed to be the largest surveillance operation in American history.

Boumediene v. Bush, 2008

In the *Boumediene* case, the court determined that the Military Commissions Act (2006), as passed by Congress, had unconstitutionally denied meaningful habeas relief without suspending the writ of habeas corpus under the Suspension Clause.

Obama on Signing Statements, 2009

Just a few weeks after taking office, President Obama issued a memorandum directing all agency heads to disregard the earlier constitutional objections from the Bush-era signing statements.

Detainee Policy under Obama, 2009

President Obama issued an executive order establishing a Task Force to review the status of the remaining detainees at Guantanamo Bay, Cuba. A new set of guidelines for the military commissions was established following the court's decision in *Boumediene*.

State Secrets Privilege, 2009

Very early in his presidency, President Obama issued a memorandum to agency and department heads establishing a general policy of transparency. Before long, however, it was clear he would continue the practice of asserting the state secrets privilege to block lawsuits that might require the disclosure of national security secrets.

Drone Strikes and Targeted Killings, 2010

The targeted killing of alleged terrorists by drone strikes became a frequently employed, but highly controversial, element of the counterterror efforts of the Obama administration. The growing frequency of these targeted killings alarmed many international human rights organizations, foreign leaders, as well as many in Congress.

Military Intervention in Libya, 2011

In 2011, the United States took military action against the Libyan dictator Colonel Muammar Qaddafi. President Obama's legal advisors determined that the president was obligated, under the War Powers Act, to seek approval from Congress for the continuation of hostilities after 60 days. He declined to do so, however, citing the supporting role that U.S. forces played in the NATO action.

Syria and War Powers, 2013

President Obama had repeatedly called upon Syrian President Bashar al-Assad to step down for his role in leading a brutal civil war that had claimed over 100,000 lives. When it was clear that Assad had used chemical weapons in contravention of international law, President Obama sought authorization from Congress to take military action against Assad.

Recess Appointments, 2014

Obama made three appointments to the National Labor Relations Board in 2012 during a very brief (three-day) recess of the Senate rather than during the longer intersession period when recess appointments typically are made. The court upheld the so-called intrasession appointments in principle, but determined that three days is insufficient to trigger the Recess Appointments Clause.

New AUMF for ISIS, 2015

The United States carried out thousands of airstrikes in Syria and Iraq, targeting the terrorist organization known as the Islamic State. The Obama administration sought congressional approval for the military action against ISIS, even though the administration's position was that the president had the authority under existing statutes to take direct military action under the 2001 AUMF and the 2002 Iraq War resolution.

Snowden Leaks and a Revision of FISA, 2015

An NSA contractor named Edward Snowden leaked sensitive files documenting the existence and broad scale of a secret governmental electronic surveillance program that collected bulk phone records of Americans. After several federal courts ruled the program illegal, Congress passed the USA FREEDOM Act, which required the NSA and federal investigators to submit a warrant with their phone record requests on a case-by-case basis to telecommunication companies for specific counterterror investigations.

Further Readings

Ball, Howard. 2007. *Bush, the Detainees, and the Constitution: The Battle over Presidential Power in the War on Terror*. Lawrence: Kansas University Press.

Bawn, Kathleen. 1995. "Political Control versus Expertise: Congressional Choices about Administrative Procedures." *American Political Science Review* 89:62–73.

Bond, Jon R., and Richard Fleisher. 1990. *The President in the Legislative Arena*. Chicago: University of Chicago Press.

Bond, Jon R., and Richard Fleisher. 2000. *Polarized Politics: Congress and the President in a Partisan Era*. Washington, DC: CQ Press.

Borelli, Maryanne, Karen Hult, and Nancy Kassop. 2001. "White House Counsel's Office." *Presidential Studies Quarterly* 31:561–584.

Cameron, Charles. 2000. *Veto Bargaining*. New York: Cambridge University Press.

Carey, John M., and Matthew Soberg Shugart, eds. 1998. *Executive Decree Authority*. Cambridge, UK: Cambridge University Press.

Cooper, Phillip. 2002. *By Order of the President: The Use and Abuse of Executive Direct Action*. Lawrence: University of Kansas Press.

Cronin, Thomas, and Michael Genovese. 2004. *The Paradoxes of the American Presidency*. Oxford: Oxford University Press.

Edelson, Chris. 2013. *Emergency Presidential Power: From the Drafting of the Constitution to the War on Terror*. Madison: University of Wisconsin Press.

Edwards, George C., III. 2009. *The Strategic President: Persuasion and Opportunity in Presidential Leadership*. Princeton, NJ: Princeton University Press.

Edwards, George C., III. 2012. *Overreach: Leadership in the Obama Presidency*. Princeton, NJ: Princeton University Press.

Edwards, George C., III., and Stephen J. Wayne. 2014. *Presidential Leadership: Politics and Policymaking*, 9th ed. New York: Cengage Learning.

Ellis, Richard J. 2012. *The Development of the American Presidency*. New York: Routledge Press.

Epstein, David, and Sharyn O'Halloran. 1999. *Delegating Powers: A Transaction Cost Politics Approach to Policy Making Under Separate Powers.* Cambridge, UK: Cambridge University Press.

Fisher, Louis. 1978. *The Constitution between Friends: Congress, the President, and the Law.* New York: St. Martin's Press.

Fisher, Louis. 2005. *Nazi Saboteurs on Trial: A Military Tribunal and American Law,* 2nd ed. Lawrence: Kansas University Press.

Fisher, Louis. 2007. *Constitutional Conflicts between Congress and the President,* 5th ed. Lawrence: Kansas University Press.

Fisher, Louis. 2007. "Signing Statements: Constitutional and Practical Limits." *William & Mary Bill of Rights Journal* 16:183–210.

Fisher, Louis. 2008. *The Constitution and 9/11: Recurring Threats to America's Freedoms.* Lawrence: Kansas University Press.

Fisher, Louis. 2013. *Presidential War Power,* 3rd ed. Lawrence: Kansas University Press.

Goldsmith, Jack. 2009. *The Terror Presidency: Law and Judgment inside the Bush Administration.* New York: Norton.

Greenberg, Karen. 2009. *The Least Worst Place: Guantanamo's First 100 Days.* Oxford: Oxford University Press.

Halstead, T.J. 2007. "Presidential Signing Statements: Constitutional and Institutional Implications." Congressional Research Service Report for Congress. http://www.gao.gov/new.items/d08553t.pdf.

Harward, Donald W. 1974. *Crisis in Confidence: The Impact of Watergate.* Boston: Little, Brown and Co.

Howell, William G. 2003. *Power without Persuasion: The Politics of Direct Presidential Action.* Princeton, NJ: Princeton University Press.

Howell, William, Saul Jackman, and Jon Rogowski. 2013. *The Wartime President: Executive Influence and the Nationalizing Politics of Threat.* Chicago: University of Chicago Press.

Huber, John, and Charles Shipan. 2002. *Deliberate Discretion? The Institutional Foundations of Bureaucratic Autonomy.* Cambridge, UK: Cambridge University Press.

Huber, John D., Charles R. Shipan, and Madelaine Pfahler. 2001. "Legislatures and Statutory Control of Bureaucracy." *American Journal of Political Science* 45:330–345.

Jones, Charles O. 1994. *The Presidency in a Separated System.* Washington, DC: Brookings Institution.

Kautz, Steven, Arthur Melzer, Jerry Weinberger, and M. Richard Zinman, eds. 2009. *The Supreme Court and the Idea of Constitutionalism.* Philadelphia: University of Pennsylvania Press.

Kelley, Christopher, ed. 2006. *Executing the Constitution: Putting the President Back into the Constitution.* Albany, NY: SUNY Press.

Kelley, Christopher, ed. 2007. "A Matter of Direction: The Reagan Administration, the Signing Statement, and the 1986 Westlaw Decision." *William & Mary Bill of Rights Journal* 16:283–306.

Kelley, Christopher S., and Bryan W. Marshall. 2008. "Assessing Presidential Power: Signing Statements and Veto Threats as Coordinated Strategies." *American Politics Research* 37:508–533.

Kernell, Samuel. 2005. *Presidential Veto Threat in Statements of Administration Policy: 1985–2004*, version 1.0, CD-ROM distributed by CQ Press.

Kernell, Samuel. 2007. *Going Public: New Strategies of Presidential Leadership.* Washington, DC: CQ Press.

Kleinerman, Benjamin. 2009. *The Discretionary President: The Promise and Peril of Executive Power.* Lawrence: Kansas University Press.

Lewis, David. 2003. *Presidents and the Politics of Agency Design.* Palo Alto, CA: Stanford University Press.

Light, Paul C. 1999. *The President's Agenda: Domestic Policy Choice from Kennedy to Clinton*, 3rd ed. Baltimore, MD: The Johns Hopkins University Press.

Mayer, Kenneth M. 1999. "Executive Orders and Presidential Power." *The Journal of Politics* 61:445–466.

Mayer, Kenneth M. 2001. *With the Stroke of a Pen: Executive Orders and Presidential Power.* Princeton, NJ: Princeton University Press.

McCubbins, Mathew D., Roger G. Noll, and Barry R. Weingast. 1989. "Structure and Process, Politics and Policy: Administrative Arrangements and the Political Control of Agencies." *Virginia Law Review* 75:431–482.

McCubbins, Mathew D., and Thomas Schwartz. 1984. "Congressional Oversight Overlooked: Police Patrols versus Fire Alarms." *American Journal of Political Science* 28:165–179.

Moe, Terry M., and Scott A. Wilson. 1994. "Presidents and the Politics of Structure." *Law and Contemporary Problems* 57:1–44.

Neustadt, Richard. 1960. *Presidential Power.* New York: John Wiley.

Ogul, Morris S. 1976. *Congress Oversees the Bureaucracy: Studies in Legislative Supervision.* Pittsburgh, PA: University of Pittsburgh Press.

Pfiffner, James P. 2008. *Power Play: The Bush Presidency and the Constitution.* Washington, DC: Brookings Institution.

Pika, Joseph A., and John A. Maltese. 2013. *The Politics of the Presidency.* Los Angeles: Sage Press.

Poole, Keith T., and Howard Rosenthal. 1997. *Congress: A Political-Economic History of Roll Call Voting.* New York: Oxford University Press.

Rohde, David W., and Dennis M. Simon. 1985. "Presidential Vetoes and Congressional Response: A Study of Institutional Conflict." *American Journal of Political Science* 29:397–427.

Rossiter, Clinton. 1960. *The American Presidency.* New York: Harcourt, Brace and World.

Rourke, Frances E. 1960. "Administrative Secrecy: A Congressional Dilemma." *American Political Science Review* 54:684–694.

Rudalevige, Andrew. 2006. *The New Imperial Presidency.* Ann Arbor: University of Michigan Press.

Savage, Charlie. 2007. *Takeover: The Return of the Imperial Presidency and the Subversion of American Democracy*. New York: Little, Brown and Co.

Schlesinger, Arthur M., Jr. 1974. *The Imperial Presidency*. Boston: Houghton Mifflin Co.

Skowronek, Stephen. 2011. *Presidential Leadership in Political Time*. Lawrence: University Press of Kansas.

Sievert, Joel, and Ian Ostrander. 2013. "The Logic of Presidential Signing Statements." *Political Research Quarterly* 66:141–153.

Thurber, James, ed. 2013. *Rivals for Power: Presidential-Congressional Relations*, 5th ed. Plymouth, UK: Rowman & Littlefield.

Warshaw, Shirley Anne. 2009. *The Co-Presidency of Bush and Cheney*. Stanford, CA: Stanford University Press.

Whittington, Keith. 2007. *Political Foundations of Judicial Supremacy: The Presidency, the Supreme Court, and Constitutional Leadership in U.S. History*. Princeton, NJ: Princeton University Press.

Whittington, Keith. 2009. "Constitutional Constraints in Politics." In *The Supreme Court and the Idea of Constitutionalism*, edited by Steven Kautz, Arthur Melzer, Jerry Weinberger, and M. Richard Zinman. Philadelphia: University of Pennsylvania Press.

Wood, B. Dan. 2009. *The Myth of Presidential Representation*. Cambridge, UK: Cambridge University Press.

Index

About the Author

Brian M. Harward, PhD, is associate professor of Political Science and director of the Center for Political Participation at Allegheny College in Meadville, PA. He teaches constitutional law, philosophy of law, and courses in American politics. His recent scholarly journal publications explore issues related to executive power, presidential campaigns, congressional oversight, and teaching and learning. He is also the author of *The 2012 Presidential Election* (Pearson) and the coauthor of *Presidential Campaigns: Documents Decoded* (ABC-CLIO). In addition to multiple campus and disciplinary teaching awards, Harward was the 2013 recipient of the American Political Science Association/CQ Press Award for Teaching Innovation in Political Science.